TELEPEN
0084265024

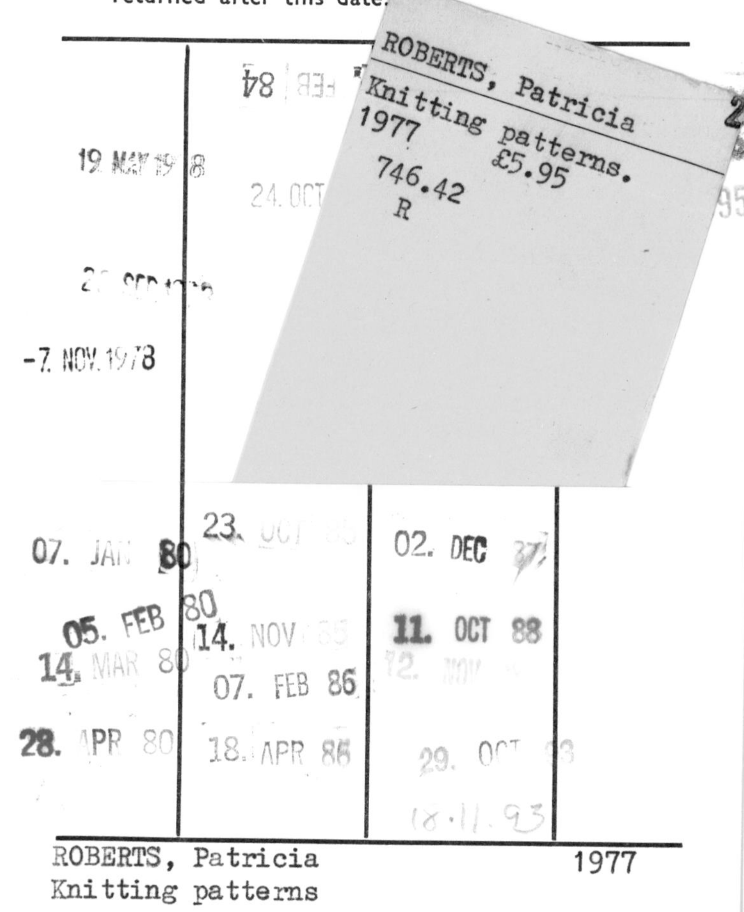

PATRICIA ROBERTS
KNITTING PATTERNS
EXCLUSIVE KNITWEAR DESIGNS FOR ALL THE FAMILY

MACDONALD AND JANE'S · LONDON

All photography by John Carter

Illustrations by Michael Wells

ISBN 0354 08508 5

Published by Macdonald and Jane's Publishers Limited,
Paulton House, 8 Shepherdess Walk, London N1 7LW.

Printed and bound in Great Britain by Morrison and Gibb Limited,
London and Edinburgh

ACKNOWLEDGEMENTS
Ziggy
Trousers by Salmon and Green.
Rough Stuff
Trousers by Wendy Dagworthy. Shirt by Margaret Howell, 13 South Molton Street, London W.1.
Yours and Mine
Shirt by Pinkerton's. Photographed at La Popote, Walton Street, London S.W.3.
Hoodwinked
Trousers by Rosella Goldsmidt for Daily Blue from Bombacha, 104 Fulham Road, London S.W.7. Shirt by Wendy Dagworthy. Shoes by Kickers.
Nostalgia Trip
Trousers by Wendy Dagworthy. Shirt by Margaret Howell, 13 South Molton Street, London W.1.
Hodge
Knickerbockers by Krizia. Handbag by Nigel Lofthouse.
Rag, Tag & Bobtail
Trousers by Jap from The Jap Shop, Brompton Road, London S.W.3.
All That Glitters
Skirt by Jap from The Jap Shop, Brompton Road, London S.W.3. Brooch from Bombacha, 104 Fulham Road, London S.W.7.
Folk Isle
Woman's trousers by Rosella Goldsmidt for Daily Blue from Bombacha, 104 Fulham Road, London S.W.7. Woman's shirt by Margaret Howell, 13 South Molton Street, London W.1. Gold necklace by Patricia Roberts. Man's trousers by Wendy Dagworthy. Man's shirt from Margaret Howell.
Brown Study
Hat by Patricia Roberts.
A Pocketful of Posies
Trousers by Daniel Hector. Photographed at The Conservatory, Fulham Road, London S.W.3.
Blue Moon
Smith's jeans from Joseph at The Jap Shop, Brompton Road, London S.W.3.
Cold Shoulder
Trousers by Rosella Goldsmidt for Daily Blue from Bombacha, 104 Fulham Road, London S.W.7. Photographed at the Curzon House Club, Curzon Street, London W.1.
Lily of the Valley
Skirt by Daniel Hector.
Stripe Me Pink
Trousers by Salmon and Green.
In The Pink and **Pansygirl**
Skirts and scarves by Wendy Dagworthy.
Double Cream and **Single Cream**
Skirts and shirt by Wendy Dagworthy.
Swansong
Skirt and hat by Jap from The Jap Shop, Brompton Road, London S.W.3. Photographed outside La Brasserie, Brompton Road, London S.W.3.
Silver
Shirt by Margaret Howell, 13 South Molton Street, London W.1. Trousers by Rosella Goldsmidt for Daily Blue from Bombacha, 104 Fulham Road, London S.W.7. Photographed at the Curzon House Club, Curzon Street, London W.1.
Picture Pullovers
Trousers from Môme, 27 Harrington Road, London S.W.7.
Polo Set
Trousers by Rosella Goldsmidt for Daily Blue from Bombacha, 104 Fulham Road, London S.W.7.
Cream of the Crop
Skirt by La Maison Bleue from Joseph, 33 Kings Road, London S.W.3. Cashmere scarf by Patricia Roberts.
Dreamy
Leggings by Multiply by Patricia Roberts.
Child's Play
Trousers from Môme, 27 Harrington Road, London S.W.7.
Diamond
Trousers by Wendy Dagworthy. Shirt by Margaret Howell, 13 South Molton Street, London W.1.
Long Tall Sally
Trousers by Rosella Goldsmidt for Daily Blue from Bombacha, 104 Fulham Road, London S.W.7. Shirt by Wendy Dagworthy. Shoes by Kickers.
Classic Cool
Trousers by Wendy Dagworthy. Shirt by Wendy Dagworthy.
Crown of Glory
Parachute trousers by Jap from The Jap Shop, Brompton Road, London S.W.3. Brooch from Bombacha, 104 Fulham Road, London S.W.7. Cashmere scarf by Patricia Roberts. Handbag by Nigel Lofthouse.
Jacket In
Sweater and scarf by Patricia Roberts.
Lacey
Skirt by Enrico Coveri from the Elle Italian Shop, 20 Sloane Street, London S.W.1; also from the Elle Shop in Reigate, Manchester and Brighton.
Plain Dealing
Dress by Pinkerton's.
Ibble-Obble
Cream trousers by Jap from the Jap Shop, Brompton Road, London S.W.3. Hat and mittens by Patricia Roberts.
Tea Cosy
Shirt by Salmon and Green. Hat and scarf by Patricia Roberts.
Easy Rib
Trousers and matching shirt by Rosella Goldsmidt for Daily Blue from Bombacha, 104 Fulham Road, London S.W.7.
Walking the Dog
Culottes by Suzuya from Joseph, 33 Kings Road, London S.W.3. Hat by Patricia Roberts.

FIRST HAND INFORMATION

To cast on stitches
There are several methods of casting on stitches. The 'thumb' method is the one most frequently used at the start of work, and the 'through the stitch' method is normally used for casting on once a piece of knitting has been started.

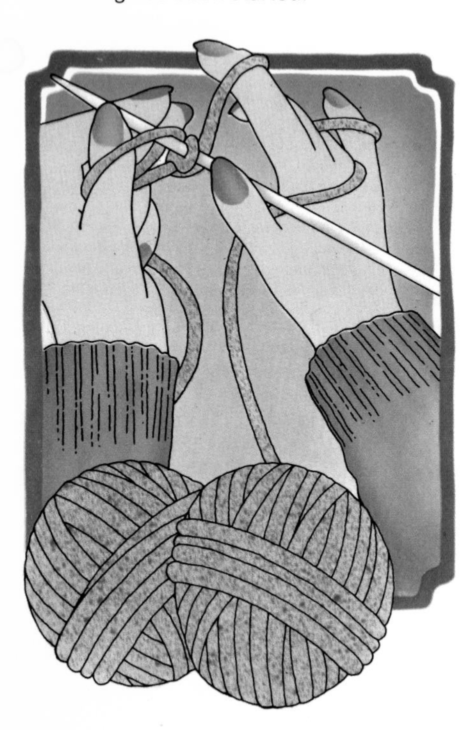

1. *The through the stitch method*
Make a loop and place it on the needle held in the left hand. Insert the right-hand needle into this loop, wind the yarn round the needle, draw the loop through and place this loop onto left-hand needle. Continue working into the last loop formed on the left-hand needle each time.

2. *The thumb method*
Leaving a length of yarn sufficient to make the required number of stitches, make a loop and place it on the needle held in the right hand, the yarn from the ball in the right hand. Take the loose end of yarn in the left hand and form a loop on the left thumb. Insert the point of the right-hand needle into the loop on thumb, wrap the yarn round the point of the needle and draw the loop through that on the thumb, at the same time as slipping the loop from the thumb and gently tightening the left-hand thread. Continue is this way.

To work knit stitches
With the needle containing the cast on stitches in the left hand, insert the right-hand needle into the front of the first loop on the left-hand needle, so that the point of the right-hand needle passes towards the back of the work beneath the left-hand needle. Wind yarn round the right-hand needle and draw this loop through the loop of the left-hand needle, at the same time as slipping the loop from the left-hand needle. Keep the yarn to the back of the work throughout.

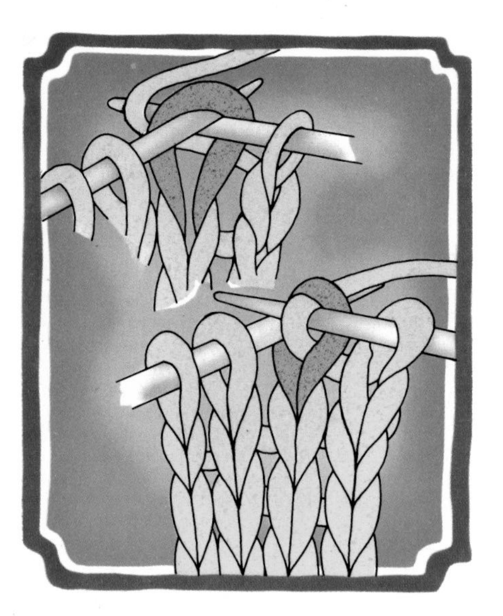

To work purl stitches
With the yarn to the front of the work, insert the right-hand needle into the front of the first stitch on the left-hand needle as shown in the diagram. Wind the yarn round the needle and draw the loop through, allowing the stitch to fall from the left-hand needle.

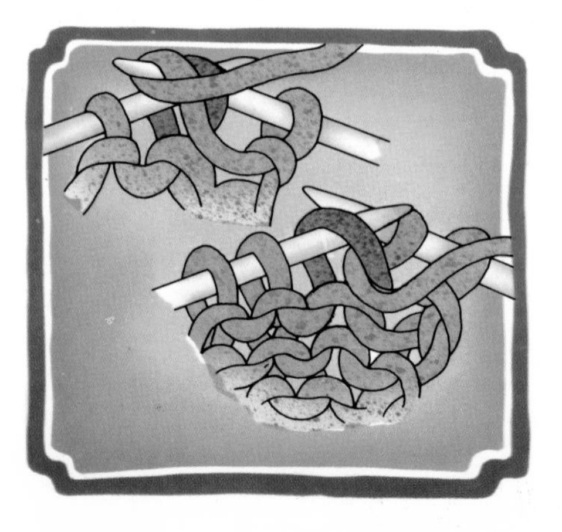

To cast off stitches
Casting off should be worked as follows: k. 2, slip the first of these 2 stitches now on right-hand needle over the second stitch, * k. 1, then pass previous stitch over this one. Repeat from * for required number of stitches. If you cast off to the end of the row, break off the yarn at the end, pass it through the final stitch and draw up. When casting off, care should be taken not to cast off too tightly; to avoid this a needle of a larger size may be used if required.

To pick up and knit stitches
Keep the yarn at back of the work throughout. With the right side of the work facing you rejoin the yarn. Hold the knitting in the left hand then, with the needle in the left hand, insert the needle into the knitting at the required edge, wind the yarn round the needle and draw the loop through. Continue in this way.

To work invisible seams
Place the first finger of the left hand between the two pieces of knitting to be sewn up, hold them edge to edge, with the right sides of the work facing you. Secure the yarn at one edge, making sure that the needle is on the right side of the work when commencing the seam. Taking the needle to the second edge, insert it under the thread that lies between the first and second stitches with the point of the needle towards the top of the pieces being seamed. Then draw the needle and yarn through. Take the needle to the first edge and insert it into the place through which the last thread on the side was drawn, and under the loop between the first and second stitches as before. Continue in this way.

Check your tension before commencing work
The correct tension for each garment is given at the beginning of each pattern. First check your tension using the size needles suggested in the pattern. If your tension is too tight using the size needles suggested, test it again using larger needles. If it is still too tight, try again with even larger needles and so on until your tension is correct. If your tension is too loose, test your tension with smaller needles until it is correct. A garment knitted at the correct tension will have the measurements given in the knitting pattern.

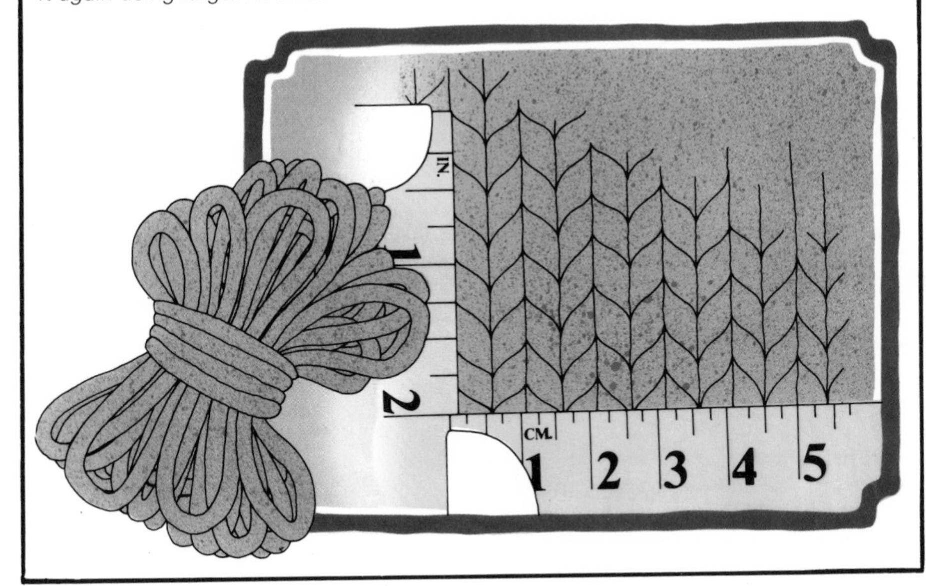

Read the abbreviations paragraph
As you knit a garment, do not take it for granted that you understand all the abbreviated stitches. Read the abbreviations paragraph to ensure that you are working the stitches correctly for that particular pattern.

Pin out knitting before pressing
Pin out each piece of knitting to the measurements given at the beginning of the pattern. Use a lot of pins, pinning them approximately four centimetres (one and a half inches) apart all round the outer edges. Ironing boards are often too small for pinning out knitting. A table or the floor covered by blankets or foam and an ironing sheet are best.

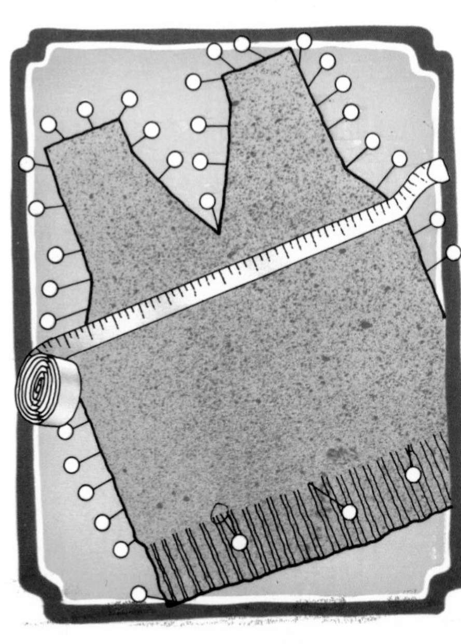

Correct pressing
Place a cloth, dry, wet, or damp according to the pattern, over the wrong side of the knitting, which has already been pinned to size. Press the knitting with an upwards downwards movement, that is lifting the iron into the air and then placing it down on the knitting. If you press the knitting with a sideways motion you may press it out of shape. Remove the cloth after pressing and leave the knitting pinned to size until it is cool; then the pins may be removed.

Make up your garment neatly
Use either the same yarn as the knitting or a finer matching yarn to make up a garment. Use small stitches so that the seams will not show. Invisible seaming is a particularly successful method of making up, although a fine back stitch seam can be very neat.

Press seams
After making up the garment press the seams, using a dry, wet, or damp cloth and an iron at the same temperature as that used for the main pressing.

Hand wash hand-knitting
Hand washing is better for hand-knitted garments than dry cleaning. Wash garments according to the instructions given on the yarn label.

Dry garments flat
Do not dry knitting on a washing line or it will become misshapen. Lay knitting flat on a towel to dry away from any direct heat or sunlight.

Yarn and knitting enquiries
For any enquiries concerning the knitting patterns or yarns used in this book write, enclosing a stamped, self-addressed envelope, to the Patricia Roberts Knitting Shop, 60 Kinnerton Street, London SW1X 8ES.

ZIGGY

Big needles and big stitches make this mohair jacket quick to knit. Mohair colours are so lustrous and rich that you can have great fun choosing your own colour combinations to brighten up a cold day in the garden.

Materials:
10 (11) (12) 25 gram balls of Emu Filigree in main colour, sea grotto—H704, and 9 (10) (11) balls in first contrast colour, black—L751; 4 (4) (5) balls in second colour, scarlet—K239; a pair each of No. 4 and No. 5 knitting needles; 8 buttons.

Tension:
7 stitches and 10 rows to 5 cm (2 in.) over the stocking stitch using No. 4 needles. If you cannot obtain the correct tension using the size needles suggested, use larger or smaller needles accordingly.

Abbreviations:
K., knit; p., purl; st., stitch; tog., together; dec., decrease (by working 2 sts. tog.); inc., increase (by working twice into same st.); y.r.n., yarn round needle; s.s., stocking stitch (k. on the right side and p. on the wrong side); double rib is k. 2 and p. 2 alternately; garter stitch is k. plain on every row; m.b., make bobble thus, k. 1, y.r.n., k. 1, y.r.n., k. 1, turn, p. 5, turn, k. 5, turn, p. 5, turn, k. 5, turn, p. 5, pass 2nd, 3rd, 4th and 5th sts. over first st. on left hand needle, then k. 1 through back of st.; m., main colour; a., first contrast; b., second contrast; up 1, pick up the loop that lies between the needles, slip it on to left hand needle, then k. into back of it.

Note:
The instructions are given for the small size. Where they vary work the figures in the first brackets for the medium size or the figures in the second brackets for the large size.

Measurements:
The measurements are given in centimetres followed by inches in square brackets.

To fit sizes		
small (10)	medium (12)	large (14)
All round at underarms		
92.5 [37]	97.5 [39]	102.5 [41]
side seam		
55 [22]	55 [22]	55 [22]
Length		
76 [30½]	77.5 [31]	77.5 [31]
Sleeve seam (excluding cuffs)		
41 [16½]	41 [16½]	41 [16½]

The back:
With No. 5 needles and m. cast on 56 (60) (64) sts. and work 15 rows in double rib.
Increase row: Rib 4 (6) (8), * up 1, rib 8; repeat from * ending last repeat rib 4 (6) (8)—63 (67) (71) sts.
Change to No. 4 needles, join in a. and work in pattern as follows: it is *not* necessary to weave in the colours not in use, but great care should be taken to avoid pulling colours not in use tightly across the back of the work. The pattern is worked entirely in s.s.—except for the bobbles—so only the colour details are given.
1st and 2nd rows: All a. in s.s.
3rd row: 3 (5) (7) a., * 2 m., 9 a.; repeat from * ending last repeat 3 (5) (7) a.
4th row: 2 (4) (6) a., * 4 m., 7 a.; repeat from * ending last repeat 2 (4) (6) a.
The last 4 rows set the position of the pattern given in the chart. Now work the 5th to 26th rows from chart as set.
Continuing in pattern as set pattern 70 rows more.
To shape the raglan armholes: Maintaining the continuity of the pattern as set dec. 1 st. at each end of the next row and the 20 (21) (22) following alternate rows.
On 21 (23) (25) sts. work 1 row, then cast off.

The pocket backs *(both alike)***:**
With No. 4 needles and m. cast on 16 sts. and beginning with a k. row s.s. 24 rows, then leave these sts. on a spare needle until required.

The left front:
With No. 5 needles and m. cast on 28 (30) (32) sts. and work 15 rows in double rib.
Increase row: Rib 10 (11) (12), up 1, rib 8, up 1, rib 10 (11) (12)—30 (32) (34) sts.
Change to No. 4 needles and work in pattern—in s.s. as follows, noting the information given for back.
1st and 2nd rows: All a. in s.s.
3rd row: 3 (5) (7) a., 2 m., 9 a., 2 m., 9 a., 2 m., 3 a.
4th row: 2 a., 4 m., 7 a., 4 m., 7 a., 4 m., 2 (4) (6) a.
The last 4 rows set the position of the pattern given in the chart. Now work the 5th to 26th rows from the chart as set, then work the first 8 rows again.
Pocket row: Pattern 7 (9) (11), slip next 16 sts. on to a stitch-holder and leave at front of work, in their place work across the 16 sts. of one pocket back, work to end as set.
Pattern 61 rows more.
***To shape the neck and the raglan armhole:* Dec. 1 st. at each end of the next row, work 1 row back to armhole edge, dec. 1 st. at the beginning—armhole edge on the next row, then work 1 row straight.
Repeat the last 4 rows 7 (8) (9) times more—6 (5) (4) sts.
Dec. 1 st. at the beginning—armhole edge on the next row and the 3 (2) (1) following alternate rows—2 sts.
P. 2, then k. 2 tog. and fasten off.

The right front:
With No. 5 needles and m. cast on 28 (30) (32) sts. and work 15 rows in double rib.
Increase row: Rib 10 (11) (12), up 1, rib 8, up 1, rib 10 (11) (12)—30 (32) (34) sts.
Change to No. 4 needles and work in pattern as follows, noting the information given for back.
1st and 2nd rows: All a.
3rd row: 3 a., 2 m., 9 a., 2 m., 9 a., 2 m., 3 (5) (7) a.
4th row: 2 (4) (6) a., 4 m., 7 a., 4 m., 7 a., 4 m., 2 a.
The last 4 rows set the position of the pattern given in the chart. Now work the 5th to 26th rows from the chart as set, then work the first 8 rows again.
Pocket row: Pattern 7, slip next 16 sts. on to a stitch-holder and leave at front of work, in their place work across the 16 sts. of one pocket back, work to end as set.
Pattern 62 rows more.
Now work as given for left front from ** to end.

The sleeves *(both alike)***:**
With No. 5 needles and m. cast on 3 sts. and k. 15 (16) (17) rows increasing 1 st. at each end of each row.
On 33 (35) (37) sts. k. 7 (6) (5) rows.
Change to No. 4 needles and work in pattern as follows: noting the information given for back and beginning with the 13th pattern row.
13th pattern row: In s.s. all m.
14th to 17th rows: In s.s. all a.
18th row: 3 (4) (5) a., 5 b., 17 a., 5 b., 3 (4) (5) a.
19th row: 1 (2) (3) a., 9 b., 13 a., 9 b., 1 (2) (3) a.
The last 2 rows set the position of the pattern given in the chart.
Continuing in pattern as set work 5 rows more.
Now working extra sts. into the pattern as they occur inc. 1 st. at each end of the next row and the 5 following 12th rows.
On 45 (47) (49) sts. pattern 11 rows.
To shape the raglan sleevetop: Dec. 1 st. at each end of the next row and the 20 (21) (22) following alternate rows.
On 3 sts. work 1 row, then cast off.

The pocket tops *(both alike)*:
With right side of work facing rejoin m. to the 16 sts. left on stitch-holder and using No. 5 needles k. 6 rows, then cast off.

The button band and half collar:
With No. 5 needles and m. cast on 7 sts. and k. 96 rows.
**To shape for the collar inc. 1 st. at the beginning of the next row and the 20 (21) (22) following alternate rows.
On 28 (29) (30) sts. work 1 row.
Cast on 14 (15) (16) sts. at the beginning of the next row.
On 42 (44) (46) sts. k. 30 rows.
Cast off loosely.

The buttonhole band and half collar:
With No. 5 needles and m. cast on 7 sts. and k. 4 rows.
1st Buttonhole row: K. 2, cast off 3, k. to end.
2nd Buttonhole row: K. 2, turn, cast on 3, turn, k. to end.
K. 16 rows.
Repeat the last 18 rows 4 times more, then work the 2 buttonhole rows again.
Now work as given for buttonband and half collar from ** to end.

To make up the cardigan:
Pin out to size, then press all s.s. parts on the wrong side with a warm iron over a damp cloth. Join raglan seams so that the sts. cast off at top of sleeves form part of neck edge. Join sleeve and side seams. Join the half collars along the row ends of the last 30 rows for centre back neck. Sew bands and collar in place so that the first collar increases are in line with the first front edge decreases. Neatly sew pocket backs and row ends of pocket tops in position. Fold garter st. cuffs to right side and secure point of each cuff with a button. Sew on buttons. Press seams.

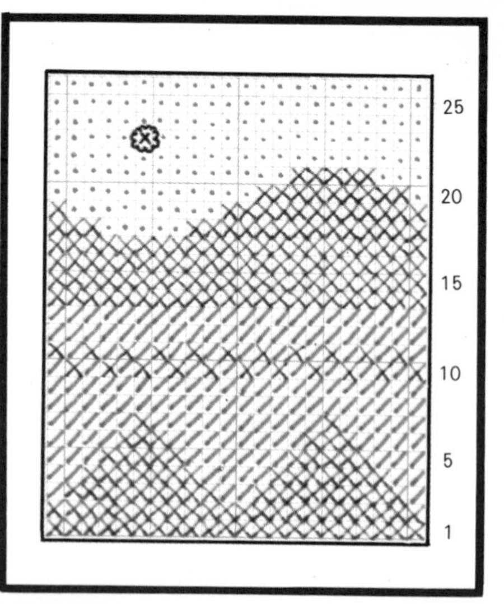

ROUGH STUFF

The softest wool ever, spun thick and thin, combined with simple knit and purl stitches, make this the easiest to knit, most luxury jacket imaginable. It's just as good for ladies too.

Materials:
50 ounces of 'Woollybear' soft chunky 100% wool slub; a pair each of size 8 mm (No. 0) and size 6 mm (No. 4) Aero knitting needles; a 55 cm (22 in.) open-ended zip fastener. The 'Woollybear' wool for this garment may be obtained by mail order from the Patricia Roberts Knitting Shop, 60 Kinnerton Street, London SW1, price inclusive of postage and V.A.T. £22.70.

Tension:
8 stitches—1 repeat of the pattern to 7.5 cm (3 in.) in width and 8 rows to 5 cm (2 in.) in depth using size 8 (No. 0) needles.

Abbreviations:
K., knit; p., purl; st., stitch; tog., together; dec., decrease (by working 2 sts. tog.); inc., increase (by working twice into same st.); single rib is k. 1 and p. 1 alternately; s.s., stocking stitch is k. on the right side and p. on the wrong side.

Note:
The instructions are given for the small size. Where they vary work the figures in the first brackets for the medium size, or the figures in the second brackets for the large size.

Measurements:

The measurements are given in centimetres followed by inches in square brackets.

small	medium	large
All round at underarms		
105 [42]	112.5 [45]	120 [48]
Side seam		
40 [16]	40 [16]	40 [16]
Length		
65 [26]	66 [26½]	67 [27]
Sleeve seam		
47.5 [19]	47.5 [19]	47.5 [19]

The back:
With size 6 mm (No. 4) needles cast on 56 (60) (64) sts. and work 20 rows in single rib.
Change to size 8 mm (No. 0) needles and work in pattern as follows: *1st row:* All k.
2nd row: * K. 4, p. 4, repeat from * ending last repeat p. 4 (k. 4) (p. 4).
3rd row: P. 1 (k. 1, p. 4) (p. 1), * k. 4, p. 4; repeat from * ending last repeat p. 3.
4th row: K. 2, * p. 4, k. 4; repeat from * ending last repeat k. 2 (p. 2)(k. 2).
5th row: P. 3 (k. 3, p. 4) (p. 3), * k. 4, p. 4; repeat from * ending last repeat p. 1.
6th row: * P. 4, k. 4; repeat from * ending last repeat k. 4 (p. 4) (k. 4).
7th row: All k.
8th row: * K. 4, p. 4; repeat from * ending last repeat p. 4 (k. 4) (p. 4).
9th row: K. 4 (p. 4, k. 4) (k. 4), * p. 4, k.4; repeat from * ending last repeat p. 4.
10th and 11th rows: As 8th and 9th rows.
12th row: All p.
13th row: P. 4 (k. 4, p. 4) (p. 4), * k. 4, p. 4; repeat from * ending last repeat k. 4.
14th row: K. 1, * p. 4, k. 4; repeat from * ending last repeat k. 3, (p. 3) k. 3).
15th row: P. 2 (k. 2, p. 4) (p. 2), * k. 4, p. 4; repeat from * ending last repeat p. 2.
16th row: K. 3, * p. 4, k. 4; repeat from * ending last repeat k. 1(p. 1) (k. 1).
17th row: K. 4 (p. 4, k. 4) (k. 4), * p. 4, k. 4; repeat from * ending last repeat p. 4.
18th row: All p.
19th row: P. 4 (k. 4, p. 4) (p. 4), * k. 4, p. 4; repeat from * ending last repeat k. 4.
20th row: * P. 4, k. 4; repeat from * ending last repeat k. 4 (p. 4) (k. 4).
21st and 22nd rows: As 19th and 20th rows.
The last 22 rows from the pattern; repeat them once more.
To slope the raglan armholes: Maintaining the continuity of the pattern as set dec. 1st at each end of the next row and the 2 following 4th rows then at each end of the 14 (15) (16) following alternate rows.
On 22 (24) (26) sts. work 1 row. Cast off.

The left front:
With size 6 mm (No. 4) needles cast on 28 (30) (32) sts. and work in rib with garter st. edging as follows.
1st row: * K. 1, p. 1; repeat from * until 2 remain, k. 2.
2nd row: K. 3, p. 1, * k. 1, p. 1; repeat from * to end.
Repeat the last 2 rows 9 times more.
Change to size 8 mm (No. 0) needles and work in pattern with garter st. edging as follows:
1st row: All k.
2nd row: K. 2, p. 2, * k. 4, p. 4; repeat from * ending last repeat with p. 4 (k. 2) (k. 4).
3rd row: P. 1 (3) (k. 1, p. 4), * k. 4, p. 4; repeat from * until 3 remain k. 3.
4th row: K. 6, * p. 4, k. 4; repeat from * ending last repeat k. 2 (k. 4) (p. 2).
The last 4 rows set the position of the pattern given for back, with 2 sts. garter st. edging at front edge.
Pattern 40 rows more as set.
***To slope the raglan armhole:* Dec. 1 st. at the beginning of the next row and the 2 following 4th rows, then on the 8 (9) (10) following alternate rows.
To shape the neck: While continuing to slope the raglan as before on every alternate row cast off 5 (6) (7) sts. at the beginning of the next row, then dec. 1 st. at the neck edge on the next row and the 4 following alternate rows.
P. 2, then k. 2 tog. and fasten off.

The right front:
With size 6 mm (No. 4) needles cast on 28 (30) (32) sts. and work in rib with garter st. edging as follows:

1st row: K. 2, * p. 1, k. 1, repeat from * to end.
2nd row: * P. 1, k. 1; repeat from * ending last repeat k. 3.
Repeat the last 2 rows 9 times more.
Change to size 8 mm (No. 0) needles and work in pattern with garter stitch edging as follows:
1st row: All k.
2nd row: P. 4 (k. 2, p. 4) (k. 4, p. 4), * k. 4, p. 4; repeat from * ending last repeat p. 2, k. 2.
The last 2 rows set the position of the pattern given for back with 2 st. garter st. edging at front edge.
Pattern 43 rows more as set.
Now work as given for left front from ** to end.

The sleeves *(both alike)*:
With size 6 mm (No. 4) needles cast on 40 (44) (48) sts. and work 10 rows in single rib.
Change to size 8 mm (No. 0) knitting needles and work 22 rows in pattern as given for back.
Continuing in pattern as set; inc. 1 st. at each end of the next row and the 3 following 10th rows.
On 48 (52) (56) sts. pattern 13 rows.
To shape the raglan sleeve top: Work as given for raglan armhole shaping on back, to end when 14 (16) (18) sts. will remain.
Cast off.

The collar:
First join raglan seams, so that the sts. cast off at top of sleeves from part of neck edge.
With right side of work facing rejoin yarn and using size 6 mm (No. 4) needles pick up and k. 22 (23) (24) sts. from right front neck edge, 24 (26) (28) sts. from top of right sleeves, 36 (38) (40) sts. from back neck edge, 24 (26) (28) sts. from top of left sleeve and 22 (23) (24) sts. from left front neck edge—128 (136) (144) sts.
Work 7 rows in single rib.
Decrease 1 st. at each end of the next 8 rows.
Cast off in rib.

The pocket backs *(two alike)*:
With size 8 mm (No. 0) needles cast on 16 sts. and s.s. 48 rows then cast off.

To make up the jacket:
Pin out to size and press all parts except the ribbing on the wrong side with a warm iron over a damp cloth. Fold pocket backs in half and join row end edges. Join sleeve and side seams, inserting pockets in side seams above ribbing. Neatly sew zip fastener in place. Press seams.

YOURS AND MINE

A multi-patterned cardigan to suit the whole family. It looks as attractive on men as it does on women, and is flattering regardless of age. It can be knitted quickly in Paton's double knitting yarn, and the chain stripes in contrasting colours are easy to do.

Materials:

7(8) (9) 50 gram balls of Patons Double Knitting; 3(4) (4) balls in first contrast colour and 1 (2) (2) balls in each of the 2 other contrasting colours; a pair each of No.10 and No.11 knitting needles; 6 buttons.

Tension:
13 stitches to 5 cm (2 in.) in width and 22 rows—1 repeat of the pattern to 5 cm (2 in.) in length over the pattern or 13 stitches and 17 rows to 5 cm (2 in.) over stocking stitch both using No.10 needles. If you cannot obtain the correct tension using needles of the size suggested, use larger or smaller needles accordingly.

Abbreviations:
K., knit; p., purl; st., stitch; tog., together; dec., decrease (by working 2sts. tog.); inc., increase (by working twice into same st.); sl., slip; m., main colour; a., first contrast colour; b., second contrast; c., third contrast; s.s., stocking stitch (k. on the right side and p. on the wrong side); garter st. is k. on every row; y.f., yarn forward; y.b., yarn back.

Note:
The instructions are given for the small size. Where they vary, work the figures in the first brackets for the medium size or the figures in the second brackets for the large size.

Measurements:
The following measurements are given in centimetres first, followed by inches in brackets.

small (10)	medium (12)	large (14)
All round at underarms		
85(34)	92.5(37)	100(40)
Side seam		
40(16)	40(16)	40(16)
Length		
60(24)	60.5(24¼)	61 (24½)
Sleeve seams excluding cuffs		
42.5(17)	42.5(17)	42.5(17)

The back:
With No.11 needles and a., cast on 110 (120) (130) sts. and k.12 rows.
Change to No.10 needles and work in pattern in the following way, joining in and breaking off colours as required.
1st to 4th rows: With m. beginning with a k. row s.s. these 4 rows.
5th and 6th rows: With b. all k. **
7th row: With m. sl.1, * k.8, sl.2; repeat from * ending last repeat sl.1.
8th row: With m. sl.1 p.wise, * p.8, sl.2 p. wise; repeat from * ending last repeat sl.1 p.wise.
9th row: With b. as 7th row.
10th row: With b. all k.
11th to 14th rows: With m. in s.s.
15th and 16th rows: With c. all k.
17th row: With m. k.4, * sl.2, k.8; repeat from * ending last repeat k.4.
18th row: With m. p.4, * sl.2 p.wise, p.8; repeat from * ending last repeat p.4.
19th row: With c. as 17th row.
20th row: With c. all k.
21st to 24th rows: With m. all k.
25th row: With a. k.1, * sl. 1, k.6, sl. 1, k.2; repeat from * ending last repeat k.1.
26th row: With a., * k.1, y.f., sl.1, y.b., k.6, y.f., sl.1, y.b., k.1; repeat from * to end.
27th and 28th rows: With m. in s.s.
29th row: With a. k.3, * sl.1, k.2, sl.1, k.6; repeat from * ending last repeat k.3.
30th row: With a. k.3, * y.f., sl.1, y.b., k.2, y.f., sl. 1, y.b., k.6; repeat from * ending last repeat k.3.
These 30 rows form the pattern; repeat them 4 more times, then work the first 16 rows again.
To shape the armholes: Maintaining the continuity of the pattern cast off 5sts. at the beginning of the next 2 rows, then dec. 1st. at each end of the next 10(12) (14) rows.
On 80(86) (92) sts. pattern 68(70) (72) rows.
To slope the shoulders: Cast off 5sts. at the beginning of the next 6 rows and 5(7) (9) sts. on the 2 following rows.
Cast off the remaining 40(42) (44) sts.

The pocket backs *(two alike)*:
With No.10 needles and m. cast on 34sts. and beginning with a k. row s.s. 54 rows, then cast off.

The left front:
With No.11 needles and a. cast on 50(55) (60) sts. and work as for back to **.
7th row: With m. sl.1, * k.8, sl.2; repeat from * ending last repeat sl.1 (sl.2, k.4) (sl.1).
8th row: With m. sl.1 p.wise (p.4, sl.2 p. wise) (sl.1 p.wise), * p.8, sl.2 p.wise; repeat from * ending last repeat sl.1 p. wise.
9th row: With b. as 7th row.
10th row: With b. all k.
The last 10 rows set the position of the pattern given for back.
Continuing in pattern as set pattern 22 more rows.
*** Cast off 10sts. at the beginning of the next row for pocket opening.
On 40(45) (50) sts., pattern 55 rows.
Cast on 10sts. at the beginning of the next row to close pocket opening.
On 50(55) (60) sts., pattern 45 more rows.

To slope the front edge: Continuing in pattern as set, dec. 1st. at end—front edge—next row and the 5 following 6th rows.
Pattern 1 row back to side seam edge.

To shape the armhole and to slope the front edge: Still decreasing 1st. at front edge on every 6th row from previous front edge dec., cast off 5sts. at beginning of next row, work 1 row back to armhole edge, then dec. 1st. at armhole edge on each of the next 10(12) (14) rows.
Pattern a further 41 (45) (49) rows decreasing 1st. at front edge on every 6th row as before.
On 20(22) (24) sts., pattern 27(25) (23) rows.
To slope the shoulder: Cast off 5sts. at the beginning of the next row and the 2 following alternate rows. On 5(7) (9) sts., work 1 row, then cast off.

The right front:
Work as for back to **.
7th row: With m. k. nil (4) (nil), sl.1 (2) (1), * k.8, sl.2; repeat from * ending last repeat sl.1.
The last 7 rows set the position of the pattern for back. Continuing in pattern as set pattern 26 more rows.
Now work as for left front from *** to end.

The pocket tops *(both alike)*:
With right side of work facing rejoin a. and using No.11 needles pick up and k.33sts. from row end edge of pocket opening. K.12 rows, then cast off.

The frontband:
With No.11 needles and a. cast on 14sts. and k.12 rows.
1st buttonhole row: K.5, cast off 4, k. to end
2nd buttonhole row: K.5, turn, cast on 4, turn, k. to end.
K.22 rows.
Repeat the last 24 rows 4 more times, then work the 2 buttonhole rows again.
Continue in garter stitch until the band is long enough to fit up right front, across back neck edge, then down left front edge.
Cast off when correct length is assured.

The sleeves *(both alike)*:
With No.11 needles and a. cast on 66(70) (74) sts. and k.24 rows.
Change to No.10 needles, break off a., join in m. With m. beginning with a k. row s.s.18 rows.
Inc. 1st. at each end of the next row and the 6 following 18th rows.
On 80(84) (88) sts. s.s.17 rows.
To shape the sleevetop: Cast off 5sts. at the beginning of the next 2 rows, then dec. 1st. at each end of the next row and the 5(7) (9) following alternate rows—58sts. Work 1 row.
Dec. 1st. at each end of next 12 rows.
Cast off 3sts. at beginning of next 8 rows.
Cast off remaining 10sts.

To make up the jacket:
Press all parts on the wrong side with a warm iron over a damp cloth. Join shoulder seams. Set in sleeves, sew pocket backs in place, then sew row ends of pocket tops in place. Join sleeve and side seams. Sew front band in place. Sew on buttons. Press seams. Fold cuffs to right side.

SHINE ON

Knit this simple swimsuit as a shining complement to the glitter bikini, in a different shade of the same yarn. The colour combination in our picture is gold, pink, silver and blue lurex entwined.

Materials:
5(6) (6) 20 gram balls of Wendy Minuit; a pair each of No. 12 and No. 13 knitting needles.

Tension:
16 stitches and 20 rows to 5 cm (2 in.) over the stocking stitch using No. 12 needles.

Abbreviations:
K., knit; p., purl; st., stitch; tog., together; dec., decrease (by working 2 sts. tog.); up 1, pick up the loop which lies between the needles slip it onto left-hand needle, then k. into back of it; s.s., stocking stitch (k. on the right side and p. on the wrong side); garter st. is k. plain on every row; sl., slip; p.s.s.o., pass sl. st. over.

Note:
The instructions are given for the small size. Where they vary work the figures in the first brackets for the medium size or the figures in the second brackets for the large size.

Measurements:
The measurements are given in centimetres followed by inches in square brackets.

To fit bust sizes		
80 [32]	85 [34]	90 [36]
All round at underarms		
61 [24½]	65 [26]	69 [27½]
Side seam		
35 [14]	35 [14]	35 [14]

Special note:
The measurements of this garment are smaller than those of the wearer for improved fit.

The back:
With No. 12 needles cast on 34 sts. and work in s.s. with garter st. edging and increase as follows:
1st row: K. 3, up 1, k. until 3 remain, up 1, k. 3.
2nd row: K. 3, p. until 3 remain, k. 3.
3rd row: As 1st row.
4th row: K. 3, up 1, p. until 3 remain, up 1, k. 3.
Repeat the last 4 rows 15 (16) (17) times more.
Mark each end of the last row with a coloured thread—130 (136) (142) sts.
Now continuing in s.s. only—without the garter st. edging—work as follows:
S.s. 50 rows.
1st Dec. row: K. 18 (21) (24), * sl. 1, k. 2 tog., p.s.s.o., k. 10; repeat from * ending last repeat k. 18 (21) (24)—114 (120) (126) sts.
S.s. 19 rows.
2nd Dec. row: K. 17 (20) (23), * sl. 1, k. 2 tog., p.s.s.o., k. 8; repeat from * ending last repeat k. 17 (20) (23)—98 (104) (110) sts.
S.s. 28 rows.
Now divide the sts. for the back: *Next row (wrong side):* P. 41 (42) (43) and leave these sts. on a spare needle until required for second half back, p. 16 (20) (24) and leave these sts. on a stitch-holder until required for edging, p. to end and continue on these 41 (42) (43) sts. for the first half back.
The first half back:
To shape the neck: Dec. 1 st. at end of the next row and at the same edge—inner edge—on each of the next 38 (39) (40) rows. Take the 2 remaining sts. tog. and fasten off.
The second half back:
With right side of work facing rejoin yarn to inner edge of sts. left on spare needle. Dec. 1 st. at the beginning—inner edge of next row and at the same edge on the next 38 (39) (40) rows. Take the 2 remaining sts. tog. and fasten off.

The front:
With No. 12 needles cast on 34 sts. and work in s.s. with garter st. edging as follows:
1st row: K. 3, k. 2 tog., k. until 5 remain, k. 2 tog., k. 3.
2nd row: K. 3, p. until 3 remain, k. 3.
Repeat the last 2 rows 4 times more.
On 24 sts. continue as follows:
1st row: All k.
2nd row: K. 3, p. until 3 remain, k. 3.
Repeat the last 2 rows 13 times more.
Now increase as follows: *1st row:* K. 3, up 1, k. until 3 remain, up 1, k. 3.
2nd row: K. 3, p. until 3 remain, k. 3.
Repeat the last 2 rows 16 (17) (18) times more—58 (60) (62) sts.
Next row: K. 3, up 1, k. until 3 remain, up 1, k. 3.
Next row: K. 3, up 1, p. until 3 remain, up 1, k. 3.
Repeat the last 2 rows 9 (10) (11) times more—98 (104) (110) sts. Mark each end of the last row with coloured threads.
Beginning with a k. row s.s. 140 rows.
To shape the top: 1st and 2nd turning rows: K. until 5 remain, turn, p. until 5 remain, turn.
3rd and 4th turning rows: K. until 10 remain, turn, p. until 10 remain, turn.
5th and 6th turning rows: K. until 15 remain, turn, p. until 15 remain, turn.
7th and 8th turning rows: K. until 20 remain, turn, p. until 20 remain, turn.
9th and 10th turning rows: K. until 25 remain, turn, p. until 25 remain, turn.
Change to No. 13 needles and work as follows: *Next row:* K. to end of row.
Next row: K. to end of row.
On all 98 (104) (110) sts. k. 4 rows, then cast off.

The back edging:
With right side of work facing rejoin yarn to the top of one half of back, using No. 13 needles pick up and k. 41 (42) (44) sts. from shaped row ends at inner edge of half back, k. across the 16 (20) (24) sts. at centre back, then pick up and k. 41 (42) (44) sts. from shaped row ends of other half back.
K. 5 rows, then cast off.

The straps *(2 alike):*
With No. 13 needles cast on 5 sts. and work in garter stitch until the straps are 60 cm (24 in.) long, then cast off.

To make up the swimsuit:
Pin out to size and press all s.s. parts lightly on the wrong side with a cool iron over a dry cloth. Join side seams from marking threads upwards. Join cast on edges of back and front. Make 2 chain loops at top of back each 4 cm (1½ in.) from centre back. Sew straps in place at front. Cross straps at back, thread through chain loops, then tie together. Press seams.

HOODWINKED

As simple to knit as it is easy to wear. Knit it in pastel shades for summer or darker tones for winter.

Materials:
22 (23) (24) 25 gram balls of Hayfield Gossamer; a pair each of size 6 mm (No. 4) and size 5 mm (No. 6) Aero knitting needles; 8 buttons.
Tension:
8 stitches and 10 rows to 5 cm (2 in.) over the stocking stitch using size 6 mm (No. 4) knitting needles.
Abbreviations:
K., knit; p., purl; st., stitch; tog., together; dec., decrease (by working 2 sts tog.); inc., increase (by working twice into same stitch); s.s., stocking stitch (k. on the right side and p. on the wrong side); y.r.n., yarn round needle; m.b., make bobble thus, k. 1, y.r.n., k. 1, y.r.n., k. 1, all into next st., turn p. 5, turn, k. 5, turn, p. 5, pass 2nd, 3rd, 4th and 5th sts. over first st. on left hand needle, k. 1 remaining st; single rib is k. 1 and p. 1 alternately; up 1., pick up the loop that lies between the needles, slip it onto left hand needle, then k. into back of it.
Note:
The instructions are given for the small size. Where they vary work the figures in the first brackets for the medium size or the figures in the second brackets for the large size.

Measurements:

The measurements are given in centimetres followed by inches in square brackets.

	small	medium	large
All round at underarms	95 [38]	100 [40]	105 [42]
Side seam	41 [16½]	41 [16½]	41 [16½]
Length	61 [24½]	62.5 [25]	64 [25½]
Sleeve seam	42.5 [17]	42.5 [17]	42.5 [17]

The back:
With size 5 mm (no. 6) needles cast on 65 (69) (73) sts. and work 21 rows in single rib.
Eyelet hole row: Rib 2, * y.r.n., k. 2 tog., rib 2; repeat from * ending last repeat rib 1.
Rib 1 row.
Increase row: Rib 5 (7) (9), * up 1, rib 5; repeat from * ending last repeat rib 5 (7) (9)—77 (81) (85) sts.
Change to size 6 mm (No. 4) needles and beginning with a k. row s.s. 6 rows.
Now work in pattern as follows:
1st row: k. 2 (4) (6) * m.b., k. 7; repeat from * ending last repeat k. 2 (4) (6).
2nd to 6th rows: s.s 5 rows.
7th row: K. 6 (8) (2), * m.b., k. 7, repeat from * ending last repeat k. 6 (8) (2).
8th to 12th rows: s.s. 5 rows.
The last 12 rows from the pattern; repeat them 3 times more, than work the first 8 rows again, mark each end of the last row with coloured threads to mark armhole.
To shape the raglan armholes: Maintaining the continuity of the pattern as set, dec. 1st at each end of the next row and the 14 following alternate rows.
Dec. 1 st. at each end of the next 11 (13) (15) rows.
Cast off the 25 remaining sts.

The left front:
With size 5 mm (No. 6) needles cast on 30 (32) (34) sts. and work 21 rows in single rib.
Eyelet hole row: Rib 2, * y.r.n., k. 2 tog., k. 2; repeat from * ending last repeat k. 2 (k. 2 tog.) (k. 2).
Rib 1 row.
Increase row: Rib 2 (3) (4), * up 1, rib 5; repeat from * ending last repeat rib , rib 3 (4) (5)—36 (38) (40) sts.
Change to size 6 mm (No. 4) needles and beginning with a k. row s.s. 6 rows.**
Now work in pattern as follows:
1st row: K. 2 (4) (6) * m.b., k. 7; repeat from * ending last repeat k. 1.
2nd to 6th rows: S.s. 5 rows.
7th row: K. 6 (8) (2), * m.b., k. 7; repeat from * ending last repeat k. 5.
8th to 12th rows: S.s. 5 rows.
The last 12 rows form the pattern; repeat them 3 times more, then work the first 8 rows again, marking the end of last row with a coloured thread to mark armhole.
****To slope the raglan armhole:* Dec. 1 st. at the beginning of the next row and the 9 following alternate rows.
To shape the neck and continue to slope the raglan armhole: Cast off 3 sts. at the beginning of the next row. Pattern 7 rows decreasing 1 st. at neck edge on each row and at the same time decreasing 1 st. at armhole edge on the first of these rows and the 3 following alternate rows.
Pattern 1 row straight.
Now dec. 1 st. at raglan armhole edge on each of the next 10 (12) (14) rows.
Take the 2 remaining sts. tog. and fasten off.

The right front:
Work as given for left front until ** is reached.
Now work in pattern as follows:
1st row: K. 1, * m.b., k. 7; repeat from * ending last repeat k. 2 (4) (6).
The last row sets the position of the pattern given for back. Pattern 56 rows more as set. Mark the end of the last row with a coloured thread to mark armhole.
Now work as given for left front from *** to end.

The sleeves *(both alike):*
With size 5 mm (No. 6) needles cast 31 (33) (35) sts. and work 21 rows in single rib.
Increase row: Rib 1, * up 1, rib 1, repeat from * to end.
Change to size 6 mm (No. 4) needles and on 61 (65) (69) sts and work 68 rows in pattern as given for back. Mark each end of the last row with coloured threads to mark sleeve top.
To shape the raglan sleeve top: Work as given for raglan shaping on back to end, when 9 sts. will remain, cast off.

The left front band:
With size 5 mm (No. 6) needles cast on 7 sts. and work 106 rows in single rib, then cast off.

The right front band:
With size 5 mm (No. 6) needles cast on 7 sts. and work 4 rows in single rib.
1st Buttonhole row: Rib 2, cast off 3, rib to end.
2nd Buttonhole row: Rib 2, turn, cast on 3, turn, rib to end.
Rib 12 rows.
Repeat the last 14 rows 6 times, then work the 2 buttonhole rows again.
Rib 2 rows.
Cast off.

The pocket backs *(two alike):*
With size 6 mm (No. 4) Needles cast on 20 sts. and work 50 rows in s.s., then cast off.

The hood:
First join raglan seams, so that the sts. cast off at top of sleeves form part of neck edge. With right side of work facing rejoin yarn and using size 5 mm (No. 6) needles pick up and k. 26 sts. from right front neck edge, 9 sts. from top of right sleeve; 25 sts. from back neck edge, 9 sts. from top of left sleeve and 26 sts. from left front neck edge—95 sts.
Now work in bobble pattern with ribbed edgings as follows:
1st row: Rib 5, k until 5 remain, rib 5.
2nd row: Rib 5, p. until 5 remain, rib 5.
3rd and 4th row: As 1st and 2nd rows.
5th row: Rib 5, k. 2, * m.b., k. 7, repeat from * ending last repeat k. 2, rib 5.
6th row: As 2nd row.
7th to 10th rows: Repeat 1st and 2nd rows twice.
11th row: Rib 5, k. 6, * m.b., k. 7; repeat from * ending last repeat k. 6, rib 5.
12th row: As 2nd row.
Repeat the last 12 rows 5 times more, then cast off.

The chord:
Cut 3 lengths of yarn each 450 cm (180 in.) long. Knot one end, then twist firmly in one direction. Fold in half allowing the two halves to twist together. Knot each end.

To make up the jacket:
Pin out to size and press all parts except the ribbing on the wrong side with a warm iron over a damp cloth. Fold pocket backs in half and join row end edges. Join sleeve and side seams, inserting pockets above ribbing at side seams. Sew front bands in place. Press seams. Sew on buttons. Thread chord through eyelet holes.

FISHERMAN'S LUCK

A fisherman's sweater for those men who sit by the river every weekend—or for those who simply stay at home and think about it! The sweater's cross-over ribbed collar makes it easy to wear with or without a shirt. It is knitted in Robin's Rusticana double knitting yarn, which is obtainable in lovely muted autumn shades.

Materials:
21(22)(23) 25 gram balls of Robin Rusticana Double Knitting in main colour; and 1 ball of the same yarn in each of 5 contrasting colours; a pair each of No. 10 and No. 11 knitting needles.

Tension:
13 stitches and 17 rows to 5 cm (2 in.) over stocking stitch using No.10 needles. If you cannot obtain the correct tension using needles of the size suggested, use larger or smaller ones accordingly.

Abbreviations:
K., knit; p., purl; st., stitch; tog., together; dec., decrease (by working 2 sts. tog.); inc., increase (by working twice into same st.); double rib is k.2 and p.2 alternately; s.s., stocking stitch (k. on the right side and p. on the wrong side); m., main colour; a., first contrast colour; b., second contrast colour.

Note:
The instructions are given for the small size. Where they vary, work the figures in the first brackets for the medium size or the figures in the second brackets for the large size.

Measurements:
The following measurements are given in centimetres first, followed by inches in brackets.

small	medium	large
All round at underarms		
92.5(37)	97.5(39)	102.5(41)
Side seam		
40(16)	40(16)	40(16)
Length		
64(25½)	65(26)	66(26½)
Sleeve seam		
47.5(19)	47.5(19)	47.5(19)

The back:
With No.11 needles and m. cast on 122 (128)(134) sts. and work 40 rows in double rib.
Change to No.10 needles and beginning with a k. row s.s.102 rows.
To shape the raglan armholes: Dec. 1st. at each end of the next row and the 39 (41)(43) following alternate rows.
On 42(44)(46) sts. work 1 row.
Change to No. 11 needles and work 54 rows in double rib, then cast off in rib loosely.

The front:
Work as given for back until 20 rows have been worked in s.s.
Now work the fisherman motif in the following way. This is worked entirely in s.s. so only the colour details follow. Take great care not to pull colours not in use tightly across the back of the work or it will become puckered. Join in and break off colours as required.
1st row: 35(38)(41) m., 3a., 1m., 6a., 51m., 2a., 24(27)(30) m.
2nd row: 24(27)(30) m., 2a., 1m., * 2b., 2m.; repeat from * 9 more times, 2b., 8m., 10a., 35(38)(41) m.
These 2 rows set the position of the pattern given in the chart, now work the 3rd to 58th rows from the chart.
Continuing with m. only s.s.23 rows.
Now divide the sts. for the neck: *Next row:* (wrong side): P.51(53)(55), and leave these sts. on a spare needle until required for right front shoulder, cast off 20(22)(24) sts. for neck opening, then p. to end and continue on these 51(53)(55) sts. for the left front shoulder.
The left front shoulder: To shape the raglan armhole and to shape the neck: Pattern 78(82)(86) rows decreasing 1st. at the armhole edge on every right side row *and at the same time* dec. 1st. at the neck edge on the first of these rows and the 9 following 8th rows.
Take the 2 remaining sts. together and fasten off.
The right front shoulder: With right side of work facing rejoin m. to inner edge of sts.

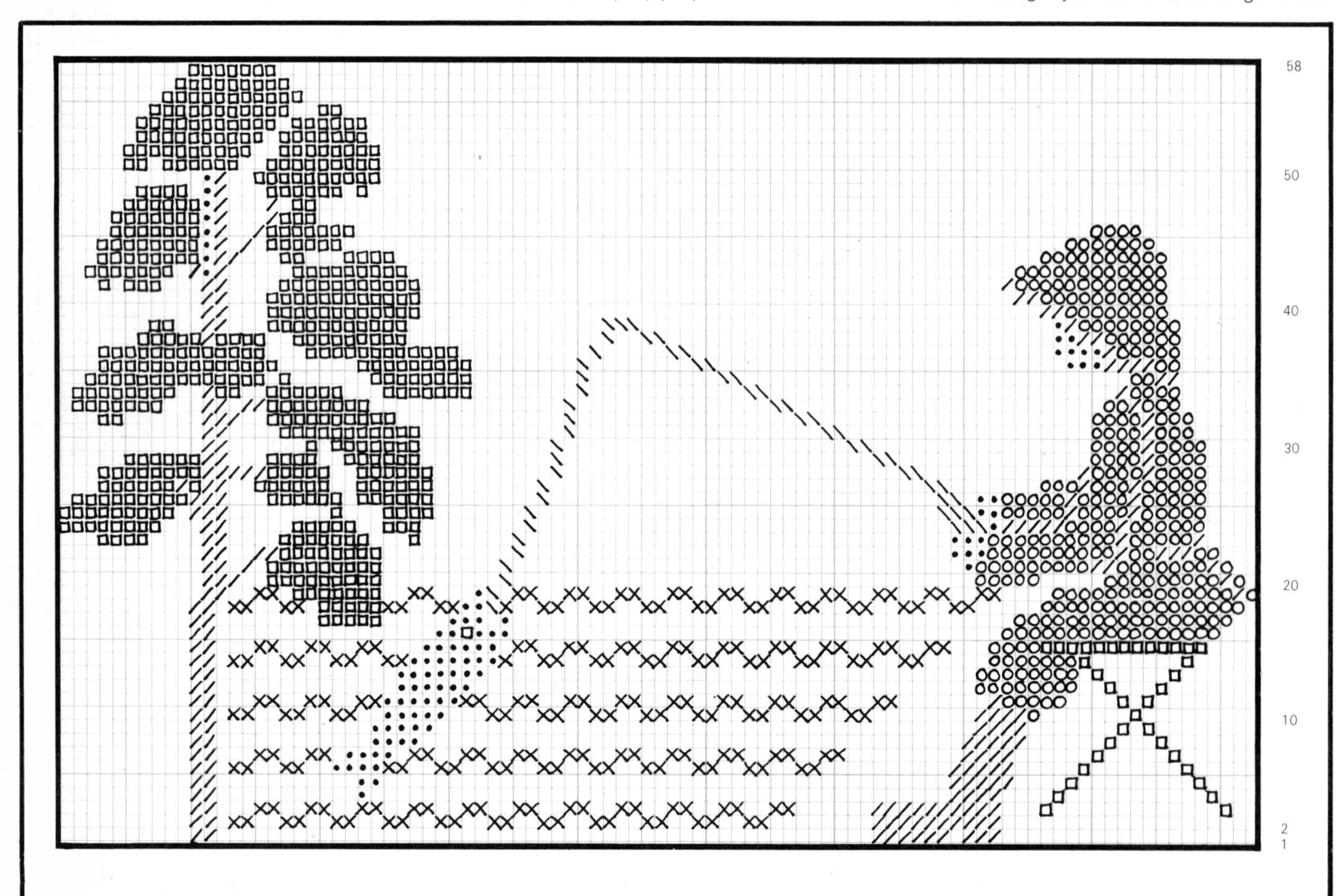

left on spare needle and work as given for left front shoulder to end.

The sleeves *(both alike):*
With No.11 needles and m. cast on 64 (68) (72) sts. and work 40 rows in double rib.
Change to No.10 needles and beginning with a k. row s.s.6 rows.
Inc. 1st. at each end of the next row and the 11 following 12th rows.
On 88 (92) (96) sts. s.s.5 rows.
To shape the raglan sleevetop: Dec. 1st. at each end of the next row and the 39 (41) (43) following alternate rows.
On 8 sts. work 1 row, then cast off.

The pocket:
With No. 11 needles and m. cast on 26sts. and k.8 rows.
Change to No.10 needles and work as follows:
1st row: All k. *2nd row:* K.4, p.18, k.4.
Repeat these 2 rows 14 more times.
Change to No.11 needles and k.16 rows, then cast off.

The left and right half collars
(both alike as the fabric is reversible):
With No.11 needles and m. cast on 20 (22) (24) sts. and work 2 rows in double rib. Continuing in rib inc. 1st. at the beginning of the next row and the 19 (20) (21) following 4th rows.
On 40 (43) (46) sts. work 1 row.
Cast on 8sts. at the beginning of the next row.
On 48 (51) (54) sts. rib 53 rows, then cast off.

To make up the sweater:
Press all parts except the ribbing on the wrong side with a warm iron over a damp cloth. Set in raglan sleeves, so that the sts. cast off at top of sleeves form part of neck edge. Join sleeve and side seams. Neatly sew left half collar in position so that the cast on edge is sewn to sts. cast off for neck at centre front, the 8 sts. cast on groups at shaped edge of collar is sewn to the 8sts. cast off at top of sleeves and the 53 straight row end edge is sewn to row end edge of back collar. Now sew right half collar in place so that the cast on edge is sewn behind that of left front edge. Neatly sew pocket in place on left sleeve, folding the 12k. rows at top to right side and catching in place. Press seams.

CLOWNABOUT

Follow the colour chart carefully, and you will find it easier than you think to reproduce this brightly coloured clown motif. A black bobble makes the nose, while the pocket back is red—the collar could also be knitted in red for a different look.

Materials:
8 (10) (12) 25 gram balls of Patons Purple Heather 4-ply in main colour and one ball in each of the 5 contrast colours—here snow white, lipstick red, steel grey mix, black and tan; a pair each of No. 12 and No. 13 knitting needles; 1 button.

Tension:
16 stitches and 20 rows to 5 cm (2 in.) over stocking stitch using No. 12 needles. If you cannot obtain the correct tension using the size needles suggested, use larger or smaller ones accordingly.

Abbreviations:
K., knit; p., purl; st., stitch; tog., together; dec., decrease (by working 2 sts. tog.); single rib is k.1 and p.1 alternately; s.s., stocking stitch (k. on the right side and p. on the wrong side); up 1, pick up the loop that lies between the needles, slip it on to left hand needle, then k. into back of it; inc., increase (by working twice into same st.); sl., slip; p.s.s.o., pass sl. st. over; m.b. make bobble thus, k.1, p.1, k.1, p.1, k.1 all into next st., turn, p.5, turn, k.5, turn, p.2 tog., p.1, p.2 tog., turn, sl.1, k.2 tog., p.s.s.o.; m., main colour; a., first contrast—white; b., black; c., tan; d., red; e., grey.

Note:
The instructions are given for the first size. Where they vary work the figures in the first brackets for the second size or the figures in the second brackets for the third size.

Measurements:
The measurements are given in centimetres followed by inches in square brackets.

To fit chest sizes		
60 [24]	65 [26]	70 [28]
All round at underarms		
60 [24]	65 [26]	70 [28]
Side seam		
25 [10]	29 [11½]	32.5 [13]
Length		
39 [15½]	44 [17½]	49 [19½]
Sleeve seam (with cuffs folded in half)		
27.5 [11]	31 [12½]	35 [14]

The back:
With No. 13 needles and m. cast on 88 (96) (104) sts. and work 25 (27) (29) rows in single rib.

Increase row: Rib 9 (13) (17), * up 1, rib 10; repeat from * ending last repeat rib 9 (13) (17).

Change to No. 12 needles and on 96 (104) (112) sts. beginning with a k. row s.s. 78 (90) (102) rows.

To shape the raglan armholes: Cast off 2 (2) (3) sts. at the beginning of the next 2 rows, then dec. 1 st. at each end of the next row and the 25 (28) (30) following alternate rows.

On 40 (42) (44) sts. p.1 row, then cast off.

The pocket back:
With No. 12 needles and d. cast on 18 (20) (22) sts. and beginning with a k. row s.s. 22 (24) (26) rows, then leave these sts. on a stitch-holder until required.

The front:
Work as given for back until the increase row has been worked.

Change to No. 12 needles and on 96 (104) (112) sts. beginning with a k. row s.s. 2 (6) (12) rows.

Now work the clown motif as follows. This is worked entirely in s.s. so only the colour details are given. Take great care to avoid pulling colours not in use tightly across the back of the work or it will become puckered.

1st row: 73 (77) (81) m., 8 a., 15 (19) (23) m.

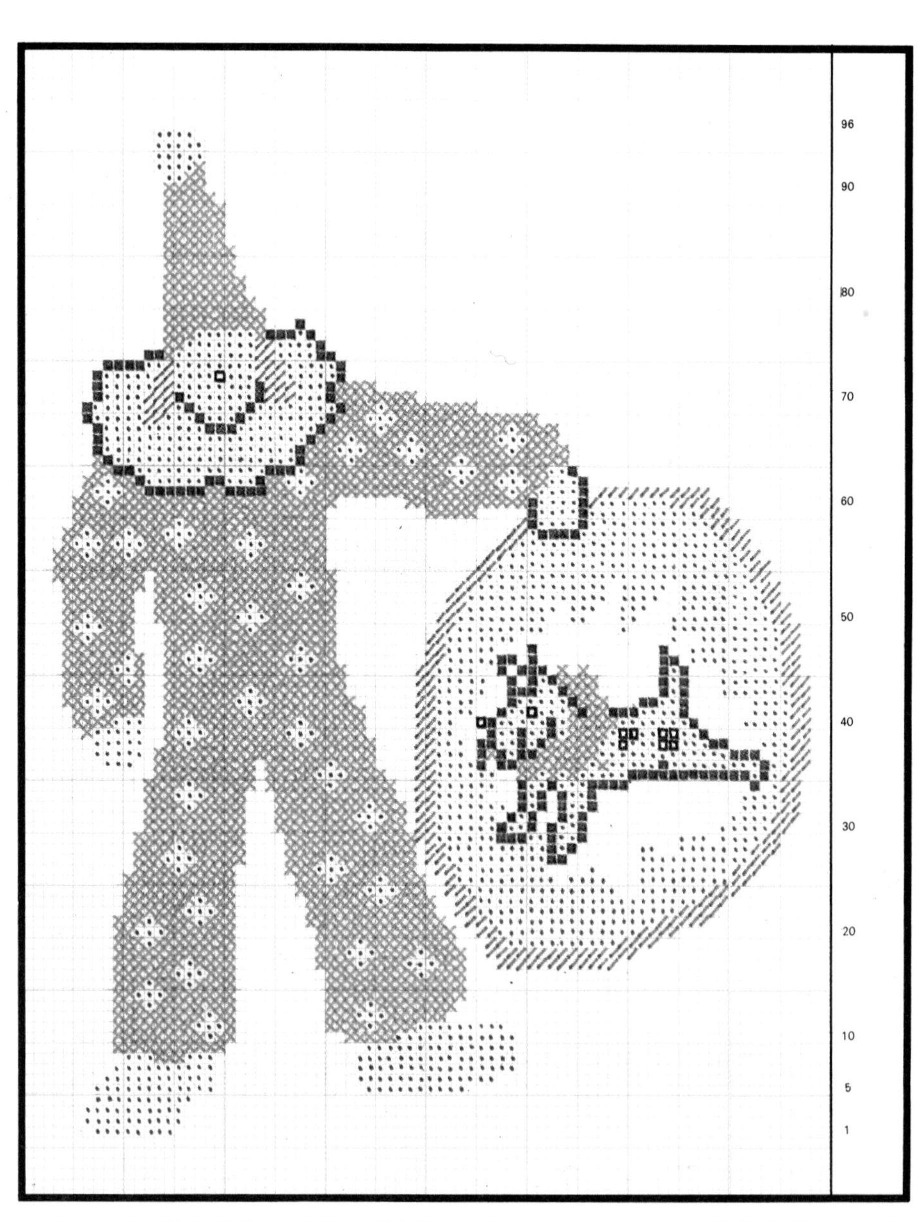

2nd row: 14 (18) (22) m., 10 a., 72 (76) (80) m.

These 2 rows set the position of the pattern given in the chart, now work the 3rd to 72nd rows from the chart as set.

73rd row: 56 (60) (64) m., 1 e., 5 a., 3 c., 3 a., with b. m.b.—see abbreviations—4 a., 2 c., 5 a., 1 e., 15 (19) (23) m.

Now work the 74th row as set.

Pocket row: 16 (18) (20) m., slip next 18 (20) (22) sts. on to a stitch-holder until required and in their place with m. k. across the 18 (20) (22) sts. of pocket back, work to end in pattern as set.

Pattern 1 (9) (15) row(s) as set.

To shape the raglan armholes: Continuing in pattern as set, cast off 2 (2) (3) sts. at the beginning of the next 2 rows, then dec. 1 st. at each end of the next row and the 5 (7) (9) following alternate rows—80 (84) (86) sts.

Now divide the sts. for the neck: *Next row:* P. 34 (36) (37) and leave these sts. on a spare needle until required for right front shoulder, cast off next 12 sts., p. to end and continue on these 34 (36) (37) sts. for the left front shoulder.

The left front shoulder:
Dec. 1 st. at the beginning of the next row for raglan and the 7 following alternate rows.

On 26 (28) (29) sts. work 1 row.

To shape the neck and continue to slope the

raglan: While decreasing 1 st. at the armhole edge as before on each alternate row, dec. 1 st. at the neck edge on each of the next 13 (14) (15) rows.
Still decreasing for raglan on each alternate row, s.s. a further 9 (10) (9) rows—2 sts.
Take the 2 remaining sts. tog. and fasten off.
The right front shoulder:
With right side of work facing rejoin yarn to inner edge of sts. on spare needle and work to end of row. Now work as given for left front shoulder to end.
The pocket top:
With right side of work facing rejoin m. to the 18 (20) (22) sts. left on stitch-holder and using No. 13 needles work 4 rows in single rib, then cast off.
The sleeves *(both alike)***:**
With No. 13 needles and m. cast on 40 (42) (44) sts. and work 44 rows in single rib.
Change to No. 12 needles and beginning with a k. row s.s. 8 rows.
Continuing in s.s. inc. 1 st. at each end of the next row and the 9 (11) (13) following 8th rows.
On 60 (66) (72) sts. s.s. 9 (7) (7) rows.
To shape the raglan sleevetop: Work as given for raglan armhole shaping on back to end, when 4 sts. will remain, cast off.
The neckbands and collar:
With No. 13 needles and m., cast on 18 sts. and work 8 rows in single rib.
1st Buttonhole row: Rib 6, cast off 6, rib to end.
2nd Buttonhole row: Rib 6, turn, cast on 6, turn, rib to end.
Rib 6 rows.
To shape for the collar: Inc. 1 st. at the beginning of the next row and at the same edge on each of the next 23 (25) (25) rows.
On 42 (44) (44) sts., rib 60 (62) (64) rows.
Dec. 1 st. at the beginning of the next row and at the same edge on each of the next 23 (25) (25) rows.
On 18 sts. rib 16 rows, then cast off.

To make up the sweater:
Pin out to size and press all s.s. parts on the wrong side with a warm iron over a damp cloth. Join raglan seams, so that the sts. cast off at top of sleeves form part of neck edge. Join sleeve and side seams. Neatly sew pocket back in place. Fold pocket top down to right side and neatly catch row ends in place. Sew shaped row end edge of collar and front neckbands in place. Sew on button. Press seams.

BUMPER-JUMPER

A cardigan for boys or girls. Wear it to school or for best. There are so many colours knitted into the pattern, that the garment could be worn with almost any colour. The hood will keep you warm and cosy on wintry days.

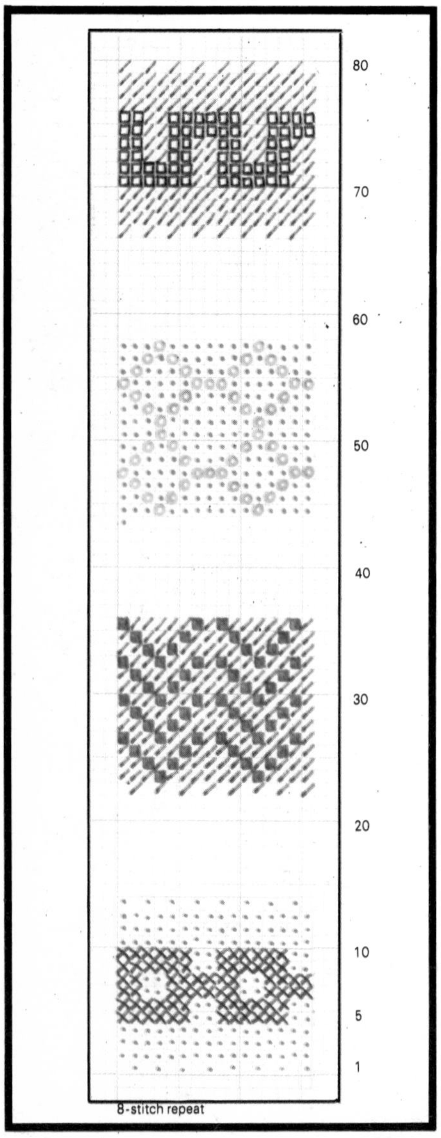

8-stitch repeat

Materials:
8 (10) (12) 25 gram balls of Paton's Purple Heather 4-ply in main colour, and two ball in each of the 6 contrast colours; a pair each of No. 12 and No. 13 knitting needles; 7 (8) (9) buttons.
Tension:
16 stitches and 20 rows to 5 cm (2 in.) over the stocking stitch using No. 12 needles. If you cannot obtain the correct tension using the size needles suggested use larger or smaller ones accordingly.
Abbreviations:
K., knit; p., purl; st., stitch; tog., together; dec., decrease (by working 2 sts. tog.); inc., increase (by working twice into same st.); s.s., stocking stitch (k. on the right side and p. on the wrong side); single rib is k. 1 and p. 1 alternately; up 1, pick up the loop that lies between the needles, slip it on to left hand needle, then k. into back of it; m., main colour; a., first contrast colour; b., second contrast colour.
Note:
The instructions are given for the first size. Where they vary work the figures in the first brackets for the second size or the figures in the second brackets for the third size.

Measurements:
The measurements are given in centimetres followed by inches in square brackets.

To fit chest sizes		
60 [24]	65 [26]	70 [28]
All round at underarms		
62.5 [25]	67.5 [27]	72.5 [29]
Side seam		
25 [10]	29 [11½]	32.5 [13]
Length		
39 [15½]	44 [17½]	49 [19½]
Sleeve seam (with cuffs folded in half)		
27.5 [11]	31 [12½]	35 [14]

The back:
With No. 13 needles and m. cast on 88 (96) (104) sts. and work 25 (27) (29) rows in single rib.
Increase row: Rib 9 (13) (17), * up 1, rib 10; repeat from * ending last repeat rib 9 (13) (17).
Change to No. 12 needles and on 96 (104) (112) sts. beginning with a k. row s.s. 4 rows.
Now work in pattern as follows. This is worked entirely in s.s. so only the colour details are given. Take great care to avoid pulling colours not in use tightly across the back of the work or it will become puckered.
1st row: * 1 m., 1 a.; repeat from * to end.
2nd, 3rd, and 4th rows: All a.
5th row: 1 a., * 6 b., 2 a.; repeat from * ending last repeat 1 a.
6th row: As 5th row.
The last 6 rows set the position of the pattern given in the chart. Now work the 7th to 74th (86th) (88th) rows from the chart.
For the third size only: Work the 1st to 10th pattern rows again.
For all sizes—to shape the raglan armholes: Continuing in pattern from chart as set cast off 2 (2) (3) sts. at the beginning of the next 2 rows, then dec. 1 st. at each end of the next row and the 25 (28) (30) following alternate rows.
On 40 (42) (44) sts. work 1 row, then cast off.
The pocket backs *(both alike)***:**
With No. 12 needles and m. cast on 20 (22) (24) sts. and beginning with a k. row s.s. 30 rows, then leave these sts. on a stitch-holder until required.
The left front:
With No. 13 needles and m. cast on 44 (48) (52) sts. and work 25 (27) (29) rows in single rib.
Increase row: Rib 9 (13) (17), * up 1, rib 10; repeat from * ending last repeat rib 5.
Change to No. 12 needles and on

48 (52) (56) sts., beginning with a k. row s.s. 4 rows.
Now work in pattern as follows, noting the information given for the back.
1st row: * 1 m., 1 a.; repeat from * to end.
2nd to 4th rows: All a.
5th row: 1 a., * 6 b., 2 a.; repeat from * ending last repeat 1 a. (3 b.) (1 a.).
The last 5 rows set the position of the pattern given in the chart. Now work the 6th to 38th rows from the chart as set.
Pocket row: Work as set across 14 (15) (16) sts., slip next 20 (22) (24) sts. on to a stitch-holder and leave at front of work, in their place work across the 20 (22) (24) sts. of one pocket back, work to end of row.
Pattern 35 (47) (59) rows more as set.
***To shape the raglan armhole:* Cast off 2 (2) (3) sts. at the beginning of the next row, then work 1 row straight.
Dec. 1 st. at the beginning—armhole edge on the next row and the 5 (7) (8) following alternate rows.
Work 1 row straight.
To slope the neck and continue to slope the raglan armhole: Dec. 1 st. at each end of the next row and the 18 (19) (20) following alternate rows—2 sts. P. 2, then k. 2 tog. and fasten off.

The right front:
With No. 13 needles and m. cast on 44 (48) (52) sts. and work 25 (27) (29) rows in single rib.
Increase row: Rib 5, * up 1, rib 10; repeat from * ending last repeat rib 9 (13) (17).
Change to No. 12 needles and on 48 (52) (56) sts. beginning with a k. row s.s. 4 rows.
Now work in pattern as follows.
1st row: * 1 a., 1 m.; repeat from * to end.
2nd to 4th rows: All a.
5th row: 1 a., (3 b., 2 a.) (1 a.), * 6 b., 2 a.; repeat from * ending last repeat 1 a.
The last 5 rows set the position of the pattern given in the chart. Work the 6th to 38th rows from the chart as set.
Work the pocket row as given for left front, then pattern 36 (48) (60) rows more as set.
Now work as given for left front from ** to end.

The pocket tops *(both alike)*:
With right side of work facing rejoin m. to the 20 (22) (24) sts. left on stitch-holder and using No. 13 needles work 6 rows in single rib, then cast off.

The sleeves *(both alike)*:
With No. 13 needles and m. cast on 42 (44) (46) sts. and work 54 (64) (72) rows in single rib.
Change to No. 12 needles and beginning with a k. row s.s. 10 rows.
Now work in pattern as follows.
1st row: * 1 m., 1 a.; repeat from * to end.
2nd to 4th rows: All a.
5th row: 2 a., (1 b., 2 a.), (2 b., 2 a.) * 6 b., 2 a.; repeat from * ending last repeat 2 a. (2 a., 1 b.) (2 a., 2 b).
6th row: As 5th row.
The last 6 rows set the position of the pattern given in the chart.
Continuing in pattern as set, inc. 1 st. at each end of the next row and the 8 (10) (12) following 8th (6th) (6th) rows.
On 60 (66) (72) sts. s.s. 3 (19) (19) rows.
To shape the raglan sleevetop: Work as given for raglan armhole shaping on back to end, when 4 sts. will remain, cast off.

The button band:
With No. 13 needles and m. cast on 12 sts. and work 118 (136) (152) rows in single rib.
Inc. 1 st. at the beginning of the next row and at the same edge on each of the next 19 (21) (23) rows, then leave these 32 (34) (36) sts. on a spare needle until required for hood.

The buttonhole band:
With No. 13 needles and m. cast on 12 sts. and work 6 rows in single rib.
1st Buttonhole row: Rib 4, cast off 4, rib to end.
2nd Buttonhole row: Rib 4, turn, cast on 4, rib to end.
Rib 16 rows.
Repeat the last 18 rows 5 (6) (7) times, then work the 2 buttonhole rows again. Rib 2 (2) (nil) rows, then inc. 1 st. at the end of the next row and at the same edge on the 19 (21) (23) following rows, then leave these 32 (34) (36) sts. on a spare needle until required for hood.

The hood:
Rejoin m. to the straight row end edge of buttonhole band and using No. 13 needles rib across these sts., turn, cast on 80 (82) (84) sts., turn, beginning at shaped edge of buttonband rib across these 32 (34) (36) sts.
On 144 (150) (156) sts. rib 60 (64) (70) rows.
Now divide the sts. for the back of the hood:
Next row: Rib 52 (54) (56), and leave these sts. on a spare needle until required, cast off 40 (42) (44) sts., rib to end and continue on these 52 (54) (56) sts.
1st half hood: On 52 (54) (56) sts. rib 20 (21) (22) rows, then cast off.
2nd half hood: With right side of work facing rejoin m. to the 52 (54) (56) sts. on spare needle and rib 20 (21) (22) rows, then cast off.

To make up the jacket:
Pin out to size and press all s.s. parts on the wrong side with a warm iron over a damp cloth. Join raglan seams so that the sts. cast off at top of sleeves form part of neck edge. Join sleeve and side seams. Sew front bands and hood in place. Join cast off edges of side pieces of hood, then join cast off sts. at centre of hood to the row end edges side pieces. Neatly sew pocket backs in place and sew row ends of pocket top in position. Press seams. Sew on buttons.

NOSTALGIA TRIP

For casual chic, knit this sweater for your man in classic shades, then borrow it for yourself.

Materials:
24 (25) (26) 25 gram balls of Sirdar Fontein Crepe 4 ply; a pair each of size 2¼ mm (No. 13) and size 3 mm (No. 11) Aero knitting needles and a cable needle; 3 buttons.
Tension:
26 stitches and 33 rows to 7.5 cm (3 in.) over the pattern using size 3 mm (No. 11) Aero knitting needles.
Abbreviations:
K., knit; p., purl; st., stitch; tog., together; dec., decrease (by working 2 sts. tog.); inc., increase (by working twice into same st.); single rib is k. 1 and p. 1 alternately; cable 6, slip next 3 sts. onto cable needle at front of work, k. 3, then k. 3 from cable needle; up 1, pick up the loop which lies between the needle, slip it onto lefthand needle, then k. into back of it; s.s., stocking st. is k. on the right side and p. on the wrong side.
Note:
The instructions are given for the small size. Where they vary work the figures in the first brackets for the medium size or the figures in the second brackets for the large size.

Measurements:

The measurements are given in centimetres followed by inches in square brackets.

small	medium	large
All round at underarms		
94 [37½]	101 [40½]	109 [43½]
Side seam		
41 [16½]	41 [16½]	41 [16½]
Length		
65 [26]	66 [26½]	67.5 [27]
Sleeve seam		
47.5 [19]	47.5 [19]	47.5 [19]

The back:
With size 2¼ mm (No. 13) needles cast on 146 (158) (170) sts. and work 43 rows in single rib.
Increase row: Rib 9 (11) (13), * up 1, rib 8: repeat from * ending last repeat rib 9 (11) (13).
Change to size 3 mm (No. 11) needles and on 163 (176) (189) sts., work in pattern as follows:
1st row: P. 1, k. 1, p. 1, k. 1, p. 1, k. 1, p. 1, * k. 6, p. 1, k. 1, p. 1, k. 1, p. 1, k. 1, p. 1; repeat from * to end.
2nd row: K. 1, p. 1, k. 1, p. 1, k. 1, p. 1, k. 1, * p. 6, k. 1, p. 1, k. 1, p. 1, k. 1, p. 1, k. 1; repeat from * to end.
3rd and 4th rows: As 1st and 2nd rows.
5th row: Rib 7 as set, * cable 6, rib 7 as set; repeat from * to end.
6th row: As 2nd row.
7th and 8th rows: As 1st and 2nd rows.
The last 8 rows form the pattern; repeat them 16 times more, then work the first 2 rows again.
Mark each end of the last row with coloured threads to mark armholes.**
Pattern 102 (108) (114) rows more.
To slope the shoulders: Cast off 51 (55) (59) sts. at the beginning of the next 2 rows—61 (66) (71) sts.
Change to size 2¼ mm (No. 13) needles and work in moss st. as follows: Next row: K. 1 (k. 2 tog.) (k. 1), * p. 1, k. 1; repeat from * to end.
Pattern row: * K. 1, p. 1; repeat from * ending last repeat k. 1.
Repeat the last row 14 times more.
Cast off loosely.

The front:
Work as given for back until ** is reached.
Pattern 1 (5) (9) row(s) more.
Now divide the sts. for the front opening: Next row: Pattern 72 (79) (85) and leave these sts. on a spare needle until required for right front shoulder, cast off 19 (18) (19), pattern to end and continue on these 72 (79) (85) sts. for the left front shoulder.
The left front shoulder: Pattern 51 rows.
To shape the neck: Cast off 3 (4) (4) sts. at the beginning of the next row, then dec. 1 st. at the neck edge on each of the next 18 (20) (22) rows—51 (55) (59) sts.
Pattern 30 rows more, then cast off.
The right front shoulder: With right side of work facing rejoin yarn to inner edge of sts. left on spare needle, pattern to end of row, then work as given for left front shoulder to end.

The sleeves *(both alike)*:
With size 2¼ mm (No. 13) needles cast on 85 (90) (94) sts. and work 66 rows in single rib.
Change to size 3 mm (No. 11) needles and work in pattern as follows: 1st row: Beginning with p. 1, rib 7 (3) (5), * k.6, beginning with p. 1, rib 7; repeat from * ending last repeat rib 7 (3) (5).

The last row sets the position of the pattern given for back; pattern 3 rows more as set. Continuing in pattern as set and working the extra sts. into the pattern as they occur, inc. 1 st. at each end of the next row and the 35 (37) (39) following 4th rows.
On 157 (166) (174) sts. pattern 31 (23) (15) rows, then cast off.

The right front band:
With size 2¼ mm (No. 13) needles cast on 19 sts. and work in moss st. as follows:
Pattern row: K. 1, * p. 1, k. 1; repeat from * to end.
Repeat the last row 51 times more.
Next row: Using the needle holding the 19 sts., pick up and k. 51 (54) (56) sts. from right front neck edge.
On 70 (73) (75) sts. moss st. 15 rows as set.
Cast off.

The left front band:
With size 2¼ mm (No. 13) needles cast on 19 sts. and work 10 rows in moss st. as given for right front band.
1st Buttonhole row: Moss st. 7, cast off 5, moss st. to end.
2nd Buttonhole row: Moss st. 7, turn, cast on 5, turn, moss st. to end.
Moss st. 22 rows, work the 2 buttonhole rows again, then moss st. 16 rows.
Now with right side of work facing rejoin yarn and using the empty needle, pick up and k. 51 (54) (56) sts. from left front neck edge, then moss st. across the 19 sts. of frontband—70 (73) (75) sts.
Moss st. 5 rows.
Next Buttonhole row: Moss st. 58 (61) (63), turn, cast off 5, moss st. to end.
Next Buttonhole row: Moss st. 7, turn, cast on 5, turn, moss st. to end.
Moss st. 8 rows, then cast off.

The pocket backs *(two alike)*:
With size 3 mm (No. 11) needles cast on 40 sts. and beginning with a k. row s.s. 100 rows, then cast off.

To make up the sweater:
Pin out to size all parts of the sweater and lightly press on the wrong side with a warm iron over a damp cloth. Join shoulder seams continuing seams across neck bands. Set in sleeves between the marking threads on back and front. Fold pocket backs in half and join row end edges. Join sleeve and side seams, inserting pockets above the ribbing at side seams. Neatly sew left and right front bands in place, sewing cast on edge of right front band behind that of left front band. Press seams. Sew on buttons.

HODGE

This Aran pattern is knitted in Shetland 4-ply to make a new classic suitable for any age and for any occasion. The Shetland yarn can be purchased from The Patricia Roberts Knitting Shop, 60 Kinnerton Street, London S.W.1. Mail order service available. The many colours available include green tweed; brown tweed; oatmeal tweed; plain red; cream; blue.

Materials:
12 ounces of special Shetland 4-ply equivalent; a pair each of No.12 and No.13 knitting needles; a cable needle.

Tension:
15 stitches and 19 rows to 5 cm (2 in.) over reversed stocking stitch using No.12 needles. If you cannot obtain the correct tension using needles of the size suggested, use larger or smaller ones accordingly.

Abbreviations:
K.,knit; p.,purl; st.,stitch; tog.,together; dec.,decrease (by working 2sts. tog.); inc.,increase (by working twice into same st.); double rib is k.2 and p.2 alternately; m.b.,make bobble thus—k.1, p.1, k.1, p.1, all into next st., turn, p.4, turn, k.4, turn, p.2 tog., p.2 tog., turn, k.2 tog. through back of sts.; cr.3 rt., cross 3 right thus—slip next st. onto cable needle and leave at back of work, k.2, then p.1 from cable needle; cr.3 lt., cross 3 left thus—slip next 2sts. onto a cable needle and leave at front of work, p.1, then k.2 from cable needle; cable 8 thus—slip next 4sts. onto cable needle and leave at back of work, k.4, then k.4 from cable needle; r.s.s., reversed stocking stitch (p. on the right side and k. on the wrong side).

Note:
The instructions are given for the small size. Where they vary, work the figures in the brackets for the medium size or the figures in the second brackets for the large size.

Measurements:
The following measurements are given in centimetres first, followed by inches in brackets.

small (10)	medium (12)	large (14)
All round at underarms		
80 (32)	85 (34)	90 (36)
Side seam		
35 (14)	35 (14)	35 (14)
Length		
55 (22)	55.5 (22¼)	56 (22½)
Sleeve seam		
42.5 (17)	42.5 (17)	42.5 (17)

The back:
With No.13 needles and m. cast on 104 (112) (120) sts. and work 43 rows in double rib.
Increase row: Rib 7 (3) (7), * up 1, rib 6 (7) (7); repeat from * ending last repeat rib 7 (4) (8)—120 (128) (136) sts.
Change to No.12 needles and work as follows:
1st row: P.2 (6) (2), m.b., * p.7, m.b.; repeat from * once (once) (twice), p.6, k.8, p.6, m.b., p.3, m.b., p.3, m.b., p.10, k.4, p.10, m.b., p.3, m.b., p.3, m.b., p.6, k.8, p.6, * m.b., p.7; repeat from last * ending last repeat p.2 (6) (2).
2nd row: K.25 (29) (33), p.8, k.25, p.4, k.25, p.8, k.25 (29) (33).
3rd row: P.25 (29) (33), k.8, p.24, cr.3 rt., cr.3 lt., p.24, k.8, p.25 (29) (33).
4th row: K.25 (29) (33), p.8, k.24, p.2, k.2, p.2, k.24, p.8, k.25 (29) (33).
5th row: P.25 (29) (33), k.8, p.23, cr. 3 rt., p.2, cr.3 lt., p.23, k.8, p.25 (29) (33).
6th row: K.25 (29) (33), p.8, k.23, p.2, k.4, p.2, k.23, p.8, k.25 (29) (33).
7th row: P.6 (2) (6), * m.b., p.7; repeat from * once (twice) (twice) more, p.3 more, cable 8, p.10, m.b., p.11, cr.3 rt., p.4, cr.3 lt., p.11, m.b., p.10, cable 8, p.10, * m.b., p.7; repeat from last * ending last repeat p.6 (2) (6).
8th row: K.25 (29) (33), p.8, k.22, p.2, k.6, p.2, k.22, p.8, k.25 (29) (33).
9th row: P.25 (29) (33), k.8, p.21, cr.3 rt., p.6, cr.3 lt., p.21, k.8, p.25 (29) (33).
10th row: K.25 (29) (33), p.8, k.21, p.2, k.8, p.2, k.21, p.8, p.25 (29) (33).
11th row: P.25 (29) (33), k.8, p.20, cr.3 rt., p.8, cr.3 lt., p.20, k.8, p.25 (29) (33).
12th row: K.25 (29) (33), p.8, k.20, p.2, k.10, p.2, k.20, p.8, k.25 (29) (33).
13th row: P.2 (6) (2), m.b., * p.7, m.b.; repeat from * once (once) (twice), p.6, k.8, p.19, cr.3 rt., p.10, cr.3 lt., p.19, k.8, p.6, * m.b., p.7; repeat from * ending last repeat p.2 (6) (2).
14th row: K.25 (29) (33), p.8, k.19, p.2, k.12, p.2, k.19, p.8, k.25 (29) (33).
15th row: P.25 (29) (33), k.8, p.18, cr.3 rt., p.12, cr.3 lt., p.18, k.8, p.25 (29) (33).
16th row: K.25 (29) (33), p.8, k.18, p.2, k.14, p.2, k.18, p.8, k.25 (29) (33).
17th row: P.25 (29) (33), k.8, p.17, cr.3 rt., p.14, cr.3 lt., p.17, k.8, p.25 (29) (33).
18th row: K.25 (29) (33), p.8, k.17, p.2, k.16, p.2, k.17, p.8, k.25 (29) (33).
19th row: P.6 (2) (6), * m.b., p.7; repeat from * once (twice) (twice), p.3 more, cable 8, p.17, k.2, p.16, k.2, p.17, cable 8, p.10, * m.b., p.7; repeat from last * ending last repeat p.6 (2) (6).
20th row: As 18th row.
21st row: P.25 (29) (33), k.8, p.17, cr.3 lt., p.14, cr.3 rt., p.17, k.8, p.25 (29) (33).
22nd row: As 16th row.
23rd row: P.25 (29) (33), k.8, p.18, cr. 3 lt., p.12, cr.3 rt., p.18, k.8, p.25 (29) (33).
24th row: As 14th row.
25th row: P.2 (6) (2), m.b., * p.7, m.b.; repeat from * once (once) (twice), p.6, k.8, p.19, cr.3 lt., p.10, cr.3 rt., p.19, k.8, p.6, * m.b., p.7; repeat from * last ending last repeat p.2 (6) (2).
26th row: As 12th row.
27th row: P.25 (29) (33), k.8, p.20, cr.3 lt., p.8, cr.3 rt., p.20, k.8, p.25 (29) (33).
28th row: As 10th row.
29th row: P.25 (29) (33), k.8, p.21, cr.3 lt., p.6, cr.3 rt., p.21, k.8, p.25 (29) (33).
30th row: As 8th row.
31st row: P.6 (2) (6), * m.b., p.7, repeat from * once (twice) (twice), p.3 more, cable 8, p.10, m.b., p.11, cr.3 lt., p.4, cr.3 rt., p.11, m.b., p.10, cable 8, p.10, * m.b., p.7; repeat from last * ending last repeat p.6 (2) (6).
32nd row: As 6th row.
33rd row: P.25 (29) (33), k.8, p.23, cr.3 lt., p.2, cr.3 rt., p.23, k.8, p.25 (29) (33).
34th row: As 4th row.
35th row: P.25 (29) (33), k.8, p.24, cr.3 lt., cr.3 rt., p.24, k.8, p.25 (29) (33).
36th row: As 2nd row.
These 36 rows form the pattern. Repeat them once more.
** Work the first 24 rows again.
To shape the armholes: Maintaining the continuity of the pattern as set, cast off 8sts. at the beginning of the next 2 rows, then dec. 1st. at each end of the next row and 7 (9) (11) following alternate rows.
On 88 (92) (96) sts. pattern 53 rows.
To slope the shoulders: Cast off 8 sts. at the beginning of the next 4 rows, then 7 (8) (9) sts. on the 2 following rows.
Cast off the 42 (44) (46) remaining sts.

The pocket back:
With No.12 needles cast on 20sts. and beginning with a p. row r.s.s. 24 rows, then leave these sts. on a stitch holder until required.

The front:
Work as given for back until 24 rows have been worked in pattern.
Pocket row: Pattern 81 (85) (89) as set, slip next 20sts. onto a stitch holder and leave until required for pocket top, then in their place pattern across the 20sts. of pocket back, pattern to end.
Pattern 70 rows more as set.
Now divide the sts. for the neck: *Next row* (wrong side): Pattern 56 (60) (64) and leave these sts. on a spare needle until required for right front shoulder, pattern 8 and leave these sts. on a safety pin until required for right front neckband pattern to end and continue on these 56 (60) (64) sts. for the left front shoulder.
The left front shoulder: To shape the armhole: Maintaining the continuity of the pattern as set, cast off 8sts. at the beginning of the next row. Work 1 row back to armhole edge. Dec. 1st. at beginning—armhole on the next row and the 7 (9) (11) following alternate rows.
On 40 (42) (44) sts. pattern 28 rows.
To shape the neck: Cast off 4 (5) (6) sts. at the beginning of the next row, then dec. 1st. at the neck edge on each of the next 13 rows.
On 23 (24) (25) sts. pattern 11 more rows.
To slope the shoulder: Cast off 8 sts. at the beginning of the next row and following alternate row.
On 7 (8) (9) sts. work 1 row, then cast off.
The left front shoulder: With right side of work facing rejoin yarn to inner edge of sts. left on spare needle and work to end

of row. Now work as given for left front shoulder to end.

The sleeves *(both alike)*:
With No.13 needles cast on 64 (68) (72) sts. and work 60 rows in double rib.
Change to No.12 needles and work in pattern as follows:
1st row: P.5 (7) (1), m.b., * p.7, m.b.; repeat from * once (once) (twice) more, p.6, k.8, p.6, * m.b., p.7; repeat from last * ending last repeat p.5 (7) (1).
2nd row: K.28 (30) (32), p.8, k.28 (30) (32).
3rd row: P.28 (30) (32), k.8, p.28 (30) (32).
4th and 5th rows: As 2nd and 3rd rows.
6th row: As 2nd row.
7th row: P.1 (3) (5), m.b., * p.7, m.b.; repeat from * once, p.10, cable 8, p.10, * m.b., p.7; repeat from last * ending last repeat p.1 (3) (5).
8th to 12th rows: As 2nd to 6th rows.
These 12 rows form the pattern. Continuing in pattern as set inc.1 st. at each end of the next row and the 12 following 8th rows.
On 90 (94) (98) sts. pattern 23 rows.
To shape the sleevetop: Cast off 8sts. at the beginning of the next 2 rows, then dec. 1st. at each end of the next row and the 17 (19) (21) following alternate rows —38sts.
Cast off 4sts. at the beginning of the next 8 rows. Cast off the 6 remaining sts.

The pocket top:
With right side of work facing rejoin yarn to the 20sts. left on stitch holder at front of work. Using No.13 needles work 4 rows in double rib, then cast off.

The right front neckband:
With right side of work facing rejoin yarn to the 8sts. left on safety pin at centre front and using No.13 needles work 46 rows in single rib, then cast off.

The left front neckband:
With No.13 needles cast on 8sts. and work 46 rows in single rib, then cast off.

The collar:
With No.13 needles cast on 191 (195) (199) sts. and work 4 rows in double rib.
Next row: Cast off 32 for row end edging, rib 126 (130) (134) sts., cast off 32sts.
Rejoin yarn to centre 127 (131) (135) sts.
Change to No.12 needles and beginning with a p. row s.s.4 rows.
Now work in pattern as follows:
1st row: P.3 (5) (1), * m.b., p.5; repeat from * ending last repeat p.3 (5) (1).
2nd to 4th rows: R.s.s. 3 rows.
5th row: P.6 (2) (4), * m.b., p.5; repeat from * ending last repeat p.6 (2) (4).
6th to 8th rows: All r.s.s.
These 8 rows form the pattern; work the first 4 rows again.
Continuing in pattern as set, dec. 1st. at each end of the next row and the 2 following 8th rows.
On 121 (125) (129) sts., work 1 row, then cast off.

To make up the sweater:
Press all parts except the ribbing with a warm iron over a damp cloth. Join shoulder seams. Set in sleeves. Join sleeve and side seams. Neatly sew pocket back and row end edges of pocket top in place. Sew cast off edges of ribbing on collar to the row end edges on collar, then sew collar in place all round neck edge. Sew left and right front neckbands in position. Press seams.

RAG, TAG & BOBTAIL

On the front of the jacket the rabbits are dressed in their pyjamas, on the way to bed with their candles. On the back they are already in bed asleep. Knit this snuggly jacket and matching hat and scarf in the colours we suggest, or in black or cream with either bright or subtle contrasts.

Materials:
16 (17) (18) 50 gram balls of Sirdar Pullman in main colour—light navy; 5 (5) (6) balls in each of the 2 main contrast colours— scarlet and roman pink; one ball in each of three other contrast colours, driftwood, white and burnt almond; a pair each of No. 7 and No. 6 knitting needles; 6 buttons.
Tension:
8 stitches and 10 rows to 5 cm (2 in.) over the stocking stitch, using No. 6 knitting needles.
Abbreviations:
K., knit; p., purl; st., stitch; tog., together; dec., decrease (by working 2 sts. tog.); inc., increase (by working twice into same st.); s.s., stocking stitch (k. on the right side and p. on the wrong side); single rib is k. 1 and p. 1 alternately; garter st. is k. plain on every row; m.b., make bobble thus, k. 1, yarn round needle, k. 1 all into next st., turn, k. 3, turn, sl. 1, k. 2 tog., p.s.s.o.; sl., slip; p.s.s.o., pass sl. st. over; m., main colour—navy; a., scarlet; b., roman pink; c., driftwood.
Note:
The instructions are given for the small size. Where they vary work the figures in the first brackets for the medium size or the figures in the second brackets for the large size.

Measurements:
The measurements are given in centimetres followed by inches in square brackets.

small (10)	medium (12)	large (14)
All round at underarms		
95 [38]	100 [40]	105 [42]
Side seam		
55 [22]	55 [22]	55 [22]
Length		
77.5 [31]	77.5 [31]	77.5 [31]
Sleeve seam		
44 [17½]	44 [17½]	44 [17½]

THE JACKET
The back:
With No. 7 needles and m. cast on 77 (81) (85) sts. and work in garter st. in stripes as follows: 2 rows m., 2 rows a., 2 rows m., 2 rows b., 2 rows m.
Change to No. 6 needles and with m. beginning with a k. row s.s. 4 rows.
Now work in bobble pattern, taking great care to avoid pulling contrast colours not in use tightly across the back of the work.
1st row: With m. k. 2, * with a., m.b., with m. k. 3; repeat from * ending last repeat with m. k. 2.
2nd to 4th rows: With m. in s.s.
5th row: With m. k. 4, * with b., m.b., with m., k. 3; repeat from * ending last repeat k. 4.
6th to 8th rows: With m. in s.s.
The last 8 rows form the bobble pattern. Repeat them 4 times more.
Now work the rabbits motif as follows, and at the same time work the bobble pattern at each side as set. For easier working use a separate ball of m. and b. for bobbles at each side of motif throughout and a separate ball of a. for bobbles at each side of motif on rows 25 to 38.
1st row: Work in bobble pattern as set across 13 (15) (17) sts., with a. k. 51, work in bobble pattern to end as set.
2nd row: With m. p. 13 (15) (17), with a, p. 51, with m. p. to end.
These 2 rows set the position of the pattern given in the chart. Now work the 3rd to 38th rows from the chart as set with bobble pattern at each side.
Now continuing in bobble pattern only, pattern 22 rows more.
To shape the armholes: Cast off 8 (9) (10) sts. at the beginning of the next 2 rows—61 (63) (65) sts.
Pattern 38 (40) (42) rows more as set.
To slope the shoulders: Cast off 9 sts. at the beginning of the next 4 rows.
Cast off the 25 (27) (29) remaining sts.
The left front:
With No. 7 needles and m. cast on 35 (37) (39) sts. and work in garter st. in stripes as follows: 2 rows m., 2 rows a., 2 rows m., 2 rows b., 2 rows m.
Change to No. 6 needles and with m. beginning with a k. row s.s. 4 rows.
Now work in bobble pattern as follows taking great care to avoid pulling colours not in use tightly across the back of the work or it will become puckered.
1st row: With m. k. 1 (2) (1), * with a., m.b., with m. k. 3; repeat from * ending last repeat with m. k. 1 (2) (1).
2nd to 4th rows: With m. in s.s.
5th row: With m. k. 3 (4) (3), * with b. m.b., with m. k. 3; repeat from * ending last repeat k. 3 (4) (3).
6th to 8th rows: With m. in s.s.
The last 8 rows form the bobble pattern, repeat them 3 times more, then work the first 6 rows again. Work 1 extra row here when working right front.
Cast off 4 sts. for pocket opening at the beginning of the next row.
Now work the rabbit motif which is worked entirely in s.s. so only the colour details are given as follows. At the same time work the bobble pattern at each side as set. For easier working use a separate ball of m. and also a. and b. at each side of motif.
1st row: Work as set across 8 (9) (10) sts., 4 c., 7 m., 8 c., work to end as set.
2nd row: Work as set across 3 (4) (5) sts., 9 c., 6 m., 7 c., work to end as set.
These 2 rows set the position of the rabbit motif given in the chart. Now work the 3rd to 29th rows from the chart as set.
Continuing to work the rabbit motif as set, cast on 4 sts. to close the pocket opening at the beginning of the next row.
Now work the 31st to 47th pattern rows as set.
Continuing in bobble pattern as before, work 14 rows more.
To shape the armhole: Cast off 8 (9) (10) sts. at the beginning of the next row—27 (28) (29) sts.
Pattern 18 (20) (22) rows more.
To shape the neck: Cast off 3 (4) (5) sts. at the beginning of the next row, then dec. 1 st. at the neck edge on each of the next 6 rows.
On 18 sts. pattern 14 rows.
To slope the shoulder: Cast off 9 sts. at the beginning of the next row. On 9 sts. work 1 row, then cast off.
The right front:
Work as given for left front noting the variation in the number of rows before working the pocket opening. Also note that the rabbit motif will be reversed.
The pocket backs *(two alike)*:
With No. 6 needles and m. cast on 21 sts. and beginning with a k. row s.s. 30 rows, then cast off.
The pocket tops *(both alike)*:
With right side of work facing rejoin b. and using No. 7 needles pick up and k. 25 sts. from row ends of pocket opening.
Work in garter st. in stripes as follows: 1 row b., 2 rows m., 2 rows a., 2 rows m. Cast off.
The sleeves *(both alike)*:
With No. 7 needles and m. cast on 49 (51) (53) sts. and work in garter stitch in stripes as follows: 2 rows m., 2 rows a., 2 rows m., 2 rows b., 2 rows m.
Change to No. 6 needles and beginning with a k. row s.s. 4 rows.
Now work in bobble pattern as follows: *1st row:* With m. k. 2 (3) (4), * with a., m.b., with m. k. 3; repeat from * ending last repeat with m. k. 2 (3) (4).
2nd to 4th rows: With m. in s.s.
5th row: With m. k. 4 (1) (2), * with b., m.b., with m. k. 3; repeat from * ending last repeat with m. k. 4 (1) (2).
6th to 8th rows: With m. in s.s.
Continuing in pattern as set, inc. 1 st. at each end of the next row and the 7 following 8th rows.
On 65 (67) (69) sts. pattern 11 rows.
Mark each end of the last row with coloured threads.
Now working in garter st. work in stripes of 2 rows m., 2 rows a., 2 rows m., 2 rows b., 2 (3) (4) rows m. then cast off.
The button band and half collar:
With No. 7 needles and m. cast on 7 sts. and work 134 rows in single rib.
**Inc. 1 st. at the beginning of the next row and at the same edge on each of the next 7 (9) (9) rows. Leave these 15 (17) (17) sts. on a spare needle until required.

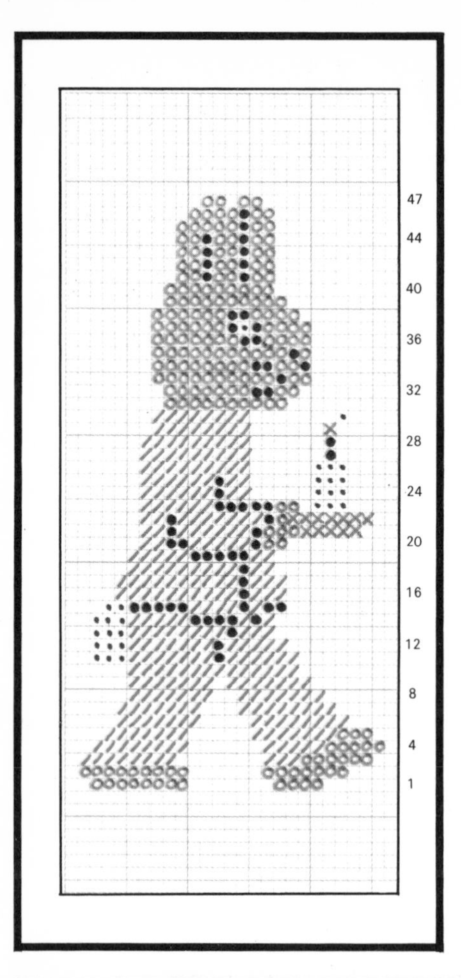

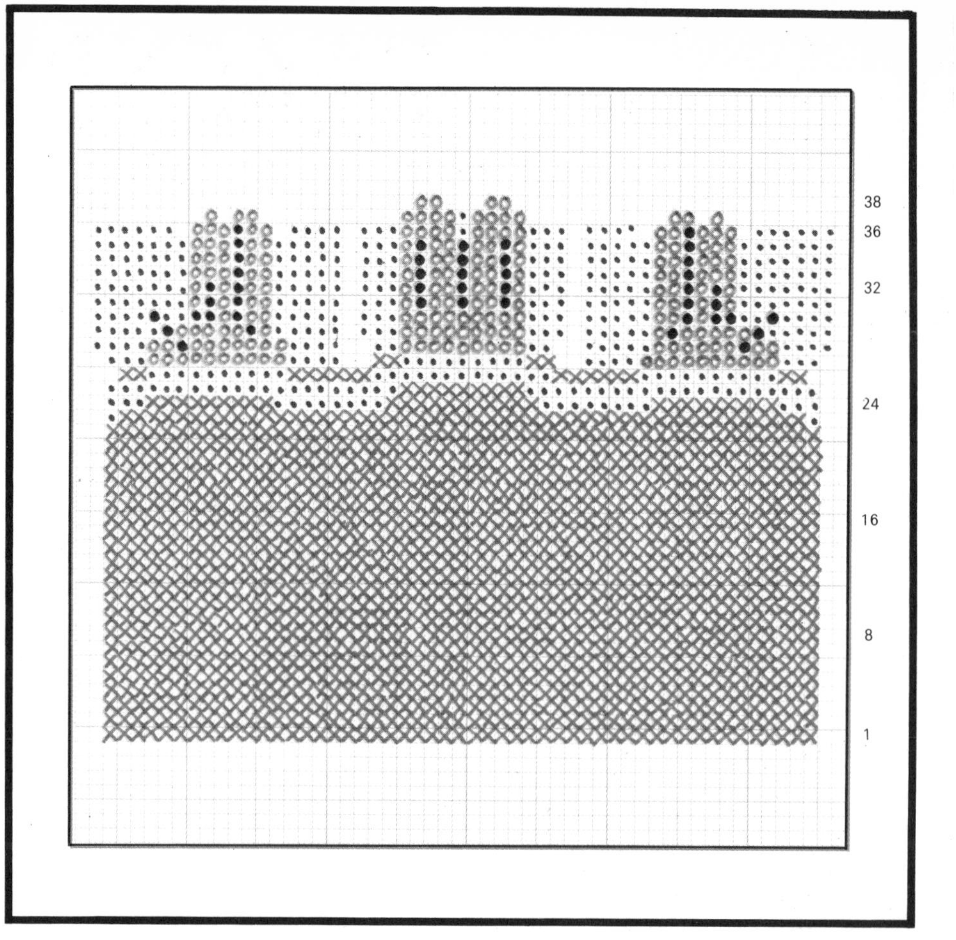

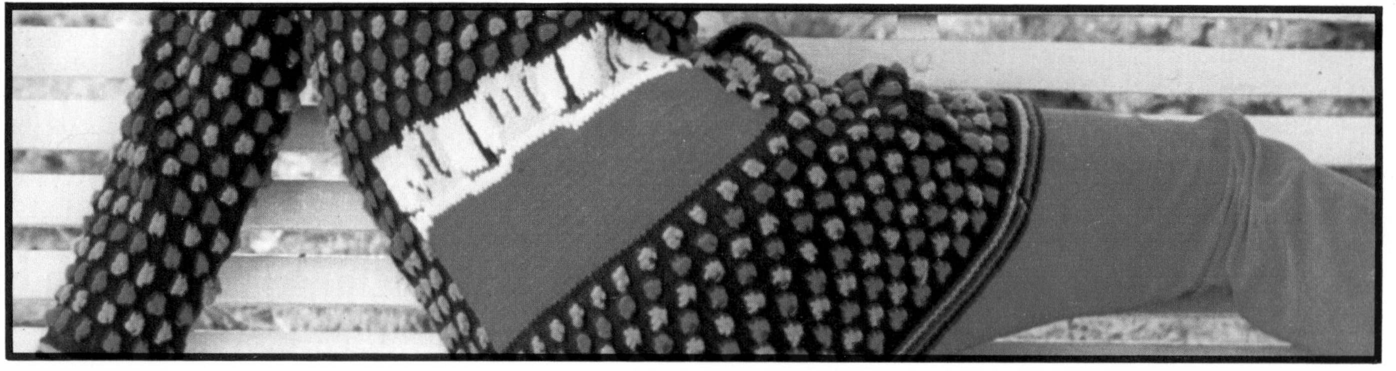

For the back half collar: Cast on 29 sts. and work 20 rows in single rib.
Next row: Rib across the 29 sts. of back collar, turn, cast on 17 sts, turn, rib across the 15 (17) (17) sts. of front half collar.
On 61 (63) (63) sts. rib 26 rows.
Dec. row: Rib 3, sl. 1, k. 2 tog., p.s.s.o., rib until 6 remain, sl. 1, k. 2 tog., p.s.s.o., rib 3.
Rib 1 row.
Repeat the last 2 rows once more, then cast off.

The buttonhole band and half collar:
With No. 7 needles and m. cast on 7 sts. and work 6 rows in single rib.
1st Buttonhole row: Rib 2, cast off 3, rib to end.
2nd Buttonhole row: Rib 2, turn, cast on 3, turn, rib to end.
Rib 22 rows.
Repeat the last 24 rows 4 times more, then work the 2 buttonhole rows again.
Rib 5 rows.
Now work as given for buttonband and half collar from ** to end.

To make up the jacket:
Pin out to size and press all parts except the ribbing lightly on the wrong side with a warm iron over a damp cloth. Sew row ends of pocket tops in place. Sew pocket backs in place, so that one row end edge of each pocket will form part of side seam. Join shoulder seams. Set in sleeves so that the row ends above the marking threads are sewn to the sts. cast off at underarms. Join sleeve and side seams. Join the cast on edges of the 2 half back collar pieces. Sew front bands and collar in place all round neck edge. Sew on buttons. Press seams.

THE SCARF

To work: With No. 7 needles and m. cast on 26 sts. and working in garter st. work in stripes as follows: 2 rows m., 2 rows a., 2 rows m., 2 rows b.
Repeat the last 8 rows 47 times more, with m. k. 2 rows.
Cast off.
Press lightly.

THE HAT

To work: With No. 7 needles and m. cast on 73 sts. and working in garter st. work in stripes as follows: 2 rows m., 2 rows a., 2 rows m., 2 rows b.; repeat these 8 rows 3 times.
Change to No. 6 needles and beginning with a. k. row s.s. 4 rows.
Now work in bobble pattern as follows: *1st row:* With m. k. 2, * with a. m.b., with m. k. 3; repeat from * ending last repeat k. 2.
2nd to 4th rows: With m. in s.s.
5th row: With m. k. 4, * with b. m.b., with m. k. 3; repeat from * ending last repeat k. 4.
6th to 8th rows: With m. in s.s.
Repeat the last 8 rows once more.
Break off a. and b. and continue with m. only in s.s.
1st dec. row: K. 1, * k. 2 tog., k. 6; repeat from * to end—64 sts.
Beginning with a p. row s.s. 3 rows.
2nd dec. row: K. 1, * k. 2 tog., k. 5; repeat from * to end—55 sts.
P. 1 row.
Thus working 1 st. less after the decreases on each successive repeat of the dec. row.
Repeat the last 2 rows 3 times more, then work the dec. row again—19 sts.
Next row: P. 1, * p. 2 tog.; repeat from * to end—10 sts.
Break off m. leaving a long end, thread this through the remaining 10 sts. draw up firmly and secure, then using long end neatly join row ends. Fold striped edging in half to wrong side and slip st. in place. Press lightly on wrong side.

THE GOLDRUSH

Here's a complete evening outfit to knit in gold or silver yarn. The jacket, skirt and top are all knitted in a leaf pattern, which looks intricate but which is, in fact, quite easy to do. The skirt flares from the ribbed hip band, which gives the appearance of a full skirt without having unflattering bulges at the waist. The top can always be worn as a suntop when the hot weather arrives, and the full jacket can be worn over an evening dress, or in a more casual way with jeans.

Materials:
For the skirt 22(23)(23) balls of Robin Moonlight; a pair of No.10, No.11, No.12 and No.13 knitting needles; a 6 in. zip fastener; one button; a waist length of elastic.
For the top: 16(17)(18) balls of Robin Moonlight; a pair each of No.12 and No.13 knitting needles; 2 buttons.
For the jacket: 28(29)(30) balls of Robin Moonlight; a pair each of No.12 and No.13 knitting needles.

Tension:
16 stitches and 20 rows to 5 cm (2 in.) over the leaf pattern using No.12 needles; 15 stitches and 19 rows to 5 cm (2 in.) using No.11 needles; 14 stitches and 18 rows to 5 cm (2 in.) using No.10 needles.

Abbreviations:
K.,knit; p.,purl; st.,stitch; tog.,together; dec.,decrease (by working 2 sts. tog.); inc.,increase (by working twice into same st.); s.s.,stocking stitch (k. on the right side and p. on the wrong side); sl.,slip; p.s.s.o.,pass sl. st. over; y.r.n.,yarn round needle to make a stitch; garter stitch is k. plain on every row; s.s.k., sl.1, k.1, p.s.s.o.; m.b., make bobble thus—k.1, y.r.n., k.1, y.r.n., k.1 all into next st., turn, k.5, turn, p.5, turn, k.1, sl.1, k.2 tog., p.s.s.o., k.1, turn, p.3 tog.

Note:
The instructions are given for the small size. Where they vary, work the figures in the first brackets for the medium size or the figures in the second brackets for the large size.

Measurements:
The following measurements are given in centimetres first, followed by inches in brackets.

	small (10)	medium (12)	large (14)
THE SKIRT			
To fit hip sizes	87.5(35)	92.5(37)	97.5(39)
All round at hem	135(54)	142.5(57)	150(60)
Length	72.5(29)	72.5(29)	72.5(29)
THE TOP			
To fit bust sizes	82.5(33)	87.5(35)	92.5(37)
All round at underarms	62.5(25)	69(27½)	75(30)
Side seam	34(13½)	34(13½)	34(13½)
THE JACKET			
To fit bust sizes	82.5(33)	87.5(35)	92.5(37)
All round at underarms	120(48)	130(52)	140(55½)
Side seam	39(15½)	39(15½)	39(15½)
Length	64(25½)	65(26)	66(26¼)
Sleeve seam	39(15½)	39(15½)	39(15½)

THE SKIRT

The back and front *(both alike):*
With No.11 needles cast on 191(201)(211) sts. and k.4 rows.
Change to No.10 needles and work in pattern as follows:
1st row: K.1, * y.r.n., k.3, sl.1, k.2 tog., p.s.s.o., k.3, y.r.n., k.1; repeat from * to end.
2nd row and every wrong side row: All p.
3rd row: K.2, * y.r.n., k.2, sl.1, k.2 tog., p.s.s.o., k.2, y.r.n., k.3; repeat from * ending last repeat k.2.
5th row: K.3, * y.r.n., k.1, sl.1, k.2 tog., p.s.s.o., k.1, y.r.n., k.5; repeat from * ending last repeat k.3.
7th row: K.4, * y.r.n., sl.1, k.2 tog., p.s.s.o., y.r.n., k.7; repeat from * ending last repeat k.4.
9th row: Sl.1, k.1, p.s.s.o., * k.3, y.r.n., k.1, y.r.n., k.3, sl.1, k.2 tog., p.s.s.o.; repeat from * ending last repeat k.2 tog. instead of sl.1, k.2 tog., p.s.s.o.
11th row: Sl.1, k.1, p.s.s.o., * k.2, y.r.n., k.3, y.r.n., k.2, sl.1, k.2 tog., p.s.s.o.; repeat from * ending last repeat sl.1, k.1, p.s.s.o.
13th row: Sl.1, k.1, p.s.s.o., * k.1, y.r.n., k.5, y.r.n., k.1, sl.1, k.2 tog., p.s.s.o.; repeat from * ending last repeat sl.1, k.1, p.s.s.o.
15th row: Sl.1, k.1, p.s.s.o., * y.r.n., k.7, y.r.n., sl.1, k.2 tog., p.s.s.o.; repeat from * ending last repeat sl.1, k.1, p.s.s.o.
16th row: All p.
These 16 rows form the pattern; repeat them 3 more times, then work the first 4 rows again.
Change to No.11 needles and pattern 80 rows as set.
Work should now measure 40 cm (16¼ in.) from beginning.
Change to No.12 needles and pattern 68 rows as set; work should now measure 57.5 cm (23 in.) from beginning.
Change to No. 13 needles and work as follows:
Decrease row: K.1(1)(2), * k.2 tog., k.2; repeat from * ending last repeat k.2 tog. (k.2)(k.3)—143(151)(159) sts.
Now work in rib as follows:
1st row: P.1, * k.1, p.1; repeat from * to end.
Rib 29 rows as set.
Next decrease row: Rib 7(11)(15), * sl.1, k.2 tog., p.s.s.o., rib 15; repeat from * ending last repeat rib 7(11)(15)—127(135)(143) sts.
Rib 31 rows.
Next decrease row: Rib 6(10)(14), * sl.1, k.2 tog., p.s.s.o., rib 13; repeat from * ending last repeat rib 6(10)(14)—111(119)(127) sts.
Rib 5 rows.
Next row: All p. on the right side to form fold line.
Rib 5 rows, then cast off very loosely.

To make up the skirt:
Pin out and press all parts on the wrong side with a cool iron over a dry cloth, taking care to press the ribbing only very lightly. Make sure all measurements are correct. Join left side seam. Join right side seam to base of ribbing. Fold ribbing at foldline and sew in place neatly. Thread elastic through waistband, securing each end at left side seam. Sew zip fastener in place at left side seam. Sew button to waistband at back of left side opening and make a buttonhole loop at waistband at front of opening. Press seams.

THE TOP

The back:
With No.12 needles cast on 131(131)(157) sts. and k.4 rows.
Now work the mimosa border as follows:
1st row: P.1, * k.25, p.1; repeat from * to end.
2nd and each wrong side row: K.1, * p.25, k.1; repeat from * to end.
3rd row: P.1, * k.1, y.r.n., k.1, y.r.n., k.7, s.s.k., sl.1, k.2 tog., p.s.s.o., k.2 tog., k.7, y.r.n., k.1, y.r.n., k.1, p.1; repeat from * to end.
5th row: P.1, * k.2, y.r.n., k.1, y.r.n., k.2, m.b., k.3, s.s.k., sl.1, k.2 tog., p.s.s.o., k.2 tog., k.3, m.b., k.2, y.r.n., k.1, y.r.n., k.2, p.1; repeat from * to end.
7th row: P.1, * m.b., k.2, y.r.n., k.1, y.r.n., k.2, m.b., k.2, s.s.k., sl.1, k.2 tog., p.s.s.o., k.2 tog., k.2, m.b., k.2, y.r.n., k.1, y.r.n., k.2, m.b., p.1; repeat from * to end.
9th row: P.1, * k.1, m.b., k.2, y.r.n., k.1, y.r.n., k.2, m.b., k.1, s.s.k., sl.1, k.2 tog., p.s.s.o., k.2 tog., k.1, m.b., k.2, y.r.n., k.1, y.r.n., k.2, m.b., k.1, p.1; repeat from * to end.
11th row: P.1, * k.2, m.b., k.2, y.r.n., k.1, y.r.n., k.2, m.b., s.s.k., sl.1, k.2 tog., p.s.s.o., k.2 tog., m.b., k.2, y.r.n., k.1, y.r.n., k.2, m.b., k.2, p.1; repeat from * to end.
13th row: P.1, * k.3, m.b., k.2, y.r.n., k.1, y.r.n., k.2, s.s.k., sl.1, k.2 tog., p.s.s.o., k.2 tog., k.2, y.r.n., k.1, y.r.n., k.2, m.b., k.3, p.1; repeat from * to end.
15th row: As 1st row.
16th row: All p.
This completes the border pattern.
Decrease row: K.2 tog., k.1(3)(1), * k.2 tog., k.3(5)(3), k.2 tog., k.2(5)(2); repeat from * ending last repeat k.2(3)(1), k.2 tog.—101(111)(121) sts.
P.1 row **.
Now work 108 rows in leaf pattern as given for skirt.
Change to No.13 needles and k.10 rows, then cast off.

The front:
Work as given for back until ** is reached.
Work 107 rows in leaf pattern as given for skirt.
Now divide the sts. for the neck: *Next row:*

P.50(55)(60) and leave these sts. on a spare needle until required for right front point, p.2 tog., p. to end and continue on these 50(55)(60)sts. for the left front point.
The left front point: Dec.1st. at each end of the next 24(26)(29) rows, then take the 2(3)(2) remaining sts. tog. and fasten off.
The right front point: With right side of work facing rejoin yarn and work as given for left front point to end.

The front edging:
With right side of work facing rejoin yarn and using No.13 needles pick up and k.29 (32)(34)sts. from side up to top of left front point, 29(32)(34)sts. from top of left front point to centre front, 29(32)(34) sts. from centre front to top of right front point and 29(32)(34)sts. from right front point to side seam edge—116(128)(136) sts.
K.9 rows, increasing at top of each front point and decreasing 1st. at centre front on each row—125(137)(145) sts.
Next row: Cast off 29(32)(34), k.9 and leave these sts. on a safety pin until required, cast off 49(55)(59)sts., k. next 9sts. and leave these 9sts. on a safety pin until required, cast off the remaining 29(32)(34)sts.

The shoulder straps *(both alike):*
Rejoin yarn to the 9sts. left on safety pin and using No.13 needles work in garter stitch until the straps measure 12 in. or for length required. Cast off.

To make up the top:
Press all parts lightly on the wrong side with a cool iron over a dry cloth. Join side seams. Secure shoulder straps with buttons. Press seams.

THE JACKET

The back:
With No.13 needles cast on 191(201) (211)sts. and k.4 rows.
Change to No.12 needles and work 152 rows in leaf pattern as given for skirt.
To slope the raglan armholes: Maintaining the continuity of the pattern as set dec.1st. at each end of the next row and the 49(51)(53) following alternate rows—91(97)(103)sts.
** Change to No.13 needles and k.8 rows.
Eyelet hole row: K.2(3)(3), * y.r.n., k.2 tog., k.3; repeat from * ending last repeat k.2(2)(3).
K.9 rows.
Cast off.

The left front:
With No.13 needles cast on 97(107)(117) sts. and k.4 rows.
Change to No.12 needles and work in pattern with garter stitch front edging as follows:
1st row: Work in leaf pattern as given for skirt until 6 remain, k.6.
2nd row: K.6, p. to end.
Work 150 rows in leaf pattern with garter stitch edging as set.
To slope the raglan armhole: Dec.1st. at the beginning of the next row and the 32(34)(36) following alternate rows.
To shape the neck: Next row: K.6, pattern 20(26)(32) and leave these sts. on a spare needle until required for neckband, work to end as set.
While continuing to dec.1st. at the armhole edge on each alternate row, dec.1st. at the neck edge on each of the next 20(22)(24) rows.
Pattern 12(10)(8) rows decreasing 1st. at armhole edge on each alternate row as before.
Take the 2 remaining sts. tog. and fasten off.

The right front:
With No.13 needles cast on 97(107)(117) sts. and k.4 rows.
Change to No.12 needles and work in pattern with garter stitch front edgings as follows:
1st row: K.6, work in leaf pattern as given for skirt to end.
2nd row: P. until 6 remain, k.6.
Work 151 rows in leaf pattern with garter stitch edging as set.
To slope the raglan: Work as given for left front raglan armhole shaping to end.

The sleeves *(both alike):*
With No.13 needles cast on 121(131) (141)sts. and k.4 rows.
Change to No.12 needles and work 152 rows in leaf pattern as given for skirt.
To shape the raglan sleeve top: Dec.1st. at each end of the next row and the 49(51)(53) following alternate rows—21(27)(33)sts.
Work as given for back from ** to end.

The left front neckband:
With right side of work facing rejoin yarn and using No.13 needles pick up and k.35sts. from left front neck edge, then k. across the 26(32)(38)sts. left on spare needle—61(67)(73)sts.
Work as given for back from ** to end.

The right front neckband:
With right side of work facing rejoin yarn and using No.13 needles k. across the 26(32)(38)sts. left on spare needle, then pick up and k.35 sts. from right front neck edge—61(67)(73)sts.

FLASHBACK

This is a glitter knit sweater in an eyelet check pattern, which is slit from neck to waist to show off a well-shaped back. Wear it in the evenings with gold lamé trousers or a chiffon skirt, and a pretty brooch on the front.

Work as given for back from ** to end.

The cord:
Cut 3 lengths of yarn each 80 in. long, knot one end. Twist yarn until firm, fold cord in half and knot the cut ends allowing cords to twist together to form 1 cord 27½ in. long.

The bobbles *(two alike):*
Cut 2 pieces of card 5 cm (2 in.) in diameter with a central hole 1.5 cm (⅝ in.) in diameter. Now make bobbles in the usual way.

To make up the jacket:
Press all parts lightly on the wrong side with a cool iron over a dry cloth. Join raglan seams continuing seams across neckband. Join sleeve and side seams. Press seams. Thread cord through eyelet holes in neckband and draw up neckband. Secure one bobble at each end of cord.

Materials:
19(20)(21) balls of Robin Moonlight; a pair each of No.12 and No.13 knitting needles; 6 buttons.

Tension:
16 stitches and 20 rows to 5 cm (2 in.) over the pattern using No.12 needles. If you cannot obtain the correct tension using needles of the size suggested, use larger or smaller ones accordingly.

Abbreviations:
K.,knit; p.,purl; st.,stitch; tog.,together; dec.,decrease (by working 2sts. tog.); inc.,increase (by working twice into same st.); double rib is k.2 and p.2 alternately; y.r.n.,yarn round needle; garter st. is k. plain on every row.

Note:
The instructions are given for the small size. Where they vary, work the figures in the first brackets for the medium size or the figures in the second brackets for the large size.

Measurements:
The following measurements are given in centimetres first, followed by inches in brackets.

small (10)	medium (12)	large (14)
All round at underarms		
81 (32½)	86 (34½)	91 (36½)
Side seam		
37.5 (15)	37.5 (15)	37.5 (15)
Length		
57 (22¾)	57.5 (23)	58 (23¼)
Sleeve seam		
6 (2½)	6 (2½)	6 (2½)

The front waistband:
With No.13 needles cast on 48sts. and work 132(140)(148) rows in double rib, then cast off.

The half back waistbands *(two alike):*
With No.13 needles cast on 48sts. and work 66(70)(74) rows in double rib, then cast off.

The front:
With right side of waistband for front facing rejoin yarn and using No.12 needles pick up and k.131(139)(147) sts. from one row end edge, then p.1 row.
Now work in pattern as follows:
1st row: K.2, * p.3, k.5; repeat from * ending last repeat k.6.
2nd row: P.6, * k.3, p.5; repeat from * ending last repeat p.2.
3rd row: K.2, * p.1, y.r.n., p.2 tog., k.5; repeat from * ending last repeat k.6.
4th row: As 2nd row.
5th row: As 1st row.
6th row: All p.
7th row: K.6, * p.3, k.5; repeat from * ending last repeat k.2.
8th row: P.2, * k.3, p.5; repeat from * ending last repeat p.6.
9th row: K.6, * p.1, y.r.n., p.2 tog., k.5; repeat from * ending last repeat k.2.
10th row: As 8th row.
11th row: As 7th row.
12th row: All p.
These 12 rows form the pattern. Repeat them 9 more times.
To shape armholes: Cast off 8sts. at the beginning of the next 2 rows, then dec. 1st. at each end of the next 10(12)(14) rows.
On 95(99)(103) sts. pattern 25 rows.
Now divide the sts. for the neck: *Next row:* Pattern 35(36)(37) and leave these sts. on a spare needle until required for right front shoulder, cast off 25(27)(29) sts. at centre front, work to end and continue on the 35(36)(37) remaining sts. for left front shoulder.
The left front shoulder: To shape the neck: Dec. 1st. at the neck edge on each of the next 12 rows.
On 23(24)(25) sts. pattern 22 rows.
To slope the shoulder: Cast off 8sts. at the beginning of next row and following alternate row.
On 7(8)(9) sts., work 1 row, then cast off.
The right front shoulder: With right side of work facing rejoin yarn to inner edge of sts. left on spare needle and work to end of row, then work as given for left front shoulder to end.

The right half back:
With right side of one half back waistband facing rejoin yarn and using No.12 needles pick up and k.65(69)(73) sts. from one row end edge.
P.1 row.
Now work in pattern as follows:
1st row: K.1(3)(1), * p.3, k.5; repeat from * ending last repeat k.5(7)(5).
2nd row: P.5(7)(5), * k.3, p.5; repeat from * ending last repeat p.1(3)(1).
The last 2 rows set the position of the pattern given for front. Pattern 118 more rows as set. Work 1 extra row here on left half back.
To shape the armhole: Cast off 8sts. at the beginning of the next row, work 1 row back to armhole edge, then dec. 1st. at the armhole edge on each of the next 10(12)(14) rows.
On 47(49)(51) sts. pattern 60 rows.
To slope the shoulder: Cast off 8sts. at the beginning of the next row and the following alternate row, then 7(8)(9) sts. on the next alternate row—24(25)(26) sts.
Change to No.13 needles and k.6 rows for back neckband, then cast off.

The left half back:
Work as given for right half back noting the extra row to be worked before shaping armhole.

The front neckband:
With right side of work facing rejoin yarn and using No.13 needles pick up and k. 36sts. from left front neck edge, 26(28) (30) sts. from centre front neck edge and 36sts. from right front neck edge—98(100)(102) sts.
K.5 rows, then cast off.

The right half back edging:
With No.13 needles and right side of work facing pick up and k.136(138) (140) sts. from row ends of right half back at centre back edge and 32 sts. along end of ribbing—168(170)(172) sts.
K.5 rows, then cast off.

The left half back edging:
With No.13 needles and right side of work facing pick up and k.32sts. along end of waist ribbing and 136(138)(140) sts. from row ends of left half back at centre back edge, ending at top of left half back—168(170)(172) sts.
K.4 rows—ending at top edge.
1st Buttonhole row: K.3, cast off 3, k. until 32 remain, * cast off 3, k. next 6sts.; repeat from * twice more, cast off 3, k.2 more.
2nd Buttonhole row: All k. but casting on 4sts. over each group of 3sts. cast off on previous row.
Cast off.

The sleeves *(both alike):*
With No.13 needles cast on 99sts. and beginning with a k. row s.s.5 rows.
Next row: All k. on the wrong side to mark hemline.
Change to No.12 needles and work 24 rows in pattern as given for back.
To shape the sleevetop: Cast off 8sts. at the beginning of the next 2 rows. Dec. 1st. at each end of the next row and the 19(20)(21) following alternate rows. Work 1 row straight.
Cast off 4sts. at the beginning of the next 8 rows. Cast off the 11(9)(7) remaining sts.

To make up the top:
Press all parts except the ribbing on the wrong side with a cool iron over a dry cloth. Join shoulder seams. Set in sleeves. Join sleeve and side seams. Fold hem on sleeves to wrong side and neatly sew in place. Press seams. Sew on buttons.

ALL THAT GLITTERS

An ideal sweater for beginners to attempt. Knitted in just two pieces and elasticated at the waist. The top, back and front are bordered with a flower pattern and the front is laced with diamonds. Buttoned on the shoulders, the little top can also be worn over a shirt.

Materials:
12(13)(14) balls of Robin Moonlight; a pair of No.11 knitting needles; a waist length of elastic; 6 buttons; a size 2.50 crochet hook.

Tension:
16 stitches and 20 rows to 5 cm (2 in.) over stocking stitch using No.11 needles.

Abbreviations:
K.,knit; p.,purl; st.,stitch; tog.,together; dec.,decrease (by working 2sts. tog.); inc.,increase (by working twice into same st.); s.s.,stocking stitch (k. on the right side and p. on the wrong side); y.r.n.,yarn round needle; sl.,slip; p.s.s.o., pass sl. st. over; garter stitch is k. plain on every row; k.1 long, k.1 winding yarn round needle 3 times; cr.3 rt.,cross 3 right thus—k. into front of 3rd st. on left-hand needle, then k. into first and 2nd sts. allowing loops to fall from left-hand needle; cr.3 lt., cross 3 left thus—slip next st. from left-hand needle and leave at front of work, k.2, then k. st. left at front of work; m.b.,make bobble thus—k.1, p.1, k.1 all into next st., turn, p.3, turn, k.3, turn, sl.1, k.2 tog., p.s.s.o., turn, p.1 through back of st.

Note:
The instructions are given for the small size. Where they vary, work the figures in the first brackets for the medium size or the figures in the second brackets for the large size.

Measurements:
The following measurements are given in centimetres first, followed by inches in brackets.

small (10)	medium12)	large (14)
All round at underarms		
84(33½)	89(35½)	94(37½)
Side seam		
31(12½)	31(12½)	31(12½)
Length		
53(21¼)	53(21¼)	54(21½)

The back:
With No.11 needles cast on 135(143) (151) sts. and beginning with a k. row s.s.5 rows.
Next row: All k. on the wrong side to mark fold line.
Beginning with a k. row s.s.124 rows.
To shape the armholes: Dec. 1st. at each end of the next row and the 3(4)(5) following alternate rows—127(133) (139) sts. **.
S.s. 61 rows.
Now work in pattern as follows:
1st to 5th rows: All k.
6th row: All p.
7th row: All k.
8th row: K.7(5)(8), * k.1 long, k.1 long, k.1 long, k.7; repeat from * ending last repeat k.7(5)(8).
9th row: K.3(1)(4), * sl.1, k.3, sl.3 long sts. allowing extra loops to drop from needle, k.3; repeat from * until 4(2)(5) remain, sl.1, k.3(1)(4).
10th row: P.3(1)(4), * sl.1, p.3, sl.3, p.3; repeat from * until 4(2)(5) remain, sl.1, p.3 (1)(4).
11th row: K.7(5)(8), * sl.3, k.7; repeat from * ending last repeat k.7(5)(8).
12th row: P.7(5)(8), * sl.3, p.7; repeat from * ending last repeat p.7(5)(8).
13th row: K.5(3)(6), * cr.3 rt., k.1, cr.3 lt., k.3; repeat from * ending last repeat k.5(3)(6).
14th row: P.5(3)(6), * m.b., p.2, m.b., p.2, m.b., p.3; repeat from * ending last repeat p.5(3)(6).
15th row: All k.
16th row: All p.
17th to 20th rows: All k. Cast off.

The front:
Work as given for back until ** is reached.
Work 1 row.
Now work the diamond pattern as follows:
1st row: K.61(64)(67), k.2 tog., y.r.n., k.1, y.r.n., sl.1, k.1, p.s.s.o., k. to end.
2nd row and each wrong side row: All p.
3rd row: K.60(63)(66), k.2 tog., y.r.n., k.3, y.r.n., sl.1, k.1, p.s.s.o., k. to end.
5th row: K.59(62)(65), k.2 tog., y.r.n., k.5, y.r.n., sl.1, k.1, p.s.s.o., k. to end.
7th row: K.58(61)(64), k.2 tog., y.r.n., k.7, y.r.n., sl.1, k.1, p.s.s.o., k. to end.
9th row: K.57(60)(65), k.2 tog., y.r.n., k.9, y.r.n., sl.1, k.1, p.s.s.o., k. to end.
11th row: K.58(61)(64), y.r.n., sl.1, k.1, p.s.s.o., k.7, k.2 tog., y.r.n., k. to end.
13th row: K.59(62)(65), y.r.n., sl.1, k.1, p.s.s.o., k.5, k.2 tog., y.r.n., k. to end.
15th row: K.60(63)(66), y.r.n., sl.1, k.1, p.s.s.o., k.3, k.2 tog., y.r.n., k. to end.
17th row: K.61(64)(67), y.r.n., sl.1, k.1, p.s.s.o., k.1, k.2 tog., y.r.n., k. to end.
19th row: K.62(65)(68), y.r.n., sl.1, k.2 tog., p.s.s.o., y.r.n., k. to end.
20th row: All p.
These 20 rows form the pattern; repeat them twice more. Now work the 20 row flower pattern given for back.

To make up the sweater:
Press all parts on the wrong side with a cool iron over a dry cloth. Join side seams up to first armhole dec. Fold hem at lower edge to wrong side and slip stitch in place, leaving an opening for elastic; thread through elastic and secure.

The armhole edgings *(both alike):*
With right side of work facing rejoin yarn at one shoulder and using No.11 needles pick up and k.132 sts. from all round armhole edge.
K.5 rows, then cast off.

The buttonhole edging:
With right side of work facing rejoin yarn to top of front at left front shoulder and using crochet hook work 126(132)(138) d.c. along cast off edge of front, turn.
Buttonhole row: 2ch. to stand for first d.c., 1d.c. into each of next 2d.c., * 4ch., miss 3d.c., 1d.c. into each of next 4d.c., 4ch., miss 3d.c., 1d.c. into each of next 4d.c., 4ch., miss 3d.c., * 1d.c. into each of next 86(92)(98) d.c.; repeat from * to *, 1d.c. into each of next 3d.c., fasten off.

The button edging:
With right side of work facing rejoin yarn to top of back and with crochet hook work 126(132)(138) d.c. along cast off edge of back, turn, and work a row of d.c. over d.c. Fasten off. Sew on buttons. Press.

FOLK ISLE

A waistcoat for everyone in lovely soft Shetland wool. There are a great many colours available. Ask for cream, beige grey or dark navy as base colours, with either bright or subtle contrast colours.

Materials:
8 ounces of 'Woollybear' 100% Shetland wool in main colour and one ounce in each of the 4 contrast colours; a pair each of size 3 mm (No. 11) and size 2¼ mm (No. 13) Aero knitting needles; 6 buttons. The wool for this garment is available by mail order from the Patricia Roberts Knitting Shop, 60 Kinnerton Street, London SW1, price £4.35 including postage and V.A.T.

Tension:
18 stitches and 16 rows to 5 cm (2 in.) over the stocking stitch using size 3 (No. 11) knitting needles.

Abbreviations:
K., knit; p., purl; st., stitch; tog., together; dec., decrease (by working 2 sts. tog.); inc., increase (by working twice into same st.); s.s., stocking stitch (k. on the right side and p. on the wrong side); single rib is k. 1 and p. 1 alternately; m., main colour; a., first contrast colour; b., second contrast colour; c., third contrast colour; d., fourth contrast colour; up 1, pick up the loop which lies between the needles, slip it onto left hand needle, then k. into back of it.

Note:
The instructions are given for the first size. Where they vary work the figures in the first brackets for the second size; the figures in the second brackets for the third size.

Measurements:

The measurements are given in centimetres followed by inches in square brackets.

small	medium	large
All round at underarms		
90 [36]	95 [38]	100 [40]
Side seam		
34 [13½]	34 [13½]	34 [13½]
Length		
57.5 [23]	59 [23½]	60 [24]

The back:
With size 2¼ mm (No. 13) needles and m. cast on 128 (136) (144) sts. and work 49 rows in single rib.
Increase row: Rib 14 (2) (6), * up 1, rib 3 (4) (4); repeat from * ending last repeat rib 15 (2) (6)—162 (170) (178) sts.
Change to size 3 mm (No. 11) needles and beginning with a k. row. s.s. 2 rows.
Now work in pattern as follows: 1st row: 2 m. (4a., 2 m.) (2 m.) * 6 a., 2 m., repeat from * ending last repeat 2 m. (4 a.) (2 m.).
The last row sets the position of the first 7 pattern rows given in chart, now work the 2nd to 7th rows from the chart as set.
8th row: 2 m. (2 m., 2 b., 2m.) (1 m., 1 b., 1 m., 1 b., 2 m., 2 b., 2 m.), * 2 b., 2 m., 1 b., 1 m., 1 b., 4 m., 3 b., 2 m., 3 b., 4 m., 1 b., 1 m., 1 b., 2 m., 2 b., 2m.; repeat from * until nil (4) (8) remain, nil (2 b., 2 m.) (2 b., 2 m., 1 b., 1 m., 1 b., 1m.).
The last row sets the position of the rest of the pattern.
Continuing in pattern as set, work 62 rows more from the chart as set.
To shape the armholes: Cast off 4 sts. at the beginning of the next 2 rows.
Dec. 1 st. at each end of the next row and the 8 (10) (12) following alternate rows.
On 136 (140) (144) sts., pattern 57 rows.
To slope the shoulders: Cast off 37 (38) (39) sts. at the beginning of the next 2 rows.
Cast off the remaining 62 (64) (66) sts.

The pocket backs *(two alike)*:
With size 3 mm (No. 11) needles and m. cast on 35 sts. and beginning with a k. row s.s. 40 rows, then leave these sts. on a spare needle until required.

The left front:
With size 2¼ mm (No. 13) needles and m. cast on 64 (68) (72) sts. and work 49 rows in single rib.
Increase row: Rib 2 (4) (6), * up 1, rib 5; repeat from * ending last repeat rib 2 (4) (6).
Change to size 3 mm (No. 11) needles and on 77 (81) (85) sts., beginning with a k. row s.s. 2 rows.**
Now work in Fair Isle pattern as follows:
1st row: 2 m. (4 a., 2m.) (2 m.), * 6 a., 2 m.; repeat from * ending last repeat 3 a.
The last row sets the position of the first 7 pattern rows given in the chart, now work the 2nd to 7th rows from the chart.
8th row: 4 m., 1 b., 1 m., 1 b., 2 m., 2 b., * 2 m., 2 b., 2 m., 1 b., 1 m., 1 b., 4 m., 3 b., 2 m., 3 b., 4 m., 1 b., 1 m., 1 b., 2 m., 2 b.; repeat from * ending last repeat 2 m. (2 m., 2 b., 2 m.), (2 m., 2b., 2 m., 1 b., 1 m., 1 b., 1 m.).
The last row sets the position of the rest of the pattern; work 10 rows more as set.
Pocket row: Pattern 21 (23) (25), slip next 35 sts. onto a stitch-holder at front of work and in their place pattern across the 35 sts. of pocket back, pattern to end.
Pattern 41 rows.
****To slope the neck edge:* Dec. 1 st. at the end-neck edge on the next row and at the same edge on the 3 following 3rd rows.
To shape the armhole and continue to slope the front edge: While decreasing at front edge on every 3rd row as before, cast off 4 sts. at the beginning of the next row, then dec. 1 st. at the beginning—armhole edge on the 9 (11) (13) following alternate rows.
Still decreasing at front edge on every 3rd row as before, pattern 50 rows more.
On 37 (38) (39) sts., work 7 rows.
To slope the shoulder: Cast off.

The right front:
Work as given for left front until ** is reached.
Now work in Fair Isle pattern as follows:
1st row: 3 a., * 2 m., 6 a.; repeat from * ending last repeat 2 m. (4 a.) (2 m.).
The last row sets the position of the first 7 pattern rows given in the chart, now work the 2nd to 7th rows from the chart.
8th row: 2 m. (2 m., 2 b., 2 m.) (1 m., 1 b., 1 m., 1 b., 2 m., 2 b., 2 m.), * 2 b., 2 m., 1 b., 1 m., 1 b., 4 m., 3 b., 2 m., 3 b., 4 m., 1 b., 1 m., 1 b., 2 m., 2 b., 2 m.; repeat from * until 11 remain, 2 b., 2 m., 1 b., 1 m., 1 b., 4 m.
The last row sets the position of the rest of the pattern; work 10 rows more as set.
Pocket row: Pattern 21 (23) (25), slip next 35 sts. onto a stitch-holder at front of work and in their place pattern across the 35 sts. of pocket back, pattern to end.
Pattern 42 rows.
Now work as given for let front from *** to end.

The front band:
With size 2¼ mm (No. 13) needles and m. cast on 12 sts. and work 10 rows in single rib.
1st Buttonhole row: Rib 4, cast off 4, rib to end.
2nd Buttonhole row: Rib 4, turn, cast on 4, turn, rib to end.
Rib 18 rows more.
Repeat the last 20 rows 4 times more, then work the 2 buttonhole rows again.
Continue in rib, until the band is long enough to fit up left front so that the top buttonhole is in line with the first front decrease, along back neck edge and down right front edge. Cast off when correct length is assured.

The pocket tops *(both alike):*
With right side of work facing rejoin m. to sts. left at front of work and using size 2¼ mm (No. 13) needles work 6 rows in single rib, then cast off.

The armbands *(both alike):*
First join shoulder seams. With right side of work facing rejoin m. and using size 2¼ mm (No. 13) needles pick up and k. 160 (168) (176) sts. from all round armhole edge. Work 9 rows in single rib, then cast off.

To make up the waistcoat:
Pin out to size and press on the wrong side with a warm iron over a damp cloth. Join side seams. Sew front bands in place. Neatly sew pocket backs and row ends of pocket tops in place. Press seams. Sew on buttons.

BROWN STUDY

Two shades of brown mohair are used together here to give a marled effect; cream and oatmeal would also be a good combination. Why not knit the pansy sweater (Pansygirl) *to wear beneath the cape? A plum coloured sweater with red mohair flowers would be stunning beneath a red and plum cape.*

Materials:
26 (28) 25 gram balls of Jaeger Mohair in each of 2 toning colours—here brushwood and mole; a pair of No. 2 knitting needles; 2 buttons; a cable needle.

Tension:
20 stitches—1 repeat of the side panel pattern to 14 cm (5½ in.) in width and 24 rows—1 repeat of the side panel pattern to 17.5 cm (7 in.) in depth using No. 2 needles and mohair double. 7 stitches and 8 rows to 5 cm (2 in.) over the garter stitch using No. 2 needles and mohair double.

Abbreviations:
K., knit; p., purl; st., stitch; tog., together; dec., decrease (by working 2 sts. tog.); garter st. is k. plain on every row; inc., increase (by working twice into same st.); cr. 2 f., cross 2 front thus, slip next st. on to cable needle at front of work, p. 1, then k. 1 from cable needle; cr. 2 b., cross 2 back thus, slip next st. on to cable needle at back of work, k. 1, then p. 1 from cable needle; k. or p. b., k. or p. through back of sts.; m.b., make bobble thus, k. across next 4 sts., turn, p. 4, turn, k. 4, turn, p. 4, turn, k. 4, turn, p. 4, turn, pick up a loop from first row of bobble and k. this tog. with next st., k. 2, then pick up loop from 1st row of bobble and k. this tog. with next st.

Note:
The instructions are given for the small size. Where they vary, work the figures in the first brackets for the medium size or the figures in the second brackets for the large size.

Measurements:
The measurements are given in centimetres followed by inches in square brackets.

Sizes	small	medium
All round at hem	170 [68]	175 [70]
Length	117.5 [47]	119 [47½]

Special note:
Two strands—one in each colour mohair—are used together throughout.

The side panels *(two alike)*:
With No. 2 needles and using 2 strands of mohair together, here 1 strand of mole and 1 strand of brushwood, cast on 62 sts. and k. 6 rows.
Now work in pattern as follows:
1st row: P. 5, * cr. 2 f., cr. 2 f., cr. 2 f., cr. 2 b., cr. 2 b., cr. 2 b., p. 8; repeat from * ending last repeat p. 5.
2nd row: K. 6, * p. 1 b., k. 1, p. 1 b., k. 1, p. 2 b., k. 1, p. 1 b., k. 1, p. 1 b., k. 10; repeat from * ending last repeat k. 6.
3rd row: P. 6, * k. 1 b., p. 1, k. 1 b., m.b.—see abbreviations—k. 1 b., p. 1, k. 1 b., p. 10; repeat from * ending last repeat p. 6.
4th row: K. 6, * p. 1 b., k. 1, p. 1 b., k. 1, p. 2 b., k. 1, p. 1 b., k. 1, p. 1 b., k. 10; repeat from * ending last repeat k. 6.
5th row: P. 5, * cr. 2 b., cr. 2 b., cr. 2 b., cr. 2 f., cr. 2 f., cr. 2 f., p. 8; repeat from * ending last repeat p. 5.
6th row and every wrong side row: K. all k. sts. and p. into back of all p. sts.
7th row: P. 4, * cr. 2 b., cr. 2 b., cr. 2 b., p. 2, cr. 2 f., cr. 2 f., cr. 2 f., p. 6; repeat from * ending last repeat p. 4.
9th row: P. 3, * cr. 2 b., cr. 2 b., cr. 2 b., p. 4, cr. 2 f., cr. 2 f., cr. 2 f., p. 4; repeat from * ending last repeat p. 3.
11th row: P. 2, * cr. 2 b., cr. 2 b., cr. 2 b., p. 6, cr. 2 f., cr. 2 f., cr. 2 f., p. 2; repeat from * to end.
13th row: P. 1, * cr. 2 b., cr. 2 b., cr. 2 b., p. 8, cr. 2 f., cr. 2 f., cr. 2 f.; repeat from * until 1 remains, p. 1.
15th row: P. 1, m.b., k. 1 b., * p. 10, k. 1 b., p. 1, k. 1 b., m.b., k. 1 b., p. 1, k. 1 b.; repeat from * until 16 remain, p. 10, k. 1 b., m.b., p. 1.
16th row (wrong side): K. 1, * p. 1 b., k. 1, p. 1 b., k. 1, p. 1 b., k. 10, p. 1 b., k. 1, p. 1 b., k. 1, p. 1 b.; repeat from * until 1 remains, k. 1.
17th row: P. 1, * cr. 2 f., cr. 2 f., cr. 2 f., p. 8, cr. 2 b., cr. 2 b., cr. 2 b.; repeat from * until 1 remains, p. 1.
19th row: P. 2, * cr. 2 f., cr. 2 f., cr. 2 f., p. 6, cr. 2 b., cr. 2 b., cr. 2 b., p. 2; repeat from * to end.
21st row: P. 3, * cr. 2 f., cr. 2 f., cr. 2 f., p. 4, cr. 2 b., cr. 2 b., cr. 2 b., p. 4; repeat from * ending last repeat p. 3.
23rd row: P. 4, * cr. 2 f., cr. 2 f., cr. 2 f., p. 2, cr. 2 b., cr. 2 b., cr. 2 b., p. 6; repeat from * ending last repeat p. 4.
24th row: K. 5, * p. 1 b., k. 1, p. 1 b., k. 1, p. 1 b., k. 2, p. 1 b., k. 1, p. 1 b., k. 1, p. 1 b, k. 8; repeat from * ending last repeat k. 5.
The last 24 rows form the pattern.
Continuing in pattern as set, dec. 1 st. at each end of the next row and the 9 following 10th rows.
On 42 sts. pattern 7 (9) rows or until work measures 90 (91) cm [36 (36½) in.]
Dec. 1 st. at each end of the next row and the 17 following alternate rows.
On 6 sts. work 1 row, then cast off.

The centre back panel:
With No. 2 needles cast on 58 (61) sts. and k. 24 rows.
Continuing in garter st. dec. 1 st. at each end of the next row and the 11 following 10th rows.
On 34 (37) sts. k. 13 rows or until work measures 92.5 cm [37 in.] from beginning.
Dec. 1 st. at each end of the next row and the 4 (5) following 10th (8th) rows.
On 24 (25) sts. work 3 (5) rows, then cast off.

The left front:
With No. 2 needles cast on 33 (35) sts. and k. 24 rows.
Continuing in garter st., dec. 1 st. for the side edge at the beginning of the next row and the 11 following 10th rows.
On 21 (23) sts. k. 13 rows ending at shaped edge or until work measures 92.5 cm [37 in.] from beginning.**
Dec. 1 st. at the beginning of the next row and the 2 (3) following 10th (8th) rows.
On 18 (19) sts. k. 4 (2) rows.
****To shape the neck:* K. 6 (7) and leave these sts. on a safety pin until required for collar, k. to end—12 sts.
Dec. 1 st. at the neck edge on each of the next 8 rows and at the same time dec. 1 st. at side edge on the 5th of these rows.
On 3 sts. k. 6 (4) rows.
Dec. 1 st. at the beginning of the next row.
On 2 sts. k. 3 (5) rows, then take these 2 sts. tog. and fasten off.

The right front:
Work as given for left front until ** is reached.
Dec. 1 st. at the beginning of the next row.
K. 1 (3) rows—20 (22) sts.
1st Buttonhole row: K. until 8 remain, cast off 3, k. to end.
2nd Buttonhole row: K. 5, turn, cast on 3, turn, k. to end.
K. 14 rows decreasing 1 st. at side seam edge on the 7th (3rd and 11th) of these rows.
Work the 2 buttonhole rows again.
K. 5 rows decreasing 1 st. at the side edge on the first (3rd) of these rows.
Now work as given for left front from *** to end.

The left and right half collars *(both alike as the fabric is reversible)*:
Rejoin yarn to the inner edge of the 6 (7) sts. left on safety pin and working in garter st., inc. 1 st. at the beginning—inner edge of the next row and at the same edge on each of the next 15 rows.
On 22 (23) sts. k. 16 (17) rows, then cast off.

To make up the cape:
Pin to size and press all parts lightly on the wrong side with a warm iron over a damp cloth. Join side seams so that the 6 sts. cast off at top of side panels form part of neck edge and leaving an opening 17.5 cm [7 in.] long between front and side panels, starting 62.5 cm [25 in.] above lower edge and finishing 80 cm [32 in.] from lower edge. Join cast off edges of the 2 half collar pieces. Sew shaped row end edges of collar in place all round neck edge. Press seams. Sew on buttons.

RAINY DAY BLOUSON

An easy-to-knit blouson for men of all ages, knitted in a special soft double knitting yarn. The wool is available in tweed and plain shades from The Patricia Roberts Knitting Shop, 60 Kinnerton Street, London S.W.1. Mail order service available. Colours to choose from include blue and mauve tweed; green and brown tweed; brown and olive tweed; plain olive; cherry; grey.

Materials:
10 2 ounce hanks of Special Shetland D.K.; a pair each of No.10 and No.11 knitting needles; 1 button.

Tension:
13 stitches and 17 rows to 5 cm (2 in.) over the reversed stocking stitch using No.10 needles. If you cannot obtain the correct tension using needles of the size suggested, use larger or smaller ones accordingly.

Abbreviations:
K.,knit; p.,purl; st.,stitch; tog.,together; dec.,decrease (by working 2sts. tog.); inc.,increase (by working twice into same st.); double rib is k.2 and p.2 alternately; r.s.s.,reversed stocking stitch (p. on the right side and k. on the wrong side).

Note:
The instructions are given for the small size. Where they vary, work the figures in the first brackets for the medium size or the figures in the second brackets for the large size.

Measurements:
The following measurements are given in centimetres first, followed by inches in brackets.

small	medium	large
All round at underarms		
90(37)	95(39)	100(41)
Side seam		
40(16)	40(16)	40(16)
Length		
64(25½)	65(26)	66(26½)
Sleeve seam		
49(19)	49(19)	49(19)

The back:
With No.11 needles cast on 122(128) (134) sts. and work 40 rows in double rib.
Change to No.10 needles and beginning with a p. row r.s.s.102 rows.
To shape the raglan armholes: Dec. 1st. at each end of the next row and the 39 (41)(43) following alternate rows.
On 42(44)(46) sts. work 1 row.
Change to No.11 needles and work 12 rows in double rib, then cast off loosely.

The front:
Work as given for back until 91 rows have been worked in r.s.s.
Now divide the sts. for the neck: *Next row* (wrong side): K.61(64)(67) and leave these sts. on a spare needle until required for right front shoulder, k. to end and continue on these 61(64)(67) sts. for the left front shoulder.
The left front shoulder: To shape the neck: Dec. 1st. at the end—neck edge on the next row and the 2 following 4th rows.
Work 1 row back to armhole edge.
To shape the raglan armhole and continue to slope the neck: While decreasing 1st. at neck edge on every 4th row as before, dec. 1st. at the beginning—armhole edge on the next row and the 35(37)(39) following alternate rows—4sts.
Work 1 row back to armhole edge, then dec. for raglan at the beginning of the next row and the following alternate row.
Work 1 row, then p.2 tog. and fasten off.
The right front shoulder: With right side of work facing rejoin yarn to inner edge of sts. left on spare needle and work to end of row. Now work as given for left front shoulder to end.

The left and right front neckbands *(both alike):*
With right side of work facing rejoin yarn and using No.11 needles pick up and k. 72(76)(80) sts. from appropriate neck edge and work 1 row in double rib.
Continuing in double rib, dec. 1st. at centre front edge on the next row and the 4 following alternate rows.
Work 1 more row, then cast off in rib.

The sleeves *(both alike):*
With No.11 needles cast on 64(68)(72) sts. and work 40 rows in double rib.
Change to No. 10 needles and beginning with a p. row r.s.s.6 rows.
Inc. 1st. at each end of the next row and the 11 following 12th rows.
On 88(92)(96) sts. r.s.s.5 rows.
To shape the raglan sleevetop: Dec. 1st. at each end of the next row and the 39 (41)(43) following alternate rows.
On 8 sts. work 1 row.
Change to No.11 needles and work 12 rows in double rib, then cast off.

The collar:
With No. 11 needles cast on 120sts. and k.8 rows.
Change to No.10 needles and work as follows:
1st row: K.4, p. until 4 remain, k.4.
2nd row: All p.
Repeat the last 2 rows once more.
Decrease row: K.4, p.2 tog., p.until 6 remain, p.2 tog.b., k.4.
Work 7 rows in r.s.s. with garter stitch edging as set.
Repeat the last 8 rows 3 more times, then work the decrease row again.
Work 3 rows as set.
Cast off loosely.

The pocket:
With No.11 needles cast on 26sts. and k.8 rows.
Change to No.10 needles and work 30 rows in r.s.s. with 4st. garter st. edging as for collar.
Change to No.11 needles and k.16 rows, then cast off.

To make up the blouson:
Pin out and press all r.s.s. parts on the wrong side with a warm iron over a damp cloth. Join raglan seams. Join sleeve and side seams. Neatly sew cast off edge of collar in place at base of neck ribbing (on wrong side). Sew pocket in position at left front, so that the 16 rows in garter stitch are folded to right side and secured with a button at centre. Press seams.

A POCKETFUL OF POSIES

Textures are important to the design of this pretty smock. The flowers are knitted in soft mohair yarn against a plain background, and the basket is knitted in garter stitch in a contrasting shade of plain yarn. The handle of the basket is sewn into place at the centre of the flower basket, so that each side of the basket can be used as a large pocket.

Materials:
16(17)(18) 50 gram balls of Hayfield's Gaylon Chunky in main colour and 2 balls of the same yarn in fourth contrast colour, one ball of Hayfield Gossamer in each of the following colours—red; green; blue and lemon; a pair each of No. 4 and No. 5 knitting needles.

Tension:
7 stitches and 10 rows to 5 cm (2 in.) over the stocking stitch using No.4 needles.

Abbreviations:
K.,knit; p.,purl; st.,stitch; tog.,together; dec.,decrease (by working 2sts. tog.); inc.,increase (by working twice into same st.); s.s.,stocking stitch (k. on the right side and p. on the wrong side); m., main colour; a., first contrast colour—mohair; b., second contrast—mohair; c., third contrast—mohair; d., fourth contrast—double D.K.

Note:
The instructions are given for the small size. Where they vary, work the figures in the first brackets for the medium size or the figures in the second brackets for the large size.

Measurements:
The following measurements are given in centimetres first, followed by inches in brackets.

small (10)	medium (12)	large (14)
All round at underarms		
85 (34)	90 (36)	95 (38)
Side seam		
50 (20)	50 (20)	50 (20)
Length		
70 (28)	71 (28½)	72 (28¾)
Sleeve seam		
32.5 (13)	32.5 (13)	32.5 (13)

The back:
With No.5 needles and m. cast on 79 (83) (87) sts. and k.10 rows.
Change to No.4 needles and beginning with a k. row s.s.12 rows **
Dec. 1st. each end of the row and the 9 following 8th rows.
On 59 (63) (67) sts. s.s.9 rows.
To shape the armholes: Cast off 3 sts. at the beginning of the next 2 rows, then dec. 1st. at each end of the next row and the 1 (2) (3) following alternate rows.
On 49 (51) (53) sts. s.s.33 rows.
To slope the shoulder: Cast off 10(11) (12) sts. at the beginning of the next 2 rows—29 sts.
Cast off.

The front:
Work as given for back until ** is reached.
Dec. 1st. at each end of the next row and the 3 following 8th rows.
On 71 (75) (79) sts. s.s.1 row.
Now work the flower pattern in the following way. This is worked entirely in s.s. so only the colour details follow. For easier working use a different ball of m. at each side of motif and using mohair double throughout, use a separate small ball of contrast colours for each flower motif.
1st row: 3(5)(7) m., 4a., 7b., 1a., 2c., 3a., 2c., 3a., 2b., 3a., 3b., 5a., 3b., 3a., 2b., 3a., 2c., 3a., 2c., 1a., 7b., 4a., 3(5) (7) m.
2nd row: 2(4)(6) m., 4a., 8b., 4c., 1a., 4c., 1a., 4b., 1a., 5b., 3a., 5b., 1a., 4b., 1a., 4c., 1a., 4c., 8b., 4a., 2(4)(6) m.
These 2 rows set the position of the motif

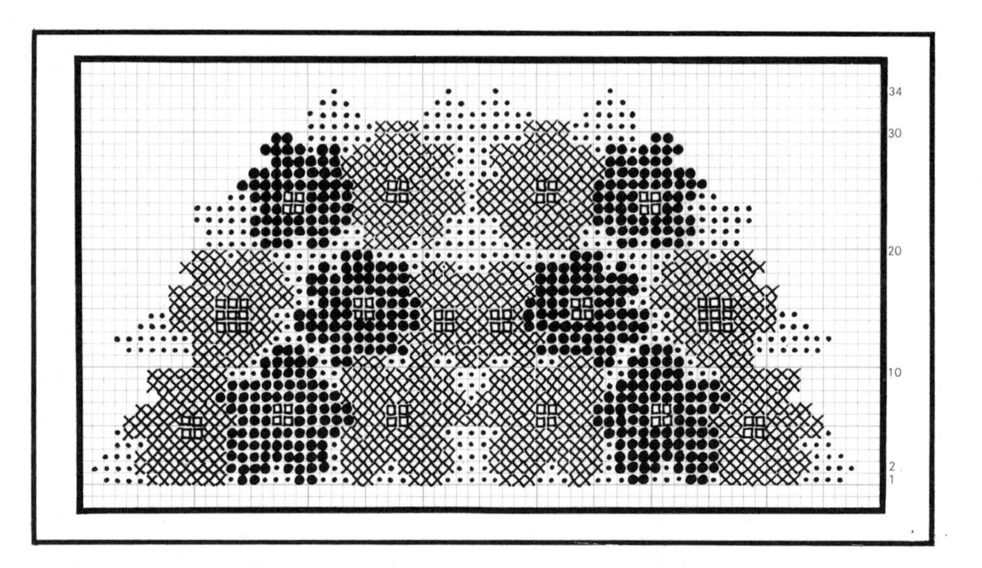

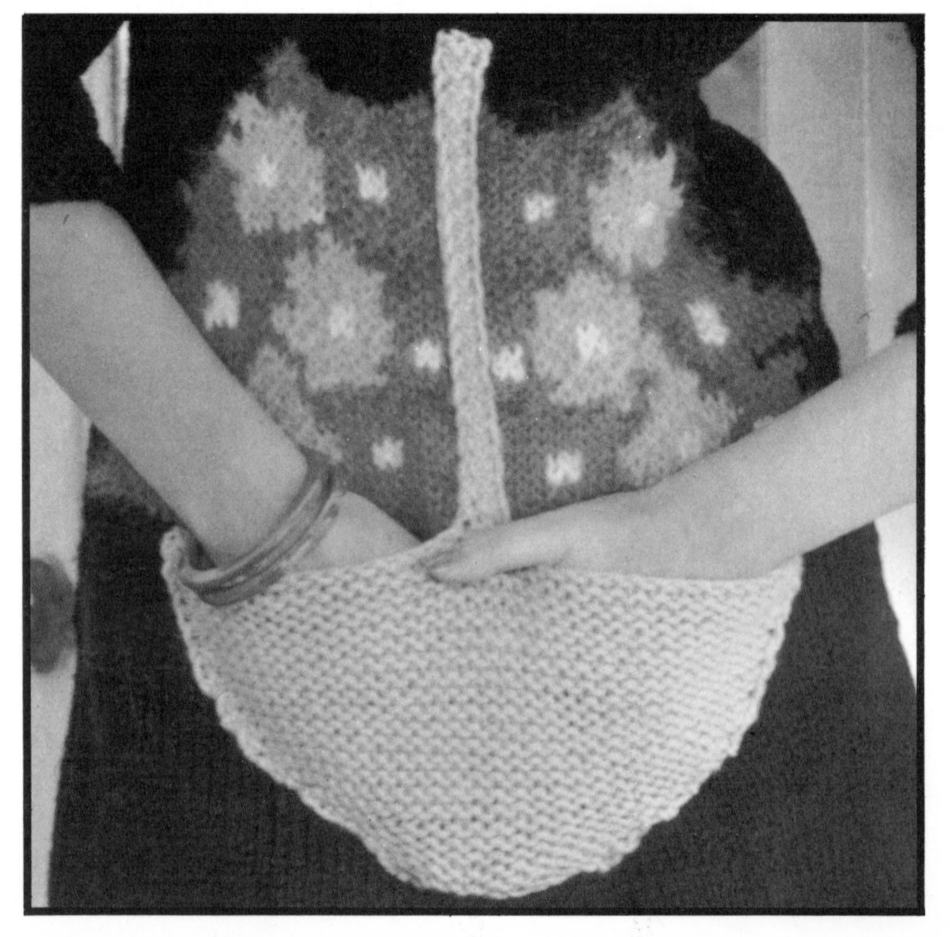

given in the chart. Now work the 3rd to 34th rows from the chart and at the same time decrease 1st. at each end of the 7th pattern row and 3 following 8th rows. Continuing with m. only s.s.4 rows.
Dec. 1st. at each end of the next row and the following 8th rows.
On 59(63)(67) sts. s.s.2 rows.
Now divide the sts. for the neck: *Next row:* P.29(31)(33) and leave these sts. on a spare needle until required for right front shoulder, p.2 tog., p. to end and continue on these 29(31)(33) sts. for the left front shoulder.
The left front shoulder: To shape the neck: Dec. 1st. at the neck edge on the next row and the following 3rd row.
Work 2 rows ending at armhole edge.
To shape the armhole and continue to slope the neck: While decreasing at neck edge on every 3rd row from previous neck edge dec. cast off 3sts. at the beginning of the next row, then dec. 1st. at the armhole edge on the 2(3)(4) following alternate rows—20(20)(21) sts.
Still decreasing at neck edge on every 3rd row pattern 29(27)(25) rows.
On 10(11)(12) sts. work 4(6)(8) rows, then cast off.
The right front shoulder: With right side of work facing rejoin yarn to inner edge of sts. left on spare needle and work to end of row. Now work as given for left front shoulder to end.

The sleeves *(both alike):*
With No.5 needles and m. cast on 48(50)(52) sts. and k.10 rows.
Change to No.4 needles and beginning with a k. row s.s.60 rows.
To shape the sleevetop: Cast off 3 sts. at the beginning of the next 2 rows, then dec. 1st. at each end of the next 12 rows. Cast off the 18(20)(22) remaining sts.

The left half collar and neckband:
First join shoulder seams. With right side of work facing rejoin m. and using No. 5 needles pick up and k.51(53)(55) sts. between centre back neck and centre front neck.
K.8 rows, decreasing 1st. at centre front neck end on the 2nd row and the 3 following alternate rows **.
Cast off 16(18)(20) sts. at the beginning of the next row.
On 31sts. k.28 rows, then cast off.

The right half collar and neckband:
Work as given for left half collar and neckband to **.
K.1 more row.
Cast off 16(18)(20) sts. at the beginning of the next row.
On 31sts. k.27 rows, then cast off.

The basket-shaped pocket:
With No.5 needles and d. cast on 14sts.
K.8 rows, increasing 1st. at each end of each row, then inc. 1st. at each end of the 3 following 4th rows.
On 36sts. k.14 rows.
Next row: Cast off 16sts., k. next 3sts., cast off the remaining 16sts.
Rejoin a. to the 4sts. at centre and k.40 rows then cast off.

To make up the smock:
Press all parts on the wrong side with a warm iron over a damp cloth. Set in sleeves. Join sleeve and side seams. Join row end edges of collar at centre back neck and neckband at centre front. Neatly sew basket pocket in position on front, leaving the two 16 stitch cast off groups for pocket opening.

BLUE MOON

SEE MODEL ON LEFT, FOLLOWING PAGE

A simple-to-knit sweater, to wear either casually with jeans, or more formally with a suit. Knit it without the collar for a classic V-neck. Among the colours available are blue tweed as in our picture, oatmeal, grey, plum, cream and green.

Materials:
16 ounces of 'Woollybear' Shetland 4-ply; a pair each of No.12 and No.13 knitting needles. The wool for this sweater is available from the Patricia Roberts Knitting Shop, 60 Kinnerton St., London, S.W.1. Mail order service available.

Tension:
The tension is based on a tension of 16 stitches and 20 rows to 5 cm (2 in.) over stocking stitch using No.12 needles.

Abbreviations:
K., knit; p., purl; st., stitch; tog., together; dec., decrease (by working 2 sts. tog.); inc., increase (by working twice into same st.); double rib is k.2 and p.2 alternately; r.s.s., reversed stocking stitch; m.b., make bobble thus, k.1, p.1, k.1, p.1, all into next st., turn, p.4, turn, k.4, turn, p.2 tog., p.2 tog., turn, k.2 tog.b.; k.2 tog.b., k.2 tog. through back of sts.; cr.3 rt., cross 3 right thus, slip next st. on to cable needle and leave at back of work, k.2, then p.1 from cable needle; cr.3 lt., cross 3 left, slip next 2 sts. on to cable needle and leave at front of work, p.1, then k.2 from cable needle; cable 8 thus, slip next 4 sts. on to cable needle and leave at back of work, k.4 then k.4 from cable needle; up 1, pick up the loop which lies between the needles, slip it on to left hand needle, then k. into back of it.

Note:
The instructions are given for the 36 in. chest size. Where they vary work the instructions in the first brackets for the 38 in. chest size or the instructions in the second brackets for the 40 in. chest size.

Measurements:
The measurements are given in centimetres followed by inches in square brackets.

To fit chest sizes		
90 [36]	95 [38]	100 [40]
All round at underarms		
90 [36]	95 [38]	100 [40]
Side seam		
41 [16½]	41 [16½]	41 [16½]
Length		
63 [25¼]	64 [25¾]	65.5 [26¼]
Sleeve seam (with cuffs folded in half)		
47.5 [19]	47.5 [19]	47.5 [19]

The back:
With No.13 needles cast on 128 (136) (144) sts. and work 47 rows in double rib.
Increase row: Rib 4 (8) (12), * up 1, rib 8; repeat from * ending last repeat rib 4 (8) (12)—144 (152) (160) sts.
Change to No.12 needles and work as follows:
1st row: P.6 (2) (6), m.b., * p.7, m.b.; repeat from * twice (3 times) (3 times), p.6, k.8, p.6, m.b., p.3, m.b., p.3, m.b., p.10, k.4, p.10, m.b., p.3, m.b., p.3, m.b., p.6, k.8, p.6, * m.b., p.7; repeat from last * ending last repeat p.6 (2) (6).
2nd row: K.37 (41) (45), p.8, k.25, p.4, k.25, p.8, k.37 (41) (45).
3rd row: P.37 (41) (45), k.8, p.24, cr.3 rt., cr.3 lt., p.24, k.8, p.37 (41) (45).
4th row: K.37 (41) (45), p.8, k.24, p.2, k.2, p.2, k.24, p.8, k.37 (41) (45).
5th row: P.37 (41) (45), k.8, p.23, cr.3 rt., p.2, cr.3 lt., p.23, k.8, p.37 (41) (45).
6th row: K.37 (41) (45), p.8, k.23, p.2, k.4, p.2, k.23, p.8, k.37 (41) (45).
7th row: P.2 (6) (2), m.b., * p.7, m.b.; repeat from * twice (twice) (3 times) more, p.10, cable 8, p.10, m.b., p.11, cr.3 rt., p.4, cr.3 lt., p.11, m.b., p.10, cable 8, p.10, * m.b., p.7; repeat from last * ending last repeat p.2 (6) (2).
8th row: K.37 (41) (45), p.8, k.22, p.2, k.6, p.2, k.22, p.8, k.37 (41) (45).
9th row: P.37 (41) (45), k.8, p.21, cr.3 rt., p.6, cr.3 lt., p.21, k.8, p.37 (41) (45).
10th row: K.37 (41) (45), p.8, k.21, p.2, k.8, p.2, k.21, p.8, p.37 (41) (45).
11th row: P.37 (41) (45), k.8, p.20, cr.3 rt., p.8, cr.3 lt., p.20, k.8, p.37 (41) (45).
12th row: K.37 (41) (45), p.8, k.20, p.2, k.10, p.2, k.20, p.8, k.37 (41) (45).
13th row: P.6 (2) (6), m.b., * p.7, m.b.; repeat from * twice (3 times) (3 times), p.6, k.8, p.19, cr.3 rt., p.10, cr.3 lt., p.19, k.8, p.6, * m.b., p.7; repeat from last * ending last repeat p.6 (2) (6).
14th row: K.37 (41) (45), p.8, k.19, p.2, k.12, p.2, k.19, p.8, k.37 (41) (45)
15th row: P.37 (41) (45), k.8, p.18, cr.3 rt., p.12, cr.3 lt., p.18, k.8, p.37 (41) (45).
16th row: K.37 (41) (45), p.8, k.18, p.2, k.14, p.2, k.18, p.8, k.37 (41) (45).
17th row: P.37 (41) (45), k.8, p.17, cr.3 rt., p.14, cr.3 lt., p.17, k.8, p.37 (41) (45).
18th row: K.37 (41) (45), p.8, k.17, p.2, k.16, p.2, k.17, p.8, k.37 (41) (45).
19th row: P.2 (6) (2), m.b., * p.7, m.b.; repeat from * twice (twice) (3 times), p.10, cable 8, p.17, k.2, p.16, k.2, p.17, cable 8, p.10, * m.b., p.7; repeat from last * ending last repeat p.2 (6) (2).
20th row: As 18th row.
21st row: P.37 (41) (45), k.8, p.17, cr.3 lt., p.14, cr.3 rt., p.17, k.8, p.37 (41) (45).
22nd row: As 16th row.
23rd row: P.37 (41) (45), k.8, p.18, cr.3 lt., p.12, cr.3 rt., p.18, k.8, p.37 (41) (45).
24th row: As 14th row.
25th row: P.6 (2) (6), m.b., * p.7, m.b.; repeat from * twice (3 times) (3 times), p.6, k.8, p.19, cr.3 lt., p.10, cr.3 rt., p.19, k.8, p.6, * m.b., p.7; repeat from last * ending last repeat p.6 (2) (6).
26th row: As 12th row.
27th row: P.37 (41) (45), k.8, p.20, cr.3 lt., p.8, cr.3 rt., p.20, k.8, p.37 (41) (45).
28th row: As 10th row.
29th row: P.37 (41) (45), k.8, p.21, cr.3 lt., p.6, cr.3 rt., p.21, k.8, p.37 (41) (45).
30th row: As 8th row.
31st row: P.2 (6) (2), m.b., * p.7, m.b.; repeat from * twice (twice) (3 times), p.10, cable 8, p.10, m.b., p.11, cr.3 lt., p.4, cr.3 rt., p.11, m.b., p.10, cable 8, p.10, * m.b., p.7; repeat from last * ending last repeat p.2 (6) (2).
32nd row: As 6th row.
33rd row: P.37 (41) (45), k.8, p.23, cr.3 lt., p.2, cr.3 rt., p.23, k.8, p.37 (41) (45).
34th row: As 4th row.
35th row: P.37 (41) (45), k.8, p.24, cr.3 lt., cr.3 rt., p.24, k.8, p.37 (41) (45).
36th row: As 2nd row.
These 36 rows form the pattern. Repeat them twice more.**
Work the first 14 rows again.
To shape the armholes: Maintaining the continuity of the pattern as set, cast off 8 sts. at the beginning of the next 2 rows, then dec. 1 st. at each end of next row and 8 (10) (12) following alternate rows.
On 110 (114) (118) sts. pattern 63 rows.
To slope the shoulders: Cast off 10 sts. at the beginning of the next 4 rows, then 11 (12) (13) sts. on the 2 following rows.
Change to No.13 needles and on 48 (50) (52) sts. work 10 rows in double rib, then cast off in rib.

The front:
Work as given for back until ** is reached. Pattern 1 row more.
Now divide the sts. for the neck: *Next row:* Pattern as set across 72 (76) (80) and leave these sts. on a spare needle until required for right half front, work as set to end and continue on these 72 (76) (80) sts. for the left half front.
The left half front:
To slope the neck: Dec. 1 st. at the end of the next row and at the same edge on the 2 following 4th rows.
Pattern 3 rows ending at side seam edge.
To shape the armhole and continue to slope the neck: While decreasing at neck edge on every 4th row from previous neck dec., cast off 8 sts. at the beginning of the next row, then dec. 1 st. at the armhole edge on the 9 (11) (13) following alternate rows.
Still decreasing 1 st. at neck edge on every 4th row pattern 62 rows—31 (32) (33) sts.
Work 1 row back to armhole edge.
To slope the shoulder: Cast off 10 sts. at the beginning of the next row and following alternate row. On 11 (12) (13) sts., work 1 row, then cast off.
The right half front:
With right side of work facing rejoin yarn to inner edge of sts. left on spare needle and work to end of row, now work as given for left half front to end.

The front neckband:
With right side of work facing rejoin wool

and using No.13 needles pick up and k.96 (100) (104) sts. from left front neck edge and 96 (100) (104) sts. from right front neck edge.
Next row: Work in double rib to within 2 sts. of centre front, k. 2 tog.b., k. 2 tog., work in double rib to end.
Repeat the last row 10 times more then cast off in rib.

The sleeves *(both alike)* **:**
With No.13 needles cast on 76 (80) (84) sts. and work 56 rows in double rib.
Change to No.12 needles and work in pattern as follows:
1st row: P.3 (5) (7), m.b., * p.7, m.b.; repeat from * twice more, p.6, k.8, p.6, * m.b., p.7; repeat from last * ending last repeat p.3 (5) (7).
2nd row: K. 34 (36) (38), p. 8, k. 34 (36) (38).
3rd row: P. 34 (36) (38), k. 8, p. 34 (36) (38).
4th and 5th rows: As 2nd and 3rd rows.
6th row: As 2nd row.
7th row: P.7 (1) (3), m.b., * p.7, m.b.; repeat from * once, p.10, cable 8, p.10, * m.b., p.7; repeat from last * ending last repeat p.7 (1) (3).
8th to 12th rows: As 2nd to 6th rows.
These 12 rows form the pattern. Continuing in pattern as set, inc. 1 st. at each end of the next row and the 15 following 8th rows.
On 108 (112) (116) sts. pattern 31 rows.
To shape the sleevetop: Cast off 8 sts. at the beginning of the next 2 rows, then dec. 1 st. at each end of the next row and the 25 (27) (29) following alternate rows.
Cast off 4 sts. at the beginning of the next 8 rows.
Cast off the 8 remaining sts.

The collar:
With No.13 needles cast on 197 sts. and work 5 rows in double rib.
Next row: Cast off 30 sts., rib next 136 sts., cast off the 30 remaining sts.
Rejoin wool to the centre 137 sts. and work in bobble pattern as follows:
1st to 4th rows: Beginning with a p. row in r.s.s.
5th row: P.4, * m.b., p.7; repeat from * ending last repeat p.4.
6th to 10th rows: Beginning with a p. row in r.s.s.
11th row: P.8, * m.b., p.7; repeat from * ending last repeat p.8.
12th row: All k.
While working in pattern as set dec. 1 st. at each end of the next row and the 3 following 6th rows.
On 129 sts., pattern 5 rows, then cast off.

To make up the sweater:
Pin all pieces out to size and press on the wrong side lightly with a warm iron over a damp cloth. Join shoulder seams. Set in sleeves. Join sleeve and side seams. Sew cast off groups at side of collar to row end edges of collar. Sew collar in place. Press seams.

CADILLAC BLUES

SEE MODEL ON RIGHT, FOLLOWING PAGE

Fair Isle made easy. Just the two fronts of this jacket are in Fair Isle, while the back and sleeves are in reversed stocking stitch, which makes it quicker to knit. Base colours with appropriate contrast colours are blue as in our picture, grey, oatmeal, cream, plum and black.

Materials:
13 ounces of 'Woolly bear' 100% Shetland wool in main colour, 2 ounces of first contrast and 1 ounce in each of the 3 other contrast colours; a pair each of No.11 and No.12 and No.13 knitting needles; 8 buttons. The wool is available from the Patricia Roberts Knitting Shop, 60 Kinnerton Street, London, S.W.1. Mail order service available.

Tension:
14 stitches and 18 rows to 5 cm (2 in.) over the reversed stocking stitch using No.11 needles; 18 stitches and 18 rows to 5 cm (2

Abbreviations:
K., knit; p., purl; st., stitch; tog., together; dec., decrease (by working 2 sts. tog.); inc., increase (by working twice into same st.); r.s.s., reversed stocking stitch (p. on the right side and k. on the wrong side); single rib is k.1 and p.1 alternately; up 1, pick up the loop that lies between the needles, slip it on to left hand needle, then k. into back of it; s.s., stocking stitch (k. on the right side and p. on the wrong side); m., main colour; a., first contrast colour; b., second contrast colour; c., third contrast colour; sl., slip; p.s.s.o., pass sl. st. over.

Note:
The instructions are given for the small size. Where they vary work the figures in the first brackets for the medium size or the figures in the second brackets for the large size.

Measurements:
The measurements are given in centimetres followed by inches in square brackets.

To fit chest sizes		
small	medium	large
90–92.5 [36–37]	95–97.5 [38–39]	100–102.5 [40–41]
All round at underarms		
95 [38]	100 [40]	105 [42]
Side seam		
44 [17½]	44 [17½]	44 [17½]
Length		
67.5 [27]	69 [27½]	70 [28]
Sleeve seam (with cuffs folded in half)		
45 [18]	45 [18]	45 [18]

The back:
With No.13 needles and m. cast on 120 (128) (135) sts. and work 29 rows in single rib.
Inc. row: Rib 4 (8) (12), * up 1, rib 8; repeat from * ending last repeat rib 4 (8) (11).
Change to No.11 needles and on 135 (143) (150) sts. beginning with a p. row r.s.s. 144 rows. Work should now measure 16 in. from beginning of *r.s.s.*
To shape the armholes: Cast off 8 (10) (12) sts. at the beginning of the next 2 rows.
On 119 (123) (126) sts., r.s.s. 80 (84) (88) rows.
To slope the shoulders: Cast off 17 sts. at the beginning of the next 2 rows and 16 (17) (18) sts. on the 2 following rows.
Cast off the remaining 53 (55) (56) sts.

The sleeves *(both alike)* **:**
With No.13 needles and m. cast on 76 (80) (84) sts. and work 40 rows in single rib.
Change to No.11 needles and beginning with a p. row r.s.s. 6 rows.
Continuing in r.s.s., inc. 1 st. at each end of the next row and the 21 following 6th rows.
On 120 (124) (128) sts., r.s.s. 11 rows, marking each end of the last row with coloured threads.
R.s.s. 10 (12) (14) rows more, then cast off.

The two large pocket backs *(both alike)* **:**
With No.11 needles and m. cast on 45 sts. and beginning with a p. row r.s.s. 50 rows then leave these sts. on a stitch-holder until required.

The small pocket back:
With No.11 needles and m. cast on 19 sts. and beginning with a p. row r.s.s. 40 rows, then leave these sts. on a stitch-holder until required.

The left front:
With No.13 needles and m. cast on 61 (65) (69) sts. and work 29 rows in single rib.
Inc. row: Rib 2 (4) (6), * up 1, rib 3; repeat from * ending last repeat rib 2 (4) (6).
Change to No.12 needles and on 81 (85) (89) sts. beginning with a k. row s.s. 2 rows.
Now work in Fair Isle pattern as follows. This is worked entirely in s.s. so only the colour details are given. Take great care to avoid pulling colours not in use tightly across the back of the work or it will become puckered.
1st Pattern row: 1 m. (1 c., 2 m.) (2 m.), 1 b. * 2 m., 1 c., 2 m., 1 b.; repeat from * until 1 (3) (2) remain, 1 m. (2 m., 1 b.) (2 m.).
The last row sets the position of the pattern

given in the chart. Work the 2nd to 12th rows from the chart as set.

13th Pattern row: 1 (3) (5) a., * 7 c., 11 a.; repeat from * ending last repeat 1 (3) (5) a. The last row sets the position of the rest of the pattern. Work the 14th to 56th rows from the chart as set.

Pocket row: Work across 18 (20) (22) sts., slip next 45 sts. on to a stitch-holder and leave at front of work, in their place work across the 45 sts. of one large pocket back, work to end.

Pattern 85 rows more as set.**

To shape the armhole: Continuing in pattern as set, cast off 10 (12) (14) sts. at the beginning of the next row.

On 71 (73) (75) sts. pattern 44 (48) (52) rows more.

To shape the neck: Cast off 12 (13) (14) sts. at the beginning of the next row, then dec. 1 st. at the neck edge on each of the next 20 rows.

On 39 (40) (41) sts. pattern 16 rows.

To slope the shoulder: Cast off 20 sts. at the beginning of the next row.

On 19 (20) (21) sts. work 1 row, then cast off.

The right front:

Work as given for left front until ** is reached.

2nd Pocket row: Pattern 31 (33) (35), slip next 19 sts. on to a stitch-holder and leave at front of work, in their place pattern across the 19 sts. of small pocket back, pattern to end.

Now work as given for left front armhole shaping to end.

The collar:

With No. 13 needles and m. cast on 220 (226) (230) sts. and work 4 rows in single rib.

Next row: Rib 3, sl. 1, k. 2 tog., p.s.s.o., rib until 6 remain, sl. 1, k. 2 tog., p.s.s.o., rib 3.

Rib 3 rows.

Repeat the last 4 rows 14 times more.

Cast off the remaining 160 (166) (170) sts.

The left front band:

With No. 13 needles and m. cast on 12 (14) (14) sts. and work 14 (16) (18) rows in single rib.

1st Buttonhole row: Rib 4 (5) (5), cast off 4, rib to end.

2nd Buttonhole row: Rib 4 (5) (5), turn, cast on 4 (5) (5), turn, rib to end.

Rib 24 rows.

Repeat the last 26 rows 6 times more, then work the 2 buttonhole rows again.

Rib 6 (8) (10) rows.

Cast off in rib.

The right front band:

With No. 13 needles and m. cast on 12 sts and work 204 (208) (212) rows in single rib, then cast off.

The pocket tops *(all 3 alike)*:

With right side of work facing rejoin m. to the sts. left at front of work. Using No. 13 needles rib 6 rows, then cast off in rib.

To make up the jacket:

Pin out to size all the s.s. and r.s.s. pieces and press with a warm iron over a damp cloth. Join shoulder seams. Set in sleeves so that the straight row ends above the marking threads are sewn to the sts. cast off at underarms. Join sleeve and side seams. Neatly sew row ends of pocket tops and pocket backs in place. Sew cast off edge of collar in place all round neck edge. Fold ribbing at lower edge in half to wrong side and slip st. in place. Sew front bands in position. Sew on buttons. Press seams.

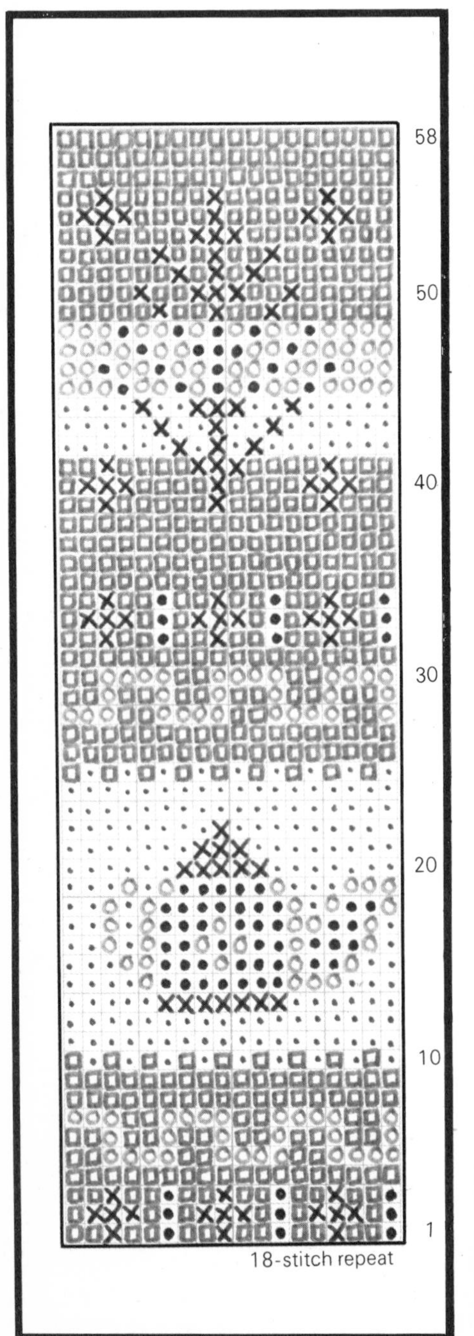

18-stitch repeat

COLD SHOULDER

If you want to look sexy, wear this sweater off one shoulder, or to look demure wear it with both shoulders covered. Not a sweater for beginners.

Materials:
20 (21) (22) 20 gram balls of Wendy Minuit; a pair each of size 2¾ (No. 12) and size 2¼ (No. 13) Aero knitting needles; a small Aero cable needle: a long circular size 2¼ mm (No. 13) Aero knitting needle.

Tension:
Work at such a tension that 83 sts.—1 repeat of the pattern between the stars *, measures 21 cm (8½ in.) in width and 50 rows—1 repeat of the pattern measure 10.5 cm (4¼ in.) in length, using size 2¾ (No. 12) needles.

Abbreviations:
K., knit; p., purl; st., stitch; tog., together; dec., decrease (by working 2 sts. tog.); inc., increase (by working twice into same st.); y.f., yard forward; y.r.n.,yarn round needle; m.b., make bobble thus, k. 1, y.r.n., k. 1, y.r.n., k. 1 all into next st., turn, p. 5, turn, k. 5, turn, p. 5, turn, pass 2nd, 3rd, 4th and 5th sts. on left hand needle over first st., y.f., p. 1 remaining st.; cable 6 thus, slip next 3 sts. onto cable needle and leave at front of work, k. 3, then k. 3 from cable needle; c. 3rt., cross 3 right thus, slip next st. onto cable needle at back of work, k. 2, then p. 1 from cable needle; c. 31t., cross 3 left thus, slip next 2 sts. onto cable needle at front of work, p. 1, then k. 2, from cable needle; cable 6b., as cable 6, but leaving sts. on cable needle at back of work; cr. 5, thus, slip next 2 sts. onto a cable needle at front of work, k. 2, p. 1, then k. 2 from cable needle; double rib is k. 2 and p. 2 alternately; up 1, pick up the loop which lies between the needles, slip it onto left hand needle, then k. into back of it; single rib is k. 1 and p. 1 alternately; sl., slip; p.s.s.o., pass sl. st. over; 3 from 1, k. 1, y.r.n., k. 1, all in next st.

Note:
The instructions are given for the small size. Where they vary work the figures in the first brackets for the medium size or the figures in the second brackets for the large size.

Measurements:

The measurements are given in centimetres followed by inches in square brackets.

small	medium	large
All round at underarms		
90 [36]	95 [38]	100 [40]
Side seam		
51 [20½]	51 [20½]	51 [20½]
Length		
67 [26¾]	67.5 [27]	68 [27¼]
Sleeve seam with cuff folded in half		
42.5 [17]	42.5 [17]	42.5 [17]

The back:
With size 2¼ mm (No. 13) needles cast on 128 (136) (144) sts. and work 107 rows in double rib.

Increase row: Rib 1 (5) (9), * up 1, rib 2, up 1, rib 3; repeat from * until 2 (6) (10) remain, up 1, rib 1 (5) (9), inc in last st.—180 (188) (196) sts.

Change to size 2¾ mm (No. 12) needles and work in pattern as follows:

1st row: K. 1 (3) (5), * p. 4, k. 1, p. 4, k. 1, p.4, m.b., p. 4 (5) (6), k. 6, p. 2, k. 5, p. 7, k. 2, m.b., k. 2, p. 7, k. 5, p. 2, k. 6, p. 4 (5) (6), m.b., p. 4, k. 1, p. 4, k. 1, p. 4 *, k. 1, p. 2, k. 6, p. 2, k. 1; repeat from * to *, k. 1 (3) (5).

2nd row: P. 1 (3) (5), * k. 4, p. 1, k. 4, p. 1, k. 4, p. 1, k. 4 (5) (6), p. 6, k. 2, p. 5, k. 7; p. 5, k. 7, p. 5, k. 2, p. 6, k. 4 (5) (6), p. 1, k. 4, p. 1, k. 4, p. 1, k.4, * p. 1, k. 2, p. 6, k.2, p. 1; repeat from * to *, p. 1 (3) (5).

3rd row: K. 1 (3) (5), * p. 4, k. 1, p. 4, k. 1, p. 3, m.b., k. 1, m.b., p. 3 (4) (5), cable 6, p. 2, k. 5, p. 6, c. 3rt., k. 1, c. 3lt., p. 6., k. 5, p. 2, cable 6, p. 3 (4) (5), m.b., k. 1, m.b., p. 3, k. 1, p.4, k. 1, p.4, * k. 1, p. 2, cable 6, p. 2, k. 1; repeat from * to *, then, k. 1 (3) (5).

4th row: P. 1 (3) (5), * k. 4, p. 1, k. 4, p. 1, k. 4, p. 1, k. 4 (5) (6), p. 6, k. 2, p. 5, k. 6, p. 2, k. 1, p. 1, k. 1, p. 2, k. 6, p. 5, k. 2, p. 6, k. 4 (5) (6), p. 1, k. 4, p. 1, k. 4, p. 1, k. 4, *, p. 1, k. 2, p. 6, k. 2, p. 1,; repeat from * to *, p. 1 (3) (5).

5th row: K. 1 (3) (5), * p. 4, k. 1, p. 4, k. 1, p. 2, m. b., p. 1, m. b., p. 1, m.b., p. 2 (3) (4), k. 6, p. 2, k. 5, p. 5, c. 3rt., p. 1, k. 1, p. 1, c. 3lt., p. 5, k. 5, p. 2, k. 6, p. 2 (3) (4), m.b., p. 1, m.b., p. 1, m.b., p. 2, k. 1, p. 4, k. 1, p. 4 *, k. 1, p. 2, k. 6, p. 2, k. 1; repeat from * to *, then k. 1 (3) (5).

6th row: P. 1 (3) (5), * k. 4, p. 1, k. 4, p. 1, k. 4, p. 1, k. 4 (5) (6), p. 6, k. 2, p. 5, k. 5, p. 3, k. 1, p. 1, k. 1, p. 3, k. 5, p. 5, k. 2, p. 6, k. 4 (5) (6), p. 1, k. 4, p. 1, k. 4, p. 1, k. 4, *, p. 1, k. 2, p. 6, k. 2, p. 1; repeat from * to *, then p. 1 (3) (5).

7th row: K. 1(3) (5), * p. 4, m.b., p. 4, k. 1, p. 4, k. 1, p. 4 (5) (6), k. 6, p. 2, k. 2, m.b., k. 2, p. 4, c. 3rt., k. 1, p. 1, k. 1, p. 1, k. 1, c. 3lt., p. 4, k. 2, m.b., k. 2, p. 2, k. 6, p. 4 (5) (6), k. 1, p. 4, k. 1, p. 4, m.b., p. 4 *, k. 1, p. 2, k. 6, p. 2, k. 1; repeat from * to *, then k. 1 (3) (5).

8th row: P. 1 (3) (5), * k. 4, p. 1, k. 4, p. 1, k. 4, p. 1, k. 4 (5) (6), p. 6, k. 2, p. 5, k. 4, p. 2, k. 1, p. 1, k. 1, p. 1, k. 1, p. 1, k. 1, p. 2, k. 4, p. 5, k. 2, p. 6, k. 4 (5) (6), p. 1, k. 4, p. 1, k. 4., p. 1, k. 4, * p. 1, k. 2, p. 6, k. 2, p. 1; repeat from * to *, then p. 1 (3) (5).

9th row: K. 1 (3) (5), * p. 3, m.b., k. 1, m.b., p. 3, k. 1, p. 4, k. 1, p. 4 (5) (6), k. 6, p. 2, k. 1, m.b., k. 1, m.b., k. 1, p. 3, c. 3rt., p. 1, k. 1, p. 1, k. 1, p. 1, k. 1, p. 1, c. 3lt., p. 3, k. 1, m.b., k. 1, m.b., k. 1, p. 2, k. 6, p. 4 (5) (6), k. 1, p. 4, k. 1, p. 3, m.b., k. 1, m.b., p. 3, * k. 1, p. 2, k. 6, p. 2, k. 1; repeat from * to *, then k. 1 (3) (5).

10th row: P. 1 (3) (5), * k. 4, p. 1, k.4, p. 1, k. 4, p. 1, k. 4 (5) (6), p. 6, k. 2, p. 5, k. 3, p. 3, k. 1, p. 1, k. 1, p. 1, k. 1, p. 1, k. 1, p. 3, k. 3, p. 5, k. 2, p. 6, k. 4 (5) (6), p. 1, k. 4, p. 1, k. 4, p. 1, k. 4, * p. 1, k. 2, p. 6, k. 2, p. 1; repeat from * to *, then p. 1 (3) (5).

11th row: K. 1 (3) (5), * p. 2, m.b., p. 1, m.b., p. 1, m.b., p. 2, k. 1, p. 4, k. 1, p. 4 (5) (6), cable 6, p. 2, k. 5, p. 2, c. 3rt., k. 1, p. 1, k. 1, p. 1, k. 1, p. 1, k. 1, p. 1, k. 1, c. 3lt., p. 2, k. 5, p. 2, cable 6, p. 4 (5) (6), k. 1, p. 4, k. 1, p. 2, m.b., p. 1, m.b., p. 1, m.b., p. 2 *, k. 1, p. 2, cable 6, p. 2, k. 1; repeat from * to *, k. 1 (3) (5).

12th row: P. 1 (3) (5), * k. 4, p. 1, k. 4, p. 1, k. 4, p. 1, k. 4 (5) (6), p. 6, k. 2, p. 5, k. 2, p. 2, k. 1, p. 1, k. 1, p. 1, k. 1, p. 1, k. 1, p. 1, k. 1, p. 1, k. 1, p. 2, k. 2, p. 5, k. 2, p. 6, k. 4 (5) (6), p. 1, k. 4, p. 1, k. 4, p. 1, k. 4 *, p. 1, k. 2, p. 6, k. 2, p. 1; repeat from * to *, then p. 1 (3) (5).

13th to 24th rows: As 1st to 12th rows.

25th row: K. 1 (3) (5), * p. 11, cr. 5, p. 5, k. 9, p. 2, k. 1, p. 3 (4) (5), m.b., p. 2, cr. 5, p. 2, m.b., p. 3 (4) (5), k. 1, p. 2, k. 9, p. 5, cr. 5, p. 11 *, k. 1, p. 2, k. 6, p. 2, k. 1; repeat from * to *, k. 1 (3) (5).

26th row: P. 1 (3) (5), * k. 11, p. 2, k. 1, p. 2, k. 5, p. 9, k. 2, p. 1, k. 6, p. 2, k. 1, p. 2, k. 6, p. 1, k. 2, p. 9, k. 5, p. 2, k. 1, p. 2, k. 11 *, p. 1, k. 2, p. 6, k. 2, p. 1; repeat from * to *, p. 1 (3) (5).

27th row: K. 1 (3) (5), *, p. 3, m.b., p. 6, c. 3rt., p. 1, c. 3lt., p. 4, cable 6, k. 3, p. 2, k. 1, p. 5 (6) (7), c. 3rt., p. 1, c. 3lt., p. 5 (6) (7), k. 1, p. 2, cable 6, k. 3, p. 4, c. 3rt., p. 1, c. 3lt., p. 6, m.b., p. 3 *, k. 1, p. 2, cable 6, p. 2, k. 1; repeat from * to *, k. 1 (3) (5).

28th row: P. 1 (3) (5), * k. 10, p. 2, k. 3, p. 2, k. 4, p. 9, k. 2, p. 1, k. 5 (6) (7), p. 2, k. 3, p. 2, k. 5 (6) (7), p. 1, k. 2, p. 9, k. 4, p. 2, k. 3, p. 2, k. 10 *, p. 1,k. 2, p. 6, k. 2, p. 1; repeat from * to *, p. 1 (3) (5).

29th row: K. 1 (3) (5), * p. 9, c. 3rt., p. 3, c. 3lt., p. 3, k. 9, p. 2, k. 1, p. 4 (5) (6), c. 3rt., p. 3, c. 3lt., p. 4 (5) (6), k. 1, p. 2, k. 9, p. 3, c. 3rt., p. 3, c. 3lt., p. 9 *, k. 1, p. 2, k. 6, p. 2, k. 1; repeat from * to *, k. 1 (3) (5).

30th row: P. 1 (3) (5), * k. 9, p. 2, k. 5, p. 2, k. 3, p. 9, k. 2, p. 1, k. 4 (5) (6), p. 2, k. 5, p. 2, k. 4 (5) (6), p. 1, k. 2, p. 9, k. 3, p. 2, k. 5, p. 2, k. 9 *, p. 1, k. 2, p. 6, k. 2, p. 1; repeat from * to *, p. 1 (3) (5).

31st row: K. 1 (3) (5), * p. 1, m.b., p. 3, m.b., p. 3, k. 2, p. 5, k. 2, p. 3, k. 3, cable 6b., p. 2, k. 1, p. 3 (4) (5), c. 3rt., p. 2, m.b., p. 2, c. 3lt., p. 3 (4) (5), k. 1, p. 2, k. 3, cable 6b., p. 3, k. 2, p. 5, k. 2, p. 3, m.b., p. 3, m.b., p. 1 *, k. 1, p. 2, k. 6, p. 2, k. 1; repeat from * to *, k. 1 (3) (5).

32nd row: P. 1 (3) (5), * k. 9, p. 2, k. 5, p. 2, k. 3, p. 9, k. 2, p. 1, k. 3 (4) (5), p. 2, k. 7, p. 2, k. 3 (4) (5), p. 1, k. 2, p. 9, k. 3, p. 2, k. 5, p. 2, k. 9 *, p. 1, k. 2, p. 6, k. 2, p. 1; repeat from * to *, p. 1 (3) (5).

33rd row: K. 1 (3) (5), * p. 9, c. 3lt., p. 3, c. 3rt., p. 3, k. 9, p. 2, k. 1, p. 2 (3) (4), c. 3rt., p. 7, c. 3lt., p. 2 (3) (4), k. 1, p. 2, k. 9, p. 3, c. 3lt., p. 3, c. 3rt., p. 9, *, k. 1, p. 2, k. 6, p. 2, k. 1; repeat from * to *, k. 1 (3) (5).

34th row: P. 1 (3) (5), * k. 10, p. 2, k. 3, p. 2, k. 4, p. 9, k. 2, p. 1, k. 2 (3) (4), p. 2, k. 9, p. 2, k. 2 (3) (4), p. 1, k. 2, p. 9, k. 4, p. 2, k. 3, p. 2, k. 10 *, p. 1, k. 2, p. 6, k. 2, p. 1; repeat from * to *, p. 1 (3) (5).

35th row: K. 1 (3) (5), * p. 3, m.b., p. 6, c. 3lt., p. 1, c. 3rt., p. 4, cable 6, k. 3, p. 2, k. 1, p. 1 (2) (3) c. 3rt., p. 2, m.b., p. 3., m.b., p. 2, c. 3lt., p. 1 (2) (3), k. 1, p. 2, cable 6, k. 3, p. 4, c. 3lt., p. 1, c. 3rt., p. 6, m.b., p. 3 *, k. 1, p. 2, cable 6, p. 2, k. 1; repeat from * to *, k. 1 (3) (5).

36th row: P. 1 (3) (5), * k. 11, p. 2, k. 1, p. 2, k. 5, p. 9, k. 2, p. 1, k. 1 (2) (3), p. 2, k. 11, p. 2, k. 1 (2) (3), p. 1, k. 2, p. 9, k. 5, p. 2, k. 1, p. 2, k. 11 *, p. 1, k. 2, p. 6, k. 2, p. 1; repeat from * to *, p. 1 (3) (5).
37th row: K. 1 (3) (5), * p. 11, cr. 5, p. 5, k. 9, p. 2, k. 1, p. 1 (2) (3), k. 2, p. 11, k. 2, p. 1 (2) (3), k. 1, p. 2, k. 9, p. 5, cr. 5, p. 11 *, k. 1, p. 2, k. 6, p. 2, k. 1; repeat from * to *, k. 1 (3) (5).
38th row: As 36th row.
39th row: K. 1 (3) (5), * p. 1, m.b., p. 3, m.b., p. 4, c. 3rt., p. 1, c. 3lt., p. 4, k. 3, cable 6b., p. 2, k. 1, p. 1 (2) (3), c. 3lt., p. 2, m.b., p. 3, m.b., p. 2, c. 3rt., p. 1 (2) (3), k. 1, p. 2, k. 3, cable 6b., p. 4, c. 3rt., p. 1, c. 3lt., p. 4, m.b., p. 3, m.b., p. 1 *, k. 1, p. 2, cable 6, p. 2, k. 1; repeat from * to *, k. 1 (3) (5).
40th row: As 34th row.
41st row: Working c. 3rt., for c. 3lt. and c. 3lt., for c. 3rt., work as given for 33rd row.
42nd row: As 32nd row.
43rd row: K. 1 (3) (5), * p. 3, m. b., p. 5, k. 2, p. 5, k. 2, p. 3, cable 6, k. 3, p. 2, k. 1, p. 3, c. 3lt., p. 2, m.b., p.2, c. 3rt., p. 3, k. 1, p. 2, cable 6, k. 3, p. 3, k. 2, p. 5, k. 2, p. 5, m.b., p. 3 *, k. 1, p. 2, k. 6, p. 2, k. 1: repeat from * to *, k. 1 (3) (5).
44th row: As 30th row.
45th row: Working c. 3rt., for c. 3lt. and c. 3 lt., for c. 3rt., work as given for 29th row.
46th row: As 28th row.
47th row: K. 1 (3) (5), * p. 1, m.b., p. 3, m.b., p. 4, c. 3lt., p. 1, c. 3rt., p. 4, k. 3, cable 6b., p. 2, k. 1, p. 5, c. 3lt., p. 1, c. 3rt., p. 5, k. 1, p. 2, k. 3, cable 6b., p. 4, c. 3 lt., p. 1, c. 3rt., p. 4., m.b., p. 3, m.b., p. 1 *, k. 1, p. 2, cable 6, p. 2, k. 1; repeat from * to *, k. 1 (3) (5).
48th row: As 26th row.
49th and 50th rows: As 25th and 26th rows.
The last 50 rows form the pattern; repeat them once more, then work the first 36 rows again.
To shape the raglan armholes: Maintaining the continuity of the pattern as set cast off 4 (6) (8) sts. at the beginning of the next 2 rows.
Dec. 1 st. at each end of the next 14 rows.
Dec. 1 st. at each end of the next row and the 9 (10) (11) following alternate rows—124 (126) (128) sts.
Now divide the sts. for the neck: Next row: Pattern 42 and leave these sts. on a spare needle until required for second point, cast off 40 (42) (44) sts., pattern to end and continue on these 42 sts. for the first point.
The first point: To shape the neck and continue to slope the raglan.
1st row: Dec. 1 st. at the beginning pattern to end.
2nd row: Cast off 3 sts., pattern to end.
Repeat the last 2 rows 5 times more.
Pattern 10 rows more decreasing 1 st. at armhole edge as before on every alternate row and decreasing 1 st. at the neck edge on each row—3 sts.
S1.1, k. 2, tog. p.s.s.o. Fasten off.
The second point: With right side of work facing rejoin yarn to inner edge of sts. left on spare needle and work to end of row, then work as given for first point to end.

The front:
Work as given for back.

The sleeves (both alike):
With size 2¼ mm (No. 13) needles cast on 56 (60) (64) sts. and work 59 rows in double rib.
Increase row: K. 1 (3) (5), * 3 from 1; repeat from * until nil (2) (4), remain, k. nil (2) (4)—166 (170) (174) sts.
Change to size 2¾ mm (No. 12) needles and work in pattern as follows:
1st row: Work from * to * on 17th pattern row given for back, then repeat from * to * again.
Thus continuing to work the pattern given between * and * twice on each pattern row given for back, beginning with the 18th pattern row work 169 rows.
Mark each end of the last row with coloured threads.
Pattern 4 (6) (8) rows.
To shape the raglan: Dec. 1 st. at each end of the next 31 (33) (35) rows.
Now divide the sts. for the top of the sleeve: Dec, pattern 25 and leave these sts. on a spare needle until required for second point, cast off 50, pattern until 2 remain, dec., then continue on these 26 sts. for the first point.
The first point: Dec. 1 st. at each end of the next 12 rows.
Take the 2 remaining sts. tog. and fasten off.
The second point: With right side of work facing rejoin yarn to inner edge of sts. left on spare needle and work as given for first point.

The pockets *(2 alike):*
With size 2¾ mm (No. 12) needles cast on 28 sts. and work 114 rows in s.s., then cast off.

The neckband:
First join raglan seams so that the sts. cast off at underarms are sewn to the straight row ends of sleeves above the marking threads.
Rejoin yarn to top of left back raglan seam and using a long circular size 2¼ mm (No. 13) knitting needle, pick up and k. 70 sts. from top of left sleeve, 100 sts. from front neck edge, 70 sts. from top of right sleeve and 100 sts. from back neck edge—340 sts.
Work 7 rounds in single rib.
1st decrease row: Rib 7, * sl. 1, k. 2 tog., p.s.s.o., rib 14; repeat from * ending last repeat rib 7—300 sts.
Rib 7 rows.
2nd decrease row: Rib 6, * sl. 1, k. 2 tog., p.s.s.o., rib 12; repeat from * ending last repeat rib 6.
Rib 4 rows. Cast off the 260 remaining sts.

To make up the sweater:
Pin out to size all parts and press on the wrong side with a cool iron over a dry cloth. Join row ends of back and front ribbing. Fold pockets in half and join the row end edges at each side. Neatly sew pockets in place at side seams above ribbing. Join rest of sleeve and side seams. Press seams.

BEELINE

A hooded coat which looks equally stunning with straight skirts or long dresses. To emphasise the different textures of the yarns used, the tweed stripes are in garter stitch, and the mohair ones in stocking stitch. Wear the hat under the hood for one of the newest looks, or over it, as we have, for a more Eastern effect.

Materials:
For the coat: 14 (15) (16) 50 gram balls of Jaeger Catkin in main colour and 10(11)(12) 25 gram balls of Jaeger Mohair-spun in contrast colour; a pair of No.5 knitting needles; 7 buttons.
For the hat: One ball of Jaeger Pebble-spun; one ball of Jaeger Mohair; a pair of No.5 knitting needles.

Tension:
7 stitches to 5 cm (2 in.) in width and 14 rows—1 repeat of the pattern to 5.5 cm ($2\frac{1}{4}$ in.) in length using No.5 needles. If you cannot obtain the correct tension using needles of the size suggested, use larger or smaller ones accordingly.

Abbreviations:
K.,knit; p.,purl; st.,stitch; tog.,together; dec.,decrease (by working 2 sts. tog.); inc.,increase (by working twice into same st.); s.s.,stocking stitch (k. on the right side and p. on the wrong side); garter stitch is k. plain on every row; m., main colour—Pebblespun; c.,contrast colour—mohair; sl.,slip; p.s.s.o.,pass sl. st. over; s.k.p.,slip 1, k.1, p.s.s.o.

Note:
The instructions are given for the small size. Where they vary, work the figures in the first brackets for the medium size or the figures in the second brackets for the large size.

Measurements:
The following measurements are given in centimetres first, followed by inches in brackets.

small (10)	medium (12)	large (14)
All round at underarms		
85 (34)	90 (36)	95 (38)
Side seam		
74 ($30\frac{1}{2}$)	74 ($30\frac{1}{2}$)	74 ($30\frac{1}{2}$)
Length		
96 ($39\frac{1}{2}$)	97.5 (40)	99 ($40\frac{1}{2}$)
Sleeve seam		
33 ($13\frac{1}{2}$)	33 ($13\frac{1}{2}$)	33 ($13\frac{1}{2}$)

The back:
With No.5 needles and m. cast on 90 (94) (98) sts. and work in stripe pattern as follows:
1st to 8th rows: With m. all k.
9th to 14th rows: Join in c. and beginning with a k. row s.s. 6 rows. These 14 rows form the stripe pattern. Repeat them twice more, then work the first 8 rows again.
1st Decrease row: With c. k.13 (15) (17), s.k.p., k.2 tog., k.26, s.k.p., k.2 tog., k.26, s.k.p., k.2 tog., k.13 (15) (17)—84 (88) (92) sts.
Work 27 rows in pattern as set.
2nd Decrease row: With c. k.12 (14) (16), s.k.p., k.2 tog., k.24, s.k.p., k.2 tog., k.24, s.k.p., k.2 tog., k.12 (14) (16)—78 (82) (86) sts.
Work 27 rows in pattern as set.
3rd Decrease row: With c. k.11 (13) (15), s.k.p., k.2 tog., k.22, s.k.p., k.2 tog., k.22, s.k.p., k.2 tog., k.11 (13) (15)—72 (76) (80) sts.
Work 27 rows in pattern as set.
4th Decrease row: With c. k.10 (12) (14), s.k.p., k.2 tog., k.20, s.k.p., k.2 tog., k.20, s.k.p., k.2 tog., k.10 (12) (14)—66 (70) (74) sts.
Work 27 rows in pattern as set.
5th Decrease row: With c. k.9 (11) (13), s.k.p., k.2 tog., k.18, s.k.p., k.2 tog., k.18, s.k.p., k.2 tog., k.9 (11) (13)—60 (64) (68) sts.
Work 25 rows in pattern as set.
To shape the armholes: Continuing in pattern as set cast off 5 (6) (7) sts. at the beginning of the next 2 rows.
On 50 (52) (54) sts. pattern 54 (56) (58) rows.
To slope the shoulders: Cast off 13 (14) (15) sts. at the beginning of the next 2 rows.
Cast off the 24 remaining sts.

The pocket backs *(two alike):*
With No.5 needles and m. cast on 20sts. and work 36 rows in stripe pattern given for back, then leave these sts. on a stitch holder until required.

The left front:
With No.5 needles and m. cast on 42 (44) (46) sts. and work 50 rows in stripe pattern given for back.
1st Decrease row: K.13 (15) (17), s.k.p., k.2 tog., k.23, s.k.p.—39 (41) (43) sts.
Work 27 rows in stripes as set.
2nd Decrease row: K.12 (14) (16), s.k.p., k.2 tog., k.21, s.k.p.—36 (38) (40) sts.
Work 13 rows as set.
Pocket row: With c. k.8 (9) (10), then k. across the 20 sts. of one pocket back, with m. cast off 20sts., then with c. work to end.
Work 13 rows as set.
3rd Decrease row: K.11 (13) (15), s.k.p., k.2 tog., k.19, s.k.p.—33 (35) (37) sts.
Work 27 rows as set.
4th Decrease row: K.10 (12) (14), s.k.p., k.2 tog., k.17, s.k.p.—30 (32) (34) sts.
Work 27 rows as set.
5th Decrease row: K.9 (11) (13), s.k.p., k.2 tog., k.15, s.k.p.—27 (29) (31) sts.
Work 25 rows as set.
** *To shape the armhole and to slope the front edge:* Cast off 5 (6) (7) sts. at the beginning and dec. 1st. at the end of the next row.
Work 3 rows as set.
Dec. 1st. at the front edge on the next row and the 7 following 4th rows.
On 13 (14) (15) sts. work 23 (25) (27) rows as set.
To slope the shoulder: Cast off the 13 (14) (15) remaining sts.

The right front:
With No.5 needles and m. cast on 42 (44) (46) sts. and work 50 rows in stripe pattern given for back.
1st Decrease row: K.2 tog., k.23, s.k.p., k.2 tog., k.13 (15) (17)—39 (41) (43) sts.
Work 27 rows in stripes as set.
2nd Decrease row: K.2 tog., k.21, s.k.p., k.2 tog., k.12 (14) (16)—36 (38) (40) sts.
Work 13 rows as set, then work the pocket row given for left front.
Work 13 rows as set.
3rd Decrease row: K.2 tog., k.19, s.k.p., k.2 tog., k.11 (13) (15)—33 (35) (37) sts.
Work 27 rows as set
4th Decrease row: K.2 tog., k.17, s.k.p., k.2 tog., k.10 (12) (14)—30 (32) (34) sts.
Work 27 rows as set.
5th Decrease row: K.2 tog., k.15, s.k.p., k.2 tog., k.9 (11) (13)—27 (29) (31) sts.
Work 26 rows as set.
Now work as for left front from ** to end.

The sleeves *(both alike):*
With No.5 needles and m. cast on 46 (48) (50) sts. and work 20 rows in stripe pattern given for back.
Continuing in stripe pattern as set inc. 1st. at each end of the next row and the 7 following 8th rows.
On 62 (64) (66) sts. work 7 rows. For longer sleeves, work more rows here, but end with 6 rows c. Mark each end of the last row with coloured threads.
With m. k.10 (12) (14) rows then cast off.

The left front band and left half hood:
With No.5 needles and m. cast on 7sts. and k.188 rows.
** *To shape for the hood and collar:* Inc. 1st. at the beginning of the next row and the 8 following 4th rows—16sts.
K.3 rows.
Cast on 24 (25) (26) sts. at the beginning of the next row.
On 40 (41) (42) sts. k.79 rows.
Cast off 12sts. for centre back hood at the beginning of the next row.
On 28 (29) (30) sts. k.28 rows, then cast off.

The right front band and right half hood:
With No.5 needles and m. cast on 7sts. and k.18 rows.
1st Buttonhole row: K.2, cast off 3, k. to end.
2nd Buttonhole row: K.2, turn, cast on 3, turn, k. to end.
K.26 rows.
Repeat the last 28 rows 5 more times, then work the 2 buttonhole rows again.
Now work as given for left front band and half hood from ** to end.

To make up the coat:
Press all parts lightly on the wrong side with a warm iron over a damp cloth. Join shoulder seams. Set in sleeves so that the straight row ends above the marking threads are sewn to the sts. cast off at underarms. Join sleeve and side seams. Sew pocket backs in place. Neatly sew front bands in place, so that the shaped row end and cast on edges are sewn to the neck edge—with the first front edge dec. in line with the first increase on collar. Join row ends of hood at centre

back up to cast off groups. Join final cast off edges of hood, then sew straight row end edge above cast off groups to the cast off groups. Sew on buttons. Press seams.

THE HAT

To work:
With No.5 needles and c. cast on 72 sts. and beginning with a k. row s.s.24 rows. Break off c., join in m.
With m. k.16 rows.
1st Decrease row: K.2 tog., k.7; repeat from * to end—64sts.
K.5 rows.
2nd Decrease row: K.2 tog., k.6; repeat from * to end.
On 56sts. k.5 rows.
3rd Decrease row: K.2 tog., k.5; repeat from * to end.
On 48sts. k.3 rows.
4th Decrease row: K.2 tog., k.4; repeat from * to end.
On 40sts. k.3 rows.
5th Decrease row: K.2 tog., k.3; repeat from * to end.
On 32sts. k.3 rows.
6th Decrease row: K.2 tog., k.2; repeat from * to end.
On 24sts. k.1 row.
7th Decrease row: K.2 tog., k.1; repeat from * to end.
On 16sts. k.1 row.
Next Decrease row: * K.2 tog.; repeat from * to end.
Break off m. leaving a long end. Thread through remaining 8sts., draw up and secure firmly.

To complete:
Press lightly on the wrong side with a warm iron over a damp cloth. Join row end edges. Roll mohair edging to right side and slip stitch in place. Press seams.

GLITTER BAND

Look glamorous on the beach and save your pennies at the same time. This bikini takes only three balls of Wendy Minuit and is very quick to knit. The yarn is made up of black, emerald, rust, royal blue and pink lurex, prettily entwined.

Materials:
Three 20 gram balls of Wendy Minuit; a pair each of No. 12 and No. 13 knitting needles.

Tension and size:
Worked at a tension of 16 stitches and 24 rows to 5 cm (2 in.) over the pattern using No. 12 needles, the bikini will be suitable for bust sizes 80–85 cm (32–34 in.) and 87.5–92.5 cm (35–37 in.) and for hip sizes 85–90 cm (34–36 in.) and 92.5–97.5 cm (37–39 in.).

Abbreviations:
K., knit; p., purl; st., stitch; tog., together; dec., decrease (by working 2 sts. tog.); inc., increase (by working twice into same st.); garter st. is k. plain on every row; up 1, pick up the loop that lies between the needles, slip it onto left hand needle, then k. into back of it; sl., slip; p.s.s.o., pass sl. st. over.

Note:
The instructions are given for the smaller size. Where they vary work the figures given in brackets for the medium size.

BIKINI TOP

The base strap:
With No. 13 needles cast on 5 sts. and k. 180 (190) rows, marking the end of the last row with a red coloured thread, k. 55 (59) rows, marking the beginning of the last row with a red coloured thread, k. 55 (59) rows, marking the end of the last row with a yellow coloured thread, k. 180 (190) rows. Cast off.

The right bra cup:
With right side of work facing rejoin yarn to the strap at red marking thread at centre and using No. 12 needles pick up and k. 55 (59) sts. from row ends of strap between the red marking threads—1 stitch from each row end.
Next row: K. 3, p. until 3 remain, k. 3.
Now work as follows: *To shape for the dart:*
1st row: K. 2, k. 2 tog., k. 16 (18), up 1, k. 1, up 1, k. 30 (32), k. 2 tog., k. 2.
***2nd row:* K. 3, p. until 3 remain, k. 3.
3rd row: All k.
4th row: All k.
5th and 6th rows: As 1st and 2nd rows.
7th row: All k.
8th row: As 2nd row.
9th row: As 1st row.
10th row: All k.
11th row: All k.
12th row: As 2nd row.
These 12 rows form the pattern and dart shaping. Repeat the first 8 rows again.
Now work as follows: *1st row:* K. 2, k. 2 tog., k. until 4 remain, k. 2 tog., k. 2.
2nd row: All k.
3rd row: As 1st row.
4th row: K. 3, p. until 3 remain, k. 3.
5th and 6th rows: As 3rd and 4th rows.
Repeat the last 6 rows 5 times more (5 times more then the first 4 rows)—19 sts.
Next row: K. 1, * k. 2 tog.; repeat from * to end—10 sts.
Next row: * K. 2 tog.; repeat from * to end—5 sts.
For the strap:
Change to No. 13 needles and work in garter stitch until the strap is 30 cm (12 in.) long or for length required, then cast off.

The left bra cup:
With right side of work facing rejoin yarn to the base strap at yellow marking thread and using No. 12 needles pick up and k. 55 (59) sts. from row end edges of strap between the yellow and red marking threads—1 stitch from each row end.
Next row: K. 3, p. until 3 remain, k. 3.
Now work as follows: *1st row:* K. 2, k. 2 tog., k. 30 (32), up 1, k. 1, up 1, k. 16 (18), k. 2 tog., k. 2.
Now work as given for right bra cup from ** to end noting that on 5th and 9th rows the 1st row will be worked as that above.

To complete the top:
Press very lightly on the wrong side with a cool iron over a dry cloth.

BIKINI BOTTOM

The back hip strap:
With No. 13 needles cast on 5 sts. and k. 72 (82) rows, marking the end of the last row with a coloured thread, k. 144 (152) rows, marking the end of the last row with a coloured thread, k. 72 (82) rows, then cast off.

The back:
With right side of back hip strap facing rejoin yarn to the row end edge at first marking thread, then using No. 12 needles pick up and k. 144 (152) sts. from the row ends between the marking threads—1 stitch from each row end.
Next row: K. 3, p. until 3 remain, k. 3.
Now work as follows: *1st row:* K. 2, k. 2 tog., k. until 4 remain, k. 2 tog., k. 2.
2nd row: K. 3, p. until 3 remain, k. 3.
3rd row: K. 3, sl. 1, k. 2 tog., p.s.s.o., k. until 6 remain, sl. 1, k. 2 tog., k. 3.
4th row: As 2nd row.
5th row: As 1st row.
6th row: All k.
7th and 8th rows: As 3rd and 4th rows.
9th and 10th rows: As 1st and 2nd rows.
11th row: As 3rd row.
12th row: All k.
Work the last 12 rows 5 times more, then work the first 2 (6) rows again.
Cast off the remaining 34 (36) sts.

The front hip strap:
With No. 13 needles cast on 5 sts. and k. 72 (82) rows marking the end of the last row with a coloured thread, k. 96 (102) rows marking the end of the last row with a coloured thread, k. 72 (82) rows, then cast off.

The front:
With right side of front hip strap facing rejoin yarn to the row end edge at first marking thread then using No. 12 needles pick up and k. 96 (102) sts. from row ends between the marking threads—1 st. from each row end.
Next row: K. 3, p. until 3 remain, k. 3.
Now work as follows: *1st row:* K. 2, k. 2 tog., k. until 4 remain, k. 2 tog., k. 2.
2nd row: K. 2, k. 2 tog., p. until 4 remain, k. 2 tog., k. 2.
3rd and 4th rows: As 1st and 2nd rows.
5th row: As 1st row.
6th row: As 1st row.
Repeat the last 6 rows twice more—60 (66) sts.
Now continue as follows: *1st row:* K. 2, k. 2 tog., k. until 4 remain, k. 2 tog., k. 2.
2nd row: K. 3, p. until 3 remain, k. 3.
3rd and 4th rows: As 1st and 2nd rows.
5th row: As 1st row.
6th row: All k.
Repeat the last 6 rows 5 times more (5 times more, then the first 4 rows again)—24 (26) sts.
Now work straight as follows: *1st row:* All k.
2nd row: K. 3, p. until 3 remain, k. 3.
3rd and 4th rows: As 1st and 2nd rows.
5th and 6th rows: All k.
Repeat the last 6 rows 3 times more, then work the first 4 rows again.
Now increase as follows: *1st row:* K. 3, up 1, k. until 3 remain, up 1, k. 3.
2nd row: All k.
3rd row: As 1st row.
4th row: K. 3, p. until 3 remain, k. 3.
5th and 6th rows: As 3rd and 4th rows.
Work the 1st to 4th rows again—34 (36) sts. Cast off.

To complete the pants:
Press as for top. Join cast off edges of back and front, press seams.

APPLE CANDY

Quick and easy summer knitting to make in the pastel shades photographed or in shades of sand, cream and khaki.

Materials:
For the sweater: 18 ounces of 'Wollybear' 100% chunky cotton in main colour and 4 ounces in each of the 3 contrast colours.
For the hat: 4 ounces of the same yarn in main colour.
For the scarf: 6 ounces of the same yarn in main colour and 1 ounce in each of the 3 contrast colours.
For the shorts: 11 ounces of the same yarn in main colour and 4 ounces in each of the 3 contrast colours.
For all garments: A pair each of size 4½ mm (No. 7) and size 4 mm (No. 8) Aero knitting needles. The 'Woollybear' cotton for these garments may be obtained by mail order from the Patricia Roberts knitting Shop, 60, Kinnerton Street, London, SW1. Prices: all inclusive of postage within the U.K. and V.A.T. For the sweater: £10.55; for the hat: £1.45; for the scarf: £3.30; for the shorts: £5.50.
Tension: 10 stitches and 13 rows to 5 cm (2 in.) over the stocking stitch using size 4½ mm (No. 7) knitting needles.
Abbreviations:
K., knit; p., purl; st., stitch; tog., together; dec., decrease (by working 2 sts. tog.); inc., increase (by working twice into same st.); s.s., stocking stitch is k. on the right side and p. on the wrong side; single rib is k. 1 and p. 1 alternately; up 1, pick up the loop which lies between the needles, slip it onto left hand needle, then k. into back of it; m., main colour; a., first contrast colour—green; b., second contrast—pink; c., third contrast colour—blue; y.r.n., yarn round needle.
Note:
The instructions are given for the small size. Where they vary work the figures in the first brackets for the medium size or the figures in the second brackets for the large size.

Measurements:

The measurements are given in centimetres followed by inches in square brackets.

THE SWEATER

small	medium	large
All round at underarms		
95 [38]	100 [40]	105 [42]
Side seam		
44 [17½]	44 [17½]	44 [17½]
Length		
69 [27½]	69.5 [27¾]	70 [28]
Sleeve seam		
15 [6]	15 [6]	15 [6]

THE SHORTS

All round at hips		
100 [40]	105 [42]	110 [44]
Inside leg		
15 [6]	15 [6]	15 [6]
Length		
40 [16]	41 [16½]	42.5 [17]

The Hat:
Suitable for an average head size.
The Scarf:
22.5 (9) in width and 150 (60) in length before knotting ends.

THE SWEATER
The back:
With size 4 mm (No. 8) needles and m. cast on 85 (91) (95) sts. and work 27 rows in single rib.
Increase row: Rib 6 (9) (11), * up 1, rib 8; repeat from * ending last repeat rib 7 (10) (12)—95 (101) (105) sts.
Change to size 4½ mm (No. 7) needles and work in stripe pattern as follows:
1st to 4th rows: With m. beginning with a k. row s.s. 4 rows.
5th to 6th rows: With a. all k.
7th to 10th rows: As 1st to 4th rows.
11th and 12th rows: With b. all k.
13th to 16th rows: As 1st to 4th rows.
17th and 18th rows: With c. all k.
The last 18 rows form the stripe pattern; repeat them once more.
Now work the apples and cloud motif with stripes as before at each end of the rows. Use a separate ball of m. at each side of centre motif.
1st to 4th rows: With m. s.s. 11 (14) (16), with a. s.s. 73, with m., s.s. to end.
5th row: With a. all k.
6th row: With a., k. 11 (14) (16), p. 73; k. 11 (14) (16).
7th and 8th rows: As 1st and 2nd rows.
The centre motif—73 sts. is completely in s.s. so only the colour details are given and the 11 (14) (16) stitches at each end of each row are worked in the 18 row stripe pattern given at beginning.
9th row: Work 11 (14) (16) in stripe pattern as set, 7 a., * 5 b., 3 a., 5 b., 10 a.; repeat from * twice more, ending last repeat 7 a., work 11 (14) (16) in stripe pattern as set.
10th row: Work 11 (14) (16) as set, 6 a., * 7 b., 1 a., 7 b., 8 a.; repeat from * once more, 7 b., 1 a., 7 b., 8 a.; repeat from * once more, 7 b., 1 a., 7 b., 6 a.; work 11 (14) (16) as set.
11th row: Work 11 (14) (16) as set., 5 a., 17 b., 6 a., 17 b., 6 a., 17 b., 5 a., work to end as set.
12th row: Work 11 (14) (16) as set, 4 a., 19 b., 4 a., 19 b., 4 a., 19 b., 4 a., work to end as set.
13th to 18th rows: As 12th row.
19th to 22nd rows: As 11th row.
23rd row: Work 11 (14) (16) as set, 6 a., 15 b., 8 a., 15 b., 8 a., 15 b., 6 a., work to end as set.
24th row: Work 11 (14) (16) as set, 7 a., * 6 b., 1 a., 6 b., 10 a.; repeat from * once more, 6 b., 1 a., 6 b., 7 a.; work to end as set.
25th and 26th rows: Work 11 (14) (16) as set; 73 a., work to end as set.
27th row: 11 (14) (16) as set, 1 a., * 1 c., 1 a.; repeat from * until 11 (14) (16) remain, work to end as set.
28th row: 11 (14) (16) as set, 1 c., * 1 a., 1 c.; repeat from * until 11 (14) (16) remain, work to end as set.
29th and 30th rows: 11 (14) (16) as set, 73 c., work to end as set.
31st to 42nd rows: 11 (14) (16) as set, 8 c., 57 m., 8 c., work to end as set.
43rd and 44th rows: As 31st row.
45th to 56th rows: As 29th row, but marking each end of the 52nd row with coloured threads to mark armholes.
57th to 72nd rows: 11 (14) (16) as set, 16 c., 41 m., 16 c., work to end as set.
73rd to 80th rows: As 29th row.
This completes the motif.**
Now work 36 rows in stripe pattern right across the rows as set.
To slope the shoulders: Cast off 25 (27) (29) sts. at the beginning of the next 2 rows.
Change to size 4 mm (No. 8) needles and with m. on 45 (47) (47) sts., work 8 rows in single rib, then cast off loosely in rib.
The front:
Work as given for back until ** is reached. Work 19 rows in stripe pattern as set. Now divide the sts. for the neck:
Next row: Work as set across 33 (35) (37) and leave these sts. on a spare needle until required for right front shoulder, pattern 29 (31) (31) and leave these sts. on a stitch-holder until required for neckband, pattern to end and continue on these 33 (35) (37) sts. for the left front shoulder.
The left front shoulder: To shape the neck: Continuing in stripe pattern as set dec. 1 st. at the neck edge on each of the next 8 rows.
Work 8 rows in stripes as set.
To slope the shoulder: Cast off the 25 (27) (29) remaining sts.
The right front shoulder:
With right side of work facing rejoin yarn to inner edge of sts. left on spare needle and work to end of row. Now work as given for left front shoulder to end.
The sleeves *(both alike):*
With size 4 mm (No. 8) needles and m. cast on 100 sts. and k. 8 rows.
Change to size 4½ (No. 7) needles and work 32 rows in stripe pattern given for back.
Cast off.
The pocket backs *(two alike):*
With size 4½ mm (No. 7) needles and m. cast on 25 sts. and beginning with a k. row s.s. 64 rows, then cast off.
The front neckband:
With right side of work facing rejoin m. and using size 4 mm (No. 8) needles, pick up and k. 10 sts. from left front neck edge, k. across the 29 (31) (31) sts. at centre front, then pick up and k. 10 sts. from right front neck edge.
On 49 (51) (51) sts. work 7 rows in single rib, then cast off loosely in rib.

To make up the sweater:
Pin out to size and press all parts except the ribbing on the wrong side with a warm iron over a damp cloth. Join shoulder seams, continuing seam across neckband. Set in sleeves, between the marking threads. Fold pocket backs in half and join row end edges. Join sleeve and side seams, inserting pocket backs at side seam above the ribbing. Press seams.

THE BAGGY SHORTS
The left and right legs *(both alike)*:
With size 4 mm (No. 8) needles and c. cast on 125 (130) (135) sts. and k. 8 rows.
Change to size 4½ (No. 7) needles and beginning with a k. row s.s. 2 rows.
Continuing in s.s. work in stripes as follows: 2 rows m., 6 rows c.; repeat the last 8 rows 3 times more.
To shape the crotch: Continuing in stripe sequence as set, cast off 6 sts. at the beginning of the next 2 rows, then dec. 1 st. at each end of the next row and the 5 following alternate rows—101 (106) (111) sts.
Work 51 (55) (57) rows in stripe pattern as set.
Change to size 4 mm (No. 8) needles and with c. only k. 4 rows.
Eyelet hole row: With c. only, * k. 2, y.r.n., k. 2 tog.; repeat from * to ending k. 1 (2) (3).
With c. only k. 3 rows, then cast off loosely.
The cord:
Cut 3 lengths of m. each 370 cm (148 in.) long. Knot one end, twist all 4 lengths together in one direction until firm. Fold in half allowing the 2 halves to twist together in the opposite direction. Knot ends.
To make up the shorts:
Press as for sweater. Join inside leg seams. Join back and front crotch seam. Thread cord through eyelet holes. Tie at centre front. Press seams.

THE SCARF
To work:
With size 4 mm (No. 8) needles and m. cast on 45 sts. and k. 8 rows.
Change to size 4½ mm (No. 7) needles and repeat 18 stripe pattern rows given for back of sweater 21 times, then work the first 4 rows again.
Change to size 4 mm (No. 8) needles and with m. only k. 8 rows.
To complete:
Pin out to size and press on the wrong side with a warm iron over a damp cloth. Fold in half lengthways and knot ends.

THE HAT
To work:
With size 4 mm (No. 8) needles and c. cast on 96 sts. and k. 50 rows.
1st decrease row: * K. 6, k. 2 tog.; repeat from * to end—84 sts.
K. 7 rows.
2nd decrease row: * K. 5, k. 2 tog.; repeat from * to end—72 sts.
K. 7 rows.
3rd decrease row: * K. 4, k. 2 tog.; repeat from * to end—60 sts.
K. 7 rows.
4th decrease row: * K. 3, k. 2 tog.; repeat from * to end —48 sts.
K. 5 rows.
5th decrease row: * K. 2, k. 2 tog.; repeat from * to end—36 sts.
K. 3 rows.
6th decrease row: * K. 1, k. 2 tog.; repeat from * to end—24 sts.
K. 1 row.
7th decrease row: * K. 2 tog.; repeat from * to end—12 sts.

To complete:
Break off yarn leaving a long end, thread through remaining sts. and draw up firmly, then using this end join row end edges.
Press.

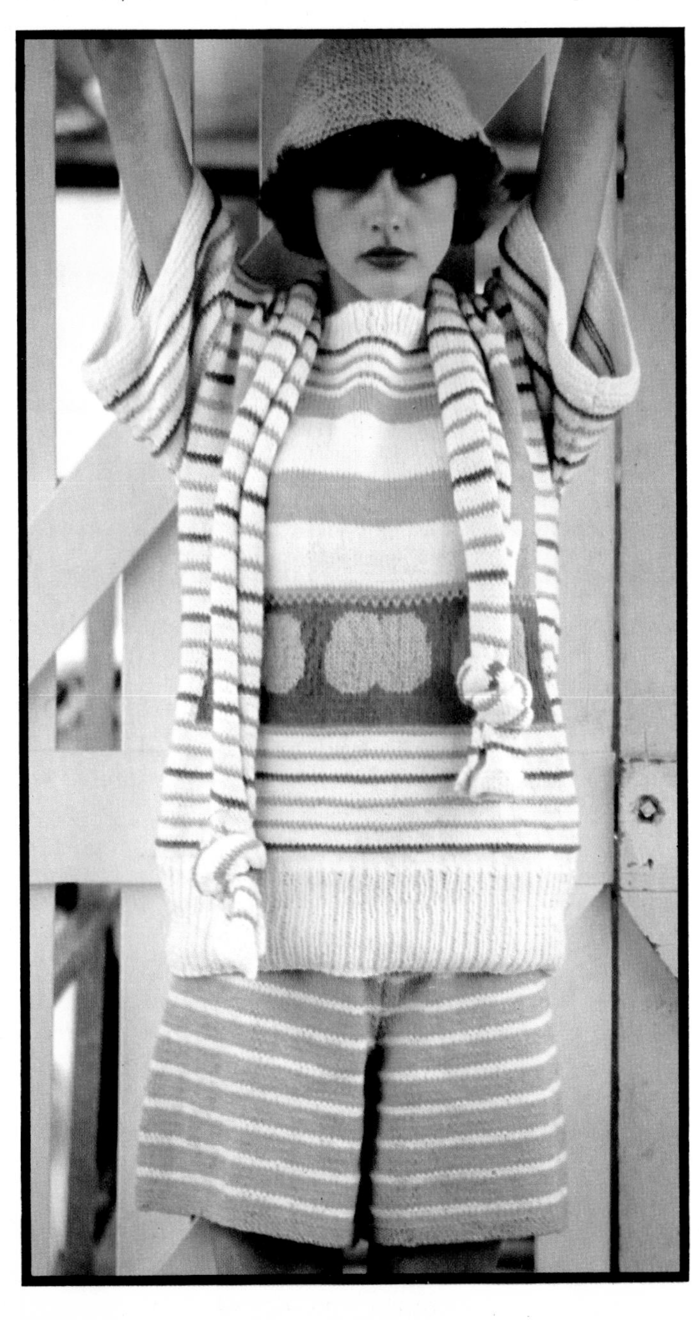

LILY OF THE VALLEY

This dainty pattern made up of bobbles and lace is called Lily of the Valley. The stitch is used in panels on both the cardigan and the sweater. The cardigan has a pretty fluted collar and the sweater has a simple V-neck with a ribbed neck-band crossing at the front, making a very attractive twinset.

Materials:
For the sweater: 13(14)(15) 25 gram balls of Sirdar Fontein crêpe 4-ply; a pair each of No. 12 and No. 13 knitting needles.
For the cardigan: 18(19)(20) 25 gram balls of Sirdar Fontein crêpe 4-ply; a pair each of No. 12 and No. 13 knitting needles; 6 buttons.

Tension:
16 stitches and 20 rows to 5 cm (2 in.) over the stocking stitch using No.12 needles. If you cannot obtain the correct tension using needles of the size suggested, use larger or smaller ones accordingly.

Abbreviations:
K., knit; p., purl; st., stitch; tog., together; dec., decrease (by working 2sts. tog.); inc., increase (by working twice into same st.); s.s., stocking stitch; single rib is k.1 and p.1 alternately; y.r.n., yarn round needle; m.b., make bobble thus—k.1, p.1, k.1, p.1 all into next st., turn, p.4, turn, sl.2, k.2 tog., p.2s.s.o., sl., slip; p.s.s.o., pass sl. st. over; up 1, pick up the loop that lies between the needles, slip it onto left-hand needle then k. into back of it.

Note:
The instructions are given for the small size. Where they vary, work the figures in the first brackets for the medium size or the figures in the second brackets for the large size.

Measurements:
The following measurements are given in centimetres first, followed by inches in brackets.

small (10) medium (12) large (14)

THE SWEATER

All round at underarms		
80(32)	85(34)	90(36)
Side seam		
32.5(13)	32.5(13)	32.5(13)
Length		
51 (20½)	51.5(20¾)	52(21)
Sleeve seam excluding ribbing		
7.5(3)	7.5(3)	7.5(3)

THE CARDIGAN

All round at underarms		
82.5(33)	87.5(35)	92.5(37)
Side seam		
36(14½)	36(14½)	36(14½)
Length		
57.5(23)	58(23)	59(23¼)
Sleeve seam excluding ribbing		
35(14)	35(14)	35(14)

THE SWEATER

The back:
With No.13 needles cast on 112(120) (128) sts. and work 48 rows in single rib. ** Change to No.12 needles.
Next row: K.3(7)(11), * up 1, k.7; repeat from * ending last repeat k.4(8)(12)—128(136)(144) sts.
P.1 row.
Now work in pattern as follows:
1st row: K.17(20)(23), * sl.1, k.1, p.s.s.o., k.6, y.r.n., k.1, y.r.n., k.1, sl.1, k.2 tog., p.s.s.o., k.1, y.r.n., k.1, y.r.n., k.6, k.2 tog., * k.48(50)(52); repeat from * to *, k.17 (20)(23).
2nd and every wrong side row: All p.
3rd row: K.17(20)(23), * sl.1, k.1, p.s.s.o., k.5, y.r.n., k.1, y.r.n., k.2, sl.1, k.2 tog., p.s.s.o., k.2, y.r.n., k.1, y.r.n., k.5, k.2 tog., * k.48(50)(52); repeat from * to *, k. to end.
5th row: K.17(20)(23), * sl.1, k.1, p.s.s.o., k.4, y.r.n., k.1, y.r.n., m.b., k.2, sl.1, k.2 tog., p.s.s.o, k.2, m.b., y.r.n., k.1, y.r.n., k.4, k.2 tog., * k.48(50)(52); repeat from * to *, k. to end.
7th row: K.17(20)(23), * sl.1, k.1, p.s.s.o., k.3, y.r.n., k.1, y.r.n., m.b., k.3, sl.1, k.2 tog., p.s.s.o., k.3, m.b., y.r.n., k.1, y.r.n., k.3, k.2 tog., * k.48(50)(52); repeat from * to *, k. to end.
9th row: K.17(20)(23), * sl.1, k.1, p.s.s.o., k.2, y.r.n., k.1, y.r.n., m.b., k.4, sl.1, k.2 tog., p.s.s.o., k.4, m.b., y.r.n., k.1, y.r.n., k.2, k.2 tog., * k.48(50)(52); repeat from * to *, k. to end.
11th row: K.17(20)(23), * sl.1, k.1, p.s.s.o., k.1, y.r.n., k.1, y.r.n., m.b., k.5, sl.1, k.2 tog., p.s.s.o., k.5, m.b., y.r.n., k.1, y.r.n., k.1, k.2 tog., * k.48(50)(52); repeat from * to *, k. to end.
13th row: K.17(20)(23), * sl.1, k.1, p.s.s.o., y.r.n., k.1, y.r.n., m.b., k.6, sl.1, k.2 tog., p.s.s.o., k.6, m.b., y.r.n., k.1, y.r.n., k.2 tog., * k.48(50)(52); repeat from * to *, k.17(20)(23).
14th row: All p. ***.
These 14 rows form the pattern; repeat them 5 more times then work the first 4 rows again.
To shape the armholes: Cast off 6sts. at the beginning of the next 2 rows.
Dec. 1st. at each end of the next 10(12) (14) rows.
On 96(100)(104) sts. pattern 58 rows.
To slope the shoulders: Cast off 8sts. at the beginning of the next 4 rows and 8(9)(10) sts. on the 2 following rows.
Cast off the 48(50)(52) remaining sts.

The front:
Work as for back until *** is reached.
Repeat the 14 row pattern 4 more times then work the first 11 rows again.
Now divide the sts. for the neck: *Next row:* Work as set across the 60(64)(68) sts. and leave these sts. on a spare needle until required for right front shoulder, p.8 and leave these sts. on a safety pin until required for neckband, work to end and continue on these 60(64)(68) sts. for the left front shoulder.
The left front shoulder: To shape the neck: Maintaining the continuity of the pattern as set dec. 1st. at the neck edge on the next row and the following 3rd row. Work 2 rows.
To shape the armhole and continue to slope the neck: Still decreasing at neck edge on every 3rd row from previous neck edge dec. cast off 6sts. at the beginning of the next row, work 1 row straight, then dec. 1st. at the armhole edge on each of the next 10(12)(14) rows.
Pattern 40(41)(42) rows decreasing 1st. at neck edge on every 3rd row as before. On 24(25)(26) sts. pattern 18(17)(16) rows.
To slope the shoulder: Cast off 8sts. at the beginning of the next row and the following alternate row. On 8(9)(10) sts. work 1 row, then cast off.
The right front shoulder: With right side of work facing rejoin yarn to inner edge of sts. left on spare needle and work to end of row, then work as given for left front shoulder to end.

The neckband:
First join shoulder seams.
With right side of work facing rejoin yarn to the 8sts. left on safety pin at centre front neck.
Increase row: K.1, * up 1, k.2; repeat from * ending last repeat k.1—12sts.
Work in single rib until the band is long enough to fit up right front neck edge, across back neck edge and down left front edge. Neatly sew band in place, casting off when correct length is assured. Sew cast off edge in place behind base of neckband.

The sleeves *(both alike)*:
With No.13 needles, cast on 104(108) (112) sts. and work 12 rows in single rib. Change to No.12 needles and beginning with a k. row s.s. 30 rows.
To shape the sleevetop: Cast off 6sts. at the beginning of the next 2 rows, then dec. 1st. at each end of the next row and the 10 following alternate rows. Work 1 row.
Dec. 1st. at each end of the next 14(16) (18) rows.
Cast off 4sts. at the beginning of the next 8 rows. Cast off the remaining 10 sts.

To make up the sweater:
Press all parts except the ribbing with a warm iron over a damp cloth. Set in sleeves, join sleeve and side seams. Press seams.

THE CARDIGAN

The back:
With No.13 needles cast on 112(120) (128) sts. and work 54 rows in single rib. Now work as given for back of sweater from ** to ***.
Repeat the 14 pattern rows 6 more times.
To shape the armholes: Cast off 6sts. at the beginning of the next 2 rows, then dec. 1st. at each end of the next 10(12) (14) rows.
On 96(100)(104) sts. pattern 66 rows.
To slope the shoulder: Cast off 8sts. at the beginning of the next 4 rows and 8(9)(10) sts. on the 2 following rows.
Cast off the 48(50)(52) remaining sts.

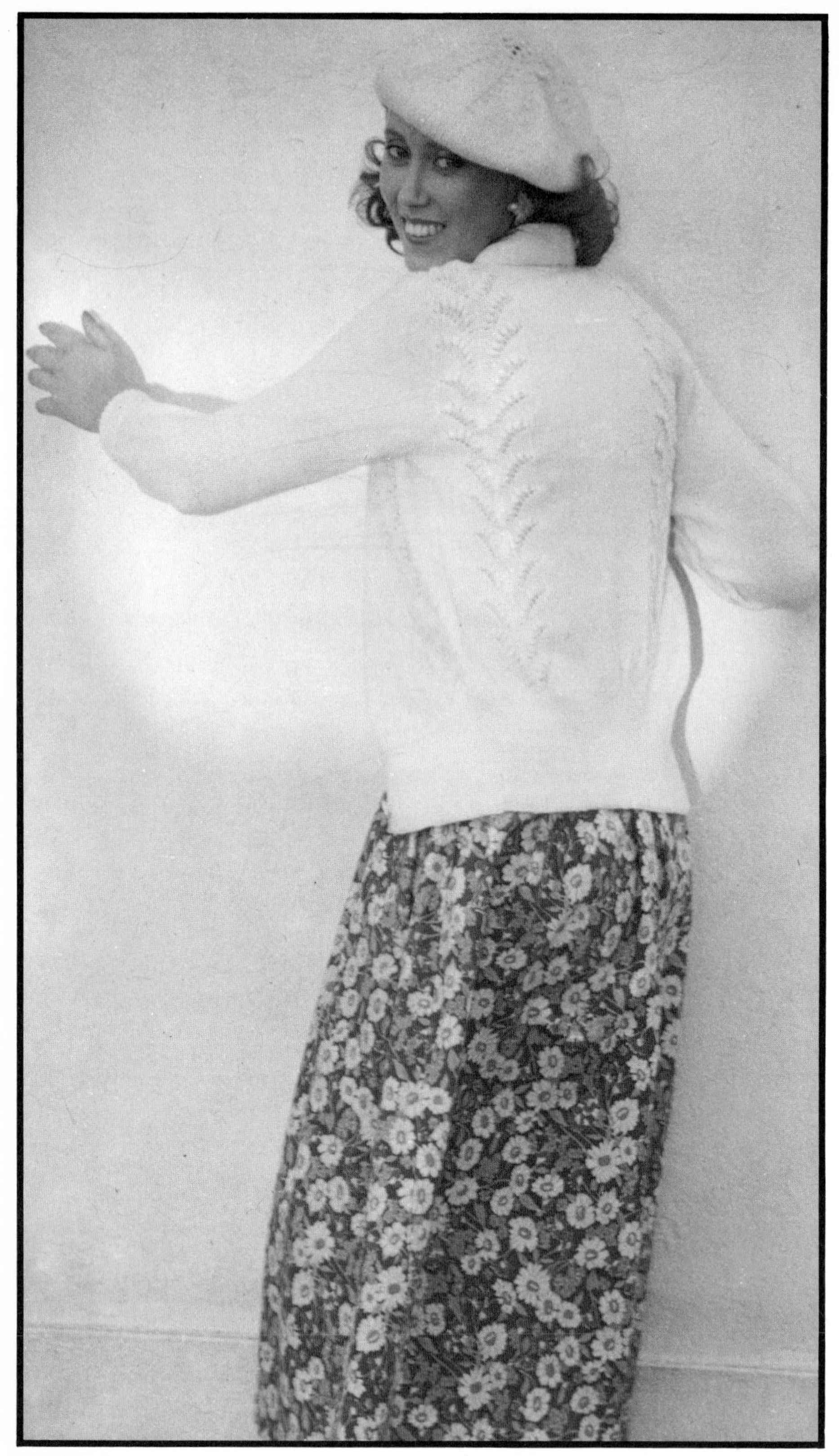

The pocket backs *(both alike):*
With No.12 needles cast on 33sts. and beginning with a k. row s.s.42 rows, then leave these sts. on a stitch holder until required.

The left front:
With No.13 needles cast on 56(60)(64) sts. and work 54 rows in single rib.
Change to No.12 needles.
Next row: K.3(5)(9), * up 1, k.7; repeat from * ending last repeat k.4(6)(10)—64(68)(72) sts.
P.1 row **.
Now work in pattern as follows:
1st row: K.17(20)(23), work from * to * on first pattern row on back of sweater, k.24(25)(26).
2nd row: All p.
These 2 rows set the position of the pattern given for back of sweater, pattern 40 more rows as set.
Pocket row: K.12(15)(18), slip next 33sts. onto a stitch holder and leave at front of work and, in their place, k. across the 33sts. of one pocket back, k.19 (20)(21).
Pattern 45 rows.
*** *To slope the front edge:* Dec. 1st. at the end of the next row and at the same edge on the 3 following 3rd rows.
To shape the armhole and continue to slope the front edge: While decreasing at front edge on every 3rd row from previous front edge dec., cast off 6sts. at the beginning of the next row, work 1 row straight, then dec. 1st. at the armhole edge on each of the next 10(12)(14) rows.
Pattern 48(49)(50) rows decreasing at front edge on every 3rd row as before.
On 24(25)(26) sts., pattern 18(17)(16) rows.
To slope the shoulder: Cast off 8sts. at the beginning of the next row and following alternate row.
On 8(9)(10) sts. work 1 row, then cast off.

The right front:
Work as given for left front to **.
Now work in pattern as follows:
1st row: K.24(25)(26), work from * to * on first pattern row on back, k.17 (20) (23).
2nd row: All p.
The last 2 rows set the position of the pattern given for back. Pattern 40 more rows as set.
Pocket row: K.19(20)(21), slip next 33sts. onto a stitch holder and leave at front of work, in their place pattern across 33sts. of other pocket back, k. to end.
Pattern 46 more rows.
Now work as given for left front from *** to end.

The pocket tops *(both alike):*
With right side of work facing rejoin yarn and using No.13 needles k.8 rows, then cast off.

The right half collar and frontband:
With No.13 needles cast on 82(84)(86) sts. and k.54 rows.
Cast off 40(41)(42) sts. at the beginning of the next row, then dec. 1st. at the end of the next row and the 29(30)(31) following alternate rows **.
On 12sts., k.3 rows.
1st Buttonhole row: K.4, cast off 4, k. to end.
2nd Buttonhole row: K.4, turn, cast on 4, turn, k. to end.
K.24 rows.
Repeat the last 26 rows 4 more times, then work the 2 buttonhole rows again.
K.10 rows, then cast off.

The left half collar and frontband:
Work as given for right half collar and frontband to **.
On 12sts. k.144 rows, then cast off.

The sleeves *(both alike):*
With No.13 needles cast on 64(68)(72) sts. and work 60 rows in single rib.
Change to No.12 needles and work as follows:
Increase row: K.3(5)(7), * up 1, k.1, up 1, k.2; repeat from * ending last repeat k.3(7)(7)—104(108)(112) sts.
Beginning with a k. row, s.s.139 rows.
To shape the sleevetop: Cast off 6sts. at the beginning of the next 2 rows, then dec. 1st. at each end of the next row and the 10 following alternate rows. Work 1 row.
Dec. 1st. at each end of the next 18(20)(22) rows.
Cast off 4sts. at the beginning of the next 6 rows. Cast off the remaining 10sts.

To make up the cardigan:
Press all parts except the ribbing with a warm iron over a damp cloth. Set in sleeves. Join sleeve and side seams. Sew front bands and collar in place. Sew on buttons. Press seams.

COBWEB

SEE MODEL ON RIGHT, FOLLOWING PAGE

Texture and colour are used together in this simply shaped polo-necked sloppy sweater. Chevrons knitted in seed stitch run into knit-twist lattices, which in turn fade into the same pattern worked in colour instead of the raised stitches.

Materials:
23(24) (25) 25 gram balls of Sirdar Fontein crepe 4-ply in main colour and 7 balls in contrast colour; a pair each of No. 12 and No. 13 knitting needles.

Tension:
10 stitches—1 repeat of the pattern to 3 cm (1¼ in.) in width and 78 rows—1 repeat of the pattern to 19.25 cm (7¾ in.) in length. If you cannot obtain the correct tension using the size needles suggested, use larger or smaller ones accordingly.

Abbreviations:
K., knit; p., purl; st., stitch; tog., together; dec., decrease (by working 2 sts. tog.); inc., increase (by working twice into same st.); s.s., stocking stitch is k. on the right side and p. on the wrong side; tw. 2 rt., twist 2 right thus, k. into front of 2nd st. on left hand needle, then into 1st st. allowing both loops to fall from left hand needle together; tw. 2 lt., twist 2 left thus, k. into back of 2nd st. on left hand needle, then into front of 1st st. allowing both loops to fall from left hand needle together; sl., slip; m., main colour; c., contrast colour; double rib is k. 2 and p. 2 alternately; up 1, pick up the loop that lies between the needles, slip it onto left hand needle, then k. into back of it.

Note:
The instructions are given for the small size. Where they vary work the figures in the first brackets for the medium size or the figures in the second brackets for the large size.

Measurements:
The measurements are given in centimetres followed by inches in square brackets.

small (8)	medium (10)	large (12)
All round at underarms		
84 [33½]	90 [36]	96 [38½]
Side seam		
52.5 [21]	52.5 [21]	52.5 [21]
Length		
74 [29½]	75.5 [30¼]	77 [30¾]
Sleeve seam (without cuff turned back)		
46 [18½]	46 [18½]	46 [18½]

The back:
With No. 13 needles and m. cast on 134 (144)(154) sts. and work 30 rows in double rib.
Change to No. 12 needles and work in pattern as follows:
1st row: K. 1, * tw. 2 rt., k. 8; repeat from * ending last repeat k. 1.
2nd row: P. 1, * sl. 2, p. 8; repeat from * ending last repeat p. 1.
3rd row: K. 2, * tw. 2 lt., k. 6, tw. 2 rt.; repeat from * until 2 remain, k. 2.
4th row: K. 1, p. 1, * k. 1, sl. 1, p. 6, sl. 1, p. 1; repeat from * until 2 remain, k. 1, p. 1.
5th row: P. 1, k. 1, * p. 1, tw. 2 lt., k. 4, tw. 2 rt., k. 1; repeat from * until 2 remain, p. 1, k. 1.
6th row: K. 1, p. 1, k. 1, p. 1, * sl. 1, p. 4, sl. 1, k. 1, p. 1, k. 1, p. 1; repeat from * to end.
7th row: P. 1, k. 1, p. 1, k. 1,* tw. 2 lt., k. 2, tw. 2 rt., p. 1, k. 1, p. 1, k. 1; repeat from * to end.
8th row: K. 1, p. 1, k. 1, p. 1, * k, 1, sl. 1, p. 2, sl. 1, p. 1, k. 1, p. 1; k. 1, p. 1; repeat from * to end.
9th row: P. 1, k. 1, p. 1, k. 1,* p. 1, tw. 2 lt., tw. 2 rt., k. 1, p. 1, k. 1, p. 1, k. 1; repeat from * to end.
10th row: K. 1, p. 1, k. 1, p. 1, * k. 1, p. 1, sl. 2, k. 1, p. 1, k. 1, p. 1, k. 1, p. 1; repeat from * to end.
11th row: P. 1, k. 1, p. 1, k. 1, * p. 1, k. 1, tw. 2 rt., p. 1, k. 1, p. 1, k. 1, p. 1, k. 1; repeat from * to end.
12th row: * K. 1, p. 1; repeat from * to end.
13th row: P. 1, * tw. 2 rt., k. 1, p. 1, k. 1, p. 1, k. 1, p. 1, k. 1, p. 1; repeat from * until 3 remain, tw. 2 rt., k. 1.
14th row: K. 1, sl. 2, p. 1, * k. 1, p. 1, k. 1, p. 1, k. 1, p. 1, k. 1, sl. 2, p. 1; repeat from * to end.
15th row: K. 2, * tw. 2 lt., p. 1, k. 1, p. 1, k. 1, p. 1, k. 1, tw. 2 rt.; repeat from * until 2 remain, k. 2.
16th row: P. 3, * sl. 1, k. 1, p. 1, k. 1, p. 1, k. 1, p. 1, sl. 1, p. 2; repeat from * ending last repeat p. 3.
17th row: K. 3, * tw. 2 lt., k. 1, p. 1, k. 1, p. 1, tw. 2 rt., k. 2; repeat from * ending last repeat k. 3.
18th row: P. 4, * sl. 1, p. 1, k. 1, p. 1, k. 1, sl. 1, p. 4; repeat from * to end.
19th row: K. 4, * tw. 2 lt., p. 1, k. 1, tw. 2 rt., k. 4; repeat from * to end.
20th row: P. 5, * sl. 1, k. 1, p. 1, sl. 1, p. 6; repeat from * ending last repeat p. 5.
21st row: K. 5, * tw. 2 lt:, tw. 2 rt., k. 6; repeat from * ending last repeat k. 5.
22nd row: P. 6, * sl. 2, p. 8; repeat from * ending last repeat p. 6.
23rd row: K. 6, * tw. 2 rt., k. 8; repeat from * ending last repeat k. 6.
24th row: As 22nd row.
25th row: K. 5, * tw. 2 rt., tw. 2 lt., k. 6; repeat from * ending last repeat k. 5.
26th row: P. 5, * sl. 1, p. 2, sl. 1, p. 6; repeat from * ending last repeat p. 5.
27th row: K. 4, * tw. 2 rt., k. 2, tw. 2 lt., k. 4; repeat from * to end.
28th row: P. 4, * sl. 1, p. 4, sl. 1, p. 4; repeat from * to end.
29th row: K. 3, * tw. 2 rt., k. 4, tw. 2 lt., k. 2; repeat from * ending last repeat k. 3.
30th row: P. 3, * sl. 1, p. 6, sl. 1, p. 2; repeat from * ending last repeat p. 3.
31st row: K. 2, * tw. 2 rt., k. 6, tw. 2 lt.; repeat from * until 2 remain, k. 2.
32nd row: P. 2, * sl. 1, p. 8, sl. 1; repeat from * until 2 remain, p. 2.
33rd row: K. 1, * tw. 2 rt., k. 8; repeat from * until 3 remain, tw. 2 rt., k. 1.
34th row: P. 1, * sl. 2, p. 8; repeat from * until 3 remain, sl. 2, p. 1.
Join in c. and continue in Fair Isle pattern as follows: This is *worked entirely in s.s. so only the colour details are given.* Great care should be taken to avoid pulling colours not in use tightly across the back of the work, or it will become puckered.
35th row: 1 m., * 2 c., 8 m.; repeat from * until 3 remain, 2 c., 1 m.
36th row: As 35th row.
37th to 66th rows: The last 2 rows set the position of the pattern given in the chart. Now work the 37th to 66th rows from the chart.
Break off c. and continue with m. only.
67th to 69th rows: As 1st, 2nd and 3rd rows.
70th row: P. 3, * sl. 1, p. 6, sl. 1, p. 2; repeat from * ending last repeat p. 3.
71st row: K. 3, * tw. 2 lt., k. 4, tw. 2 rt., k. 2; repeat from * ending last repeat k. 3.
72nd row: P. 4, * sl. 1, p. 4, sl. 1, p. 4; repeat from * to end.
73rd row: K. 4, * tw. 2 lt., k. 2, tw. 2 rt., k. 4; repeat from * to end.
74th row: P. 5, * sl. 1, p. 2, sl. 1, p. 6; repeat from * ending last repeat p. 5.
75th row: K. 5, * tw. 2 lt., tw. 2 rt., k. 6; repeat from * ending last repeat k. 5.
76th row: P. 6, * sl. 2, p. 8; repeat from * ending last repeat p. 6.
77th row: K. 6, * tw. 2 rt., k. 8; repeat from * ending last repeat k. 6.
78th row: P. 6, * sl. 2, p. 8; repeat from * ending last repeat p. 6.
The last 78 rows form the pattern. Repeat them once more, then work the first 30 rows again.
To shape the raglan armholes: Maintaining the continuity of the pattern as set dec. 1 st. at each end of the next row and the 42 (45) (48) following alternate rows.
On 48 (52) (56) sts. work 1 row, then cast off.

The pocket backs *(two alike)*:
With No. 12 needles and m. cast on 36 sts. and beginning with a k. row s.s. 48 rows, then leave these sts. on a stitch-holder until required.

The front:
Work as given for back until 66 rows have been worked in pattern as set.
Pocket row: Pattern 13 (18) (23) sts, * slip next 36 sts. on to a stitch-holder and leave at front of work, then in their place pattern

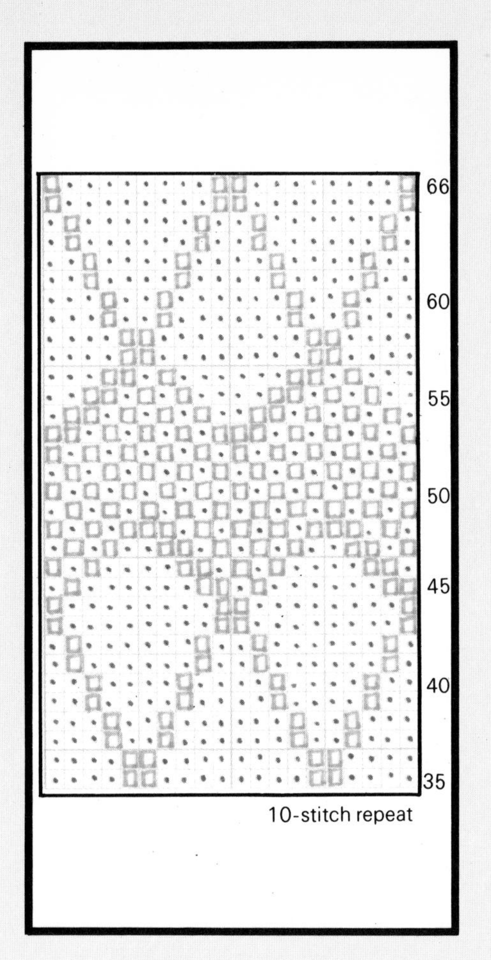

across the 36sts. of one pocket back, * pattern 36, repeat from * to *, then pattern to end.
Pattern 119 rows more.
To slope the raglan armholes: Dec. 1 st. at each end of the next row and the 21 (23) (25) following alternate rows—90 (96) (102) sts.
Now divide the sts. for the neck: *Next row:* Pattern 33 (35) (37) and leave these sts. on a spare needle until required for right front shoulder, cast off 24 (26) (28) sts. for neck, pattern to end and continue on these 33 (35) (37) sts. for the left front shoulder.
The left front shoulder: While continuing to dec. at armhole edge on every alternate row, dec. 1 st. at the neck edge on each of the next 11 (12) (13) rows.
Pattern 28 (29) (30) rows more decreasing 1 st. at armhole edge on every right side row—2 sts.
P. 2, then k. 2 tog. and fasten off.
The right front shoulder: With right side of work facing rejoin yarn to inner edge of sts. left on spare needle and work to end of row. Now work as given for left front shoulder to end.

The sleeves *(both alike)***:**
With No. 13 needles and m. cast on 48 (52) (56) sts. and work 40 rows in double rib.
Increase row: K. 2 (3) (4), * up 1, k. 1; repeat from * ending last repeat k. 1 (2) (3)—94 (100) (106) sts.
Change to No. 12 needles and p. 1 row, then continue in pattern as follows, beginning with the 35th pattern row. Join in c. and work as follows noting information given for back.
35th pattern row: 1 (9) (2) m., * 2 c., 8 m; repeat from * ending last repeat 1 (9) (2) m.
36th row: As 35th row.
The last 2 rows set the position of the pattern given in the chart. Continuing in pattern as set work the 37th to 66th rows from the chart. Break off c.
Continuing in pattern as set pattern a further 120 rows as given for back.
To slope the raglan sleevetops: Dec. 1 st. at each end of the next row and the 42 (45) (48) following alternate rows.
On 8 sts. work 1 row, then cast off.

The collar:
With No. 13 needles and m. cast on 212 (220) (228) sts. and work 144 rows in double rib, then cast off loosely.

The pocket tops *(both alike)***:**
With right side of work facing rejoin m. to the 36 sts. left on stitch-holders and using No. 13 needles work 6 rows in double rib, then cast off.

To make up the sweater:
Pin out to size and press all parts on the wrong side with a warm iron over a damp cloth. Join raglan seams so that the sts. cast off at top of sleeves form part of neck edge. Join sleeve and side seams. Neatly sew pocket backs and row ends of pocket top in position. Join row ends of collar, then sew cast off edge of collar in place all round neck edge. Press seams.

STRIPE ME PINK

SEE MODEL ON LEFT, FACING PAGE

Another sloppy sweater, but this time simple to knit. Coloured bobbles are strung together to make a very effective pattern. Instead of using just one contrast colour as we did, why not use several, so that one row of bobbles could be pink, one emerald, and another blue.

Materials:
17 (18) (19) 25 gram balls of Sirdar Fontein crepe 4-ply in main colour and 6 (7) (7) balls of the same wool in contrast colour; a pair each of No. 12 and No. 13 knitting needles.

Tension:
16 stitches and 20 rows to 5 cm (2 in.) over the pattern using No. 12 needles. If you cannot obtain the correct tension using the size needles suggested, use larger or smaller ones accordingly.

Abbreviations:
K., knit; p., purl; st., stitch; tog., together; dec., decrease (by working 2 sts. tog); inc., increase (by working twice into same st.); s.s., stocking stitch (k. on the right side and p. on the wrong side); double rib is k. 2 and p. 2 alternately; sl., slip; y.f., yarn forward, y.b., yarn back; m., main colour; c., contrast colour.

Note:
The instructions are given for the small size. Where they vary work the figures in the first brackets for the medium size or the figures in the second brackets for the large size.

Measurements:
The measurements are given in centimetres followed by inches in square brackets.

small	medium	large
All round at underarms		
90 [36]	95 [38]	100 [40]
Side seam		
52.5 [21]	52.5 [21]	52.5 [21]
Length		
74 [29½]	75 [30]	75 [30]
Sleeve seam		
42.5 [17]	42.5 [17]	42.5 [17]

The back:
With No. 13 needles and m. cast on 144 (152) (160) sts. and work 40 rows in double rib.
Change to No. 12 needles and beginning with a k. row s.s. 4 rows.
Now work in pattern as follows: *1st row:* With c., k. 11 (15) (13), turn, y.f., sl. 1, y.b., k. 3, turn, p. 4, * k. 12, turn, y.f., sl. 1, y.b., k. 3, turn, p. 4; repeat from * until 1 (5) (3) remain, k. to end.
2nd row: With c. k. 5 (9) (7), * turn, p. 4, turn, k. 3, y.f., sl. 1, y.b., k. 12; repeat from * ending last repeat k. 7 (11) (9).
3rd row: With m., k. 8 (12) (10), * sl. 2, k. 10, repeat from * ending last repeat k. 2 (6) (4).
4th to 10th rows: With m. in s.s.
11th row: With c., k. 5 (9) (7), * turn, y.f., sl. 1, y.b., k. 3, turn, p. 4, k. 12; repeat from * ending last repeat k. 7 (11) (9).
12th row: With c., k. 11 (15) (13), * turn, p. 4, turn, k. 3, y.f., sl. 1, y.b., k. 12; repeat from * ending last repeat k. 1 (5) (3).
13th row: With m., k. 2 (6) (4), * sl. 2, k. 10; repeat from * ending last repeat k. 8 (12) (10).
14th to 20th rows: With m. in s.s.
These 20 rows form the pattern; repeat them 7 times more, then work the first 10 rows again.
To shape the raglan armholes: Cast off 5 (6) (7) sts. at the beginning of the next 2 rows, then dec. 1 st. at each end of the next row and the 10 (11) (12) following alternate rows.
On 112 (116) (120) sts. work 1 row.
Change to No. 13 needles and continuing with m. only work 2 rows in double rib.
Continuing in rib as set dec. 1 st. at each end of the next row and the 29 (30) (31) following alternate rows—52 (54) (56) sts.
Work 1 row in double rib then cast off.

The pocket backs *(both alike)***:**
With No. 12 needles and m. cast on 32 sts. and beginning with a k. row s.s. 40 rows,

then leave these sts. on a spare needle until required.

The front:
Work as given for back until the 20 pattern rows have been worked. Pattern 16 rows more.
Pocket row: K. 24 (28) (32), * slip next 32 sts. on to a stitch-holder and leave at front of work, in their place pattern across the 32 sts. of one pocket back *, k. 32, repeat from * to *, k. to end.
Pattern 102 rows more as set.
Now divide the sts. for the neck: *Next row:* Pattern 72 (76) (80) and leave these sts. on a spare needle until required for right front shoulder, work to end and continue on these 72 (76) (80) sts. for the left front shoulder.
The left front shoulder:
To shape the neck: Dec. 1 st. at the neck edge on each of the next 30 rows.
To shape the armhole and continue to shape the neck: While continuing to dec. 1 st. at the neck edge on every row, cast off 5 (6) (7) sts. at the beginning of the next row, then dec. 1 st. at the armhole edge on the 11 (12) (13) following alternate rows. Dec. 1 st. at the neck edge on the next row.
Take the 2 remaining sts. tog. and fasten off.
The right front shoulder:
With right side of work facing rejoin yarn to inner edge of sts. left on spare needle and work to end of row.
Now work as given for left front shoulder to end.

The sleeves *(both alike)*:
With No. 13 needles and m. cast on 60 (64) (68) sts. and work 30 rows in double rib.
Change to No. 12 needles and beginning with a k. row, s.s. 4 rows.
Now work in pattern as follows *1st row:* With c., k. 11 (13) (15), * turn, y.f., sl. 1, y.b., k. 3; turn, p. 4, k. 12; repeat from * ending last repeat k. 1 (3) (5).
2nd row: With c., k. 5 (7) (9), * turn, p. 4, turn, k. 3, y.f., sl. 1, y.b., k. 12; repeat from * ending last repeat k. 7 (9) (11).
These 2 rows set the position of the pattern given for back. Pattern 2 rows more as set.
Continuing in pattern as set, inc. 1 st. at each end of the next row and the 13 following 10th rows.
On 88 (92) (96) sts. pattern 5 rows.
To shape the raglan sleevetop: Cast off 5 (6) (7) sts. at the beginning of the next 2 rows, then dec. 1 st. at each end of the next row and the 10 (11) (12) following alternate rows.
On 56 sts. work 1 row, then leave these sts. on a spare needle until required for neckband and collar.

The left front collar:
First join raglan shaping rows on front to those of sleeves. With right side of work facing rejoin m. to the sts. left on spare needle at top of left sleeve and using No. 13 needles k. across these 56 sts. then pick up and k. 68 (70) (72) sts. from left front neck edge—124 (126) (128) sts.
**Work 1 row in double rib, then continuing in rib as set dec. 1 st. at each end of the next row and the 29 (30) (31) following alternate rows.
On 64 sts. rib 1 row.
Next row: Cast off 56 sts., rib to end and continue on these 8 sts. for the collar.
For the collar inc. 1 st. at the end—inner edge on the next row and at the same edge on each of the next 47 rows.
On 56 sts. work in rib until collar is long enough to fit around neck edge to centre back neck, cast off.

The right front neckband and collar:
With right side of work facing rejoin m. at centre front neck and using No. 13 needles pick up and k. 68 (70) (72) sts. from right front neck edge, then k. across the 56 sts. at top of right sleeve. Work 1 row in double rib, then work as given for left front neckband and collar from ** to end.

The pocket tops *(both alike)*:
With right side of work facing rejoin m. to the 32 sts. left on stitch-holder at front of work and using No. 13 needles work 6 rows in double rib, then cast off in rib.

To make up the sweater:
Pin out to size. Press all parts except the ribbing on the wrong side with a warm iron over a damp cloth. Join back raglan seams. Join sleeve and side seams. Join cast off edges of collar for centre back neck, then neatly sew the shaped row end edges of collar pieces in place. Join shaped row end edges at centre front neck. Neatly sew pocket backs and row ends of pocket tops in place. Press seams.

IN THE PINK

SEE MODEL ON LEFT, FOLLOWING PAGE

A very feminine sweater knitted in shower stitch lace. The ribbing of the hipband is knitted sideways, then tied at one hip. The sleeves tie neatly at the wrists and the neck has a pretty ruffle edging.

Materials:
22 (23) (24) 25 gram balls of Patons Purple Heather 4-ply; a pair each of No. 12 and No. 13 knitting needles.

Tension:
12 stitches—1 repeat of the pattern to 4.5 cm ($1\frac{3}{4}$ in.) in width and 16 rows—2 repeats of the pattern to 3.75 cm ($1\frac{1}{2}$ in.) in length—using No. 12 needles. If you cannot obtain the correct tension using the size needles suggested, use larger or smaller ones accordingly.

Abbreviations:
K., knit; p., purl; st., stitch; tog., together; dec., decrease (by working 2 sts. tog.); inc., increase (by working twice into same st.); single rib is k. 1 and p. 1 alternately; y.r.n., yarn round needle; s.s.k., slip 1, k. 1, pass slip st. over; sl., slip; p.s.s.o., pass sl. st. over; p. 2 or 3 tog.b., p. 2 or 3 tog. through back of sts; up 1, pick up the loop which lies between the needles, slip it onto left hand needle, then k. into back of it.

Note:
The instructions are given for the small size. Where they vary work the figures in the first brackets for the medium size or the figures in the second brackets for the large size.

Measurements:
The measurements are given in centimetres followed by inches in square brackets.

small	medium	large
All round at underarms		
80 [32]	87.5 [35]	91 [$36\frac{1}{2}$]
Side seam excluding ribbing		
37.5 [15]	37.5 [15]	37.5 [15]
Length excluding ribbing		
55 [22]	55.5 [$22\frac{1}{4}$]	56 [$22\frac{1}{2}$]
Sleeve seam excluding cuffs		
40 [16]	40 [16]	40 [16]

The hipband:
With No. 13 needles cast on 30 sts. and work 132 rows in single rib, marking the end of the last row with a red thread.
Rib 124 (134) (140) rows more, marking the end of the last row with a blue thread.
Rib 124 (134) (140) rows more, marking the end of the last row with a yellow thread.
Rib 132 rows more, then cast off.

The back:
Rejoin yarn to hipband at blue thread mark, then using No. 12 needles pick up and k. 124 (134) (140) sts.—1 stitch from each row end— between the blue thread and yellow thread mark.
**P. 1 row.
Now work in pattern as follows: *1st row:* K. 2 (1) (4), * k. 2 tog., y.r.n., k. 2, k. 2 tog., y.r.n., y.r.n., s.s.k., k. 2, y.r.n., s.s.k.; repeat from * until 2 (1) (4) remain, k. 2 (1) (4).
2nd row: P. 5 (4) (7), * p. 2 tog.b., y.r.n., k. 1 and p. 1 into the 2 y.r.n.'s of last row, y.r.n., p. 2 tog., p. 6; repeat from * ending last repeat p. 5 (4) (7).
3rd row: K. 4 (3) (6), * k. 2 tog., y.r.n., k. 4, y.r.n., s.s.k., k. 4; repeat from * ending last repeat k. 4 (3) (6).
4th row: P. 2 (1) (4), * p. 3 tog.b., y.r.n., p. 1, y.r.n., p. 4, y.r.n., p. 1, y.r.n., p. 3 tog.; repeat from * until 2 (1) (4) remain, p. to end.
5th row: K. 2 (1) (4), y.r.n., * s.s.k., k. 2, y.r.n., s.s.k., k. 2 tog., y.r.n., k. 2, k. 2 tog., y.r.n., y.r.n.; repeat from * ending last repeat with one y.r.n., k. 2 (1) (4).
6th row: P. 3 (2) (5), * y.r.n., p. 2 tog., p. 6, p. 2 tog.b., y.r.n., k. 1, then p. 1 into the 2 y.r.n.'s of last row; repeat from * ending last repeat with k. 1 only into last y.r.n. of last row, then p. 2 (1) (4).
7th row: K. 4 (3) (6), * y.r.n., s.s.k., k. 4, k. 2 tog., y.r.n., k. 4; repeat from * ending last repeat k. 4 (3) (6).

8th row: P. 4 (3) (6), * y.r.n., p. 1, y.r.n., p. 3 tog., p. 3 tog.b., y.r.n., p. 1, y.r.n., p. 4; repeat from * ending last repeat p. 4 (3) (6).
These 8 rows form the pattern; repeat them 5 times more.
Maintaining the continuity of the pattern as set dec. 1 st. at each end of the next row and the 6 following 16th rows.
On 110 (120) (126) sts. pattern 15 rows.
To shape the armholes: Dec. 1 st. at each end of the next 5 rows.**
On 100 (110) (116) sts. pattern 65 (67) (69) rows.
To slope the shoulders: Cast off 20 (23) (24) sts. at the beginning of the next 2 rows.
Cast off the remaining 60 (64) (68) sts.

The front:
Rejoin yarn to hipband at red marking thread, then using No. 12 needles pick up and k. 124 (134) (140) sts.—1 from each row end between the place marked by the red thread and that marked by the blue thread.
Now work as given for back from ** to **
On 100 (110) (116) sts. pattern 34 (36) (38) rows.
Now divide the sts. for the neck: *Next row:* Pattern 35 (38) (39) and leave these sts. on a spare needle until required for right front shoulder, cast off 30 (34) (38) sts., pattern to end and continue on these 35 (38) (39) sts. for the left front shoulder
The left front shoulder:
To shape the neck: Dec. 1 st. at the neck edge on the next row and the 14 following alternate rows.
On 20 (23) (24) sts. work 1 row, then cast off.
The right front shoulder:
With right side of work facing rejoin yarn to inner edge of sts. left on spare needle and work to end of row.
Now work as given for left front shoulder to end.

The neckband:
With No. 12 needles cast on 11 sts. and k. 1 row, then work in pattern as follows:
1st row (right side): K. 3, y.r.n., k. 2 tog., k. 1, s.s.k., turn, cast on 4 sts., turn, k. 2 tog., k. 1—13 sts.
2nd row: K. 10, y.r.n., k. 2 tog., k. 1.
3rd row: K. 3, y.r.n., k. 2 tog., s.s.k., y.r.n., k. 1, y.r.n. k. 1, y.r.n., k. 1, y.r.n., k. 1, y.r.n., k. 2 tog.—16 sts.
4th row: K. 13, y.r.n., k. 2 tog., k. 1.
5th row: K. 3, y.r.n., k. 2 tog., s.s.k., y.r.n., k. 1, y.r.n., k. 1, y.r.n., sl. 1, k. 2 tog., p.s.s.o., y.r.n., k. 1, y.r.n., k. 1, y.r.n., k. 2 tog.—18 sts.
6th row: K. 15, y.r.n., k. 2 tog., k. 1.
7th row: K. 3, y.r.n., k. 2 tog., k. 11, k. 2 tog.—17 sts.
8th row: Cast off 6, k. next 7, y.r.n., k. 2 tog., k. 1—11 sts.
These 8 rows form the pattern. Repeat them 23 (24) (25) times, then cast off.

The sleeves *(both alike)*:
With No. 13 needles cast on 42 (46) (50) sts. and k. 1 row.
Increase row: P. 2 (4) (6), * up 1, p. 1 repeat from * ending last repeat p. 1 (3) (5)—82 (86) (90) sts.
Change to No. 12 needles and work in pattern as follows: *1st row:* K. 5 (1) (3), * k. 2 tog., y.r.n., k. 2, k. 2 tog., y.r.n., y.r.n., s.s.k., k. 2, y.r.n., s.s.k.; repeat from * ending last repeat k. 5 (1) (3).
2nd row: P. 8 (4) (6), * p. 2 tog.b., y.r.n., k. 1 and p. 1 into the 2 y.r.n.'s of last row, y.r.n., p. 2 tog., p. 6; repeat from * ending last repeat p. 8 (4) (6).
The last 2 rows set the position of the 8 row pattern given for back. Now work 168 rows in pattern as set.
To shape the sleevetop: Continuing in pattern as set dec. 1 st. at each end of the next row and the 19 following alternate rows.
On 42 (46) (50) sts. work 1 row.
Dec. 1 st. at each end of the next 2 (4) (6) rows—38 sts.
Cast off 4 sts. at the beginning of the next 6 rows. Cast off the remaining 14 sts.

The cuffs *(two alike)*:
With No. 13 needles cast on 8 sts. and work in single rib until the cuff measures 16 (16½) (17) in. then cast off.

To make up the sweater:
Press all parts except the ribbing on the wrong side with a warm iron over a damp cloth. Join shoulder seams. Set in sleeves. Join sleeve and side seams leaving sleeve seams undone for 3 in. at lower edge and do not join ribbing at left side seam. Neatly sew cuffs in place leaving 5 in. free at each end to tie at sleeve opening. Join cast on and cast off edges of neckband and sew in place. Press seams.

PANSYGIRL

SEE MODEL ON RIGHT, FOLLOWING PAGE

Pretty yet simple to knit, this sweater is versatile and easy to wear. The pansies growing out of the pocket are knitted in mohair to emphasise the motif. The square collar buttons at each shoulder, for a neat and unusual finishing touch.

Materials:
21 (22) (23) 25 gram balls of Jaeger Sheridan 4-ply in main colour—here clematis; one 25 gram ball of Jaeger mohair in each of 2 contrasting colours—here snowcap and creme de menthe; a pair each of No. 12 and No. 13 knitting needles; 6 buttons.

Tension:
16 stitches and 20 rows to 5 cm (2 in.) over the stocking stitch using No. 12 needles.

Abbreviations:
K., knit; p., purl; st., stitch; tog., together; dec., decrease (by working 2 sts. tog.); inc., increase (by working twice into same sts); s.s., stocking stitch (k. on the right side and p. on the wrong side); double rib is k. 2 and p. 2 alternately; m., main colour; c., first contrast—snowcap; b., second contrast—creme de menthe; garter st. is k. plain on every row; up 1, pick up the loop that lies between the needles, slip it on to left hand needle then k. into back of it.

Note:
The instructions are given for the small size. Where they vary work the figures in the first brackets for the medium size or the figures in the second brackets for the large size.

Measurements:
The measurements are given in centimetres followed by inches in square brackets.

small (10)	medium (12)	large (14)
All round at underarms		
85 [34]	90 [36]	95 [38]
Side seam		
45 [18]	45 [18]	45 [18]
Length		
65 [26]	65.5 [26¼]	66 [26½]
Sleeve seam		
42.5 [17]	42.5 [17]	42.5 [17]

The back:
With No. 13 needles and m. cast on 128 (136) (144) sts. and work 29 rows in double rib.
Increase row: Rib 8 (12) (16), * up 1, rib 16; repeat from * ending last repeat rib 8 (12) (16)—136 (144) (152) sts.
Change to No. 12 needles and beginning with a k. row s.s. 154 rows.
To shape the armholes: Cast off 7 (8) (9) sts. at the beginning of the next 2 rows, then dec. 1 st. at each end of the next row and the 8 (9) (10) following alternate rows.**
On 104 (108) (112) sts. s.s. 57 rows.
To slope the shoulders: Cast off 10 (11) (12) sts. at the beginning of the next 2 rows, then 10 sts. on the next 2 rows—64 (66) (68) sts.
To work the collar: Change to No. 13 needles.
***While working in garter stitch cast on 10 sts. at the beginning of the next 2 rows and 10 (11) (12) sts. on the 2 following rows.
Inc. 1 st. at each end of the next 22 rows.
K. 116 rows more, then cast off.

The pocket back:
With No. 12 needles and c. cast on 32 sts. and beginning with a k. row s.s. 40 rows, then leave these sts. on a spare needle until required.

The front:
Work as given for back until 34 rows have been worked in s.s.
Now work the flower pot as follows: *1st row:* With m., k. 88 (92) (96), join in b., with b. k. 24; join in a second ball of m. and with m. k. 24 (28) (32).
2nd row: With m. p. 24 (28) (32), with b. k. 24, with m. p. 88 (92) (96).

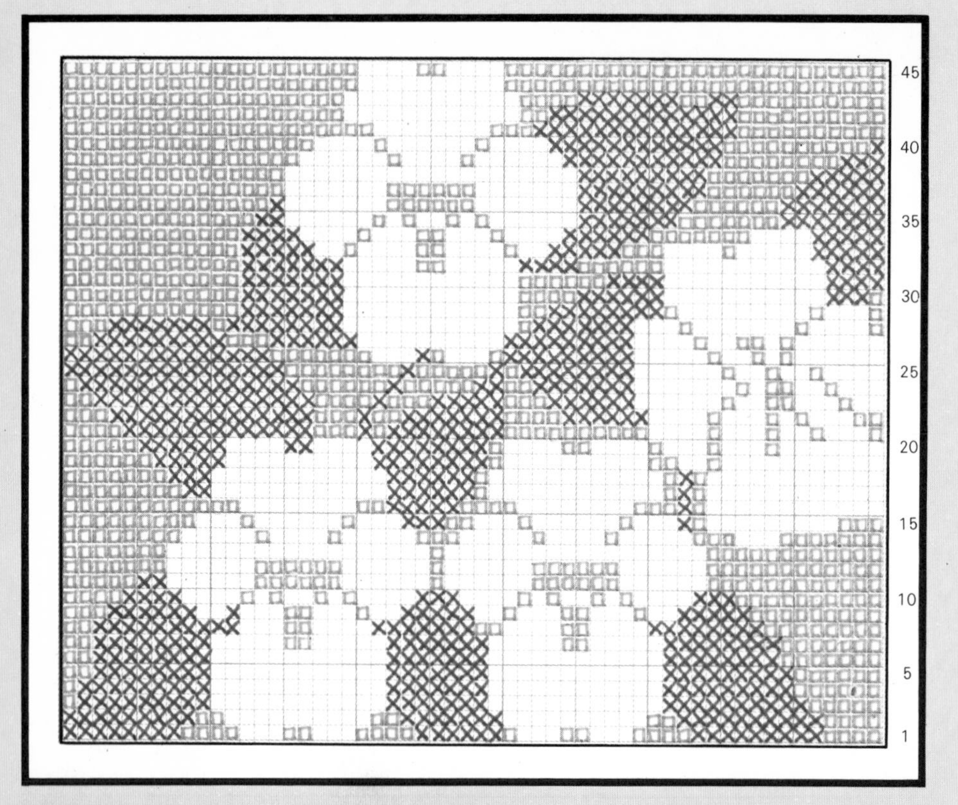

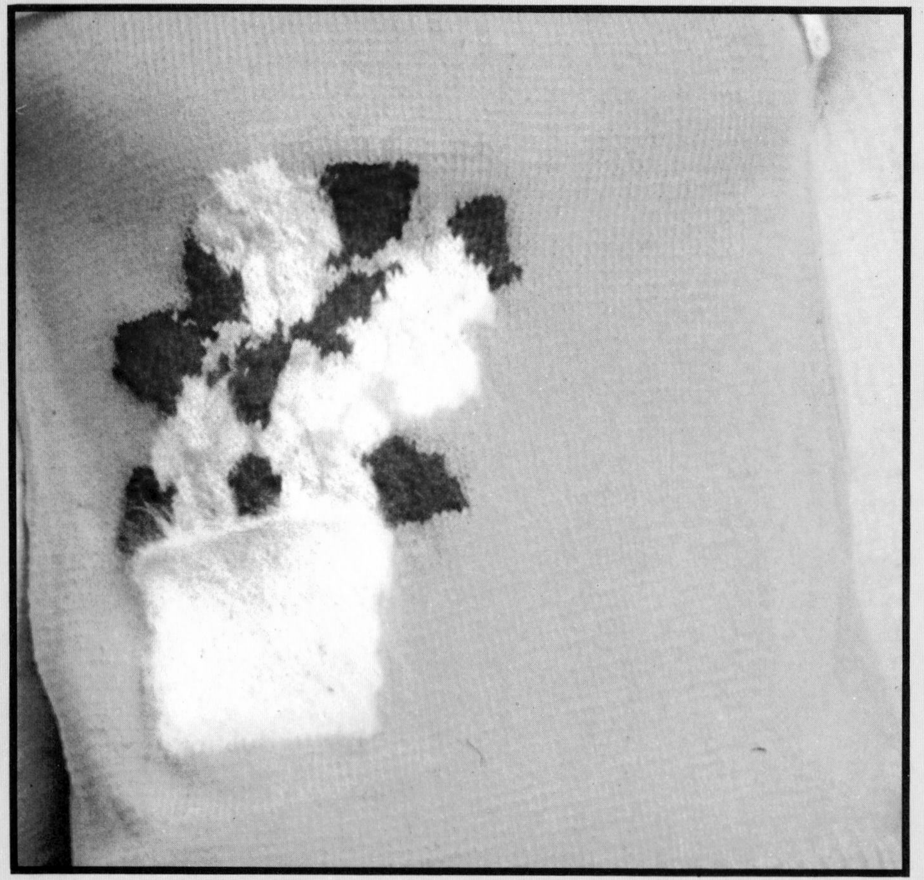

3rd row: With m. k. 88 (92) (96), with b. k. 24, with m. k. 24 (28) (32).
4th row: As 2nd row.
5th and 6th rows: As 3rd and 4th rows.
7th row: With m. k. 87 (91) (95), with b. k. 26, with m. k. 23 (27) (31).
8th row: With m. p. 23 (27) (31), with b. k. 26, with m. p. 87 (91) (95).
9th to 12th rows: Repeat 7th and 8th rows twice.
13th row: With m. k. 86 (90) (94), with b. k. 28, with m. k. 22 (26) (30).
14th row: With m. p. 22 (26) (30), with b. k. 28, with m. p. 86 (90) (94).
15th to 18th rows: Repeat 13th and 14th rows twice.
19th row: With m. k. 85 (89) (93), with b. k. 30, with m. k. to end.
20th row: With m. p. 21 (25) (29), with b. k. 30, with m. p. to end.
21st to 24th rows: Repeat 19th and 20th rows twice.
25th row: With m. k. 84 (88) (92), with b. k. 32, with m. k. 20 (24) (28).
26th row: With m. p. 20 (24) (28), with b. k. 32, with m. p. to end.
Pocket row: With m. k. 84 (88) (92), with m. k. across the 32 sts. of pocket back, with b. cast off 32 sts., with m. k. to end.
With m. p. 1 row.
Now work the pansy motif as follows: This is worked entirely in s.s. so only the colour details are given. Take great care to avoid pulling colours not in use tightly across the back of the work or it will become puckered.
1st row: 72 (76) (80) m., 9 b., 4 m., 4 c., 2 m., 3 c., 1 m., 6 b., 2 m., 3 c., 2 m., 3 c., 4 m., 8 b., 13 (17) (19) m.
2nd row: 13 (17) (19) m., 9 b., 2 m., 10 c., 7 b., 10 c., 2 m., 11 b., 72 (76) (80) m.
These 2 rows set the position of the 45 row pattern given in the chart. Now work the 3rd to 45th rows from the chart.
Continuing with m. only s.s. 47 rows.
To shape the armholes: Work as given for back up to **
On 104 (108) (112) sts. s.s. 40 rows.
Now divide the sts. for the neck: *Next row:* P. 36 (37) (38) and leave these sts. on a spare needle until required for right front shoulder, p. across next 32 (34) (36) sts. and leave these sts. on a stitch-holder until required for collar, p. to end and continue on these 36 (37) (38) sts. for the left front shoulder.
The left front shoulder:
To shape the neck: Dec. 1 st. at neck edge on each of the next 16 rows.
To slope the shoulder: Cast off 10 (11) (12) sts. at the beginning of the next row. On 10 sts. work 1 row, then cast off.
The right front shoulder:
With right side of work facing rejoin m. to inner edge of sts. left on spare needle and work to end of row, then work as given for left front shoulder to end.

The front collar:
With wrong side of work facing rejoin m. and using No. 13 needles pick up and k. 21 sts. from right front neck edge, k. across the 32 (34) (36) sts. at centre front, pick up and k. 21 sts. from left front neck edge—74 (76) (78) sts.
Now work as given for back collar from *** to end.

The sleeves *(both alike)*:
With No. 13 needles and m. cast on 64 (68) (72) sts. and work 65 rows in double rib.
Increase row: Rib 1 (3) (5), * up 1, rib 2; repeat from * ending last repeat rib 1 (3) (5)—96 (100) (104) sts.
Change to No. 12 needles and beginning with a k. row s.s. 140 rows.
To shape the sleevetop: Cast off 7 (8) (9) sts. at the beginning of the next 2 rows.
Dec. 1 st. at each end of the next row and the 16 (17) (18) following alternate rows.
On 48 sts. work 1 row.
Dec. 1 st. at each end of the next 6 rows.
Cast off 5 sts. at the beginning of the next 6 rows, then cast off the remaining 6 sts.

To make up the sweater:
Pin out to size and press all s.s. parts on the wrong side with a warm iron over a damp cloth. Neatly join the groups of sts. cast off for shoulders to those cast on for collar on back and front. Join shoulder seams for 1 cm ($\frac{1}{4}$ in.) at outer edges. Set in sleeves. Join sleeve and side seams. Sew pocket back in place. Press seams. On front make one buttonhole loop at each side of neck, one at each side of shoulder and one at each side collar at end of increases. Sew on buttons.

DOUBLE CREAM

SEE MODEL ON RIGHT, FOLLOWING PAGE

A cardigan to wear for ever and ever: you'll never tire of it, winter or summer. Knit your cardigan in cream and wear it over summer dresses, or in smart black to team with winter jerseys.

Materials:
20 (21) (22) 25 gram balls of Sirdar Superwash Wool 4-ply; a pair each of No. 12 and No. 13 knitting needles; a cable needle; 8 buttons.

Tension:
8 stitches and 10 rows to 2.5 cm (1 in.) over stocking stitch using No. 12 needles.

Abbreviations:
K., knit; p., purl; st., stitch; tog., together; dec., decrease (by working 2 sts. tog.); inc., increase (by working twice into same st.); double rib is k. 2 and p. 2 alternately; s.s., stocking stitch; m.b., make bobble thus, k. 1, p. 1, k. 1, p. 1, all into next st., turn, p. 4, turn, k. 4, turn, p. 2 tog., p. 2 tog., turn, k. 2 tog.b.; k. 2 tog.b., k. 2 tog. through back of sts.; cr. 3 rt., cross 3 right thus, slip next st. on to cable needle and leave at back of work, k. 2, then p. 1 from cable needle; cr. 3 lt., cross 3 left, slip next 2 sts. on to cable needle and leave at front of work, p. 1 then k. 2 from cable needle; cable 8 thus, slip next 4 sts. on to cable needle and leave at back of work, k. 4, then k. 4 from cable needle; single rib is k. 1 and p. 1 alternately.

Note:
The instructions are given for the small size. Where they vary work the instructions in the first brackets for the medium size or the instructions in the second brackets for the large size.

Measurements:
The measurements are given in centimetres followed by inches in square brackets.

small	medium	large
All round at underarms		
82.5 [33]	87.5 [35]	92.5 [37]
Side seam		
45 [18]	45 [18]	45 [18]
Length		
65 [26]	66 [$26\frac{1}{2}$]	67 [$27\frac{3}{4}$]
Sleeve seam (with cuffs folded in half)		
42.5 [17]	42.5 [17]	42.5 [17]

The back:
With No. 13 needles cast on 128 (136) (144) sts. and work 24 rows in double rib.
Change to No. 12 needles and work as follows:
1st row: P. 6 (2) (6), m.b., * p. 7, m.b.; repeat from * once (twice) (twice), p. 6, k. 8, p. 6, m.b., p. 3, m.b., p. 3, m.b., p. 10, k. 4, p. 10, m.b., p. 3, m.b., p. 3, m.b., p. 6, k. 8, p. 6, * m.b., p. 7; repeat from last * ending last repeat p. 6 (2) (6).
2nd row: K. 29 (33) (37), p. 8, k. 25, p. 4, k. 25, p. 8, k. 29 (33) (37).
3rd row: P. 29 (33) (37), k. 8, p. 24; cr. 3 rt., cr. 3 lt., p. 24, k. 8, p. 29 (33) (37).
4th row: K. 29 (33) (37), p. 8, k. 24, p. 2, k. 2, p. 2, k. 24, p. 8, k. 29 (33) (37).
5th row: P. 29 (33) (37), k. 8, p. 23, cr. 3 rt., p. 2, cr. 3 lt., p. 23, k. 8, p. 29 (33) (37).
6th row: K. 29 (33) (37), p. 8, k. 23, p. 2, k. 4, p. 2, k. 23, p. 8, k. 29 (33) (37).
7th row: P. 2 (6) (2) m.b., * p. 7, m.b.; repeat from * once (once) (twice) more, p. 10, cable 8, p. 10, m.b., p. 11, cr. 3 rt., p. 4, cr. 3 lt., p. 11, m.b., p. 10, cable 8, p. 10, * m.b., p. 7; repeat from last * ending last repeat p. 2 (6) (2).
8th row: K. 29 (33) (37), p. 8, k. 22, p. 2, k. 6, p. 2, k. 22, p. 8, k. 29 (33) (37).
9th row: P. 29 (33) (37), k. 8, p. 21, cr. 3 rt., p. 6, cr. 3 lt., p. 21, k. 8, p. 29 (33) (37).
10th row: K. 29 (33) (37), p. 8, k. 21, p. 2, k. 8, p. 2, k. 21, p. 8, k. 29 (33) (37).
11th row: P. 29 (33) (37), k. 8, p. 20, cr. 3 rt., p. 8, cr. 3 lt., p. 20, k. 8, p. 29 (33) (37).
12th row: K. 29 (33) (37), p. 8, k. 20, p. 2, k. 10, p. 2, k. 20, p. 8, k. 29 (33) (37).
13th row: P. 6 (2) (6), m.b., * p. 7, m.b.; repeat from * once (twice) (twice), p. 6, k. 8, p. 19, cr. 3 rt., p. 10, cr. 3 lt., p. 19, k. 8, p. 6, * m.b., p. 7; repeat from last * ending last repeat p. 6 (2) (6).
14th row: K. 29 (33) (37), p. 8, k. 19, p. 2, k. 12, p. 2, k. 19, p. 8, k. 29 (33) (37).
15th row: P. 29 (33) (37), k. 8, p. 18, cr. 3 rt., p. 12, cr. 3 lt., p. 18, k. 8, p. 29 (33) (37).
16th row: K. 29 (33) (37), p. 8, k. 18, p. 2, k. 14, p. 2, k. 18, p. 8, k. 29 (33) (37).
17th row: P. 29 (33) (37), k. 8, p. 17, cr. 3 rt., p. 14, cr. 3 lt., p. 17, k. 8, p. 29 (33) (37).
18th row: K. 29 (33) (37), p. 8, k. 17, p. 2, k. 16, p. 2, k. 17, p. 8, k. 29 (33) (37).
19th row: P. 2 (6) (2), m.b., * p. 7, m.b.; repeat from * once (once) (twice), p. 10, cable 8, p. 17, k. 2, p. 16, k. 2, p. 17, cable 8, p. 10, * m.b., p. 7; repeat from last * ending last repeat p. 2 (6) (2).
20th row: As 18th row.
21st row: P. 29 (33) (37), k. 8, p. 17, cr. 3 lt., p. 14, cr. 3 rt., p. 17, k. 8, p. 29 (33) (37).
22nd row: As 16th row.
23rd row: P. 29 (33) (37), k. 8, p. 18, cr. 3 lt., p. 12, cr. 3 rt., p. 18, k. 8, p. 29 (33) (37).
24th row: As 14th row.
25th row: P. 6 (2) (6), m.b., * p. 7, m.b.; repeat from * once (twice) (twice), p. 6, k. 8, p. 19, cr. 3 lt., p. 10, cr. 3 rt., p. 19, k. 8, p. 6, * m.b., p. 7; repeat from last * ending last repeat p. 6 (2) (6).
26th row: As 12th row.
27th row: P. 29 (33) (37), k. 8, p. 20, cr. 3 lt., p. 8, cr. 3 rt., p. 20, k. 8, p. 29 (33) (37).
28th row: As 10th row.
29th row: P. 29 (33) (37), k. 8, p. 21, cr. 3 lt., p. 6, cr. 3 rt., p. 21, k. 8, p. 29 (33) (37).
30th row: As 8th row.
31st row: P. 2 (6) (2), m.b., * p. 7, m.b.; repeat from * once (once) (twice), p. 10, cable 8, p. 10, m.b., p. 11, cr. 3 lt., p. 4, cr. 3 rt., p. 11, m.b., p. 10, cable 8, p. 10, * m.b., p. 7; repeat from last * ending last repeat p. 2 (6) (2).
32nd row: As 6th row.
33rd row: P. 29 (33) (37), k. 8, p. 23, cr. 3 lt., p. 2, cr. 3 rt., p. 23, k. 8, p. 29 (33) (37).
34th row: As 4th row.
35th row: P. 29 (33) (37), k. 8, p. 24, cr. 3 lt., cr. 3 rt., p. 24, k. 8, p. 29 (33) (37).
36th row: As 2nd row.

These 36 rows form the pattern. Repeat them 3 times more. Work the first 16 rows again.
To shape the armholes: Maintaining the continuity of the pattern as set, cast off 8 sts. at the beginning of the next 2 rows, then dec. 1 st. at each end of the next row and 9 (11) (13) following alternate rows.
On 92 (96) (100) sts. pattern 53 rows.
To slope the shoulders: Cast off 8 sts. at the beginning of the next 4 rows, then 8 (9) (10) sts. on the 2 following rows.
Cast off the remaining 44 (46) (48) sts.

The pocket backs *(both alike)*:
With No. 12 needles cast on 40 sts. and beginning with a k. row s.s. 48 rows, then leave these sts. on a spare needle until required.

The left front:
With No. 13 needles cast on 64 (68) (72) sts. and work 24 rows in double rib.
Change to No. 12 needles and work in pattern as follows: *1st row:* P. 6 (2) (6), m.b:, * p. 7, m.b.; repeat from * once (twice) (twice), p. 6, k. 8, p. 6, m.b., p. 3, m.b., p. 3, m.b., p. 10, k. 2.
2nd row: P. 2, k. 25, p. 8, k. 29 (33) (37).
3rd row: P. 29 (33) (37), k. 8, p. 24, cr. 3 rt.
4th row: K. 1, p. 2, k. 24, p. 8, k. 29 (33) (37).
The last 4 rows set the position of the 36 row pattern as given for back—working the first half of right side rows and second half of wrong side rows.
Now work 44 rows in pattern as set.
Pocket row: Pattern 12 (16) (20) as set, slip next 40 sts. on to a spare needle and leave at front of work. In their place, pattern across the 40 sts. of one pocket back, pattern to end.
Pattern 99 rows as set.
***To slope the front edge:* Continuing in pattern as set, dec. 1 st. at the end of the next row and at the same edge on the 2 following 4th rows.
Pattern 3 rows, ending at side seam edge.
To shape the armhole and continue to slope the front edge: While decreasing 1 st. at front edge on every 4th row from previous front edge dec., cast off 8 sts. at the beginning of the next row, then dec. 1 st. at the armhole edge on the 10 (12) (14) following alternate rows.
Still decreasing 1 st. at neck edge on every 4th row pattern 52 rows—24 (25) (26) sts.
Work 1 row back to armhole edge.
To slope the shoulder: Cast off 8 sts. at the

beginning of the next row and following alternate row. On 8 (9) (10) sts. work 1 row, then cast off.

The right front:
With No. 13 needles cast on 64 (68) (72) sts. and work 24 rows in double rib.
Change to No. 12 needles and work in pattern as follows: *1st row:* K. 2, p. 10, m.b., p. 3, m.b., p. 3, m.b., p. 6, k. 8, p. 6, * m.b., p. 7; repeat from last * ending last repeat p. 6 (2) (6).
2nd row: K. 29 (33) (37), p. 8, k. 25, p. 2.
3rd row: Cr. 3lt., p. 24, k. 8, p. 29 (33) (37).
4th row: K. 29 (33) (37), p. 8, k. 24, p. 2, k. 1.
The last 4 rows set the position of the pattern given for back—working the second half of all right side rows and the first half of all wrong side rows.
Work 44 rows in pattern as set.
Pocket row: Pattern 12, slip next 40 sts. on to a spare needle and leave at front of work, in their place pattern across the 40 sts. of one pocket back, pattern to end.
Pattern 100 rows as set.
Now work as given for left front from ** to end.

The sleeves *(both alike)*:
With No. 13 needles cast on 64 (68) (72) sts. and work 60 rows in double rib.
Change to No. 12 needles and work in pattern as follows:
1st row: P. 5 (7) (1), m.b., * p. 7, m.b.; repeat from * once (once) (twice) more, p. 6, k. 8, p. 6, * m.b., p. 7; repeat from last * ending last repeat p. 5 (7) (1).
2nd row: K. 28 (30) (32), p. 8, k. 28 (30) (32).
3rd row: P. 28 (30) (32), k. 8, p. 28 (30) (32).
4th and 5th rows: As 2nd and 3rd rows.
6th row: As 2nd row.
7th row: P. 1 (3) (5), m.b., * p. 7, m.b.; repeat from * once, p. 10, cable 8, p. 10, * m.b., p. 7; repeat from last * ending last repeat p. 1 (3) (5).
8th to 12th rows: As 2nd to 6th rows.
These 12 rows form the pattern. Continuing in pattern as set, inc. 1 st. at each end of the next row and the 15 following 8th rows.
On 96 (100) (104) sts. pattern 11 rows.
To shape the sleevetop: Cast off 8 sts. at the beginning of the next 2 rows, then dec. 1 st. at each end of the next row and the 19 (21) (23) following alternate rows.
Cast off 4 sts. at the beginning of the next 8 rows. Cast off the 8 remaining sts.

The pocket tops *(both alike)*:
With right side of work facing rejoin wool to the 40 sts. left on spare needle and using No. 13 needles work 6 rows in double rib, then cast off.

The front bands:
First join shoulder seams. With No. 13 needles cast on 12 sts. and work 6 rows in single rib.
1st Buttonhole row: Rib 4, cast off 4 sts., rib to end.
2nd Buttonhole row: Rib 4, turn, cast on 4, turn, rib to end.
Rib 18 rows.
Repeat the last 20 rows 6 times, then work the 2 buttonhole rows again.
Now continue in rib, until the band is long enough to fit up right front with last buttonhole in line with first front dec.—along back neck and down left front. Cast off when correct length is assured.

To make up the cardigan:
Pin all pieces out to size. Press all parts except the ribbing on the wrong side with a warm iron over a damp cloth. Set in sleeves. Join sleeve and side seams. Sew front bands in place. Sew pocket backs and row ends of pocket tops in position. Press seams. Sew on buttons.

SINGLE CREAM

SEE MODEL ON LEFT, FACING PAGE

This simple classic sweater has a sailor collar. It looks sensational knitted in black and dressed up with pretty jewellery for the evening, while in cream or grey it is comfortable and adaptable for the daytime.

Materials:
16 (17) (18) 20 gram balls of Sirdar Wash n Wear Crepe 4-ply; a pair each of No. 12 and No. 13 knitting needles.

Tension:
Work at a tension of 16 stitches and 20 rows to 5 cm (2 in.) over the stocking stitch using No. 12 needles. If you have difficulty in obtaining the correct tension using the size needles suggested, use larger or smaller ones accordingly.

Abbreviations:
K., knit; p., purl; st., stitch; tog., together; dec., decrease (by working 2 sts. tog.); inc., increase (by working twice into same st.); s.s., stocking stitch (k. on the right side and p. on wrong side); double rib is k. 2 and p. 2 alternately; sl., slip; p.s.s.o., pass sl. st. over; y.r.n., yarn round needle; p. 2 tog. b., p. 2 tog. through back of sts.; s.s.k., sl. 1, k. 1, p.s.s.o.; k. 1b., k. 1 through back of st.; garter stitch is k. plain on every row.

Note:
The instructions are given for the small size. Where they vary work the figures in the first brackets for the medium size or the figures in the second brackets for the large size.

Measurements:
The measurements are given in centimetres followed by inches in square brackets.

small (10)	medium (12)	large (14)
All round at underarms		
80 [32]	85 [34]	90 [36]
Side seam		
40 [16]	40 [16]	40 [16]
Length		
59.5 [23¾]	60 [24]	60.5 [24¼]
Sleeve seam		
38 [15¼]	38 [15¼]	38 [15¼]

The back:
With No. 13 needles cast on 130 (138) (146) sts. and work 28 rows in double rib.
Change to No. 12 needles and work in pattern as follows:
1st row: K. 1, * y.r.n., k. 1b, y.r.n., s.s.k., k. 5; repeat from * ending last repeat k. 6.
2nd row: P. 5, * p. 2 tog.b., p. 7; repeat from * ending last repeat p. 4.
3rd row: K. 1, * y.r.n., k. 1b., y.r.n., k. 2, s.s.k., k. 3; repeat from * ending last repeat k. 4.
4th row: P. 3, * p. 2 tog.b., p. 7; repeat from * ending last repeat p. 6.
5th row: K. 1, * k. 1b., y.r.n., k. 4, s.s.k., k. 1, y.r.n.; repeat from * until 1 remains, k. 1.
6th row: P. 2, * p. 2 tog.b., p. 7; repeat from * to end.
7th row: K. 6, * k. 2 tog., y.r.n., k. 1b., y.r.n., k. 5; repeat from * ending last repeat k. 1.
8th row: P. 4, * p. 2 tog., p. 7; repeat from * ending last repeat p. 5.
9th row: K. 4, * k. 2 tog., k. 2, y.r.n., k. 1b., y.r.n., k. 3; repeat from * ending last repeat k. 1.
10th row: P. 6, * p. 2 tog., p. 7; repeat from * ending last repeat p. 3.
11th row: K. 1, * y.r.n., k. 1, k. 2 tog., k. 4, y.r.n., k. 1b.; repeat from * until 1 remains, k. 1.
12th row: * P. 7, p. 2 tog.; repeat from * until 2 remain, p. 2.
These 12 rows form the pattern; repeat them 10 times more, then work the first 4 rows again.
To shape the armholes: Maintaining the continuity of the pattern as set, cast off 8 sts. *at each end* of the next row, work 1 row straight then dec. 1 st. at each end of the next row and the 9 (11) (13) following alternate rows.
On 94 (98) (102) sts. pattern 51 (49) (47) rows.
To slope the shoulders: Cast off 8 (9) (10) sts. at the beginning and end of the next row and following alternate row, then 7 sts. on the next alternate row.
Work 1 row, then cast off the 48 remaining sts.

The pocket backs *(two alike)*:
With No. 12 needles cast on 32 sts. and beginning with a k. row s.s. 34 rows, then leave these sts. on a stitch-holder until required.

The front:
Work as given for back until 34 rows have been worked in pattern.
Pocket row: Pattern 17 (21) (25), slip next 32 sts. on to a stitch-holder and leave at

front of work, in their place pattern across the 32 sts. of one pocket back, pattern 32, slip next 32 sts. on to a stitch-holder and leave at front of work, in their place, pattern across the 32 sts. of other pocket back, pattern to end.

Pattern 101 rows.

To shape the armholes: Work as given for back armhole shaping.

On 94 (98) (102) sts. pattern 7 (5) (3) rows.

Now divide the sts. for the neck: *Next row:* Pattern 41 (43) (45) as set and leave these sts. on a spare needle until required for left front shoulder, slip the next 12 sts. on to a safety pin until required, rejoin yarn and work to end of row and continue on these sts. for the right front shoulder.

The right front shoulder:

Pattern 1 row. Dec. 1 st. at the beginning—neck edge—of the next row and the 17 following alternate rows.

Pattern 9 rows—23 (25) (27) sts.

To slope the shoulder: Cast off 8 (9) (10) sts. at the end of the next row and following alternate row. Work 1 row, then cast off the 7 sts.

The left front shoulder:

With wrong side of work facing rejoin yarn to the inner edge of sts. left on spare needle. Pattern 1 row.

Dec. 1 st. at the end—neck edge—of the next row and the 17 following alternate rows.

Pattern 9 rows—23 (25) (27) sts.

To slope the shoulder: Cast off 8 (9) (10) sts. at the *beginning* of the next row and following alternate row. Work 1 row, then cast off the 7 remaining sts.

The yoke collar:

With No. 13 needles cast on 100 (104) (108) sts. and k. 8 rows.

Change to No. 12 needles and work in s.s. with garter st. edging as follows:

1st row: All k.

2nd row: K. 4, p. until 4 remain, k. 4.

Repeat the last 2 rows 32 times.

Now divide the sts. for the neck:

Next row: K. 26 (28) (30) and leave these sts. on a spare needle until required for right shoulder, cast off 48 sts., k. to end and continue on these 26 (28) (30) sts. for the left shoulder.

The left shoulder:

Work 13 rows in s.s. with garter st. edging as set.

Inc. 1 st. at the beginning of the next row and the 17 following alternate rows.

On 44 (46) (48) sts., work 1 row, then leave these sts. on a spare needle until required.

The right shoulder:

With wrong side of work facing, rejoin yarn to the inner edge of sts. left on spare needle at right shoulder. Work 13 rows in s.s. with garter st. edging as set.

Inc. 1 st. at the end of the next row and the 17 following alternate rows.

Work 1 row back to side edge.

Now join the sts. for the front:

Next row: K. across the 44 (46) (48) sts. of right shoulder, cast on 12 sts., then k. across the 44 (46) (48) sts. of left shoulder.

On 100 (104) (108) sts., work 15 rows in s.s. with garter st. edgings.

Change to No. 13 needles and k. 8 rows.

Cast off.

The sleeves *(both alike)***:**

With No. 13 needles cast on 98 (98) (106) sts. and work 14 rows in double rib.

Change to No. 12 needles and work 140 rows in pattern as given for back.

To shape the armhole: Cast off 8 sts. at each end of the next row, work 1 row, then dec. 1 st. at each end of the next row and the 19 (20) (21) following alternate rows.

Work 1 row—42 (40) (46) sts.

Cast off 5 sts. at the beginning and end of the next row and the 2 following alternate rows. Work 1 row. Cast off the 12 (10) (16) remaining sts.

The pocket tops *(both alike)***:**

With right side of work facing rejoin yarn to the 32 sts. left on stitch-holder and using No. 13 needles, k. 8 rows. Cast off.

The bow knot:

With wrong side of work facing rejoin yarn to the 12 sts. left on safety pin at centre front neck and using No. 13 needles k. 16 rows, then cast off.

To make up the sweater:

Press all parts except the ribbing with a warm iron over a damp cloth. Join shoulder seams. Set in sleeves. Join sleeve and side seams. Neatly sew pocket backs and row ends of pocket tops in place. Now sew yoke in place all round neck edge except for the 12 sts. cast off at centre front. Wrap *bow knot* at centre front over the yoke at centre front and sew cast off edge of bow knot in place at base of bow knot at centre front neck. Press seams.

SWANSONG

Pure Shetland wool and lurex combine to make this really versatile twinset. Both garments can be worn on their own, or as a twinset for parties or everyday wear. The pretty sweater, striped and collared in lurex, looks lovely with the cardigan which has a bobble drawstring at the neck. The yarns for both garments are available from The Patricia Roberts Knitting Shop, 60 Kinnerton Street, London S.W.1. Mail order service available. Among the colours available are lemon, Shetland blue, pale green and cherry red and pink and lilac.

Materials:
For the sweater: 8 ounces of Special Shetland wool 4-ply equivalent in main colour and 3 25 gram balls of Robin Moonlight in each of 2 contrast colours; 2 buttons; a pair each of No.12 and No. 13 knitting needles; a 2.50 crochet hook.
For the cardigan: 11 ounces of Special Shetland wool 4-ply equivalent in main colour and 3 25 gram balls of Robin Moonlight in each of 2 contrast shades; a pair each of No.12 and No.13 knitting needles; 11 buttons.

Tension:
15 stitches and 19 rows to 5 cm (2 in.) over the stocking stitch using No.12 needles. If you cannot obtain the correct tension using needles of the size suggested, use larger or smaller ones accordingly.

Abbreviations:
K.,knit; p.,purl; st.,stitch; tog.,together; inc.,increase (by working twice into same st.); dec.,decrease (by working 2 sts. tog.); single rib is k.1 and p.1 alternately; s.s.,stocking stitch (k. on the right side and p. on the wrong side); m., main colour—Shetland; a.,first contrast colour; b., second contrast; sl., slip; y.r.n., yarn round needle; d.c., double crochet; ch., chain.

Note:
The instructions are given for the small size. Where they vary, work the figures in the first brackets for the medium size or the figures in the second brackets for the large size.

Measurements:
The following measurements are given in centimetres first, followed by inches in brackets.

THE SWEATER

small (10)	medium (12)	large (14)
All round at underarms		
80 (32)	85 (34)	90 (36)
Side seam		
40 (16)	40 (16)	40 (16)
Length		
59.5 (23¾)	60 (24)	60.5 (24¼)
Sleeve seam excluding ribbing		
12.5 (5)	12.5 (5)	12.5 (5)

THE CARDIGAN

All round at underarms		
84 (33½)	89 (35½)	94 (37½)
Side seam		
41 (16½)	41 (16½)	41 (16½)
Length		
61 (24½)	62 (25)	64 (25½)
Sleeve seam excluding ribbing		
37.5 (15)	37.5 (15)	37.5 (15)

THE SWEATER

The back:
With No.13 needles and m. cast on 120 (128) (136) sts. and work 22 rows in single rib.
Change to No.12 needles and beginning with a k. row s.s.2 rows.
Continuing in s.s. work in stripes as follows: 2 rows a., 10 rows m., 2 rows b., 10 rows m. These 24 rows form the stripe sequence, repeat them 4 more times, then work the first 12 rows again.
To shape the armholes: Continuing in stripe sequence as set, cast off 8sts. at the beginning of the next 2 rows, then dec. 1st. at each end of the next row and the 7 (9) (11) following alternate rows.
On 88 (92) (96) sts. s.s.53 rows.
To slope the shoulders: Cast off 8sts. at the beginning of the next 4 rows, then 7 (8) (9) sts. on the 2 following rows.
Cast off the 42 (44) (46) remaining sts.

The front:
Work as given for back until the 24 stripe sequence rows have been worked 5 times altogether, then work the first 11 rows again.
Now divide the sts. for the neck: *Next row* (wrong side): P.60 (64) (68) and leave these sts. on a spare needle until required for right half front, p. to end and continue on these 60 (64) (68) sts. for the left half front.
The left half front: To shape the armhole: Cast off 8sts. at the beginning of the next row. Work 1 row back to armhole edge. Dec. 1st. at the beginning—armhole edge on the next row and the 7 (9) (11) following alternate rows.
On 44 (46) (48) sts. pattern 22 rows.
To shape the neck: Cast off 10 (11) (12) sts. at the beginning of the next row, then dec. 1st. at the neck edge on each of the next 11 rows.
On 23 (24) (25) sts. work 19 rows.
To slope the shoulder: Cast off 8sts. at the beginning of the next row and following alternate rows.
On 7 (8) (9) sts. work 1 row, then cast off.
The right front shoulder: With right side of work facing rejoin yarn to inner edge of sts. left on spare needle and work to end of row. Now work as given for left front shoulder to end.

The sleeves *(both alike):*
With No.13 needles and m. cast on 80 (84) (88) sts. and work 12 rows in single rib.
Change to No.12 needles and beginning with a k. row s.s.2 rows.
Now while working in stripe sequence of 2 rows b., 10 rows m., 2 rows a., 10 rows m., work 10 rows straight, then inc. 1st. at each end of next row and the 2 following 12th rows.
On 86 (90) (94) sts. work 13 rows in stripe sequence as set.
To shape the sleevetop: Cast off 8sts. at the beginning of the next 2 rows, then dec. 1st. at each end of the next row and the 15 following alternate rows.
On 38 (42) (46) sts. work 1 row.
Dec. 1st. at each end of the next 4 (6) (8) rows—30 sts.
Cast off 3sts. at the beginning of the next 6 rows, then cast off the remaining 12sts.

The left front neckband:
With right side of work facing rejoin m. and using crochet hook work 20d.c. along row ends of left front neck opening, turn, work 2 rows of d.c. over d.c., then fasten off.

The right front neckband:
With right side of work facing rejoin m. and using crochet hook work 20d.c. along row ends of right front neck opening, turn, work 1 row of d.c. over d.c., turn.
Next row: 2ch. for first d.c., 1d.c. into each of next 3d.c., 3ch., miss 2d.c., 1 d.c. into each of next 8d.c., 3ch., miss 2d.c., 1ch. into each of next 4d.c. Fasten off.

The collar:
With No.12 needles and a. cast on 11sts. and work in pattern as follows:
1st row: Sl.1, k.2 tog., y.r.n., y.r.n., k.2 tog., k.2 tog., y.r.n., k.1, y.r.n., k.3.
2nd row: Sl.1, k.8, p.1, k.2.
3rd row: Sl.1, k.4, k.2 tog., y.r.n., k.2, y.r.n., k.3.
4th row: Sl.1, k.12.
5th row: Sl.1, k.4, k.2 tog., y.r.n., k.3, y.r.n., k.3.
6th row: Sl.1, k.13.
7th row: Sl.1, k.2 tog., y.r.n., y.r.n., k.2 tog., k.2 tog., y.r.n., k.1, y.r.n., k.2 tog., k.1, y.r.n., k.3.
8th row: Sl.1, k.11, p.1, k.2.
9th row: Sl.1, k.4, k.2 tog., y.r.n., k.2, y.r.n., k.2 tog., k.1, y.r.n., k.3.
10th row: Sl.1, k.15.
11th row: Sl. 1, k.4, k.2 tog., y.r.n., k.3, y.r.n., k.2 tog., k.1, y.r.n., k.3.
12th row: Sl.1, k.16.
13th row: Sl.1, k.2 tog., y.r.n., y.r.n., k.2 tog., k.2 tog., y.r.n., k.1, y.r.n., k.2 tog., k.1, y.r.n., k.2 tog., k.1, y.r.n., k.3.
14th row: Sl.1, k.14, p.1, k.2.
15th row: Sl.1, k.4, k.2 tog., y.r.n., k.2, y.r.n., k.2 tog., k.1, y.r.n., k.2 tog., k.1, y.r.n., k.3.
16th row: Sl.1, k.18.
17th row: Sl.1, k.4, k.2 tog., y.r.n., k.3, y.r.n., k.2 tog., k.1, y.r.n., k.2 tog., k.1, y.r.n., k.3.
18th row: Sl.1, k.19.
19th row: Sl.1, k.2 tog., y.r.n., y.r.n., k.2 tog., k.2 tog., y.r.n., k.1, y.r.n., k.2 tog., k.1, y.r.n., k.2 tog., k.1, y.r.n., k.2 tog., k.1, y.r.n., k.3.
20th row: Sl.1, k.17, p.1, k.2.
21st row: Sl.1, k.4, k.2 tog., y.r.n., k.2, y.r.n., k.2 tog., k.1, y.r.n., k.2 tog., k.1, y.r.n., k.2 tog., k.1, y.r.n., k.3.
22nd row: Sl. 1, k.21.
23rd row: Sl.1, k.4, k.2 tog., y.r.n., k.3, y.r.n., k.2 tog., k.1, y.r.n., k.2 tog., k.1, y.r.n., k.2 tog., k.1, y.r.n., k.3.
24th row: Sl. 1, k.22.
25th row: Sl.1, k.2 tog., y.r.n., y.r.n., k.2 tog., k.2 tog., y.r.n., k.1, y.r.n., k.2 tog., k.1, y.r.n., k.2 tog., k.1, y.r.n., k.2 tog., k.1, y.r.n., k.2 tog., k.1, y.r.n., k.3.
26th row: Sl.1, k.20, p.1, k.2.
27th row: Sl.1, k.4, k.2 tog., y.r.n., k.2, y.r.n., k.2 tog., k.1, y.r.n., k.2 tog., k.1, y.r.n., k.2 tog., k.1, y.r.n., k.2 tog., k.1, y.r.n., k.3.
28th row: Sl.1, k.24.
29th row: Sl.1, k.4, k.2 tog., y.r.n., k.18.
30th row: Cast off 14, k. to end—11sts.
These 30 rows form the pattern; repeat them 5 more times, then cast off.

To make up the sweater:
Press all parts except the ribbing and the collar lightly on the wrong side with a warm iron over a damp cloth. Press collar with a cool iron over a dry cloth. Join shoulder seams. Set in sleeves. Join sleeve and side seams. Neatly sew collar in place. Press seams. Sew on buttons.

THE CARDIGAN

The back:
With No.13 needles and m. cast on 124 (132) (140) sts. and work 12 rows in single rib.
Change to No.12 needles and beginning with a k. row s.s.146 rows.
To shape the armholes: Cast off 8sts. at the beginning of the next 2 rows, then dec. 1st. at each end of the next row and the 8 (10) (12) following alternate rows.
On 90 (94) (98) sts. s.s.53 rows.
To slope the shoulders: Cast off 8sts. at the beginning of the next 4 rows, then 7 (8) (9) sts. on the 2 following rows.

Cast off the 44(46)(48) remaining sts.

The pocket backs *(both alike)*:
With No 12 needles and m. cast on 38sts. and beginning with a k. row s.s.42 rows, then leave these sts. on a stitch holder until required.

The left front:
With No.13 needles and m. cast on 60 (64)(68) sts. and work 12 rows in single rib.
Change to No.12 needles and work the swans pattern in the following way. This is worked entirely in s.s. beginning with a k. row, so only the colour details are given.
1st row: 25(29)(33) m., 3b., 32m.
2nd row: 32m., 3b.; 25(29)(33) m.
3rd row: 26(30)(34) m., 5b., 29m.
4th row: 28m., 5b., 27(31)(35) m.
These 4 rows set the position of the swans motif given in the chart. Now work the 5th to 36th rows from the chart for left front as set, then work the first 6 rows again.
Pocket row: K.11(15)(19), slip next 38sts. onto a stitch holder and leave at front of work and in their place pattern as set across the 38sts. of one pocket back, k. to end.
Now continuing in s.s. with swans motifs in contrast colours as set work 103 more rows.
***To shape the armhole:* Continuing in swans pattern as set, cast off 8sts. at the beginning of the next row. Work 1 row straight, dec. 1st. at the beginning of the next row, then work 1 row back to armhole edge.
This completes the swans motifs pattern. Break off a. and b. and continue with m. only.
Dec. 1st. at the beginning of the next row and the 7(9)(11) following alternate rows.
On 43(45)(47) sts. s.s.22 rows.
To shape the neck: Cast off 8(9)(10) sts. at the beginning of the next row, then dec. 1st. at neck edge on each of the next 12 rows.
On 23(24)(25) sts. s.s. 18 rows.
To slope the shoulder: Cast off 8sts. at the beginning of the next row and following alternate row. On 7(8)(9) sts. work 1 row, then cast off.

The right front:
With No.13 needles and m. cast on 60 (64)(68) sts. and work 12 rows in single rib.
Change to No.12 needles and work the swans pattern as follows:
1st row: 32m., 3b., 25(29)(33) m.
2nd row: 25(29)(33) m., 3b., 32m.
3rd row: 29m., 5b., 26(30)(34) m.
4th row: 27(31)(35) m., 5b., 28m.
Now work the 5th to 36th pattern rows from the chart for right front, then work the first 6 rows again.
Pocket row: K.11, slip next 38sts. on to a stitch holder and leave at front of work and in their place pattern as set across the 38sts. of one pocket back, k. to end.
Continuing to work swan motifs as set, s.s.104 rows more.
Now work as given for left front from ** to end.

The pocket tops *(both alike)*:
With right side of work facing rejoin m. to 38sts. left on stitch holder and using No.13 needles work 8 rows in single rib, then cast off.

The sleeves *(both alike)*:
With No.13 needles and m. cast on 76 (80)(84) sts. and work 12 rows in single rib.
Change to No.12 needles and beginning with a k. row s.s.18 rows.
Inc. 1st. at each end of the next row and the 6 following 18th rows.
On 90(94)(98) sts. s.s. 17 rows.
To shape the sleevetop: Cast off 8sts. at the beginning of the next 2 rows, then dec. 1 st. at each end of the next row and the 15 following alternate rows.
On 42(46)(50) sts. work 1 row.
Dec. 1st. at each end of the next 6(8)(10) rows—30sts.
Cast off 3 sts. at the beginning of the next 6 rows, then cast off the remaining 12sts.

The neckband:
First join shoulder seams. With right side of work facing rejoin m. and using No.13 needles pick up and k.42(43)(44) sts. from left front neck edge, 44(46)(48) sts. from back neck edge and 42(43)(44) sts. from right front neck edge—128 (132)(136) sts.
Work 1 row in single rib.
Eyelet row: Rib 1, * y.r.n., k.2 tog., rib 2; repeat from * ending last repeat rib 1.
Now work 9 rows in single rib.
Cast off loosely.

The left frontband:
With No.13 needles and m. cast on 12 sts. and work 212(216)(218) rows in single rib, then cast off in rib.

The right frontband:
With No.13 needles and m. cast on 12 sts. and work 6(8)(10) rows in single rib.
1st Buttonhole row: Rib 4, cast off 4, rib to end.
2nd Buttonhole row: Rib 4, turn, cast on 4, turn, rib to end.
Rib 18 rows.
Repeat the last 20 rows 9 times, then work the 2 buttonhole rows again.
Rib 4(6)(6) more rows, then cast off.

The cord:
Cut 2 lengths of a. and 2 lengths of b. each 80 in. long, knot one end. Twist yarns together until firm, fold cord in half and knot cut ends allowing cords to twist together to form 1 cord $27\frac{1}{2}$ in. long.

The bobbles *(make two alike)*:
Cut 2 circles of card 5 cm (2 in.) in diameter with a hole at centre 1.5 cm ($\frac{1}{2}$ in.) in diameter. Now make bobble as usual using b.

To make up the cardigan:
Press all parts except the ribbing with a warm iron over a damp cloth. Set in sleeves. Join sleeve and side seams. Neatly sew pocket backs in place, then sew row ends of pocket tops in position. Sew front bands in position. Sew on buttons. Press seams. Slot cord through eyelet holes in neckband and secure a bobble at each end of cord.

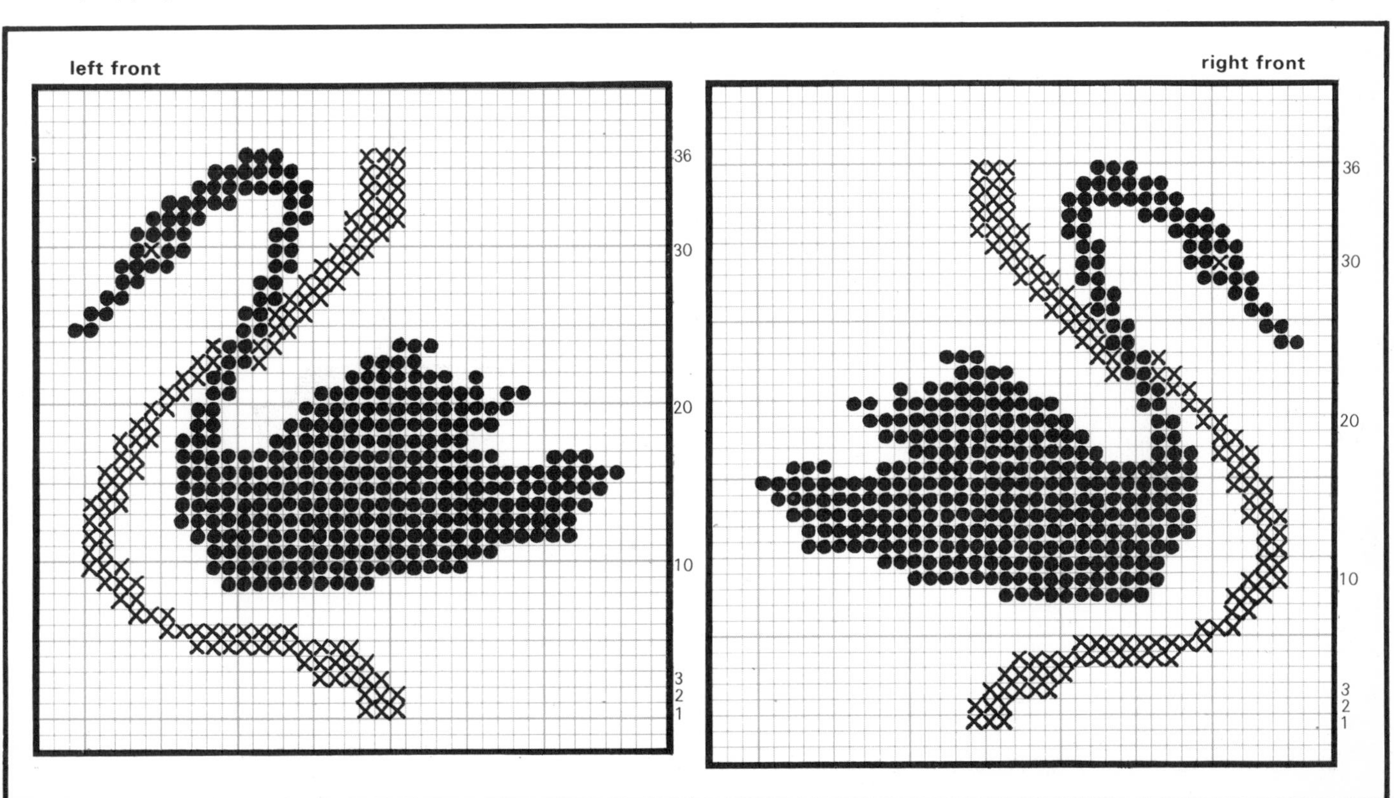

SILVER

Look glamorous in the office, fantastic on the beach or shimmering over dinner in this little waistcoat. Wear it with a tweed suit, a pretty skirt or even with your bikini.

Materials:
9 (10) (11) 20 gram balls of Wendy Minuit, a pair each of size 2¾ mm (No. 12) and size 2¼ mm (No. 13) Aero knitting needles; a medium sized Aero crochet hook; a fine Aero cable needle; 6 buttons

Tension:
16 stitches and 28 rows to 5 cm (2 in.) over the moss stitch using size 2¼ mm (No. 13) needles and one repeat of the Aran pattern 75 (79) (83) stitches to 19 (20) (21) cm (7½ (8) (8½) in.) in width and 50 rows—1 repeat of the pattern to 10.5 cm (4¼ in.) in length.

Abbreviations:
K., knit; p., purl; st., stitch; tog., together; dec., decrease (by working 2 sts. tog.); inc., increase (by working twice into same st.); y.f., yarn forward; y.r.n., yarn round needle; m.b., make bobble thus, k. 1, y.r.n., k. 1, y.r.n. k. 1 all into next stitch., turn, p. 5, turn, k. 5, turn, p. 5, turn, pass 2nd, 3rd, 4th, and 5th sts. on left hand needle over first st., y.f., p. 1 remaining st; cable 6 thus, slip next 3 sts. onto cable needle and leave at front of work, k. 3, then k. 3 from cable needle; c. 3rt., cross 3 right thus, slip next st. onto cable needle at back of work, k. 2, then p. 1 from cable needle; c. 3lt., cross 3 left thus, slip next 2 sts. onto cable needle at front of work, p. 1 then k. 2 from cable needle; cable 6 b., as cable 6, but leaving sts. on cable needle at back of work; cr. 5, thus, slip next 2 sts. onto a cable needle at front of work, k. 2, p. 1, then k. 2 from cable needle; double rib is k. 2 and p. 2 alternately; up 1, pick up the loop which lies between the needles, slip it onto left hand needle, then k. into back of it; s.s. stocking stitch is k. on the right side and p. on the wrong side; single rib is k. 1 and p. 1 alternately 3 from 1 is k. 1 p. 1, k. 1 all into next stitch; d.c., double crochet.

Note:
The instructions are given for the small size. Where they vary, work the figures in the first brackets for the medium size or the figures in the second brackets for the large size.

Measurements:

The measurements are given in centimetres followed by inches in square brackets.

small	medium	large
All round at underarms		
80[32]	85 [34]	90 [36]
Side seam		
22.5 [9]	22.5 [9]	22.5 [9]
Length		
44 [17½]	44 [17¾]	45 [18]

THE WAISTCOAT

The back:
With size 2¼ mm (No. 13) needles cast on 129 (137) (145) sts. and work in moss stitch as follows:
1st row: k. 1, * p. 1, k. 1; repeat from * to end.
2nd row: k. 1, * p. 1, k. 1; repeat from * to end. The last 2 rows form the pattern, repeat them 62 times more.
To shape the armholes: Continuing in moss st. as set, cast off 4 sts. at the beginning of the next 2 rows, then dec. 1 st. at each end of the next row and the 7 (9) (11) following alternate rows.
On 105 (109) (113) sts. pattern 97 rows more.
To slope the shoulders: Cast off 14 sts. at the beginning of the next 2 rows and 14 (15) (16) sts. on the 2 following rows.
Cast off the remaining 49 (51) (53) sts.

The pocket backs *(both alike):*
With size 2¼ mm (No. 13) needles cast on 33 sts. and work as given for back until 28 rows have been worked in moss stitch stripe pattern, then leave these sts. on a spare needle until required.

The left front:
With size 2¼ mm (No. 13) needles cast on 3 sts. and work 2 rows in moss stitch.
Continuing in moss st. as set and working the extra sts. into the pattern as they occur inc. 1 st. at each end of the next 34 (36) (38) rows.
On 71 (75) (79) sts. work 11 rows in moss st. as set.
Now divide the sts. for the front band and pocket as follows:
Next row: Pattern 12 and leave these sts. on a safety pin until required for front band, pattern 13 (15) (17), cast off next 33 sts. for pocket, pattern to end.
2nd pocket row: Pattern 13 (15) (17) across the 33 sts. of one pocket back, pattern to end—59 (63) (67) sts.
Increase row: K. 3 (1) (3) * up 1, k. 3 (4) (4) up 1, k. 4; repeat from * ending last repeat k. 4 (2) (4)—75 (79) (83) sts.**
Change to size 2¾ (12) needles and work in pattern as follows:
1st row: K. 1, p. 4, k. 1, p. 4, m.b., p. 4 (6) (8) k. 6, p. 2, k. 5, p. 7, k. 2, m.b., k. 2, p. 7, k. 5, p. 2, k. 6, p. 4 (6) (8), m.b., p. 4, k. 1, p. 4, k. 1.
******2nd row:*** p. 1, k. 4, p. 1, k. 4, p.1, k. 4 (6) (8), p. 6, k. 2, p.5, k. 7, p.5, k. 7, p. 5, k. 2, p. 6, k. 4 (6) (8), p. 1, k. 4, p. 1, k. 4, p. 1.
3rd row: K. 1, p. 4, k. 1, p. 3, m.b., k. 1, m.b., p. 3 (5) (7) cable 6, p. 2, k. 5, p. 6, c. 3rt, k. 1, c. 3lt, p. 6, k. 5, p. 2, cable 6, p. 3 (5) (7), m.b., k. 1, m.b., p. 3, k. 1, p. 4, k. 1.
4th row: P. 1, k. 4, p. 1, k. 4, p. 1, k. 4 (6) (8), p. 6, k. 2, p. 5, k.6, p. 2, k. 1, p. 1, k. 1, p. 2, k. 6, p. 5, k. 2, p. 6, k. 4 (6) (8), p. 1,, k. 4, p. 1, k. 4, p. 1.
5th row: K. 1, p. 4, k. 1, p. 2, m.b., p. 1, m.b., p. 1, m.b., p. 2 (4) (6), k. 6, p. 2, k. 5, p. 5, c. 3rt., p. 1, k. 1, p. 1, c. 3lt., p. 5, k. 5, p. 2, k. 6, p. 2 (4) (6), m.b., p. 1, m.b., p. 1, m.b., p. 2, k. 1, p. 4, k. 1.
6th row: P. 1, k. 4, p. 1, k. 4, p. 1, k. 4 (6) (8), p. 6, k. 2, p. 5, k. 5, p. 3, k. 1, p. 1, k. 1, p. 3, k. 5, p. 5, k. 2, p. 6, k. 4 (6) (8), p. 1, k. 4, p. 1, k. 4, p. 1.
7th row: M.b., p. 4, k. 1, p. 4, k. 1, p. 4 (6) (8), k. 6, p. 2, k. 2, m.b., k. 2, p. 4, c. 3rt., k. 1, p. 1, k. 1, p. 1, k. 1, c. 3lt, p. 4, k. 2, m.b., k. 2, p. 2, k. 6, p.4 (6) (8), k. 1, p. 4, k. 1, p. 4, m.b.
8th row: P. 1, k. 4, p. 1, k. 4, p. 1, k. 4 (6) (8), p. 6, k. 2, p. 5, k. 4, p. 2,k. 1, p. 1, k. 1, p. 1, k. 1, p. 1, k. 1, p. 2, k. 4, p. 5, k. 2, p. 6, k. 4 (6) (8), p. 1, k. 4, p. 1, k. 4, p. 1.
9th row: k. 1, m.b., p. 3, k. 1, p. 4, k. 1, p. 4 (6) (8), k. 6, p. 2, k. 1, m.b., k. 1, m.b., k. 1, p. 3, c. 3rt., p. 1, k. 1, p. 1, k. 1,p. 1, k. 1, p. 1, c. 3lt., p. 3, k. 1, m.b., k. 1, m.b., k. 1, p. 2, k. 6, p. 4 (6) (8), k. 1, p. 4, k. 1, p. 3, m.b., k. 1.
10th row: P. 1, k. 4, p. 1, k. 4, p. 1, k. 4 (6) (8), p. 6, k. 2, p. 5, k. 3, p. 3, k. 1, p. 1, k. 1, p. 1, k. 1, p. 1, k. 1, p. 3, k. 3, p. 5, k. 2, p. 6, k. 4 (6) (8), p. 1, k. 4, p. 1, k. 4, p. 1.
11th row: m.b., p. 1, m.b., p. 2, k. 1, p. 4, k. 1, p. 4 (6) (8), cable 6, p. 2, k. 5, p. 2, c. 3rt., k. 1, p. 1, k. 1, p. 1, k., 1, p. 1, k. 1, p. 1, k. 1, c. 3lt., p. 2, k. 5, p. 2, cable 6, p. 4 (6) (8), k. 1, p. 4, k. 1, p. 2, m.b., p. 1, m.b.
12th row: p. 1, k. 4, p. 1, k. 4, p. 1, k. 4 (6) (8), p. 6, k. 2, p. 5, k. 2, p. 2, k. 1, p. 1, k. 1, p. 1, k. 1, p. 1, k. 1, p. 1, k. 1, p. 1, k. 1, p. 2, k. 2, p. 5 k. 2, p. 6, k. 4 (6) (8), p. 1, k. 4, p. 1, k. 4, p. 1.
13th to 24th rows: As 1 to 12th rows.
25th row: p. 7, cr. 5, p. 5, k. 9, p. 2, k. 1, p. 3 (5) (7), m.b., p. 2, cr. 5, p. 2, m.b., p. 3, (5) (7), k. 1, p. 2, k. 9, p. 5, cr. 5, p. 7.
26th row: K. 7, p. 2, k. 1, p. 2, k. 5, p. 9, k. 2, p. 1, k. 6 (8) (10), p. 2, k. 1, p. 2, k. 6 (8) (10), p. 1, k. 2, p. 9, k. 5, p. 2, k. 1, p. 2, k. 7.
27th row: P. 6, c. 3rt., p. 1, c. 3lt., p. 4, cable 6, k. 3, p. 2, k. 1, p. 5 (7) (9), c. 3rt., p. 1, c. 3lt., p. 5 (7) (9), k. 1, p. 2, k. 3, cable 6b, p. 4, c. 3rt, p. 1, c. 3lt., p. 6.
28th row: K. 6, p. 2, k. 3, p. 2, k. 4, p. 9, k. 2, p. 1, k. 5 (7) (9), p. 2, k. 3, p. 2, k. 5 (7) (9), p. 1, k. 2, p. 9, k. 4, p. 2, k. 3, p. 2, k. 6.
29th row: P. 5, c. 3rt., p. 3, c. 3lt., p. 3, k. 9, p. 2, k. 1, p. 4 (6) (8), c. 3rt., p. 3, c. 3lt, p. 4 (6) (8), k. 1, p. 2, k. 9, p. 3, c. 3rt., p. 3, c. 3lt, p. 5.
30th row: K. 5, p. 2, k. 5, p. 2, k. 3, p. 9, k. 2, p. 1, k. 4 (6) (8), p. 2, k. 5, p. 2, k. 4 (6) (8), p. 1, k. 2, p. 9, k. 3, p. 2, k. 5, p. 2, k. 5.
31st row: P. 1, m.b., p. 3, k. 2, p. 5, k. 2, p. 3, k. 3, cable 6b, p. 2, k. 1, p. 3 (5) (7), c. 3rt., p. 2, m.b., p. 2, c. 3lt., p. 3 (5) (7), k. 1, p. 2, cable 6, k. 3, p. 3, k. 2, p. 5, k. 2, p. 3, m.b., p. 1.
32nd row: K. 5, p. 2, k. 5, p. 2, k. 3, p. 9, k. 2, p. 1, k. 3 (5) (7), p. 2, k. 7, p. 2, k. 3 (5) (7), p. 1, k. 2, p.9, k. 3, p. 2, k. 5, p. 2, k. 5.
33rd row: P. 5, c. 3lt., p. 3, c. 3rt., p. 3, k. 9, p. 2, k. 1, p. 2 (4) (6), c. 3rt., p. 7, c. 3lt., p. 2 (4) (6), k. 1, p. 2, k. 9, p. 3, c. 3lt., p. 3, c. 3rt., p. 5.
34th row: K. 6, p. 2, k. 3, p. 2, k. 4, p. 9, k. 2, p. 1, k. 2 (4) (6), p. 2, k. 9, p. 2, k.2 (4) (6), p. 1, k. 2, p. 9, k. 4, p. 2, k. 3, p. 2, k. 6.
35th row: P. 6, c. 3lt., p. 1, c. 3rt., p. 4, cable 6, k. 3, p. 2, k. 1, p. 1 (3) (5), c. 3rt., p. 2, m.b., p. 3, m.b., p. 2, c. 3lt., p. 1 (3) (5), k. 1, p. 2,

k.3, cable 6b, p. 4, c. 3lt., p. 1, c. 3rt., p. 6.
36th row: K. 7, p. 2, k. 1, p. 2, k. 5, p. 9, k. 2, p. 1, k. 1 (3) (5), p. 2, k. 11, p. 2, k. 1 (3) (5), p. 1, k. 2, p. 9, k. 5, p. 2, k. 1, p. 2, k. 7.
37th row: P. 7, cr. 5, p. 5, k. 9, p. 2, k. 1, p. 1 (2) (3), k. 2, p. 11, k. 2, p. 1 (2) (3), k. 1, p. 2, k. 9, p. 5, cr. 5, p. 7.
38th row: As 36th row.
39th row: P. 1, m.b., p. 4, c. 3rt., p. 1, c. 3lt, p. 4, k. 3, cable 6b, p. 2, k. 1, p. 1 (3) (5), c. 3lt., p. 2, m.b., p. 3, m.b., p. 2, c. 3rt., p. 1 (3) (5), k. 1, p. 2, cable 6, k. 3, p. 4, c. 3rt, p. 1, c. 3lt., p. 4, m.b., p. 1.
40th row: As 34th row.
41st row: Working c. 3rt., for for c. 3lt. and c. 3lt., for c. 3rt., work as given for 33rd row.
42nd row: As 32nd row.
43rd row: P. 5, k. 2, p. 5, k. 2, p. 3, cable 6, k. 3, p. 2, k. 1, p. 3 (5) (7), c. 3lt., p. 2, m.b., p. 2, c. 3rt., p. 3 (5) (7), k. 1, p. 2, k. 3, cable 6b., p. 3, k. 2, p. 5, k. 2, p. 5.
44th row: As 30th row.
45th row: Working c. 3rt., for c. 3lt. and c. 3lt., for c. 3rt., work as given for 29th row.
46th row: As 28th row.
47th row: P. 1, m.b., p. 4, c. 3lt., p. 1, c. 3rt., p. 4, k. 3, cable 6b., p. 2, k. 1, p. 5 (7) (9), c. 3lt., p. 1, c. 3rt., p. 5 (7) (9), k. 1, p. 2, cable 6, k. 3., p. 4, c. 3lt., p. 1, c. 3rt., p. 4, m.b., p. 1.
48th row: As 26th row.
49th and 50 th rows: As 25th and 26th rows.
The last 50 rows from the pattern, work the first 44 rows again.
To shape the armhole and to slope the front edge: Pattern 20 (22) (24) rows, decreasing 1 st. at the armhole edge on each row *and at the same time* decreasing 1 st. at the front edge on the 1st of these rows and the 4 (5) (5) following 4th rows—50 (51) (53) sts.
Pattern 57 (59) (61) rows, decreasing 1 st. at the front edge on the 1st (3rd) (1st) of these rows and the 14 (14) (15) following 4th rows.
On 35 (36) (37) sts. pattern 23 rows.
To slope the shoulder: Cast off 18 sts. at the beginning of the next row.
On 17 (18) (19) sts. work 1 row, then cast off.

The right front:
Work as given for left front unit ** is reached.
Change to size 2¾ (No. 12) needles and beginning with the 2nd pattern row given for left front work in pattern as given for left front from *** to end.

The pocket flaps *(both alike):*
With size 2¼ (No. 13) needles cast on 3 sts. and work 2 rows in moss st. Continuing in moss st. as set inc. 1 st. at each end of the next 4 rows.
1st Buttonhole row: Inc. in first st., moss st. 3, cast off 3 sts., moss st. next 2 sts., inc. in last st.
2nd Buttonhole row: Inc., moss st. 4, turn, cast on 3, turn, work until 1 remains, inc.
Inc. 1 st. at each end of the next 9 rows.
Cast off these 33 sts.

The left front band and half collar:
Rejoin yarn to inner edge of the 12 sts. left on safety pin using size 2¼ (No. 13) needles work 88 rows in moss st. as set.
**Inc. 1 st. at the beginning of the next row and the 16 (17) (18) following 4th rows—29 (30) (31) sts.
Work 1 row as set, then cast off.

The right front band and half collar:
Rejoin yarn to inner edge of the 12 sts. left on safety pin and work in moss st. as follows:
1st Buttonhole row: Moss st. 4, cast off 4, work to end.
2nd Buttonhole row: Moss st. 4, cast on 4, turn, work to end.
Moss st. 26 rows.
Repeat the last 28 rows twice more then work the 2 buttonhole rows again.
Moss st. 2 rows.
Now work as given for left front band and half collar from** to end.

The back collar:
With size 2¼ (No. 13) needles and m. cast on 113 (123) (133) sts. and work 40 rows in moss st.
Dec. 1 st. at each end of the next row and the 9 following alternate rows.
Cast off the remaining 93 (103) (113) sts.

Left and right front armhole edgings:
With right side facings and using crochet hook, rejoin yarn and work 1 row of d.c. along front armhole edge, turn and work 1 row of d.c. over d.c. Fasten off.

To make up the waistcoat:
Pin out to size and press all parts on the wrong side with a cool iron over a dry cloth. Join side and shoulder seams. Sew front bands and half collar in place. Neatly sew cast off edge and shaped row edges of back collar in place. Sew pocket backs in place. Sew cast off edge of pocket flaps in position. Sew on buttons. Press seams.

The purse

The back:
With size 2¼ mm (No. 13) needles cast on 3 sts. and work as given for pocket flap of waistcoat until there are 33 sts.
Change to size 2¾ mm (No. 12) needles and work in pattern as follows:
1st row: P. 2, k. 5, p. 7, k. 2, m.b., k. 2, p. 7, k. 5, p. 2.
2nd row: K. 2, p. 5, k. 7, p. 5, k. 7, p. 5, k. 2.
3rd row: P. 2, k. 5, p. 6, c. 3rt., k. 1, c. 3lt., p. 6, k. 5, p. 2.
4th row: K. 2, p. 5, k. 6, p. 2, k. 1, p. 1, k. 1, p. 2, k. 6, p. 5, k. 2.
5th row: P. 2, k. 5, p. 5, c. 3rt., p. 1, k. 1, p. 1, c. 3lt., p. 5, k. 5, p. 2.
6th row: K. 2, p. 5, k. 5, p. 3, k. 1, p. 1, k. 1, p. 3, k. 5, p. 5, k. 2.
7th row: P. 2, k. 2, m.b., k. 2, p. 4, c. 3rt., k. 1, p. 1, k. 1, p. 1, k. 1, c. 3lt., p. 4, k. 2, m.b., k. 2, p. 2.
8th row: K. 2, p. 5, k. 4, p. 2, k. 1, p. 1, k. 1, p. 1, k. 1, p. 1, k. 1, p. 2, k. 4, p. 5, k. 2.
9th row: P. 2, k. 1, m.b., k. 1, m.b., k. 1, p. 3, c. 3rt., p. 1, k. 1, p. 1, k. 1, p. 1, k. 1, p. 1, c. 3lt., p. 3, k. 1, m.b., k. 1, m.b., k. 1, p. 2.
10th row: K. 2, p. 5, k. 3, p. 3, k. 1, p. 1, k. 1, p. 1 k. 1, p. 1, k. 1, p. 3, k. 3, p. 5, k. 2.
11th row: P. 2, k. 5, p. 2, c. 3rt., k. 1, p. 1, k. 1, p. 1, k. 1, p. 1, k. 1, p. 1, k. 1, c. 3lt., p. 2, k. 5, p. 2.
12th row: K. 2, p. 5, k. 2, p. 2, k. 1, p. 1, k. 1, p. 1, k. 1, p. 1, k. 1, p. 1, k. 1, p. 1, k. 1, p. 2, k. 2, p. 5, k. 2.
13th row: P. 1, k. 9, p. 6, m.b., p. 6, k. 9, p. 1.
14th row: K. 1, p. 9, k. 6, p. 1, k. 6, p. 9, k. 1.
15th row: P. 1, k. 3, cable 6b., p. 5, m.b., k. 1, m.b., p. 5, k. 3, cable 6b., p. 1.
16th row: As 14th row.
17th row: P. 1, k. 9, p. 4, m.b., p. 1, m.b., p. 1, m.b., p. 4, k. 9, p. 1.
18th row: As 14th row.
19th row: P. 1, cable 6, k. 3, p. 6, k. 1, p. 6, cable 6, k. 3, p. 1.
20th row: As 14th row.
21st row: P. 1, k. 9, p. 2, m.b., p. 7, m.b., p. 2, k. 9, p. 1.
22nd, 24th and 26th rows: K. 1, p. 9, k. 2, p. 1, k. 7, p. 1, k. 2, p. 9, k. 1.
23rd row: P. 1, k. 3, cable 6b., p. 1, m.b., k. 1, m.b., p. 5, m.b., k. 1, m.b., p. I, k. 3, cable 6b., p. 1.
25th row: P. 1, k. 9, m.b., p. 1, m.b., p. 1, m.b., p. 3, m.b., p. 1, m.b., p. 1, m.b., k. 9, p. 1.
27th row: P. 1, cable 6, k. 3, p. 2, k. 1, p. 7, k. 1, p. 2, cable 6, k. 3, p. 1.
28th row: As 22nd row.
29th to 40th rows: As 1st to 12th rows**
Change to size 2¼ mm (No. 13) needles and working in moss st, as before dec. 1st at each end of the next 15 rows. 3 sts.
K. 3 together and fasten off. Break off yarn leaving a long end. With remaining end make a loop at top of point, which will fasten purse.

The front:
Work as given for back until ** is reached. Cast off.

To complete:
Join the back and front. Fold down triangle at top, securing loop around bobble in pattern.

The tassel:
Cut 4 lengths of yarn each 12.5 cm (5 in.) long, fold in half and using a crochet hook, pull looped ends through st. at lower point of bag, pass cut ends through looped ends and draw up firmly.

The chord:
Cut 4 lengths of yarn each 450 cm (180 in.) long. Knot together at one end and twist firmly in one direction. Fold in half allowing the the two halves to twist together. Knot 4 cm (1½ in.) from each end; cut threads at folded end and sew knots firmly to each side of lower edge, then slip st. cord in place up sides of purse.

PICTURE PULLOVERS

Sweaters for all the children. They're all the same shape, but with three different pictures to choose from—the hedgehog carrying a flag, the rabbit with a goldfish, or the kitten with a kettle. The pictures look attractive on either brightly coloured backgrounds such as pink or yellow or on grey or oatmeal.

Materials:
5(6)(7)(8)(9)(10) 25 gram balls of Patons Purple Heather 4-ply in main colour and one ball of the same yarn in each of six contrast colours; a pair each of No. 12 and No. 13 knitting needles; 3 small buttons.

Tension:
16 stitches and 20 rows to 5 cm (2 in.) over the stocking stitch using No.12 needles. If you cannot obtain the correct tension using needles of the size suggested, use larger or smaller ones accordingly.

Abbreviations:
K.,knit; p.,purl; st.,stitch; tog.,together; dec.,decrease (by working 2sts. tog.); inc.,increase (by working twice into same st.); s.s.,stocking stitch (k. on the right side and p. on the wrong side); double rib is k.2 and p.2 alternately; m., main colour; a., first contrast colour; d.c., double crochet; ch., chain.

Note:
The instructions are given for the 1½-year-old size. Where they vary, work the figures in the first brackets for the 2-year-old size; the figures in the second brackets for the 4-year-old size; the figures in the third brackets for the 6-year-old size; the figures in the fourth brackets for the 8-year-old size; or the figures in the fifth brackets for the 10-year-old size.

Measurements:
The following measurements are given in centimetres first, followed by inches in brackets.

1½ yrs	2 yrs	4 yrs
6 yrs	8 yrs	10 yrs
All round at underarms		
50(20)	55(22)	60(24)
65(26)	70(28)	75(30)
Side seam		
15(6)	17.5(7)	20(8)
22.5(9)	26(10½)	30(12)
Length		
26(10½)	30(12)	34(13½)
37.5(15)	42.5(17)	47.5(19)
Sleeve seam with cuffs folded in half		
20(8)	24(9½)	27.5(11)
31(12½)	35(14)	39(15½)

The back:
With No.13 needles and m. cast on 80 (88)(96)(104)(112)(120) sts. and work 28(34)(40)(46)(46)(46) rows in double rib.
Change to No.12 needles and beginning with a k. row s.s. 36(40)(44)(48)(62) (78) rows.
To shape the armhole: Cast off 4sts. at the beginning of the next 2 rows, then dec. 1st. at each end of the next row and the 7(8)(9)(10)(11)(12) following alternate rows.
On 56(62)(68)(74)(80)(86) sts. s.s. 23 (27)(31)(33)(37)(39) rows.
To slope the shoulders: Cast off 5(6)(7) (8)(9)(10) sts. at the beginning of the next 4 rows.
Leave the remaining 36(38)(40)(42) (44)(46) sts. on a spare needle until required.

The front:
Work as given for back until 2(4)(6)(8) (12)(16) rows have been worked in s.s.
Now work the picture pattern of your choice in the following way. The motifs are worked entirely in s.s. so only the colour details follow. Take great care not to pull colours not in use tightly across the back of the work or it will become puckered. Use separate small balls of contrast colours for each motif.
1st row: 15(19)(23)(27)(31)(35) m., 50 a., 15(19)(23)(27)(31)(35) m.
2nd row: 15(19)(23)(27)(31)(35) m., 50 a., 15(19)(23)(27)(31)(35) m.
These 2 rows set the position of the picture patterns given in charts. Now work the 3rd to 34th(36th)(38th)(40th)(50th) (50th) rows from appropriate chart.
On the largest size only: With m. s.s. 12 rows.
To shape the armholes: For all sizes: Continuing in pattern as set until completed and then continuing with m. only, cast off 4sts. at the beginning of the next 2 rows, then dec. 1st. at each end of the next row and the 7(8)(9)(10)(11)(12) following alternate rows.
On 56(62)(68)(74)(80)(86) sts. s.s. 2 (4)(6)(8)(10)(12) rows.
Now divide the sts. for the neck: *Next row:* P.21(23)(25)(27)(29)(31) and leave these sts. on a spare needle until required for right front shoulder, p.14(16) (18)(20)(22)(24) and leave these sts. on a stitch holder until required for neckband, p. to end and continue on these 21(23)(25)(27)(29)(31) sts. for the left front shoulder.
The left front shoulder: To shape the neck: Dec. 1st. at the neck edge on each of the next 11 rows.
On 10(12)(14)(16)(18)(20) sts. s.s. 9 (11)(13)(13)(15)(15) rows.
To slope the shoulder: Cast off 5(6)(7) (8)(9)(10) sts. at the beginning of the next row.
On 5(6)(7)(8)(9)(10) sts. work 1 row, then cast off.
The right front shoulder: With right side of work facing rejoin m. to inner edge of sts. left on spare needle and work to end of row. Now work as given for left front shoulder to end.

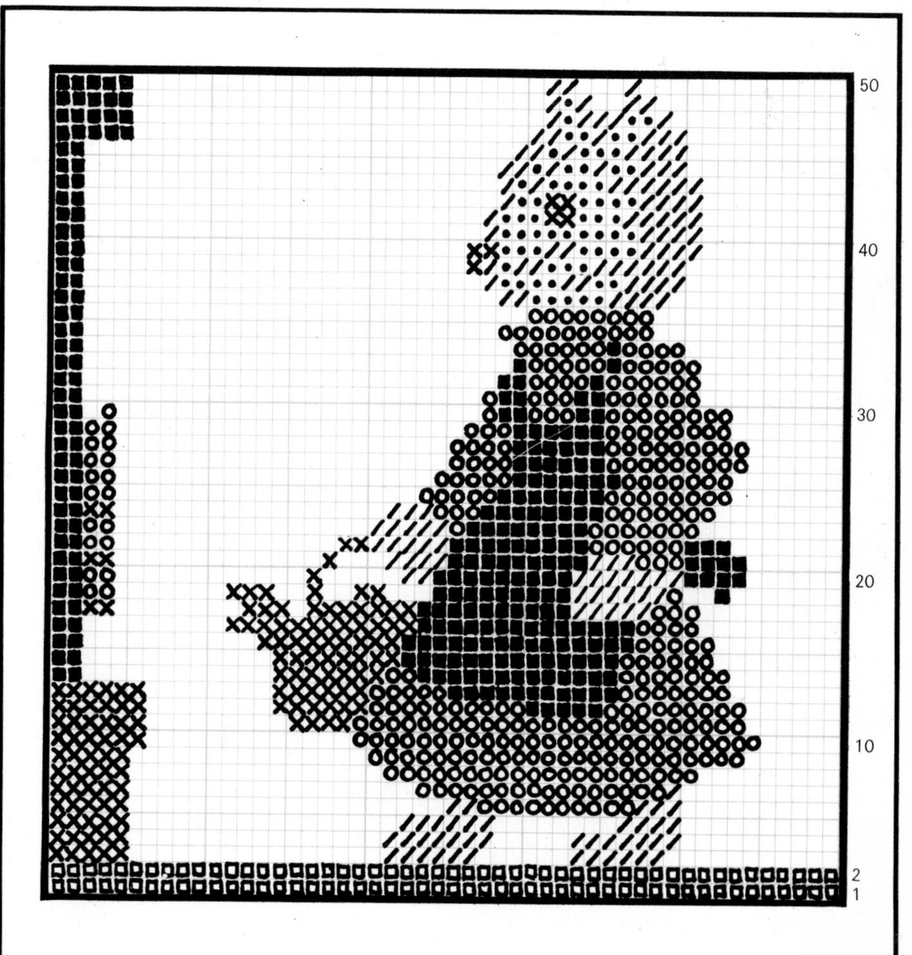

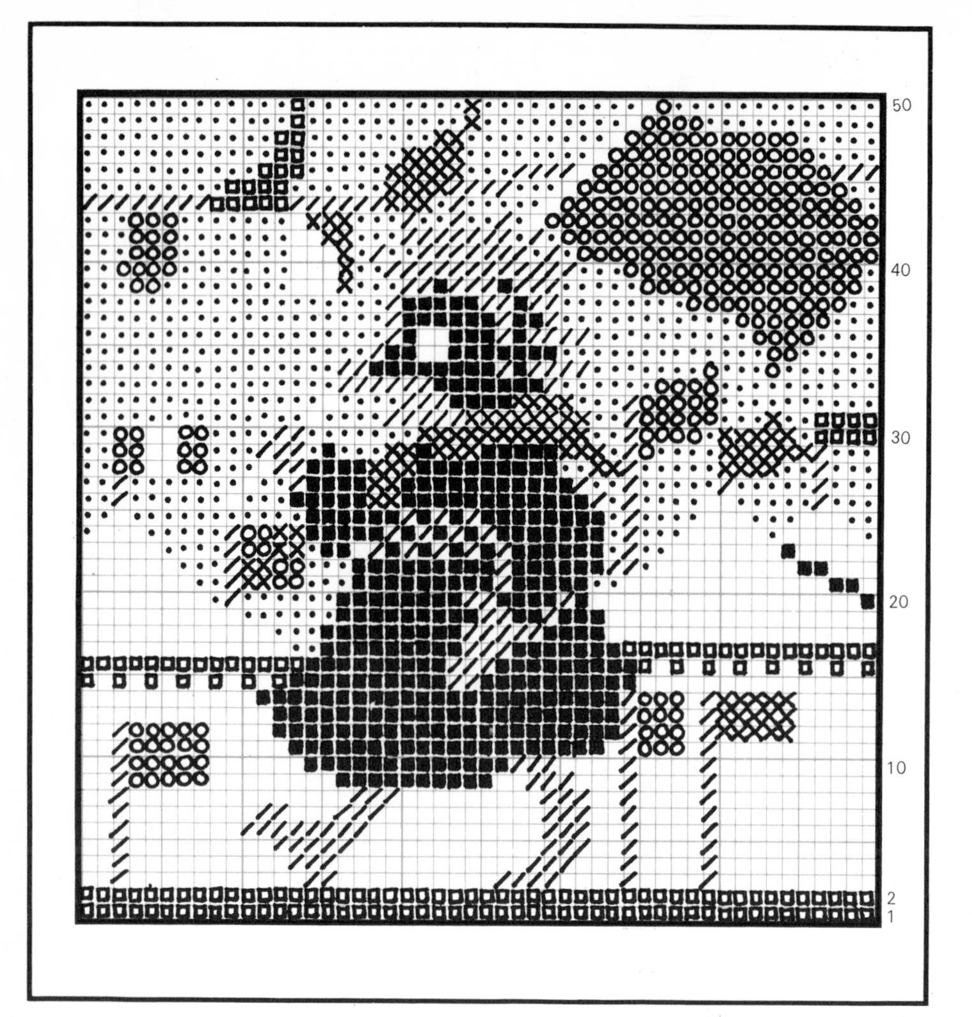

The sleeves *(both alike)*:
With No.13 needles and m., cast on 42 (46) (50) (54) (58) (62) sts. and work 38 (38) (44) (44) (50) (50) rows in double rib.
Change to No.12 needles and beginning with a k. row s.s. 2 rows.
Inc. 1st. at each end of the next row and the 6 (7) (8) (9) (10) (11) following 8th (10th) (10th) (10th) (10th) (10th) rows.
On 56 (62) (68) (74) (80) (86) sts. s.s. 11 (5) (7) (11) (11) (21) rows.
To shape the sleevetop: Cast off 4sts. at the beginning of the next 2 rows, then dec. 1st. at each end of the next row and the 11 (13) (15) (17) (19) (21) following alternate rows.
On 24 (26) (28) (30) (32) (34) sts. work 1 row.
Cast off 4sts. at the beginning of the next 4 rows.
Cast off the remaining 8 (10) (12) (14) (16) (18) sts.

The neckband:
First join right shoulder seam. With right side of work facing rejoin m. and using No.13 needles pick up and k.21 (23) (25) (25) (27) (27) sts. from left front neck edge, k. across the 14 (16) (18) (20) (22) (24) sts. left on stitch holder at centre front, pick up and k.21 (23) (25) (25) (27) (27) sts. from right front neck edge, then k. across the 36 (38) (40) (42) (44) (46) sts. left on spare needle at back neck edge —92 (100) (108) (112) (120) (124) sts.
Work 7 (7) (9) (9) (11) (11) rows in double rib.
Cast off in rib.
The left shoulder buttonhole edging: Join left shoulder seam for $\frac{1}{4}$ in. at armhole edge.
With right side of work facing rejoin m. to neckband at left shoulder and using a size 2.50 crochet hook work 16 (18) (20) (22) (24) (26) d.c. along left back shoulder, then 16 (18) (20) (22) (24) (26) d.c. along left front shoulder, turn.
Buttonhole row: 2 ch. to stand for first d.c., 1 d.c. into next d.c., * miss 2 d.c., 3 ch., 1 d.c. into each of next 4 (5) (6) (7) (8) (9) d.c.; repeat from *, miss 2 d.c., 3 ch., work in d.c. to end. Fasten off.

To make up the sweater:
Press all parts except the ribbing on the wrong side with a warm iron over a damp cloth. Set in sleeves. Join sleeve and side seams. Press seams.

POLO SET

A classic. Knit it to match the man's Classic Cool and you will have a twinset to take you anywhere, anytime.

Materials:
For the sweater: 17 (18 (19) 25 gram balls of Paton's Purple Heather 4 ply in main colour and 2 balls in each of the 4 contrast colours; a pair each of size 2¼ mm (No. 13) and size 3 mm (No. 11) Aero knitting needles.
For the scarf: 6 25 gram balls of the same yarn in main colour and 1 ball in each of the 4 contrast colours; a pair of size 2¾ mm (No. 12) Aero knitting needles.
The yarn for these garments is generally available, but should any difficulty be experienced, the yarn can be obtained by mail order from Patricia Roberts Knitting, 60 Kinnerton Street, London SW1.

Tension:
18 stitches and 16 rows to 5 cm (2 in.) over the Fair Isle pattern using size 3 mm (No. 11) needles.

Abbreviations:
K., knit; p., purl; st., stitch; tog., together; dec., decrease (by working 2 sts. tog.); inc., increase (by working twice into same st.); s.s., stocking st. is k. on the right side and p. on the wrong side; double rib is k. 2 and p. 2 alternately; up 1, pick up the loop which lies between the needles, slip it onto left hand needle, then k. 1 into back of it; m., main colour; a., first contrast colour; b., second contrast colour; c., third contrast colour; d., fourth contrast colour.

Note:
The instructions are given for the small size. Where they vary work the figures in the first brackets for the medium size or the figures in the second brackets for the large size.

Measurements:

The measurements are given in centimetres followed by inches in square brackets.

small	medium	large
All round at underarms		
90 [36]	95 [38]	100 [40]
Side seam		
40 [16]	40 [16]	40 [16]
Length		
61 [24½]	62 [24¾]	64 [25½]
Sleeve seam with cuffs folded in half		
42.5 [17]	42.5 [17]	42.5 [17]

The scarf:
Before knotting ends: 27 cm (10¾ in.) in width and 154 cm (61¾ in.) in length.

THE SWEATER

The back:
With size 2¼ mm (No. 13) needles and m. cast on 128 (136) (144) sts. and work 53 rows in double rib.
Increase row: Rib 15 (15) (2) * up 1, rib 3 (3) (4); repeat from * ending last repeat rib 14 (16) (2).
Change to size 3 mm (No. 11) needles and on 162 (172) (180) sts., beginning with a k. row s.s. 2 rows.
Now work in Fair Isle pattern as follows: The pattern is worked entirely in s.s. so only the colour details are given. Take great care not to pull colour not in use tightly across the back of the work or it will become puckered.
1st row: 2 m. (5 a., 2 m.) (1 a., 2 m.), * 6 a., 2 m.; repeat from * ending last repeat 2 m. (2 m., 5 a.) (2 m., 1 a.).
The last row sets the position of the first 7 pattern rows, work the 2nd to 7th pattern rows from the chart as set.
For the small size only: 8th row: 2 m., * 2 b., 2 m., 1 b., 1 m., 1 b., 4 m., 3 b., 2 m., 3 b., 4 m., 1 b., 1 m., 1 b., 2 m., 2 b., 2 m., * repeat from * to * to end.
For the medium size only: 8th row: 3 m., 2 b., 2 m.; repeat from * to * given for first size until 5 remain, 2 b., 3 m.
For the large size only: 8th row: 2 m., 1 b., 1 m., 1 b., 2 m., 2 b., 2 m.; repeat from * to * as given for first size until 9 remain, 2 b., 2 m., 1 b., 1 m., 1 b., 2 m.
For all sizes: The last row sets the position of the rest of the pattern. Work the 9th to 77th rows from the chart as set, then work the first 13 rows again.**
To shape the raglan armholes: Maintaining the continuity of the pattern as set, dec. 1 st. at each end of the next row and the 19 following alternate rows—then dec. 1 st. at each end of the next 29 (33) (37) rows—64 (66) (66) sts. Cast off.

The front:
Work as given for back until ** is reached.
To shape the raglan armholes: Maintaining the continuity of the pattern as set, dec. 1 st. at each end of the next row and the 18 following alternate rows.
Now divide the sts. for the neck: Next row: Pattern 52 (56) (60) and leave these sts. on a spare needle until required for right front shoulder, cast off the next 20 (22) (22) sts., pattern to end and continue on these 52 (56) (60) sts. for the left front shoulder.
The left front shoulder: The shape the neck and continue to slope the raglan: Dec. 1 st. at each end of the next 22 rows.
Dec. 1 st. at raglan armhole edge on each of the next 6 (10) (14) rows.
Take the 2 remaining sts. tog. and fasten off.
The right front shoulder: With right side of work facing rejoin yarn to inner edge of sts. left on spare needle and work to end of row.
Now work as given for left front shoulder to end.

The sleeves *(both alike):*
With size 2¼ mm (No. 13) needles and m. cast on 68 (72) (76) sts. and work 71 rows in double rib.
Increase row: Rib 3 (5) (7), * up 1, rib 2; repeat from * ending last repeat rib 3 (5) (7).
Change to size 3 mm (No. 11) needles and on 100 (104) (108) sts., beginning with a k. row, s.s. 4 rows.
Now work in pattern as follows: *59th pattern row:* 1 m. (3 m.) (2 c., 3 m.), * 2 c., 3 m., 2 c., 3 m., 1c., 1 m., 1 c., 8 m., 1 c., 1 m., 1 c., 3 m., 2 c., 3 m.; repeat from * until 3 (5) (7) remain, 2 c., 1 m. (3 m.) (3 m., 2 c.).
The last row sets the position of the pattern given in the chart, now beginning with the 60th pattern row work 107 rows in pattern as set.
To slope the raglans: Dec. 1 st. at each end of the next row and the 19 (21) (23) following alternate rows.
Dec. 1 st. at each end of the next 29 rows.
Cast off the remaining 2 sts.

The collar:
With size 2¼ mm (No. 13) needles and m. cast on 186 (196) (204) sts. and work 108 rows in double rib, then cast off.

The pocket backs *(two alike):*
With size 3 mm (No. 11) needles and m. cast on 38 sts. and work 90 rows in s.s., then cast off.

To make up the sweater:
Pin out to size and press all parts except the ribbing on the wrong side with a warm iron over a damp cloth. Join raglan seams so that the sts. cast off at top of sleeves from part of neck edge. Fold pocket backs in half and join row end edge. Join sleeve and side seams, inserting pockets in side seams above ribbing. Join row end edges of collar. Sew collar in place all round neck edge. Press seams. Fold collar in 3 to right side.

THE SCARF

To work:
With size 3 mm (No. 11) needles and m. cast on 98 sts. and beginning with a k. row s.s. 2 rows.
Now work 494 rows in pattern as given for first size on back, ending with 32nd pattern row. Cast off.

To complete the scarf:
Pin out to size and press as for sweater. Fold in half lengthways. Knot ends.

BLACKJACK

Small colour patterns are knitted in red and grey against a black background on the body and sleeves of this soft mohair sweater. The yoke, knitted in rib, may be turned back to give a narrow rolled collar.

Materials:
16 (17) (18) 25 gram balls of Emu Filigree Mohair in main colour and 3 balls in each of the 2 contrast colours; a pair each of No. 5 and No. 4 knitting needles.

Tension:
7 stitches and 9 rows to 5 cm (2 in.) over the pattern using No. 4 knitting needles.

Abbreviations:
K., knit; p., purl; st., stitch; tog., together; dec., decrease (by working 2 sts. tog.); inc., increase (by working twice into same st.); s.s., stocking stitch (k. on the right side and p. on the wrong side); single rib is k. 1 and p. 1 alternately; m., main colour; a., first contrast colour; c., second contrast; sl., slip; p.s.s.o., pass sl. st. over.

Note:
The instructions are given for the small size. Where they vary work the figures in the first brackets for the medium size or the figures in the second brackets for the large size.

Measurements:
The measurements are given in centimetres followed by inches in square brackets.

Chest sizes		
small	medium	large
All round at underarms		
92.5 [37]	99 [39½]	105 [42]
Side seam		
44 [17½]	44 [17½]	44 [17½]
Length		
71 [28½]	72.5 [29]	75 [30]
Sleeve seam		
45 [18]	45 [18]	45 [18]

The back and front *(alike)*:
With No. 5 needles and m. cast on 65 (69) (73) sts. and work 12 rows in single rib.
Change to No. 4 needles and beginning with a k. row s.s. 4 rows.
Now work in pattern as follows: This is worked entirely in s.s. so only the colour details are given. Take great care to avoid pulling colours not in use tightly across the back of the work or it will become puckered.
1st row: 1 a., * 3 m., 1 a.; repeat from * to end.
2nd row: 1 m., * 1 a., 1 m.; repeat from * to end.
3rd row: 2 m., * 1 a., 3 m.; repeat from * ending last repeat 2 m.
4th, 5th, and 6th rows: All m.
7th row: 1 m., * 3 c., 1 m.; repeat from * to end.
8th row: 2 c., * 1 m., 3 c.; repeat from * ending last repeat 2 c.
9th row: As 7th row.
10th, 11th, and 12th rows: All m.
13th to 18th rows: As 1st to 6th rows.
19th row: 2 m., * 1 c., 3 m.; repeat from * ending last repeat 2 m.
20th row: As 7th row.
21st row: As 19th row.
22nd to 24th rows: All m.
The last 24 rows form the pattern; repeat them once more, then work the first 16 rows again.
To shape the armholes: Cast off 2 sts. at the beginning of the next 2 rows, then leave these sts. on a spare needle until required for yoke.

The sleeves *(both alike)*:
With No. 5 needles and m. cast on 37 (37) (41) sts. and work 16 rows in single rib.
Change to No. 4 needles and beginning with a k. row s.s. 4 rows.
Work 6 (8) (6) rows in pattern as given for back and front.
Continuing in pattern as set and working the extra sts. into the pattern as they occur, inc. 1 st. at each end of the next row and the 5 (6) (5) following 10th (8th) (10th) rows. On 49 (51) (53) sts. pattern 7 rows more.
To shape the sleevetop: Cast off 2 sts. at the beginning of the next 2 rows, then leave these sts. on a spare needle until required for yoke.

The yoke:
With right side of work facing rejoin m. to top of one sleeve and using No. 5 needles k. across these 45 (47) (49) sts., k. across the 61 (65) (69) sts. of front, then the sts. of other sleeve, then across the 61 (65) (69) sts. of back—212 (224) (236) sts.
For the second size only: Dec. row: P. 12, * p. 2 tog., p. 16; repeat from * ending last repeat p. 12. On 212 sts., work 1 row in single rib.
For the third size only: Dec. row: P. 2, * p. 2 tog., p. 8; repeat from * ending last repeat p. 2. On 212 sts., work 3 rows in single rib.
For all sizes: Continuing with m. only work 7 rows in single rib.
1st dec. row: Rib 10, * sl. 1, k. 2 tog., p.s.s.o., rib 18; repeat from * ending last repeat rib 10.
Rib 7 rows.
2nd dec. row: Rib 9, * sl. 1, k. 2 tog., p.s.s.o., rib 16; repeat from * ending last repeat rib 9.
Thus working 1 st. less before, 2 sts. less between and 1 st. less after, the decreases on each subsequent repeat of the dec. row, repeat the last 8 rows twice more.
On 132 sts. rib 5 rows.
Next dec. row: Rib 6, * sl. 1, k. 2 tog., p.s.s.o., rib 10; repeat from * ending last repeat rib 6.
Working 1 st. less before and after, and 2 sts. less between the decreases as before, repeat the last 6 rows twice more.
On 72 sts. rib 6 rows more, then cast off.

To make up the sweater:
Pin out to size and press all parts except the ribbing on the wrong side with a warm iron over a damp cloth. Join raglan seams. Join sleeve and side seams. Press seams.

CREAM OF THE CROP

Here's a sweater which you could never knit on a machine yet, because it is knitted in very thick yarn and mohair, it can be knitted very quickly by hand. Use cream yarn for a soft effect, or brick yarn with brick mohair; ice blue yarn with Lapis blue mohair; or grey yarn with black mohair. The hat could be made to team up with almost any other sweater and jacket in this book.

Materials:
For both the sweater and the hat: 6 (6) (7) (8) 100 gram hanks of Jaeger Naturgarn in main colour; 8 (9) (10) (11) 25 gram balls of Jaeger Mohair in contrast colour; a pair each of No.5 and No.6 knitting needles; one button; a cable needle.
For the hat only: 1 ball of Jaeger Mohair; ½ hank of Jaeger Naturgarn; a pair of No.5 knitting needles; a cable needle.

Tension:
8 stitches and 10 rows to 5 cm (2 in.) over the pattern and the reversed stocking stitch using No.5 needles.

Abbreviations:
K., knit; p., purl; st., stitch; tog., together; dec., decrease (by working 2sts. tog.); inc., increase (by working twice into same st.); up 1, pick up the loop that lies between the needles, slip it onto left-hand needle, then k. into back of it; single rib is k.1 and p.1 alternately; cable 8, slip next 4sts. onto a cable needle and leave at front of work, k.4, then k.4 from cable needle; m., main colour—Naturgarn; c., contrast colour—mohair; r.s.s., reversed stocking stitch.

Note:
The instructions are given for the extra small size. Where they vary, work the figures in the first brackets for the small size; the figures in the second brackets for the medium size; or the figures in the third brackets for the large size.

Measurements:
The following measurements are given in centimetres first, followed by inches in brackets.

extra small (8)	small (10)	medium (12)	large (14)
All round at underarms			
85 (34)	90 (36)	95 (38)	100 (40)
Side seam			
45 (18)	45 (18)	45 (18)	45 (18)
Length			
64 (25½)	65 (26)	66 (26½)	67.5 (27)
Sleeve seam			
42.5 (17)	42.5 (17)	42.5 (17)	42.5 (17)

The back:
With No.6 needles and m. cast on 68 (72) (76) (80) sts. and work 12 rows in single rib.
Change to No.5 needles and work in pattern as follows, using separate balls of yarn for each vertical stripe and neatly weaving m. and c. together at each joint.
1st row: Using first ball of c. k.7 (8) (9) (10), using first ball of m. k.8, using second ball of c. k.7 (8) (9) (10), using second ball of m. k.8, using third ball of c. k.8, using third ball of m. k.8, using fourth ball of c. k.7 (8) (9) (10), using fourth ball of m. k.8, using fifth ball of c. k.7 (8) (9) (10).
2nd row: With c. p.7 (8) (9) (10), with m. p.8, with c. p.7 (8) (9) (10), with m. p.8, with c. p.8, with m. p.8, with c. p.7 (8) (9) (10), with m. p.8, with c. p.7 (8) (9) (10).
3rd to 6th rows: Repeat 1st and 2nd rows twice.
7th row: With c. k.7 (8) (9) (10), with m. cable 8, with c. k.7 (8) (9) (10), with m. cable 8, with c. k.8, with m. cable 8, with c. k.7 (8) (9) (10), with m. cable 8, with c. k.7 (8) (9) (10).
8th row: As 2nd row.
9th to 14th rows: Repeat first and second rows 3 times.
These 14 rows form the pattern, repeat them 4 more times, then work the first 8 rows again. Work should now measure 18 in. from beginning.
To shape the armholes: Maintaining the continuity of the pattern as set, cast off 7 (8) (9) (10) sts. at the beginning of the next 2 rows.
On 54 (56) (58) (60) sts. pattern 32 (34) (36) (38) rows as set.
To slope the shoulders: Cast off 8sts. at the beginning of the next 2 rows and 7 (8) (9) (10) sts. on the 2 following rows. Cast off the 24 remaining sts.

The front:
Work as given for back until 65 rows have been worked in pattern.
Now divide the sts. for the neck: *Next row:* Pattern 31 (33) (35) (37) and leave these sts. on a spare needle until required for right front shoulder; cast off 6sts., then pattern to end as set and continue on these 31 (33) (35) (37) sts. for the left front shoulder.
The left front shoulder: To shape the neck: Dec. 1 st. at the end—neck edge—on the next row and the 2 following 4th rows.
On 28 (30) (32) (34) sts. work 3 rows.
To shape the armhole and continue to slope the neck: Cast off 7 (8) (9) (10) sts. at the beginning and dec. 1 st. at the end of the next row.
Pattern 20 more rows decreasing 1 st. at neck on the 4th of these rows and the 4 following 4th rows.
On 15 (16) (17) (18) sts. pattern 13 (15) (17) (19) rows.
To slope the shoulder: Cast off 8sts. at the beginning of the next row. On 7 (8) (9) (10) sts. work 1 row, then cast off.
The right front shoulder: With right side of work facing rejoin yarns to inner edge of sts. left on spare needle and work to end of row.
Now work as given for left front shoulder to end.

The sleeves *(both alike):*
With No.6 needles and m. cast on 32 (32) (34) (34) sts. and work 15 rows in single rib.
Increase row: K.1 (1) (2) (2), * up 1, k.1, up 1, k.1, up 1, k.2; repeat from * ending last repeat k.1 (1) (2) (2)—56 (56) (58) (58) sts.
Change to No.5 needles and work in pattern as follows, noting instructions given for back:
1st row: With first ball of c. k.8 (8) (9) (9), with first ball of m. k.8, with second ball of c. k.8, with second ball of m. k.8, with third ball of c. k.8, with third ball of m. k.8, with fourth ball of c. k.8 (8) (9) (9).
This row sets the position of the 14 row cable pattern given for back. Pattern 69 rows as set, marking each end of last row with coloured threads.
Pattern 10 (10) (12) (12) more rows, then cast off.

The neckband:
With No.6 needles and m. cast on 8sts. and work 122 (126) (130) (134) rows in single rib, then cast off.

To make up the sweater:
Press all parts lightly on the wrong side with a warm iron over a damp cloth. Join shoulder seams. Set in sleeves so that the sts. cast off at underarms are sewn to the row ends above the marking threads on the sleeves. Neatly sew neckband in place so that the cast on edge is sewn to the sts. cast off at centre front and the row end edge is sewn up right front neck, along back and down left front neck edge to centre front where cast off edge is sewn behind cast on edge of neckband. Sew button in place. Press seams.

THE HAT

To work:
With No.5 needles and c. cast on 72sts. and work 16 rows in r.s.s.
1st Decrease row: * P.2 tog., p.6; repeat from * to end—63sts. R.s.s. 5 rows.
2nd Decrease row: * P.2 tog., p.5; repeat from * to end. R.s.s. 3 rows.
3rd Decrease row: * P.2 tog., p.4; repeat from * to end—45sts. R.s.s. 3 rows.
4th Decrease row: * P.2 tog., p.3; repeat from * to end—36sts. R.s.s. 1 row.
5th Decrease row: * P.2 tog., p.2; repeat from * to end—27sts. R.s.s. 1 row.
6th Decrease row: * P.2 tog., p.1; repeat from * to end—18sts. *Next row:* * K.2 tog.; repeat from * to end—9sts.
Break off c. leaving a long end, thread through remaining sts., draw up and secure, then use long end to join row end edges.

The edging:
With No.5 needles and m. cast on 8sts. and work as follows: *1st row:* All k. *2nd row:* All p. *3rd to 6th rows:* Repeat 1st and 2nd rows twice. *7th row:* Cable 8. *8th row:* All p. *9th to 12th rows:* Repeat 1st and 2nd rows twice. The last 12 rows form the pattern; repeat them 9 more times.

To complete:
Join cast on and cast off edges of edging. Neatly pin edging in place all round outer edge of hat, so that the seam in edging is placed on seam of hat, and the lower edge of edging is sewn to cast on edge of hat and the upper edge to hat in appropriate position above this. Sew edging in place along both edges. Press.

DREAMY

For the young and daring this is a mohair mini dress to wear with the leggings—for the less daring it's a baggy sweater to wear anywhere, anyday.

Materials:
20 (21) (22) 25 gram balls of Emu Filigree Mohair; a pair each of size 6 mm (No. 4) and size 5½ mm (No. 5) Aero Knitting needles, a thick Aero crochet hook.

Tension:
8 stitches and 10 rows to 5 cm (2 in.) over the cable pattern using size 6 mm (No. 4) needles.

Abbreviations:
K., knit; p., purl; st., stitch; tog., together; dec., decrease (by working 2 sts tog.); inc., increase (by working twice into same st.); single rib is k. 1 and p. 1 alternately; up 1, pick up the loop which lies between the needles, slip it onto left hand needle, then k. into back of it; cable 8, thus, slip next 4 sts. onto cable needle and leave at front of work, k. 4, then k. 4 from cable needle.

Note:
The instructions are given for the small size. Where they vary work the figures in the first brackets for the medium size or the figures in the second brackets for the large size.

Measurements:

The measurements are given in centimetres followed by inches in square brackets.

small	medium	large
All round at underarms		
95 [38]	100 [40]	105 [42]
Side seam		
52.5 [21]	52.5 [21]	52.5 [21]
Length		
77.5 [31]	77.5 [31]	77.5 [31]
Sleeve seam		
42.5 [17]	42.5 [17]	42.5 [17]

The back:

With size 5½ mm (No. 5) needles cast on 64 (68) (72) sts. and work 47 rows in single rib.

Increase row: Rib 4 (6) (8), * up 1, rib 5 repeat from * ending last repeat rib 5 (7) (9).

Change to size 6 mm (No. 4) needles and on 76 (80) (84) sts. work in cable pattern as follows:

1st row: P. 4 (6) (8), * k. 8, p. 12; repeat from * ending last repeat p. 4 (6) (8).

2nd row: K. 4 (6) (8), * p. 8, k. 12 repeat from * ending last repeat k. 4 (6) (8).

3rd to 6th rows: Repeat 1st and 2nd rows twice.

7th row: P. 4 (6) (8), * cable 8, p. 12; repeat from * ending last repeat p. 4 (6) (8).

8th row: As 2nd row.

9th to 12th rows: Repeat 1st and 2nd rows twice.

The last 12 rows form the pattern. Repeat them 4 times more, then work the first 4 rows again. Mark each end of the last row with coloured threads to mark armhole.**

Pattern 48 rows more.

To slope the shoulders: Cast off 26 (28) (30) sts. at the beginning of the next 2 rows. Cast off the remaining 24 sts.

The front:

Work as given for the back until ** is reached.

Pattern 27 rows.

Now divide the sts. for the neck: Next row: Pattern 34 (36) (38) and leave these sts. on a spare needle until required for right front shoulder, cast off 8 sts., pattern to end and continue on these 34 (36) (38) sts. for the left front shoulder.

The left front shoulder: To shape the neck: Dec. 1st at the neck edge on each of the next 8 rows.

On 26 (28) (30) sts. pattern 12 rows.

To slope the shoulder: Cast off.

The right front shoulder: with right side of work facing rejoin yarn to inner edge of sts. left on spare needle and work to end of row. Now work as given for left front shoulder to end.

The sleeves *(both alike):*

With size 5½ mm (No. 5) needles cast on 34 sts. and work 23 rows in single rib.

Increase row: Inc. in first st., * up 1, k. 1, repeat from * to end—68 sts.

Change to size 6 mm (No. 4) needles and work 64 rows in pattern as given for back. Cast off.

The collar:

With size 5½ mm (No. 5) needles cast on 100 sts. and work 60 rows in single rib. Cast off in rib.

The pocket backs *(two alike):*

With size 6 mm (No. 4) needles cast on 20 sts and work 50 rows in stocking stitch—k. on the right side and p. on the wrong side. Cast off.

To make up the sweater/dress:

Pin out to size and press all parts except the ribbing on the wrong side, with a warm iron over a damp cloth. Join shoulder seams. Set in sleeves between the marking threads on back and front. Fold pocket backs in half and join row end edges. Join sleeve and side seams, inserting pockets at side seams above ribbing. Join row ends of collar. Sew cast off edge of collar in place all round neck edge. Press seams.

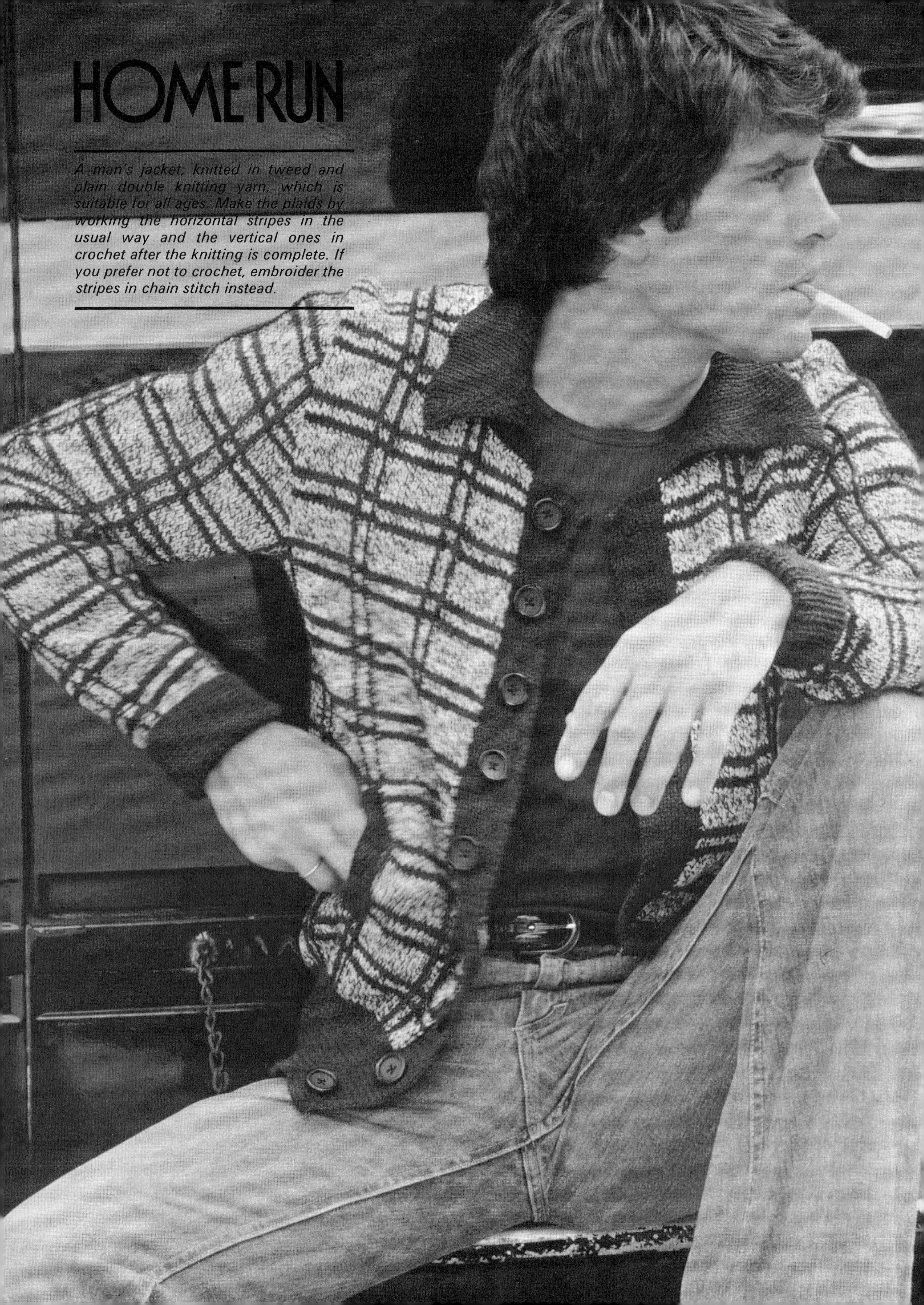

HOME RUN

A man's jacket, knitted in tweed and plain double knitting yarn, which is suitable for all ages. Make the plaids by working the horizontal stripes in the usual way and the vertical ones in crochet after the knitting is complete. If you prefer not to crochet, embroider the stripes in chain stitch instead.

Materials:

16(17)(18) 25 gram balls of Robin Gleneagle tweed Double Knitting yarn in main colour; 13(14)(15) balls of Robin Vogue D.K. in first contrast colour and 5(6)(6) balls in second contrast colour; a pair each of No.9 and No.11 knitting needles; 11 buttons; a medium sized crochet hook.

Tension:

12 stitches and 16 rows to 5 cm (2 in.) over stocking stitch using No.9 needles. If you cannot obtain the correct tension using needles of the size suggested, change to larger or smaller ones accordingly.

Abbreviations:

K.,knit; p.,purl; st.,stitch; tog.,together; dec.,decrease (by working 2sts. tog.); inc.,increase (by working twice into same st.); s.s.,stocking stitch; single rib is k.1 and p.1 alternately; m.,main colour; a., first contrast colour; b.,second contrast colour; up 1, pick up the loop that lies between the needles, slip it onto left-hand needle and k. into back of it.

Note:

The instructions are given for the small size. Where they vary, work the figures in the first brackets for the medium size or those in the second brackets for the large size.

Measurements:

The following measurements are given in centimetres first, followed by inches in brackets.

small	medium	large
All round at underarms		
95(38)	100(40)	105(42)
Side seam		
40(16)	40(16)	40(16)
Length		
64(25½)	65(26)	66(26½)
Sleeve seam		
49(19½)	49(19½)	49(19½)

The back:

With No.11 needles and a. cast on 96 (102)(108) sts. and work 31 rows in single rib.

Increase row: Rib 4(7)(10), * up 1, rib 8; repeat from * ending last repeat rib 4(7) (10)—108(114)(120) sts. Break off a., join in m.

Change to No.9 needles and work in s.s. with p.st. ridges as follows:

1st row: K.4(7)(10), * p.1, k.2, p.1, k.12; repeat from * ending last repeat k.4(7) (10).

2nd row: P.4(7)(10), * k.1, p.2, k.1, p.12; repeat from * ending last repeat p.4(7) (10).

Repeat the last 2 rows 3 more times.

Continuing in s.s. with p.st. ridges as set, work in stripe sequence as follows: 2 rows a., 2 rows m., 2 rows b., 8 rows m. These 14 rows form the stripe sequence; repeat them 5 more times then work the first 8 rows again. Work should now measure 40 cm (16 in.) from beginning.

To shape the armholes: Continuing in s.s. with p.st. ridges as set and in stripe sequence as set, cast off 6sts. at beginning of next 2 rows, then dec. 1st. at each end of the next row and 2(3)(4) following alternate rows.

On 90(94)(98) sts. work 63(65)(67) rows as set.

To slope the shoulder: Cast off 9sts. at the beginning of the next 4 rows and 9(10) (11) sts. on the 2 following rows.

Cast off the 36(38)(40) remaining sts.

The left front:

With No.11 needles and a. cast on 48(51) (54) sts. and work 31 rows in single rib.

Increase row: Rib 4, * up 1, rib 8; repeat from * ending last repeat rib 4(7)(10)—54(57)(60) sts. Break off a., join in m.

Change to No.9 needles and with m. work in s.s. with p.st. ridges as follows:

1st row: K.6(9)(12), * p.1, k.2, p.1, k.12; repeat from * to end.

2nd row: P.12, k.1, p.2, k.1; repeat from * until 6(9)(12) remain, p. to end.

These 2 rows set the position of the p.st. ridges.

Repeat the last 2 rows 3 more times.

Now while working in stripe sequence as given for back in s.s. with p.st. ridges as set work 7 rows straight.

** Now divide the sts. for the pocket:

Next row: Work as set across 30sts., and leave these sts. on a spare needle until required, cast on 30sts. for pocket back then work to end of row as set.

On 54(57)(60) sts. work 39 rows in stripe sequence as set.

Cast off 30sts. of pocket back, then without working to end of row leave the remaining 24(27)(30) sts. on a spare needle until required.

Return to the 30sts. left on spare needle at beginning of pocket opening and work 39 rows in stripe sequence as set.

Next row: Pattern across the 30sts. at centre front edge, then on to same needle across the 24(27)(30) sts. left on spare needle at side.

On 54(57)(60) sts., pattern 44 more rows.

To shape the armhole: Cast off 6sts. at the beginning of the next row, work 1 row back to armhole edge, dec. 1st. at the beginning of the next row and the 2(3)(4) following alternate rows.

On 45(47)(49) sts. pattern 32(34)(36) rows ending at front edge.

To shape the neck: Cast off 9(10)(11) sts. at the beginning of the next row, then dec. 1st. at the neck edge on each of the next 9 rows.

On 27(28)(29) sts. work 21 rows as set.

To slope the shoulder: Cast off 9sts. at the beginning of the next row and the following alternate row.

On 9(10)(11) sts. work 1 row, then cast off.

The right front:

With No.11 needles and a. cast on 48(51) (54) sts. and work 31 rows in single rib.

Increase row: Rib 4(7)(10), * up 1, rib 8; repeat from * ending last repeat rib 4—54(57)(60) sts. Break off a., join in m.

Change to No.9 needles and with m. work in s.s. with p.st. ridges as follows:

1st row: * K.12, p.1, k.2, p.1; repeat from * until 6(9)(12) remain, k. to end.

2nd row: P.6(9)(12), * k.1, p.2, k.1, p.12; repeat from * to end.

Repeat the last 2 rows 3 more times, then working in stripe sequence as given for back work 8 more rows.

Now continuing in stripe sequence as set, work as given for left front from ** to end.

The pocket tops (*both alike*):

First sew pocket backs in place. Then with right side of work facing rejoin a. to the straight row end edge of pocket opening and using No.11 needles, pick up and k.32sts. from this edge. Work 3 rows in single rib.

1st Buttonhole row: Rib 14, cast off 4, rib to end.

2nd Buttonhole row: Rib 14, turn, cast on 4sts., turn, rib to end.

Rib 2 more rows, then cast off in rib.

The sleeves (*both alike*):

With No.11 needles and a. cast on 54(58)(62) sts. and work 32 rows in single rib. Break off a., join in m.

Change to No.9 needles and with m. work in s.s. with p.st. ridges as follows:

1st row: K.9(11)(13), * p.1, k.2, p.1, k.12; repeat from * ending last repeat k.9 (11)(13).

2nd row: P.9(11)(13), * k.1, p.2, k.1, p.12; repeat from * ending last repeat p.9 (11)(13).

Repeat the last 2 rows 3 more times.

Continuing in s.s. with p.st. ridges as set and working in stripe sequence given for back, work 6 rows straight.

Then continuing in stripes as set, and working the extra sts. into the s.s. with p.st. ridges pattern as they occur, inc. 1st. at each end of the next row and the 12 following 8th rows.

On 80(84)(88) sts. pattern 17 rows.

To shape the sleevetop: Cast off 6sts. at the beginning of the next 2 rows, then dec. 1st. at each end of the next row and the 18(20)(22) following alternate rows.

Cast off 3sts. at the beginning of the next 6 rows, then cast off the 12 remaining sts.

The collar:

With No.11 needles and a. cast on 148 (152)(156) sts. and work 4 rows in single rib.

Next row: Rib 4, sl.1, k.2 tog., p.s.s.o., rib until 7 remain, sl.1, k.2 tog., p.s.s.o., rib to end.

Rib 3 rows.

Repeat the last 4 rows 8 more times then cast off the 112(116)(120) remaining sts. loosely.

The right frontband:

With No.11 needles and a. cast on 18sts. and work 174(178)(182) rows in single rib, then cast off.

The left frontband:

With No.11 needles and a. cast on 18sts. and work 6(8)(10) rows in single rib.

1st Buttonhole row: Rib 6, cast off 6, rib to end.

2nd Buttonhole row: Rib 6, turn, cast on 6, turn, rib to end.

Rib 18 more rows.

Repeat the last 20 rows 7 more times then work the 2 buttonhole rows again.

Rib 6(8)(10) more rows, then cast off.

To work the vertical stripes:

Using crochet hook with right side of work facing work in chain st. up each p.st. ridge alternating a. and b. in the following way. Insert crochet hook into st. at bottom of p.st. ridge, holding yarn at back of work, draw 1 loop through. * Insert hook through st. above, wind yarn round hook and draw loop through this st. and the loop on the hook; repeat from * to top. The vertical stripes may be embroidered.

To make up the jacket:

Press all parts on the wrong side with a warm iron over a damp cloth. Join shoulder seams. Set in sleeves. Join sleeve and side seams. Neatly sew row ends of pocket tops in place. Sew on buttons. Neatly sew cast off edge of collar in place all round neck edge. Neatly sew front bands in position. Press seams.

HOE, HOE, HOE

Easy to wear, simple to make, this lumber is knitted in chunky cotton. Colours available, in addition to the red, white and blue shown in the picture, are blossom pink, black and Venetian green.

Materials:
30 (30) (32) (32) ounces of 'Woollybear' Chunky Cotton; a pair each of No. 6 and No. 7 knitting needles; 4 buttons; a cable needle. The wool and buttons for the lumber are available from the Patricia Roberts Knitting Shop, 60 Kinnerton St., London S.W.1. Mail order service available.

Tension:
10 stitches and 12 rows to 5 cm (2 in.) over the pattern using No. 6 needles.

Abbreviations:
K., knit; p., purl; st., stitch; tog., together; dec., decrease (by working 2 sts. tog.); inc., increase (by working twice into same st.); s.s., stocking stitch; single rib is k. 1 and p. 1 alternately; cr. 3 rt., cross 3 right thus, slip next st. onto cable needle and leave at back of work, k. 2, then p. 1 from cable needle; cr. 3 lt., cross 3 left thus, slip next 2 sts. onto cable needle and leave at front of work, p. 1, then k. 2 from cable needle; m.b., make bobble thus, p. 1, k. 1, p. 1, k. 1, p. 1, all into next st., turn, k. 5, turn, p. 5, slip 2nd, 3rd, 4th and 5th sts. over first st.; p. or k. 1b., p. or k. into back of st.; k. 2 tog.b., k. 2 tog. through back of sts.; up 1, pick up the loop that lies between the needles, slip it onto left-hand needle, then k. into back of it.

Note:
The instructions are given for the 32-inch bust size. Where they vary work the figures in the first brackets for the 34-inch bust size or the figures in the second brackets for the 36-inch chest size or in the figures in the third brackets for the 38-inch chest size.

Measurements:
The measurements are given in centimetres followed by inches in square brackets.

To fit bust or chest sizes			
80 [32]	85 [34]	90 [36]	95 [38]
All round at underarms			
85 [34]	90 [36]	95 [38]	100 [40]
Side seam			
47.5 [19]	47.5 [19]	47.5 [19]	47.5 [19]
Length			
70 [28]	70.5 [28¼]	72.5 [29]	73 [29¼]
Sleeve seam			
62.5 [17]	42.5 [17]	47.5 [19]	47.5 [19]

The back:
With no. 7 needles cast on 87 (91) (97) (101) sts. and work 14 rows in single rib, beginning right side rows with k. 1 and wrong side rows with p. 1.
Change to No. 6 needles and work in pattern as follows:
1st row: P. 4 (6) (9) (11), * k. 5, ** p. 7, k. 2, m.b.—see abbreviations—k. 2, p. 7, k. 5 *, p. 4, cr. 3 rt., p. 3, m.b., p. 3, cr. 3 lt., p. 4, k. 5, p. 7, k. 2, m.b., k. 2, p. 7, k. 5, p. 4 (6) (9) (11).
2nd row: K. 4 (6) (9) (11), * p. 5, ** k. 7, p. 2, p. 1b., p. 2, k. 7, p. 5 *, k. 4, p. 2, k. 4, k. 1b., k. 4, p. 2, k. 4, p. 5, k. 7, p. 2, p. 1b., p. 2, k. 7, p. 5, k. 4 (6) (9) (11).
3rd row: P. 4 (6) (9) (11), * k. 5, ** p. 6, cr. 3 rt., k. 1b., cr. 3 lt., p. 6, k. 5 *, p. 3, cr. 3 rt., p. 9, cr. 3 lt., p. 3, repeat from * to *, p. 4 (6) (9) (11).
4th row: K. 4 (6) (9) (11), * p. 5, **, k. 6, p. 2, k. 1, p. 1b., k. 1, p. 2, k. 6, p. 5 *, k. 3, p. 2, k. 11, p. 2, k. 3; repeat from * to *, k. 4 (6) (9) (11).
5th row: P. 4 (6) (9) (11), * k. 5, ** p. 5, cr. 3 rt., p. 1, k. 1b., p. 1, cr. 3 lt., p. 5, k. 5 *, p. 2, cr. 3 rt., p. 11. cr. 3 lt., p. 2; repeat from * to *, p. to end.
6th row: K. 4 (6) (9) (11), * p. 5, ** k. 5, p. 2, p. 1b., k. 1, p. 1b., k. 1, p. 1b., p. 2, k. 5, p. 5 *, k. 2, p. 2, k. 13, p. 2, k. 2; repeat from * to *, k. 4 (6) (9) (11).
7th row: P. 4 (6) (9) (11), * k. 2, m.b., k. 2, ** p. 4, cr. 3 rt., k. 1b., p. 1, k. 1b., p. 1, k. 1b., cr. 3 lt., p. 4, k. 2, m.b., k. 2 *, p. 2, cr. 3 lt., p. 11, cr. 3 rt., p. 2; repeat from * to *, p. 4 (6) (9) (11).
8th row: K. 4 (6) (9) (11), * p. 5, ** k. 4, p. 2, k. 1, p. 1b., k. 1, p. 1b., k. 1, p. 1b., k. 1, p. 2, k. 4, p. 5 *, k. 3, p. 2, k. 11, p. 2, k. 3; repeat from * to *, k. 4 (6) (9) (11).
9th row: P. 4 (6) (9) (11), * k. 1, m.b., k. 1, m.b., k. 1, ** p. 3, cr. 3 rt., p. 1, k. 1b., p. 1, k. 1b., p. 1, k. 1b., p. 1, cr. 3 lt., p. 3, k. 1, m.b., k. 1, m.b., k. 1 *, p. 3, cr. 3 lt., p. 9, cr. 3 rt., p. 3; repeat from * to *, p. to end.
10th row: K. 4 (6) (9) (11), * p. 5, ** k. 3, p. 2, p. 1b., k. 1, p. 1b., k. 1, p. 1b., k. 1, p. 1b., k. 1, p. 1b., p. 2, k. 3, p. 5 *, k. 4, p. 2, k. 9, p. 2, k. 4; repeat from * to *, k. 4 (6) (9) (11).
11th row: P. 4 (6) (9) (11), * k. 5, ** p. 2, cr. 3 rt., k. 1b., p. 1, k. 1b., p. 1, k. 1b., p. 1, k. 1b., p. 1, k. 1b., cr. 3 lt., p. 2, k. 5 *, p. 4, cr. 3 lt., p. 7, cr. 3 rt., p. 4; repeat from * to *, p. 4 (6) (9) (11).
12th row: K. 4 (6) (9) (11), * p. 5, ** k. 2, p. 2, k. 1, p. 1b., k. 1, p. 1b., k. 1, p. 1b., k. 1, p. 1b., k. 1, p. 1b., k. 1, p. 2, k. 2, p. 5 *, k. 5, p. 2, k. 7, p. 2, k. 5; repeat from * to *, k. 4 (6) (9) (11).
These 12 rows form the pattern. Repeat them 7 times more then work the first 6 rows again. The work should now measure 47.5 cm (19 in.) from the beginning.
To shape the raglan armholes: Cast off 4 sts. at the beginning of the next 2 rows.
Next row: K. 3, k. 2 tog., pattern as set until 5 remain, k. 2 tog. b., k. 3.
Next row: P. 4, pattern as set until 4 remain, p. 4.
Repeat the last 2 rows 25 (26) (28) (29) times more.***
Leave the remaining 27 (29) (31) (33) sts. on a spare needle until required for the hood.

The front:
Work as given for back until the 12 pattern rows have been worked 3 times.
Continuing in pattern as set, cast off 4 (6) (6) (6) sts. at the beginning of the next 2 rows for pocket openings.
On 79 (79) (85) (89) sts. pattern 30 rows.
Cast on 4 (6) (6) (6) sts. at the beginning of the next 2 rows to close pocket openings.
Pattern 15 rows.
Now divide the sts. for the front opening:
Next row (wrong side): Pattern 40 (42) (45) (47) sts. as set and leave them on a spare needle until required for right half front, pattern 7 sts. and leave these sts. on a safety pin until required for right front band, pattern to end and continue on these 40 (42) (45) (47) sts. for the left half front.
The left half front: Pattern 16 rows more as set.
To shape the raglan armhole: Cast off 4 sts. at beginning of next row, then work 1 row back to armhole edge.**
Next row: K. 3, k. 2 tog., pattern to end.
Next row: Pattern until 4 remain, p. 4.
Repeat the last 2 rows 12 (13) (15) (16) times more, then work the first of these rows again—22 (23) (24) (25) sts.
To shape the neck and continue to slope the raglan: Continuing to slope raglan as before cast off 3 (4) (5) (6) sts. at beginning of next row, then dec. 1 st. at neck edge on each of the next 7 rows—8 sts.
Work 9 rows sloping raglan as set—4 sts.
Next row: K. 2, k. 2 tog.
Next row: P. 3.
Next row: K. 1, k. 2 tog.
Next row: P. 2.
K. 2 tog. and fasten off.
The right half front: With right side of work facing rejoin yarn to inner edge of sts. left on spare needle and pattern to end of row.
Now work as given for left half front until ** is reached.
Next row: P. 4, pattern to end as set.
Next row: Pattern until 5 remain, k. 2 tog., k. 3.
Repeat the last 2 rows 12 (13) (15) (16) times more then work the first of these rows again—23 (24) (25) (26) sts.
To shape the neck: Still sloping raglan as before, cast off 3 (4) (5) (6) sts. at beginning of next row, then dec. 1 st. at neck edge on each of the next 7 rows—9 sts.

Work 10 rows more, sloping raglan as before—4 sts.
Next row: K. 2 tog.b., k. 2.
Next row: P. 3.
Next row: K. 2 tog.b., k. 1.
P. 2, then k. 2 tog. b. and fasten off.

The sleeves *(both alike)*:
With No. 7 needles cast on 45 (47) (51) (53) sts. and work 23 rows in single rib.
Next row: Rib 4 (5) (7) (8),* up 1, rib 2; repeat from * ending last repeat rib 3 (4) (6) (7)—65 (67) (71) (73) sts.
Change to No. 6 needles and work in pattern as follows: *1st row:* P. 6 (7) (9) (10), work from * to * on first pattern row given for back, then work from ** to *, p. 6 (7) (9) (10).
2nd row: K. 6 (7) (9) (10), work from * to * then from ** to * on 2nd row given for back, k. 6 (7) (9) (10).
3rd row: P. 6 (7) (9) (10), work from * to *, then from ** to * on 3rd row given for back, p. 6 (7) (9) (10).
4th row: K. 6 (7) (9) (10), work from * to *, then from ** to * on 4th row given for back, k. to end.
5th to 12th rows: P. on right side or k. on wrong side, 6 (7) (9) (10), work from * to *, then from ** to * on each row, given for back, p. or k. (as appropriate) to end.
These 12 rows form the pattern. Repeat them 5 (5) (6) (6) times more, then work the first 6 rows again.
To shape the raglan sleevetop: Work as given for raglan armhole shaping on back until *** is reached.
Leave the remaining 5 sts. on a safety pin until required for hood.

The left front band:
With No. 7 needles cast on 7 sts. and work in rib as follows:
1st row: K. 2, p. 1, k. 1, p. 1, k. 2.
2nd row: K. 1, * p. 1, k. 1; repeat from * to end.
Repeat these 2 rows 22 (23) (25) (26) times, then leave sts. on a safety pin until required for hood.

The right front band:
With right side of work facing rejoin yarn to inner edge of sts. left on safety pin and using No. 7 needles work 4 (6) (8) (8) rows in rib as given for left front band.
1st Buttonhole row: Rib 2, cast off 3, rib to end.
2nd Buttonhole row: Rib 2, turn, cast on 3, rib to end.
Rib 10 rows as set.
Repeat the last 12 rows twice more, then work the 2 buttonhole rows again.
Rib 4 (4) (6) (8) rows more, then leave these 7 sts. on a safety pin until required for hood.

The hood:
First join raglan seams then sew front bands in place, so that the cast on edge of left front band is sewn behind base of right front band.
With right side of work facing rejoin yarn and using No. 7 needles rib as set across the 7 sts. of right front band, pick up and k. 25 (27) (29) (31) sts. from right front neck edge, k. across the 5 sts. at top of right sleeve, the 27 (29) (31) (33) sts. at back neck edge, and the 5 sts. at top of left sleeve, pick up and k. 25 (27) (29) (31) sts. from left front neck edge, then rib across the 7 sts. of left front band— 101 (107) (113) (119) sts.
On 101 (107) (113) (119) sts. work 62 (62) (68) (68) rows in single rib.
Now divide the sts. for the centre back: Rib 34 (36) (38) (40) and leave these sts. on a spare needle until required for second half hood, cast off 33 (35) (37) (39) sts. for centre, then rib to end and continue on these 34 (36) (38) (40) sts. for the first half hood.
The first half hood:
Rib 18 (19) (20) (21) rows, then cast off.
The second half hood:
With right side of work facing rejoin yarn to inner edge of sts. left on spare needle and rib 18 (19) (20) (21) rows, then cast off.

The pocket backs *(two alike)*:
With No. 6 needles cast on 26 sts. and beginning with a k. row s.s. 42 rows, then cast off.

The pocket tops *(both alike)*:
With right side of work facing using No. 7 needles pick up and k. 26 sts. from row ends between cast off and cast on groups at each side of front.
Work 12 rows in single rib, then cast off.

To make up the jacket:
Press all parts except the ribbing on the wrong side with a warm iron over a damp cloth. Sew pocket backs in place, fold pocket tops in half to wrong side and neatly sew in place. Join sleeve and side seams. Join cast off edges of 2 sides of hood, then sew row ends of these to centre cast off sts. Press seams. Sew on buttons.

CHILD'S PLAY

The warm woolly sweater, hat and scarf are simply knitted in stocking stitch and ribbing. The traditional Aran pullover is warm and practical for cold winter days, but could be teamed with cream shorts for special occasions. The chunky jacket isn't nearly as intricate as it looks, so it could be the first Aran you attempt, because it's small and knitted in thick yarn.

THE JACKET

Materials:
10(11)(13)(15) 50 gram balls of Hayfield Gaylon Thickerknit; a pair each of No.6 and No.7 knitting needles; 4 buttons.

Tension:
The tension is based on a stocking stitch tension of 8 stitches and 12 rows to 5 cm (2 in.) using No.6 needles. If you cannot obtain the correct tension using needles of the size suggested, use larger or smaller ones accordingly.

Abbreviations:
K.,knit; p.,purl; st.,stitch; tog.,together; dec.,decrease; inc.,increase; s.s.,stocking stitch; single rib is k.1 and p.1 alternately; k.2 tog.b., k.2 tog. through back of sts.; up 1, pick up the loop that lies between the needles, slip it onto left-hand needle and k. into back of it; tw.2, twist 2 thus—k. into front of 2nd st. on left-hand needle, then into front of first st. allowing both sts. to fall from left-hand needle at the same time; m.b.,make bobble thus—k.1, yarn round needle, k.1, yarn round needle, k.1 all into next st., turn, p.5, turn, k.5, turn, p.5, turn, pass 2nd, 3rd and 4th and 5th sts. on left-hand needle over first st. then k. into back of this st.; sl.,slip; p.s.s.o., pass sl. st. over.

Note:
The instructions are given for the 1½-year-old size. Where they vary, work the instructions in the first brackets for the 2-year-old size; the figures in the second brackets for the 4-year-old size; or the figures in the third brackets for the 6-year-old size.

Measurements:
The following measurements are given in centimetres first, followed by inches in brackets.

1½ yrs	2 yrs	4 yrs	6 yrs
All round at underarms			
55(22)	60(24)	65(26)	70(28)
Side seam			
25(10)	29(11½)	32.5(13)	36(14½)
Length			
37.5(15)	42.5(17)	47.5(19)	52.5(21)
Sleeve seam			
20(8)	24(9½)	27.5(11)	31(12½)

The back:
With No.7 needles cast on 49(53)(57)(61) sts. and work 4 rows in single rib.
Change to No.6 needles and work in pattern as follows:
1st row: * P.1(2)(3)(4), tw.2, p.5, k.2 tog., up 1, k.1, up 1, k.2 tog.b., p.5, tw.2, p.1(2)(3)(4), * k.1, ** p.1, k.1; repeat from ** twice more, then repeat from * to *.
2nd row: * P.4(5)(6)(7), k.4, p.5, k.4, p.4(5)(6)(7), * p.1, k.1, p.1, k.1, p.1, k.1, p.1; repeat from * to *.
3rd row: * P.1(2)(3)(4), tw.2, p.4, k.2 tog., up 1, k.3, up 1, k.2 tog.b., p.4, tw.2, p.1(2)(3)(4), * rib next 7sts. as set, then repeat from * to *.
4th row: * P.4(5)(6)(7), k.3, p.7, k.3, p.4(5)(6)(7), * rib next 7sts. as set; repeat from * to *.
5th row: * P.1(2)(3)(4), tw.2, p.3, k.2 tog., up 1, k.5, up 1, k.2 tog.b., p.3, tw.2, p.1(2)(3)(4), * rib 7; repeat from * to *.
6th row: * P.4(5)(6)(7), k.2, p.9, k.2, p.4(5)(6)(7), * rib 7; repeat from * to *.
7th row: * P.1(2)(3)(4), tw.2, p.2, k.2 tog., up 1, k.7, up 1, k.2 tog.b., p.2, tw.2, p.1(2)(3)(4), * rib 7; repeat from * to *.
8th row: * P.4(5)(6)(7), k.1, p.11, k.1, p.4(5)(6)(7), * rib 7; repeat from * to *.
9th row: * P.1(2)(3)(4), tw.2, p.1, k.2 tog., up 1, k.9, up 1, k.2 tog.b., p.1, tw.2, p.1(2)(3)(4), * rib 7; repeat from * to *.
10th row: P.21(23)(25)(27), rib 7, p. to end.
11th row: * P.1(2)(3)(4), tw.2, inc. in next st., k.1, m.b., k.3, sl.1, k.2 tog., p.s.s.o., k.3, m.b., k.1, inc., tw.2, p.1(2)(3)(4), * rib 7; repeat from * to *.
12th row: As 8th row.
13th row: * P.1(2)(3)(4), tw.2, p.1, inc., k.4, sl.1, k.2 tog., p.s.s.o., k.4, inc., p.1, tw.2, p.1(2)(3)(4), * rib 7; repeat from * to *.
14th row: As 6th row.
15th row: * P.1(2)(3)(4), tw.2, p.1, inc., p.1, k.1, m.b., k.1, sl.1, k.2 tog., p.s.s.o., k.1, m.b., k.1, p.1, inc., p.1, tw.2, p.1(2)(3)(4), * rib 7; repeat from * to *.
16th row: As 4th row.
17th row: * P.1(2)(3)(4), tw.2, p.1, inc., p.2, k.2, sl.1, k.2 tog., p.s.s.o., k.2, p.2, inc., p.1, tw.2, p.1(2)(3)(4), * rib 7; repeat from * to *
18th row: As 2nd row.
19th row: * P.1(2)(3)(4), tw.2, p.1, inc., p.3, k.2 tog.b., m.b., k.2 tog., p.3, inc., p.1, tw.2, p.1(2)(3)(4), * rib 7; repeat from * to *.
20th row: * P.4(5)(6)(7), k.5, p.3, k.5, p.4(5)(6)(7), * rib 7; repeat from * to *.
21st row: * P.1(2)(3)(4), tw.2, p.1, inc., p.4, sl.1, k.2 tog., p.s.s.o., p.4, inc., p.1, tw.2, p.1(2)(3)(4), * rib 7; repeat from * to *.
22nd row: * P.4(5)(6)(7), k.6, p.1, k.6, p.4(5)(6)(7), * rib 7; repeat from * to *.
23rd row: * P.1(2)(3)(4), tw.2, p.5, p.2 tog., up 1, k.1, up 1, p.2 tog., p.5, tw.2, p.1(2)(3)(4), * rib 7; repeat from * to *.
24th row: * P.4(5)(6)(7), k.5, p.3, k.5, p.4(5)(6)(7), * rib 7; repeat from * to *.
These 24 rows form the pattern. Repeat them once (once) (twice) (twice) more, then work the first 8(18)(2)(12) rows again.
To shape the armholes: Cast off 2sts. at the beginning of the next 2 rows, then dec.1st. at each end of the next row and the 2(3)(4)(5) following alternate rows. On 39(41)(43)(45)sts. pattern 21(23)(25)(27) rows.
To slope the shoulders: Cast off 8(9)(9)(10)sts. at the beginning of the next 2 rows—23(23)(25)(25)sts.
Cast off.

The pocket backs *(both alike)*:
With No.6 needles cast on 11(13)(15)(17)sts., and beginning with a k. row s.s. 24 rows, then leave these sts. on a stitch holder until required.

The left front:
With No.7 needles cast on 21(23)(25)(27)sts. and work 4 rows in single rib.
Change to No.6 needles and work from * to * on each of the 24 pattern rows given for back.
Pocket row: Pattern as set for first row across 5sts., sl. next 11(13)(15)(17)sts. onto stitch holder and leave at front of work and, in their place, pattern as set across the 11(13)(15)(17)sts. of one pocket back, then pattern to end.
Continuing in pattern as set, work 29(39)(47)(57) rows. Work 1 extra row here when working right front.
To slope the front edge: Dec.1st. at the end of the next row and the following 4th row.
Work 1 row back to armhole edge.
To shape the armhole and continue to slope the front edge: While decreasing 1st. at front edge on every 4th row from previous front edge dec. cast off 2sts. at the beginning of the next row and then dec.1st. at the armhole edge on the 3(4)(5)(6) following alternate rows.
Still decreasing at front edge on every 4th row, pattern 16(14)(16)(14) rows—8(9)(9)(10)sts.
Pattern 5(9)(9)(13) rows.
To slope the shoulder: Cast off the remaining 8(9)(9)(10)sts.

The right front:
Work as given for left front noting the variation in the number of rows before sloping front edge.

The pocket tops *(both alike)*:
With right side of work facing rejoin yarn to the sts. left on stitch holder at front and using No.7 needles work 6 rows in single rib, then cast off.

The sleeves *(both alike)*:
With No.7 needles cast on 31(33)(35)(37) sts. and work 12 rows in single rib.
Change to No.6 needles and work in pattern as follows:
1st row: P.5, then work from * to * on first pattern row given for back, then p.5—to end.
2nd row: K.5, work from * to * on 2nd pattern row on back, then k.5.
These 2 rows set the position of the pattern given between * and * on back.
Pattern 46(54)(64)(72) more rows in pattern as set.
To shape the sleevetop: Cast off 2sts. at the beginning of the next 2 rows, then dec. 1st. at each end of the next row and the 5(6)(7)(8) following alternate rows.
On 15sts. work 1 row.
Dec.1st. at each end of the next 2 rows,

then cast off 3sts., at the beginning of the next 2 rows.
Cast off the remaining 5sts.

The left front band and collar:
With No.7 needles cast on 11sts. and work 52(62)(70)(80) rows in single rib.
***To shape the collar:* Inc.1st. at the beginning of the next row and the 14(15)(16)(17) following alternate rows.
On 26(27)(28)(29)sts. work 1 row.
Cast on 27(29)(31)(33)sts. at the beginning of the next row—at shaped end.
On 53(56)(59)(62)sts. work 24 rows in single rib, then cast off in rib.

The right front band and collar:
With No.7 needles cast on 11sts. and work 8(6)(8)(12) rows in single rib.
1st Buttonhole row: Rib 4, cast off 3, rib to end.
2nd Buttonhole row: Rib 4, turn, cast on 3, turn, rib to end.
Rib 12(16)(18)(20) rows.
Repeat the last 14(18)(20)(22) rows twice more, then work the buttonhole rows again.
Work 1 row straight, then work as given for the left front band and collar from ** to end.

The belt:
With No.7 needles cast on 7sts. and work in single rib until the belt measures 90(95)(100)(105) cm or 36(38)(40)(42) in. then cast off.

To make up the jacket:
Press all parts lightly on the wrong side with a warm iron over a damp cloth. Join shoulder seams. Set in sleeves. Join sleeve and side seams. Sew pocket backs in place. Fold pocket tops to right side and sew row end edges in place. Join the 24 row end edge of collar for centre back seam. With this seam to centre back neck, neatly sew rest of shaped edge in place along back neck and down appropriate front edge. Press seams. Sew on buttons. Make belt loops at side seams.

THE PULLOVER

Materials:
5(6)(7)(8) 25 gram balls of Hayfield Gaylon D.K.; a pair each of No.11 and No.10 knitting needles; a cable needle.

Tension:
The tension is based on 13 stitches and 17 rows to 5 cm (2 in.) over stocking stitch using No.10 needles. If you cannot obtain the correct tension using needles of the size suggested, use larger or smaller ones accordingly.

Abbreviations:
K.,knit; p.,purl; st.,stitch; tog.,together; dec.,decrease (by working 2sts. tog.); inc.,increase; double rib is k.2 and p.2 alternately; m.b.,make bobble thus—k.1, p.1 then k.1 all into next st., turn, p.3, turn, k.3, turn, p.3, turn, k.3 tog.; cr.3 rt., cross 3 right thus—slip next st. onto cable needle and leave at back of work, k.2 then p.1 from cable needle; cr.3 lt., cross 3 left thus—slip next 2sts. onto cable needle and leave at front of work, p.1, then k.2 from cable needle; cable 4 thus—slip next 2sts. onto cable needle and leave at front of work, k.2 then k.2 from cable needle.

Note:
The instructions are given for the 1½-year-old size. Where they vary, work the figures in the first brackets for the 2-year-old size; the figures in the second brackets for the 4-year-old size; or the figures in the third brackets for the 6-year-old size.

Measurements:
The following measurements are given in centimetres first, followed by inches in brackets.

1½ yrs	2 yrs	4 yrs	6 yrs
All round at underarms			
50(20)	55(22)	60(24)	65(26)
Side seam			
15(6)	17.5(7)	20(8)	22.5(9)
Length			
27.5(11)	31(12½)	35(14)	39(15½)

The back:
With No.11 needles cast on 60(66)(72)(78) sts. and work 24(28)(32)(36) rows in double rib.
Change to No.10 needles and work in pattern as follows:
1st row: P.4(7)(10)(13), m.b., p.9, k.5, p.8, k.6, p.8, k.5, p.9, m.b., p.4(7)(10)(13).
2nd row: K.14(17)(20)(23), p.5, k.8, p.6, k.8, p.5, k.14(17)(20)(23).
3rd row: P.13(16)(19)(22), cr.3 rt., p.1, cr.3 lt., p.7, k.6, p.7, cr.3 rt., p.1, cr.3 lt., p. to end.
4th row: K.13(16)(19)(22), p.2, k.3, p.2, k.7, p.6, k.7, p.2, k.3, p.2, k. to end.
5th row: P.2(5)(8)(11), m.b., p.3, m.b., p.5, cr.3 rt., p.3, cr.3 lt., p.6, cable 6, p.6, cr.3 rt., p.3, cr.3 lt., p.5, m.b., p.3, m.b., p.2(5)(8)(11).
6th row: K.12(15)(18)(21), p.2, k.5, p.2, k.6, p.6, k.6, p.2, k.5, p.2, k.12(15)(18)(21).
7th row: P.11(14)(17)(20), cr.3 rt., p.5, cr.3 lt., p.5, k.6, p.5, cr.3 rt., p.5, cr.3 lt., p. to end.
8th row: K.11(14)(17)(20), p.2, k.7, p.2,

k.5, p.6, k.5, p.2, k.7, p.2, k. to end.
9th row: P.4(7)(10)(13), m.b., p.5, cr.3 rt., p.3, m.b., p.3, cr.3 lt., p.4, k.6, p.4, cr.3 rt., p.3, m.b., p.3, cr.3 lt., p.5, m.b., p.4(7)(10)(13).
10th row: K.10(13)(16)(19), p.2, k.9, p.2, k.4, p.6, k.4, p.2, k.9, p.2, k.10(13)(16)(19).
11th row: P.9(12)(15)(18), cr.3 rt., p.9, cr.3 lt., p.3, k.6, p.3, cr.3 rt., p.9, cr.3 lt., p.9(12)(15)(18).
12th row: K.9(12)(15)(18), p.2, k.11, p.2, k.3, p.6, k.3, p.2, k.11, p.2, k.9(12)(15)(18).
13th row: P.2(5)(8)(11), m.b., p.3, m.b., p.2, * k.2, p.2, m.b., p.2, m.b., p.2, m.b., p.2, k.2, * p.3, cable 6, p.3; repeat from * to *, p 2, m.b., p.3, m.b., p.2(5)(8)(11).
14th row: As 12th row.
15th row: P.9(12)(15)(18), cr.3 lt., p.9, cr.3 rt., p.3, k.6, p.3, cr.3 lt., p.9, cr.3 rt., p.9(12)(15)(18).
16th row: As 10th row.
17th and 24th rows: Reading cr.3 lt., for cr.3 rt., and cr.2 rt. for cr.3 lt., work the 9th row back to the 2nd row.
These 24 rows form the pattern; work the first 6(10)(14)(18) rows again.
To shape the armholes: Maintaining the continuity of the pattern as set, cast off 3sts. at the beginning of the next 2 rows, then dec. 1 st. at each end of next row and the 4(6)(8)(10) following alternate rows. On 44 (46)(48)(50) sts., pattern 29(29)(29)(31)rows.
To slope the shoulders: Cast off 6(7)(7)(8) sts. at the beginning of the next 2 rows.
Change to No.11 needles and on 32(32)(34)(34) sts. work 8 rows in double rib, then cast off.

The front:
Work as given for back until the 24 pattern rows have been worked once, then work the first 5(9)(13)(17) rows again.
Now divide the sts. for the neck: *Next row:* Pattern 30(33)(36)(39) and leave these sts. on a spare needle until required for right front shoulder, pattern to end and continue on these 30(33)(36)(39) sts. for the left front shoulder.
The left front shoulder: To shape the armhole and slope the neck: Maintaining the continuity of the pattern as set, cast off 3 sts. at beginning—for armhole and dec. 1 st. at end for neck on the next row.
Work 1 row straight, then dec. 1 st. at each end of the next row and the 4(6)(8)(10) following alternate rows.
Work 1 row straight then dec. 1 st. at the neck edge on the next row and the 9(7)(6)(4) following alternate rows.
On 6(7)(7)(8) sts. pattern 9(13)(15)(21) rows.
Cast off.
The right front shoulder: With right side of work facing rejoin yarn and work to end of row.
Now work as given for left front to end.

The front neckband:
With right side of work facing rejoin yarn and using No.11 needles pick up and k.34 (38)(42)(46) sts. from left front neck edge, pick up and k.1 st. from centre front, then 34(38)(42)(46) sts. up right front neck edge.
Next row: * K.2, p.2; repeat from * until within 2sts. of centre front, k.2 tog., p.1, k.2 tog.b., * p.2, k.2; repeat from last * to end.
Next row: Rib as set to within 2sts. of centre st., p.2 tog.b., k.1, p.2 tog., rib to end as set.
Continuing in rib as set and decreasing as before at each side of centre st. rib 5 more rows, then cast off loosely in rib.

The armbands (*both alike*):
First join shoulder seam. With right side of work facing rejoin yarn and using No.11 needles, pick up and k.72(80)(88)(96) sts. from all round armhole edge.
Work 7 rows in double rib, then cast off loosely in rib.

To make up the pullover:
Press all s.s. parts on the wrong side with a warm iron over a damp cloth. Join side seams. Press seams.

THE SLIT-COLLAR SWEATER

Materials:
11(12)(14)(16) 25 gram balls of Hayfield Gaylon 4-ply; a pair each of No. 12 and No. 13 knitting needles; a set of 4 double pointed No. 13 knitting needles.

Tension:
16 stitches and 20 rows to 5 cm (2 in.) over the stocking stitch using No.12 needles. If you cannot obtain the correct tension using needles of the size suggested, use larger or smaller ones accordingly.

Abbreviations:
K.,knit; p.,purl; st.,stitch; tog.,together; dec.,decrease (by working 2sts. tog.); inc.,increase (by working twice into same st.); s.s.,stocking stitch; double rib is k.2 and p.2 alternately.

The scarf:
When completed will measure 75(87.5) (100)(112.5) cm or 30(35)(40)45) in.

The hat:
Will be suitable for average children's head sizes aged 1(2)(4)(6).

Note:
The instructions are given for the 1½-year-old size. Where they vary work the figures in the first brackets for the 2-year-old size; those in the second brackets for the 4-year-old size; those in the third brackets for the 6-year-old size.

Measurements:
The following measurements are given in centimetres first, followed by inches in brackets.

1½ yrs	2 yrs	4 yrs	6 yrs
All round at underarms			
50(20)	55(22)	60(24)	65(26)
Side seam			
15(6)	17.5(7)	20(8)	22.5(9)
Length			
26(10½)	30(12)	34(13½)	37.5(15)
Sleeve seam			
20(8)	24(9½)	27.5(11)	31(12½)

The back:
With No.13 needles cast on 80(88)(96)(104) sts. and work 28(34)(40)(46) rows in double rib.
Change to No.12 needles and beginning with a k. row s.s. 36(40)(44)(48) rows.
To shape the armholes: Cast off 4sts. at beginning of next 2 rows, then dec. 1st. at each end of the next row and the 7(8)(9)(10) following alternate rows.
On 56(62)(68)(74) sts. s.s. 23(27)(31)(33) rows.
To slope the shoulders: Cast off 5(6)(7)(8) sts. at the beginning of the next 4 rows, then leave the remaining 36(38)(40)(42) sts. on a spare needle until required for collar.

The front:
Work as given for back until the armhole shaping has been worked.
S.s. 2(4)(6)(6) more rows.
Now divide the sts. for the neck: *Next row:* P.19(22)(24)(27) and leave these sts. on a spare needle until required for right front shoulder, p.9(9)(10)(10) and leave these sts. on a safety pin until required for right front collar, p.9(9)(10)(10) and leave these sts. on another safety pin until required for left front collar, p. to end and continue on these 19(22)(24)(27) sts. for the left front shoulder.
The left front shoulder: To shape the neck: Dec. 1st. at neck edge on each of the next 9(10)(10)(11) rows.
On 10(12)(14)(16) sts. s.s. 11(12)(14)(15) rows.
To slope the shoulder: Cast off 5(6)(7)(8) sts. at beginning of next row. On 5(6)(7)(8) sts. work 1 row, then cast off.
The right front shoulder: With right side of work facing rejoin yarn to inner edge of sts. left on spare needle and work to end of row, then work as given for left front shoulder to end.

The sleeves (*both alike*):
With No.13 needles cast on 42(46)(50)(54) sts. and work 38(38)(44)(44) rows in double rib.
Change to No.12 needles and beginning with a k. row s.s. 2 rows.
Inc. 1st. at each end of next row and the 6(7)(8)(9) following 8th (10th)(10th)(10th) rows.
On 56(62)(68)(74) sts. s.s. 11(5)(7)(11) rows.
To shape the sleevetop: Cast off 4sts. at beginning of next 2 rows, then dec. 1st. at each end of the next row and the 11(13)(15)(17) following alternate rows.
On 24(26)(28)(30) sts. work 1 row.
Cast off 4sts. at beginning of next 4 rows.
Cast off the remaining 8(10)(12)(14) sts.

The collar:
First join shoulder seams. With right side of work facing rejoin yarn and using the set of 4 double pointed No.13 knitting needles, k. across the 9(9)(10)(10) sts. left on safety pin at right front neck edge, pick up and k.25(26)(28)(29) sts. from right front edge, k. across the 36(38)(40)(42) sts. at back neck edge, pick up and k.25(26)(28)(29) sts. from left front edge, then k. across the 9(9)(10)(10) sts. left on safety pin at left front neck edge—104(108)(116)(120) sts.
Now work in rounds of double rib as follows, firstly marking centre front with coloured thread: *1st round:* K.1, * p.2, k.2; repeat from * ending last repeat k.1, instead of 2.
Repeat this round 4 more times.
Now divide the sts. for the split at centre front and work as follows: *Next row:* Rib to end as set, turn.
Next row: P.1, * k.2, p.2; repeat from * ending last repeat p.1.
Next row: K.1, * p.2, k.2; repeat from * ending last repeat k.1.
Repeat the last 2 rows 11(12)(13)(14) more times, then cast off in rib very loosely.

To make up the sweater:
Press all parts except the ribbing with a warm iron over a damp cloth. Set in sleeves. Join sleeve and side seams. Press seams.

THE SCARF

With No.13 needles cast on 50 sts. and work in double rib, beginning right side rows with k.2 and wrong side rows with p.2 until the scarf measures 75(87.5)(100)(112.5) cm or 30(35)(40)(45) in., then cast off in rib.
The fringing: Cut 12 pieces of yarn each 8 in long and fold in half. Using a crochet hook draw looped end through one corner of cast off edge of scarf. Pass cut ends through looped end and pull firmly to form a tassel. Work 5 more tassels along the cast off edge in the same way. In the same way work 6 tassels along the cast on edge of scarf.
Press lightly on the wrong side.

THE HAT

With No. 13 needles cast on 114(122)(130)(138) sts. and work 24(38)(44)(48) rows in double rib.
Change to No.12 needles and beginning with a k. row s.s. 16(18)(20)(22) rows.
1st Decrease row: K.2, * k.2 tog., k.12 (13)(14)(15); repeat from * to end.
S.s. 3 rows.
2nd Decrease row: K.2, * k.2 tog., k.11 (12)(13)(14); repeat from * to end.
Thus working 1st. less between the decreases on every following decrease row repeat the last 4 rows 4 more times.
P.1 row.
Next decrease row: K.2, * k.2 tog., k.6(7)(8)(9); repeat from * to end.
Still working 1st. less between the decreases on every decrease row, repeat the last 2 rows 5(6)(7)(9) more times—18sts.
Next row: * P.2 tog.; repeat from * to end.
Break off yarn leaving a long end and thread this through remaining 9sts. Draw up and fasten off securely.
To complete: Press. Join row end seam. Fold ribbing to right side.

DIAMOND

Knit it now and you will wear it for ever and ever, no matter how young or old you are.

Materials:
24 (25) (26) 25 grams balls of Sirdar Fontein Crepe 4-ply in main colour and 6 balls in contrast colour; a pair each of size 2¾ mm (No. 12) and size 2¼ mm (No. 13) Aero knitting needles; 7 buttons.

Tension:
10 stitches—1 repeat of the pattern to 3 cm (1¼ in.) in width and 78 rows—1 repeat of the pattern to 19.25 cm (7¾ in.) in length. If you cannot obtain the correct tension using the size needles suggested, use larger or smaller ones accordingly.

Abbreviations:
K., knit; p., purl; st., stitch; tog., together; dec., decrease (by working 2 sts. tog.); inc., increase (by working twice into same st.); s.s., stocking stitch is k. on the right side and p. on the wrong side; tw. 2rt., twist 2 right thus, k. into front of 2nd st. on left hand needles, then into 1st st. allowing both loops to fall from left hand needle together; tw. 2lt., twist 2 left thus, k. into back of 2nd st. on left hand needle, then into front of 1st st. allowing loops to fall from left hand needle together; sl., slip; m., main colour; c., contrast colour; double rib is k. 2, and p. 2 alternately; up 1, pick up the loop that lies between the needles, slip it onto left hand needle, then k. into back of it; single rib is k. 1 and p. 1 alternately.

Note:
The instructions are given for the small size. Where they vary work the figures in the first brackets for the medium size or the figures in the second brackets for the large size.

Measurements:

The measurements are given in centimetres followed by inches in square brackets.

small	medium	large
All round at underarms		
92.5 [37]	99 [39½]	105 [42]
Side seam (with ribbing folded in half)		
40 [16]	40 [16]	40 [16]
Length (with ribbing folded in half)		
61 [24½]	62 [24¾]	63 [25]
Sleeve seam		
42.5 [17]	42.5 [17]	42.5 [17]

The back:
With size 2¼ mm (No. 13) needles and m. cast on 128 (138) (144) sts. and work 107 rows in double rib.
Increase row: Rib 4 (9) (5), * up 1, rib 8 (8) (7); repeat from * ending last repeat rib 4 (9) (6)—144 (154) (164) sts.
Change to size 2¾ mm (No. 12) needles and work in pattern as follows:
1st row: K. 1, * tw. 2rt., k. 8; repeat from * ending last repeat k. 1.
2nd row: P. 1, * sl. 2, p. 8; repeat from * from ending last repeat p. 1.
3rd row: K. 2, * tw. 2lt., k. 6, tw. 2rt.; repeat from * until 2 remain, k. 2.
4th row: K. 1, p. 1, * k. 1, sl. 1, p. 6, sl. 1, p 1; repeat from * until 2 remain, k. 1, p. 1.
5th row: P. 1, k. 1, * p. 1, tw. 2lt., k. 4, tw. 2rt., k. 1; repeat from * until 2 remain, p. 1, k. 1.
6th row: K. 1, p. 1, k. 1, p. 1, * sl. 1, p. 4, sl. 1, k. 1, p. 1, k. 1, p. 1; repeat from * to end.
7th row: P. 1, k. 1, p. 1, k. 1, * tw. 2lt., k. 2, tw. 2rt., p. 1, k. 1, p. 1, k. 1; repeat from * to end.
8th row: K. 1, p. 1, k. 1, p. 1, * k. 1, sl. 1, p. 2, sl. 1, p. 1, k. 1, p. 1, k. 1, p. 1; repeat from * to end.
9th row: P. 1, k. 1, p. 1, k. 1, * p. 1, tw. 2lt., tw. 2rt., k. 1, p. 1, k. 1, p. 1, k. 1; repeat from * to end.
10th row: K. 1, p. 1, k. 1, p. 1, * k. 1, p. 1, sl. 2, k. 1, p. 1, k. 1, p. 1, k. 1, p. 1; repeat from * to end.
11th row: P. 1, k. 1, p. 1, k. 1, * p. 1, k. 1, tw. 2rt., p. 1, k. 1, p. 1, k. 1, p. 1, k. 1; repeat from * to end.
12th row: * K. 1, p. 1; repeat from * to end.
13th row: P. 1, * tw. 2rt., k. 1, p. 1, k. 1, p. 1, k. 1, p. 1, k. 1, p. 1; repeat from * until 3 remain, tw. 2rt., k. 1.
14th row: K. 1, sl. 2, p. 1, * k. 1, p. 1, k. 1, p. 1, k. 1, p. 1, k. 1, sl. 2, pl. 1; repeat from * to end.
15th row: K. 2, * tw. 2lt., p. 1, k. 1, p. 1, k. 1, p. 1, k. 1, tw. 2rt.; repeat from * until 2 remain, k. 2.
16th row: P. 3, * sl. 1, k. 1, p. 1, k. 1, p. 1, k. 1, p. 1, sl. 1, p. 2; repeat from * ending last repeat p. 3.
17th row: K. 3, * tw. 2lt., k. 1, p. 1, k. 1, p. 1, tw. 2rt., k. 2; repeat from * ending last repeat k. 3.
18th row: P. 4, * sl. 1, p. 1, k. 1, p. 1, k. 1, sl. 1, p. 4; repeat from * to end.
19th row: K. 4, * tw. 2lt., p. 1, k. 1, tw. 2rt., k. 4; repeat from * to end.
20th row: P. 5, * sl. 1. k. 1, p. 1, sl. 1, p. 6; repeat from * ending last repeat p. 5.
21st row: K. 5, * tw. 2lt., tw. 2rt., k. 6; repeat from * ending last repeat k. 5.

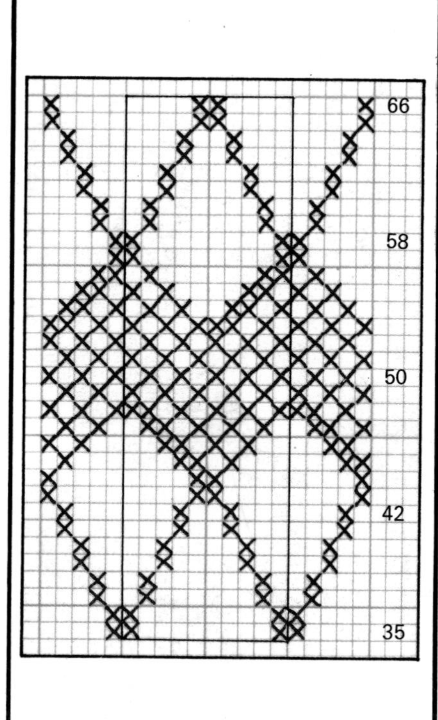

22nd row: P. 6, * sl. 2, p. 8; repeat from * ending last repeat p. 6.
23rd row: K. 6, * tw. 2rt., k. 8; repeat from * ending last repeat k. 6.
24th row: As 22nd row.
25th row: K. 5, * tw. 2rt., tw. 2lt., k. 6; repeat from * ending last repeat k. 5.
26th row: P. 5, * sl. 1, p. 2, sl. 1, p. 6; repeat from * ending last repeat p. 5.
27th row: K. 4, * tw. 2rt., k. 2, tw. 2lt., k. 4, repeat from * to end.
28th row: P. 4, * sl. 1, p. 4, sl. 1, p. 4; repeat from * to end.
29th row: K. 3, * tw. 2rt., k. 4, tw. 2lt., k. 2, repeat from * ending last repeat k. 3.
30th row: P. 3, * sl. 1, p. 6, sl. 1, p. 2; repeat from * ending last repeat p. 3.
31st row: K. 2, * tw. 2rt., k. 6, tw. 2lt.; repeat from * until 2 remain, k. 2.
32nd row: P. 2, * sl. 1, p. 8, sl. 1; repeat from * until 2 remain, p. 2.
33rd row: K. 1, * tw. 2rt., k. 8; repeat from * until 3 remain, tw. 2rt., k. 1.
34th row: P. 1, * sl. 2, p. 8; repeat from * until 3 remain, sl. 2, p. 1.
Join in c. and continue in Fair Isle pattern as follows: This is worked entirely in s.s. so only the colour details are given. Great care should be taken to avoid pulling colours not in use tightly across the back of the work, or it will become puckered.
35th row: 1 m., * 2 c., 8 m.; repeat from * until 3 remain, 2 c., 1 m.
36th row: As 35th row.
37th to 66th rows: The last 2 rows set the position of the pattern given in the chart. Now work the 37th to 66th rows from the chart.
Break off c. and continue with m. only.
67th to 69th rows: As 1st, 2nd and 3rd rows.
70th row: P. 3, * sl. 1, p. 6, sl. 1, p. 2; repeat from * ending last repeat p. 3.
71st row: K. 3, * tw. 2lt., k. 4, tw. 2rt., k. 2; repeat from * ending last repeat k. 3.
72nd row: P. 4, * sl. 1, p. 4, sl. 1, p. 4; repeat from * to end.
73rd row: K. 4, * tw. 2lt., k. 2, tw. 2rt., k. 4, repeat from * to end.
74th row: P. 5, * sl. 1, p. 2, sl. 1, p. 6; repeat from * ending last repeat p. 5.
75th row: K. 5, * tw. 2lt., tw. 2rt., k. 6; repeat from * ending last repeat k. 5.
76th row: P. 6, * sl. 2, p. 8; repeat from * ending last repeat p. 6.
77th row: K. 6, * tw. 2rt., k. 8; repeat from * ending last repeat k. 6.
78th row: P. 6, *sl. 2, p. 8; repeat from * ending last repeat p. 6.
The last 78 rows form the pattern. Repeat the first 38 rows again.
Mark each end of the last row with coloured threads to denote armholes.
Pattern 82 (86) (88) rows more.

To slope the shoulders: Cast off 45 (49) (53) sts. at the beginning of the next 2 rows.
Cast off the 54 (56) (58) remaining sts.

The left front:
With size 2¼ mm (No. 13) needles and m. cast on 64 (68) (72) sts. and work 107 rows in double rib.
Increase row: Rib 4 (6) (5), * up 1, rib 8 (7) (7); repeat from * ending last repeat rib 4 (6) (4).
Change to size 2¾ mm (No. 12) needles and on 72 (77) (82) sts. work in pattern as follows:
1st row: K. 1, * tw. 2rt., k. 8; repeat from * ending last repeat k. 9 (4) (9).
2nd row: P. 9 (4) (9), * sl. 2, p. 8; repeat from * ending last repeat p. 1.
The last 2 rows set the position of the pattern given for back. Pattern 114 rows more as set.
**Mark the end of the last row with a coloured thread to denote armhole.
To slope the front edge: Dec. 1 st. at the end—front edge—on the next row and the 26 (27) (28) following alternate rows.
On 45 (49) (53) sts. pattern 29 (31) (31) rows.
To slope the shoulder: Cast off.

The right front:
Work as given for left front until the increase row had been worked.
Change to size 2¾ mm (No. 12) needles and on 72 (77) (82) sts. work in pattern as follows:
1st row: K. 9 (4) (9), * tw. 2rt., k. 8; repeat from * ending last repeat k. 1.
The last row sets the position of the pattern giving for the back. Pattern 116 rows more. Now work as given for left front from ** to end.

The sleeves *(both alike):*
With size 2¼ mm (No. 13) needles and m. cast on 70 (72) (74) sts. and work 37 rows in double rib.

Increase row: K. 4, * up. 1, k. 1; repeat from * to end—136 (140) (144) sts.
Change to size 2¾ mm (No. 12) needles and work in pattern as follows; beginning with the 57th pattern row:
57th pattern row: 2 (4) (1) m., * 2c., 8 m.; repeat from * ending last repeat 2 (4) (1) m.
The last row sets the position of the pattern given for back. Pattern 137 rows more as set, then cast off.

The pocket backs *(both alike):*
With size 2¼ mm (No. 13) needles and m. cast on 40 sts. and s.s. 100 rows, then cast off.

The front band:
With size 2¼ mm (No. 13) needles and m. cast on 12 sts. and work 12 rows in single rib.
1st Buttonhole row: Rib 4, cast off 4, rib to end.
2nd Buttonhole row: Rib 4, turn, cast on 4, turn, rib to end.
Rib 24 rows.
Repeat the last 26 rows 5 times more, then work the 2 buttonhole rows again.
Continue in rib until the band is long enough to fit up right front edge, with last buttonhole in line with first front dec.; across back neck edge, then down left front edge, but with ribbing folded in half at lower edge.
Cast off.

To make up the cardigan:
Pin out to size and press all parts except the ribbing on the wrong side with a warm iron over a damp cloth. Join shoulder seams. Set in sleeves between the marking threads on back and front. Fold pocket backs in half and join row end edges. Join sleeve and side seams inserting pockets in side seams above ribbing, fold ribbing at lower edge in half to wrong side and slip st. in place. Sew front band in place. Press seams. Sew on buttons.

LONG TALL SALLY

No need to be long and lean to wear this chunky winter coat. Don't be put off by it's size; it's still quick to knit.

Materials:
34 50 gram balls of Wendy Naturelle; a pair each of size 8 mm [No. 0], size 7 [No. 2] and size 6 [No. 4] Aero knitting needles; a large Aero cable needle; a large Aero crochet hook; 4 buttons.
Tension:
Work at such a tension that 13 stitches measure 10 cm (4 in.) in width and 1 repeat of the pattern—120 rows measures 25 inches in length.
Abbreviations:
K., knit; p., purl; st., stitch; tog., together; dec., decrease (by working 2 sts. tog.); inc., increase (by working twice into same st.); sl., slip; y.r.n., yarn round needle; y.f., yarn forward; y.b., yarn back; 3 from 3, p. 3 tog., not allowing loops to fall from left hand needle, y.r.n., then p. 3 tog. again, but allowing the 3 sts. to fall from left hand needle in the usual way; k. 1 long, k. 1 winding yarn round needle 3 times; cr. 3rt., cross 3 right thus, slip next 2 sts. onto cable needle at back of work, k.1, then k. 2 from cable needle; cr. 3lt., cross 3 left thus, slip next st. onto cable needle at front of work, k. 2, then k. 1 from cable needle; 3 from 1, p. 1, k. 1, p. 1 all into next st.; m.b., make bobble thus, p. 3, turn, k. 3, turn, sl. 1, k. 2 tog., p.s.s.o.; p.s.s.o., pass sl. st. over; s.s.k., sl. 1, k. 1, p.s.s.o.; 5 from 1, k. 1, y.r.n., k. 1, y.r.n., k. 1, all into next st.; k. or p. 1b., k. or p. 1 through back of st.; stocking stitch is k. on the right side and p. on the wrong side; single rib is k. 1 and p. 1 alternately; d.c., double crochet.
Special note:
The first 32 pattern rows on each repeat are worked with size 8½ mm (No. 0) knitting needles and other pattern rows with size 7 mm (No. 2) needles.

Measurements:
The measurements are given in centimetres followed by inches in square brackets.

All round at underarms	133 [53]
Side seam	86 [34¼]
Length	115 [46]
Sleeve seam excluding cuffs	23 [9¼]

The back:
With size 8 mm (No. 0) needles cast on 85 sts. and work in pattern as follows:
1st row: All k.
2nd row: K. 1, * 3 from 3—see abbreviations—k. 1; repeat from * to end.
3rd row: All k.
4th row: K. 1, p. 1, k. 1, * 3 from 3, k. 1; repeat from * until 2 remain, p. 1, k. 1.
17th to 32nd rows: Repeat 1st to 4th rows. 7 times.
Change to size 7 mm [No. 2] needles.
33rd row: All k.
34th row: All p.
35th row: All k.
36th row: K. 6, * k. 1 long, k. 1 long, k. 1 long, k. 7; repeat from * ending last repeat k. 6.
37th row: K. 2, * sl. 1, k. 3, sl. 3 long sts. allowing extra loops to fall from left hand needle, k. 3; repeat from * until 3 remain, sl. 1, k. 2.
38th row: P. 2, * sl. 1, p. 3, sl. 3, p. 3; repeat from * until 3 remain, sl. 1, p. 2.
39th row: K. 6, * sl. 3, k. 7; repeat from * ending last repeat k. 6.
40th row: P. 6, * sl. 3, p. 7; repeat from * ending last repeat p. 6.
41st row: K. 4, * cr. 3rt., k. 1, cr. 3lt., k. 3; repeat from * ending last repeat k. 4.
42nd row: P. 1, sl. 3, * 3 from 1, sl. 2, 3 from 1, sl. 2, 3 from 1, sl. 3; repeat from * ending last repeat p. 1.
43rd row: K. 1, sl. 3, * y.f., m.b.—see abbreviations—y.b., sl. 2, y.f., m.b., y.b., sl. 2, y. f., m.b., y.b., sl. 3; repeat from * ending last repeat k. 1.
44th row: All p.
45th to 80th rows: Repeat 33rd to 44th rows 3 times.
81st row: K. 2, * sl. 1, k. 1, 5 from 1, k. 1; repeat from * until 3 remain, sl. 1, k. 2.
82nd row: K. 2, * y.f., sl. 1 p. wise, y.b., k. 1, p. 5 winding yarn round needle twice for each st., k. 1; repeat from * until 3 remain, y.f., sl. 1, y.b., k. 2.
83rd row: K. 4, * sl. 5 dropping extra loops, k. 3; repeat from * ending last repeat k. 4.
84th row: K. 4, * y.f., sl. 5 p. wise, y.b., k. 3; repeat from * ending last repeat k. 4 instead of k. 3.
85th row: K. 3, * k. 2 tog., sl. 3, s.s.k., k. 1; repeat from * ending last repeat k. 3.
86th row: K. 3, * p. 1, sl. 3 p. wise, p. 1, k. 1; repeat from * ending last repeat k. 3.
87th row: K. 3, * k. 2 tog., sl. 1, s.s.k., k. 1; repeat from * ending last repeat k. 3.
88th row: K. 3, * p. 1, sl. 1 p. wise, p. 1, k. 1; repeat from * ending last repeat k. 3.
89th row: K. 4, * k. 1b., k. 3; repeat from * ending last repeat k. 4.
90th row: K. 4, * p. 1b., k. 3; repeat from * ending last repeat k. 4.
91st row: K. 2, * 5 from 1, k. 1, sl. 1, k. 1; repeat from * ending last repeat k. 2 instead of k. 1, sl. 1, k. 1.
92nd row: K. 2, * p. 5 winding yarn round needle twice for each st., k. 1, y.f., sl. 1 p. wise, y.b., k. 1; repeat from * ending last repeat k. 2 *instead* of k. 1, y.f., sl. 1 p. wise, y.b., k. 1.
93rd row: K. 2, * sl. 5 dropping extra loops, k. 3; repeat from * ending last repeat k. 2.
94th row: K. 2, * y.f., sl. 5 p. wise, y.b., k. 3; repeat from * ending last repeat k. 2.
95th row: K. 1, * k. 2 tog., sl. 3, s.s.k., k. 1; repeat from * to end.
96th row: K. 1, * p. 1, sl. 3 p. wise, p. 1, k. 1; repeat from * to end.
97th row: K. 1, * k. 2 tog., sl. 1, s.s.k., k. 1; repeat from * to end.
98th row: K. 1, * p. 1, sl. 1 p. wise, p. 1, k. 1; repeat from * to end.
99th row: K. 2, * k. 1b., k. 3; repeat from * ending last repeat k. 2.
100th row: K. 2, * p. 1b., k. 3; repeat from * ending last repeat k. 2.
101th to 120th rows: As 81st to 100th rows.

Change to size 8 mm (No. 0) needles.
The last 120 rows form the pattern; work the first 44 rows again—or until work measures 86 cm (34¼ in.) from beginning.**
To shape the sleeves: Continuing in pattern as set and working the extra sts. into the pattern as they occur cast on 30 sts. at the beginning of the next 2 rows—145 sts.
Pattern 52 rows more, or until work measures 114 cm (45½ in.) from beginning.
Cast off 62 sts. at the beginning of the next 2 rows.
Cast off the remaining 21 sts.

The left front:
With size 8 (No. 0) needles cast on 45 sts. and work as given for back until ** is reached—Work 1 extra row here on right front.
To shape the sleeve: Continuing in pattern as set and working the extra sts. into the pattern as they occur cast on 30sts. at the beginning of the next row—75 sts.
Pattern 34 rows as set.
To shape the neck: Continuing in pattern as set cast off 7 sts. at the beginning of the next row, then dec. 1 st. at the neck edge on each of the next 6 rows.
On 62 sts., pattern 12 rows, then cast off.

The right front:
Work as given for left front noting the extra row before shaping the sleeve.

The pocket backs *(2 alike):*
With size 6 mm (No. 4) needles cast on 20 sts. and work 60 rows in stocking stitch, then cast off.

The cuffs *(both alike):*
First join shoulder and upper sleeve seams. With right side of work facing rejoin yarn and using size 6 mm (No. 4) knitting needles pick up and k. 20 sts. from row end edges of sleeve.
Work 15 rows in single rib, then cast off in rib.

The hood:
With right side of work facing rejoin yarn and using size 8 mm (No. 0) knitting needles pick up and k. 69 sts. from all round neck edge. p. 1 row.
Now work the first 32 pattern rows given for back, then work the first 16 rows again. Cast off. Fold cast off edge in half and join.

The front edgings:
With right side of work facing rejoin yarn and using a large crochet hook work a row of d.c. up right front edge, all round hood and down left front; turn, and work a row of d.c. over d.c., then fasten off.

The buttonhole loops:
Rejoin yarn and using crochet hook make a chain buttonhole loop at neck edge, then make 3 more loops on right front edge, each 5 inches apart.

To complete the coat:
Pin out to size and press all parts on the wrong side with a warm iron over a damp cloth. Fold pocket backs in half and join row end edges. Join underarm seams and side seams, inserting pockets 10 in. below sleeves. Press seams. Sew on buttons.

The scarf:
With size 7 mm (No. 2) needles cast on 25 sts. and work the 33rd to 80th pattern rows 4 times, then cast off.

To complete the scarf:
Join row end edges. Make 2 pom-poms each 2 in. in diameter. Gather in ends of scarf and attach a pom-pom to each end. Press.

CLASSIC COOL

SEE MODEL ON RIGHT, PREVIOUS PAGE

A man's cardigan that a lady can beg, steal or borrow, or even knit for herself. Choose cream, grey, beige or navy as base colours with either subtle or bright contrast colours.

Materials:
11 ounces of 'Woollybear' 100%shetland wool in main colour and 2 ounces in each of 4 contrast colours; 6 buttons; a pair each of size 2¼ mm (No. 13) and size 3 mm (No. 11) Aero knitting needles. The yarn for the cardigan is available by mail order from the Patricia Roberts Knitting shop, 60 Kinnerton Street, London SW1. Price £6-85 including postage, packing and VAT.

Tension:
18 stitches and 16 rows to 5 cm (2 in.) over the Fair Isle pattern using size 3 mm (No. 11) needles.

Abbreviations:
K., knit; p., purl; st., stitch; tog., together; dec., decrease (by working 2 sts. tog.); inc., increase (by working twice into same st.); s.s., stocking stitch is k. on the right side and p. on the wrong side; single rib is k. 1 and p. 1 alternately; up 1, pick up the loop, which lies between the needles, slip it onto left hand needle, then k. into back of it; m., main colour; a., first contrast colour; b., second contrast; c., third contrast; d., fourth contrast.

Note:
The instructions are given for the small size. Where they vary work the figures in the first brackets for the medium size or the figures in the second brackets for the large size.

Measurements:
The measurements are given in centimetres followed by inches in square brackets.

small	medium	large
All round at underarms		
95 [38]	100 [40]	105 [42]
Side seam		
40 [16]	40 [16]	40 [16]
Length		
64 [25½]	65 [26]	66 [26½]

Sleeve seam with cuffs 47.5 (19) 47.5 (19) 47.5 (19) folded in half.

The back:
With size 2¼ mm (No. 13) needles and m. cast on 152 (160) (168) sts. and work 49 rows in single rib.
Increase row: Rib 10 (4) (8), * up 1, rib 7 (8) (8); repeat from * ending last repeat rib 9 (4) (8).
Change to size 3 mm (No. 11) needles and on 172 (180) (188) sts., beginning with a k. row s.s. 2 rows.
Now work in Fair Isle pattern as follows: This is worked entirely in s.s. so only the colour details are given. Take great care not to pull colours not in use tightly across the back of the work or it will become puckered.
1st row: 5 (1) (5) a., * 2 m., 6 a.; repeat from * ending last repeat 5 (1) (5) a.
The last row sets the position of the first 7 pattern rows given in the chart, now work the 2nd to 7th rows from the chart as set.
For first size only: 8 th row: 1 b., 2 m., 2 b., 2 m., 2 b., 2 m., 1 b., * 1 m., 1 b., 4 m., 3 b., 2 m., 3 b., 4 m., 1 b., 1 m., 1 b., 2 m., 2 b., 2 m., 2 b., 2 m., 1 b.; repeat from * to end.
For second size only: 8th row: 2 m., 1 b., 1 m., 1 b., 2 m., 2 b., 2 m., 2 b., 2 m., 1 b., 1 m., 1 b., * 4 m., 3 b., 2 m., 3 b., 4 m., 1 b., 1 m., 1 b., 2 m., 2 b., 2 m., 2 b., 2 m., 1 b., 1 m., 1 b.; repeat from * until 2 remain, 2 m.
For third size only: 8th row: 2 b., 4 m., 1 b., 1 m., 1 b., 2 m., 2 b., 2 m., 2 b., 2 m., 1 b., 1 m., 1 b., 4 m., * 3 b., 2 m., 3 b., 4 m., 1 b., 1 m., 1 b., 2 m., 2 b., 2 m., 2 b., 2 m., 1 b., 1 m., 1 b., 4 m.; repeat from * until 2 remain, 2 b.
For all sizes: The last row sets the position of the rest of the pattern. Now work the 9th to 77th rows from the chart as set, then work the first 13 rows again. Mark each end of the last row with coloured threads to mark armholes.
Pattern 74 (78) (82) rows more.
To slope the shoulders: Cast off 55 (58) (61) sts. at the beginning of the next 2 rows.
Cast off the remaining 62 (64) (66) sts.

The left front:
With size 2¼ mm (No. 13) needles and m. cast on 73 (77) (81) sts. and work 49 rows in single rib.
Increase row: Rib 5 (7) (9), * up 1, rib 8; repeat from * ending last repeat rib 4 (6) (8).
Change to size 3 mm (No. 11) needles and on 82 (86) (90) sts., beginning with a k. row s.s. 2 rows.**
Now work in Fair Isle pattern as follows:
1st row: 5 (1) (5) a., * 2 m., 6 a.; repeat from * ending last repeat 3 a.
The last row sets the position of the rest of the first 7 pattern rows given in the chart, now work the 2nd to 7th rows from the chart.
8th row: 1 b., (2 m., 1 b., 1 m., 1 b.) (2 b., 4 m., 1 b., 1 m., 1 b.), 2 m., 2 b., 2 m., * 2 b., 2 m., 1 b., 1 m., 1 b., 4 m., 3 b., 2 m., 3 b., 4 m., 1 b., 1 m., 1 b., 2 m., 2 b., 2 m.; repeat from * until 11 remain, 2 b., 2 m., 1 b., 1 m., 1 b., 4 m.
The last row sets the position of the pattern given in the chart. Now work the 9th to 77th rows from the chart as set, then work the first 13 rows again.
***Mark the end of the last row with a coloured thread to mark armhole.
To slope the neck: Dec. 1 st. at the end of the next row and the 26 (27) (28) following alternate rows.
On 55 (58) (61) sts. pattern 21 (23) (25) rows.
Cast off.

The right front:
Work as given for left front until ** is reached.
Now work in Fair Isle pattern as follows:
1st row: 3 a., * 2 m., 6 a.; repeat from * ending last repeat 5 (1) (5) a.
The last row sets the position of the first 7 pattern rows, given in chart, now work the 2nd to 7th rows from the chart as set.
8th row: 4 m., 1 b., 1 m., 1 b., 2 m., 2 b., 2 m., 2 b., 2 m., * 1 b., 1 m., 1 b., 4 m., 3 b., 2 m., 3 b., 4 m., 1 b., 1 m., 1 b., 2 m., 2 b., 2 m., 2 b., 2 m.; repeat from * until 1 (5) (9) remain, 1 b. (1 b., 1 m., 1 b., 2 m.) (1 b., 1 m., 1 b., 4 m., 2 b.).
The last row sets the position of the rest of the pattern given in the chart. Now work the first 14 rows again.
Now work as given for left front from *** to end.

The sleeves *(both alike):*
With size 2¼ mm (No. 13) needles and m. cast on 76 (84) (92) sts. and work 44 rows in single rib.
Change in size 3 mm (No. 11) needles and beginning with a k. row s.s. 2 rows.
Now work in Fair Isle pattern as follows:
33rd row: 1 m., (1 m., 1 a., 1 m., 1 a., 1 m.) (2 a., 3 m., 1 a., 1 m., 1 a., 1 m.) 1 a., 2 m., 2 a., * 1 m., 2 a., 2 m., 1 a., 1 m., 1 a., 1 m., 1 a., 3 m., 7 a., 3 m., 1 a., 1 m., 1 a., 1 m., 1 a., 2 m., 2 a.; repeat from * until 6 (10) (14) remain, 1 m., 2 a., 2 m., 1 a. (1 a., 1 m., 1 a., 1 m., 1 a.) (1 a., 1 m., 1 a., 1 m., 1 a.; 3 m., 1 a.);
The last row sets the position of the pattern given in the chart. Now work the 34th to 36th rows from the chart as set.
Maintaining the continuity of the pattern as set and working the extra sts. into the pattern as they occur inc. 1 st. at each end of the next row and the 47 following alternate rows.
Now on 172 (180) (188) sts. pattern 35 rows, then cast off.

The pocket backs *(two alike):*
With size 3 mm (No. 11) needles and m. cast on 44 sts. and beginning with a k. row s.s. 110 rows, then cast off.

The frontband:
First join shoulder seams. With size 2¼ mm (No. 13) needles and m. cast on 12 sts. and work 10 rows in single rib.
1st Buttonhole row: Rib 4, cast off 4, rib to end.
2nd Buttonhole row: Rib 4, turn, cast on 4, turn, rib to end.
Rib 24 rows.
Repeat the last 26 rows 4 times more, then work the 2 buttonhole rows again.
Continue in rib until the band is long enough to fit up left front edge, with last buttonhole in line with first front dec., across back neck edge and down right front. Cast off when correct length is assured.

To make up the cardigan:
Pin out to size and press all parts except the ribbing on the wrong side with a warm iron over a damp cloth. Fold pocket backs in half and join row end edges. Sew cast off edges of sleeves in place at armhole edges, between the marking threads. Join sleeve and side seams, inserting pockets in side seams above the ribbing. Sew front bands in position. Press seams. Sew on buttons.

ODDS AND ENDS

Thought about your Christmas presents yet? Presents that you've made yourself are always appreciated, so surprise someone with this set of gloves and scarf. Knit them in stripes as we have, or knit them in one colour if you prefer. This is an ideal way of using up oddments of 4-ply yarn, but don't forget that you may need slightly more or less than stated in the pattern, depending upon which brand you use.

Materials:
For the scarf: 4 ounces (approximately) of 4-ply yarn in main colour and $\frac{1}{2}$ ounces in each of the 4 contrast colours (we used special Shetland 4-ply available on request from The Patricia Roberts Knitting Shop, 60 Kinnerton Street, London, S.W.1); a pair of No. 13 knitting needles.
For the gloves: One ounce (approximately—depending on wool used) in main colour and oddments in each of the four contrast colours; a set of four double pointed No. 12 and No. 13 knitting needles.

Tension:
16 stitches and 20 rows to 5 cm (2 in.) over stocking stitch using No. 12 needles and 24 stitches and 28 rows to 5 cm (2 in.) over the double rib using No. 13 needles.

Abbreviations:
K., knit; p., purl; st., stitch; tog., together; m., main colour; a., first contrast colour; b., second contrast; c., third contrast; d., fourth contrast; double rib is k.2 and p.2 alternately; s.s., stocking stitch (k. on the right side and p. on the wrong side); inc., increase (by working twice into same st.).

Size and measurements:
The scarf: 15 cm (6 in.) by 152 cm (16$\frac{3}{4}$ in.). The gloves are suitable for an average hand size.

THE SCARF

To work:
With No. 13 needles and m. cast on 72sts. and working in double rib (k.2, p.2), work in stripe sequence as follows: 10 rows m., 4 rows a., 10 rows m., 4 rows b., 10 rows m., 4 rows c., 10 rows m., 4 rows d.; repeat the last 56 rows 14 more times, then with m. rib 10 rows. Work should now measure 152 cm (60$\frac{3}{4}$ in.) from beginning. Cast off.

The fringing:
For each tassel: Cut 2 lengths of yarn each 12 in. long in each of the 5 colours used in scarf. Using a crochet hook draw all ten folded ends through one corner of cast on edge of scarf, pass looped ends through folded ends and pull firmly to form one tassel. *For the other tassels:* In the above manner make 7 more tassels along cast on edge of scarf then work 8 tassels along the cast off edge in the same way.

To complete:
Press lightly.

THE GLOVES

The left glove:
Onto 3 of the set of 4 double pointed No. 13 needles with m. cast on 52sts. and using fourth needle work 2 rounds in double rib.
Continuing in rib as set work in stripe sequence as follows: 2 rows a., 2 rows m., 2 rows b., 2 rows m., 2 rows c., 2 rows m., 2 rows d., 2 rows m. These 16 rows form the stripe sequence; repeat them once more.
Change to the set of 4 double pointed No. 12 needles and with m. only k.24 rounds.
Now divide sts. for thumb: *Next round:* K.16, slip next 10sts. onto a safety pin until required for thumb, turn, and cast on 10sts. in place of those on safety pin, turn, k. to end of round.
K.15 rounds ***.
**** Now divide sts. for fingers: *Next round:* K.5, then inc. in next st., and leave these 7sts. on a piece of yarn until required for little finger, inc., k.4, inc., and leave these 8sts. on a piece of yarn until required for third finger, inc., k.5, inc., and leave these 9sts. on a piece of yarn until required for second finger, inc., pattern 12, inc., and leave these 16sts. on a piece of yarn until required for first finger, inc., k. across 5sts., inc., and leave these 9sts. on a safety pin until required for second finger, inc., k. across 4sts., inc., and leave these sts. on a safety pin until required for third finger, inc. in next st., then k. across remaining 5sts., then k. across the 7sts. left on safety pin for little finger and continue on these 14sts.
The little finger: Using the set of 4 double pointed needles on 14sts., continuing in rounds of s.s. work 20 rounds in stripe sequence as given for ribbing at beginning of gloves.
** *Next round:* * K.2 tog.; repeat from * to end. Break off yarn leaving a long end. Thread through remaining sts., draw up and fasten off securely.
The third finger: With right side of work facing rejoin m. to one of the sets of 8sts. left for third finger and using the double pointed needles, work first across these 8sts. then across the other set of 8sts. On 16sts. work 23 rounds in stripe sequence given for ribbing at beginning, then work as for little finger from ** to end.
The second finger: With right side of work facing rejoin m. to one of the sets of sts. left for second finger, work across these sts. then across the other set of sts.
Work 27 rounds in stripe sequence given for ribbing then work as for little finger from ** to end.
The first finger: With right side of work facing rejoin m. to the 16sts. left for first finger and k.24 rounds in stripe sequence as before then work as for little finger from ** to end.
The thumb: With right side of work facing rejoin m. to the 10sts. left for thumb, cast on 10sts. and continue on these 20sts.
K.22 rounds in stripe sequence given for ribbing then work as for little finger from ** to end. Join cast on edge of thumb to 10sts. cast on beneath it.

The right glove:
Work as for left glove to ***
K. across 42sts. as set.
Now work as for left glove from **** to end.
Press with a warm iron over a damp cloth.

CROWN OF GLORY

Crown of Glory is a traditional Shetland lace pattern, and knitting it is not as difficult as it looks, providing you remember that the number of stitches used for this pattern does not remain constant throughout. The tie neck makes it an ideal sweater to wear with winter suits.

Materials:

22 (23) (24) 50 gram balls of Hayfield Gaylon 4-ply; a pair each of No. 12 and No. 13 knitting needles.

Tension:

Work at such a tension that 2 repeats of the pattern measure 9 cm ($3\frac{1}{2}$ in.) in width and 24 rows—2 repeats of the pattern in length measure 5.5 cm ($2\frac{1}{4}$ in.). If you cannot obtain the correct tension using needles of the size suggested, use larger or smaller ones accordingly.

Abbreviations:

K., knit; p., purl; st., stitch; tog., together; dec., decrease (by working 2 sts. tog.); inc., increase (by working twice into same st.); garter stitch is k. plain on every row; double rib is k.2 and p.2 alternately; y.r.n., yarn round needle; sl., slip; s.s.k., sl.1, k.1, pass sl. st. over; p.2 tog.b., p.2 tog. through back of sts.; 5 from 1, drop next 2 sts. thus making 1 large loop, k.1, p.1, k.1, p.1, k.1 all into this large loop; s.s., stocking stitch (k. on the right side and p. on the wrong side).

Note:

The instructions are given for the small size. Where they vary, work the figures in the first brackets for the medium size or the figures in the second brackets for the large size.

Special note:

When working Crown of Glory pattern the number of sts. is not constant on rows 1 to 7, therefore only count sts. on rows 8 to 12.

Measurements:

The following measurements are given in centimetres first, followed by inches in brackets.

small (10)	medium (12)	large (14)
All round at underarms		
$83 (32\frac{1}{4})$	$89 (34\frac{1}{2})$	$93.5 (36\frac{1}{4})$
Side seam		
40 (16)	40 (16)	40 (16)
Length		
60 (24)	$60.5 (24\frac{1}{4})$	$61 (24\frac{1}{2})$
Sleeve seam with cuffs folded in half		
42.5 (17)	42.5 (17)	42.5 (17)

With No. 13 needles cast on 148 (158) (166) sts. and work 26 rows in double rib, increasing 1 st. at the end of the last of these rows—149 (159) (167) sts.

Change to No. 12 needles and beginning with a k. row s.s. 4 rows.

Now work in pattern as follows:

K.4 (9) (5), * s.s.k., k.9, k.2 tog., k.3; repeat from * ending last repeat k.4 (9) (5), instead of k.3.

2nd row: P.4 (9) (5), * p.2 tog., p.7, p.2 tog.b, p.3; repeat from * ending last repeat p.4 (9) (5).

3rd row: K.4 (9) (5), * s.s.k., k.2, y.r.n., y.r.n., y.r.n., k.3, k.2 tog., k.3; repeat from * ending last repeat k.4 (9) (5).

4th row: P.4 (9) (5), * p.2 tog., p.2, 5 from 1, p.1, p.2 tog.b., p.3; repeat from * ending last repeat p.4 (9) (5).

5th row: K.4 (9) (5), * s.s.k., k.6, k.2 tog., k.3; repeat from * ending last repeat k.4 (9) (5)

6th row: P.4 (9) (5), * p.2 tog., p.9; repeat from * ending last repeat p.10 (15) (11).

7th row: K.5 (10) (6), * y.r.n., k.1, y.r.n., k.1, y.r.n., k.1, y.r.n., k.1, y.r.n., k.1, y.r.n., k.5; repeat from * ending last repeat k.5 (10) (6).

8th to 12th rows: Beginning with a p. row s.s. 5 rows.

These 12 rows form the pattern; repeat them 11 more times. Work should now measure 16 in. from beginning.

To shape the armholes: Maintaining the continuity of the pattern, cast off 16 (19) (19) sts. at the beginning of the next 2 rows.

On 117 (121) (129) sts. pattern 78 rows as set.

To slope the shoulders: Cast off 14 (15) (17) sts. at the beginning of the next 4 rows.

Cast off the 61 remaining sts.

The front:

Work as given for the back until the armhole shaping has been worked.

With 117 (121) (129) sts. after any 7th to 12th row, pattern 17 rows.

Now divide the sts. for the neck:

Next row: (an 8th pattern row): P.52 (54) (5) and leave these sts. on a spare needle until required for right front shoulder, cast off 13 sts., p. to end and continue on these 52 (54) (58) sts. for left front shoulder.

The left front shoulder: To shape the neck: Continuing in pattern as set, dec. 1 st. at the neck edge on the next row and the 23 following alternate rows.

With 28 (30) (34) sts. after 7th to 12th pattern rows, pattern 13 rows.

To slope the shoulder: Cast off 14 (15) (17) sts. at the beginning of the next row and following alternate row. Fasten off.

The right front shoulder: With right side of work facing rejoin yarn to inner edge of sts. left on spare needle and work to end of row. Now work as given for left front shoulder to end.

The sleeves *(both alike):*

With No. 13 needles cast on 80 (84) (88) sts. and work 54 rows in double rib.

Change to No. 12 needles and work as follows:

Increase row: K.1 (3) (5), * up 1, k.1, up 1, k.2; repeat from * until 1 (3) (5) remain, up 1, k.1 (3) (5).

On 133 (137) (141) sts. beginning with a p. row s.s. 3 rows.

Now work in pattern as follows:

1st row: K.4 (6) (8), * s.s.k., k.9, k.2 tog., k.3; repeat from * ending last repeat k.4 (6) (8).

This row sets the position of the pattern given for back.

Pattern 155 more rows, marking each end of the last row with coloured threads.

Work 32 (36) (36) rows in garter stitch, then cast off loosely.

The half collar *(two pieces alike):*

With No. 13 needles cast on 13 sts. and k.96 rows, marking the end of the last row with a coloured thread.

Inc. 1 st. at the beginning of the next row and the 19 following alternate rows.

On 33 sts. continue in garter stitch until the collar is long enough to fit with marking thread to neck opening at front up appropriate front edge and along back neck to centre back neck. Neatly sew *shaped* row end edge of collar in position and cast off when correct length is assured.

To make up the sweater:

Pin out to shape and size then press all parts except the ribbing on the wrong side with a warm iron over a damp cloth. Set in sleeves, so that the garter stitch rows above the marking threads are sewn to the cast off groups at underarms. Join sleeve and side seams. Join cast off edges of collar at centre back neck. Press seams. Fold cuffs in half to right side. Tie ends of collar at centre front neck.

BARTHOLO
NO
CHURCH
CE
There is a
donation box
the Church

JACKET IN

The back and sleeves of this thick jacket are knitted in single rib—very easy. The fronts are in a lace and cable pattern. A comfortable garment to wear in the car, at home, or out for a walk on the common.

Materials:
13 (13) (14) 100 gram hanks of Sirdar Norsgarn; a pair of No. 5 knitting needles; a cable needle; 4 buttons.

Tension:
10 stitches and 10 rows to 5 cm (2 in.) over the pattern and the single rib using No. 5 needles. If you have difficulty obtaining the correct tension using the size needles specified, use larger or smaller ones accordingly.

Abbreviations:
K., knit; p., purl; st., stitch; tog., together; dec., decrease (by working 2 sts. tog.); inc., increase (by working twice into same st.); single rib is k. 1 and p. 1 alternately; w.r.n., wool round needle, thus making 1 st.; cross 4 thus, slip next 2 sts. on to cable needle at back of work, k. 2 slip 2 sts. from cable needle back on to left hand needle; then on to right hand needle; cross 8 thus, slip next 4 sts. on to cable needle at back of work, k. 4, slip 4 sts. from cable needle back on to left hand needle, then on to right hand needle.

Note:
The instructions are given for the small size. Where they vary work the figures in the first brackets for the medium size or the figures in the second brackets for the large size.

Measurements:
The measurements are given in centimetres followed by inches in square brackets.
To fit chest sizes

small	medium	large
All round at underarms		
95 [38]	100 [40]	105 [42]
Side seam		
50 [20]	50 [20]	50 [20]
Length		
74 [29½]	75 [30]	76 [30½]
Sleeve seam with cuffs turned back		
45 [18]	45 [18]	45 [18]

The back:
With No. 5 needles cast on 96 (100) (104) sts. and work 100 rows in single rib.
To shape the armholes: Cast off 5 sts. at the beginning of the next 2 rows, then dec. 1 st. at each end of the next 8 (9) (10) rows.
On 70 (72) (74) sts. rib 34 (35) (36) rows more.
To slope the shoulders: Cast off 9 sts. at the beginning of the next 2 rows and 9 (10) (11) sts. on the 2 following rows.
Cast off the 34 remaining sts.

The pocket backs *(both alike)*:
With No. 5 needles cast on 26 sts. and work 24 rows in single rib, then leave these sts. on a stitch-holder until required.

The left front:
With No. 5 needles cast on 40 (42) (44) sts. and work 6 rows in single rib.
Now work in pattern as follows:
1st row: P. (3) (4) (5), * k. 3, w.r.n., k. 2 tog., k. 4, w.r.n., k. 2 tog., k. 1 *, p. 3, k. 2, w.r.n., k. 2 tog., p. 3; repeat from * to *, p. 3 (4) (5).
2nd row: K. 3 (4) (5), * p. 3, w.r.n., p. 2 tog., k. 4, w.r.n., p. 2 tog., p. 1 *, k. 3, p. 2, w.r.n., p. 2 tog., k. 3; repeat from * to *, k. 3 (4) (5).
3rd to 8th rows: Repeat 1st and 2nd rows 3 times.
9th row: P. 3 (4) (5), * k. 3, w.r.n., k. 2 tog., k. 4, w.r.n., k. 2 tog., k. 1 *, p. 3, cross 4, p. 3; repeat from * to *, p. 3 (4) (5).
10th row: As 2nd row.
11th to 20th rows: As 1st to 10th rows.
21st row: P. 3 (4) (5), k. 12, p. 3, k. 2, w.r.n., k. 2 tog., p. 3, k. 12, p. 3 (4) (5).
22nd row: K. 3 (4) (5), p. 12, k. 3, p. 2, w.r.n., p. 2 tog., k. 3, p. 12, k. 3 (4) (5).
23rd row: P. 3 (4) (5), cross 8, k. 4, p. 3, k. 2, w.r.n., k. 2 tog., p. 3, cross 8, k. 4, p. 3 (4) (5).
24th row: As 22nd row.
25th row and *Pocket row:* Work across 7 (8) (9) sts. as for 21st row, slip next 26 sts. on to a stitch-holder until required and in their place pattern across the 26 sts. of one pocket back—as on 21st pattern row, work to end as set.
26th row: As 22nd row.
27th and 28th rows: As 21st and 22nd rows.
29th row: P. 3 (4) (5), k. 4, cross 8, p. 3, cross 4, p. 3, k. 4, cross 8, p. 3 (4) (5).
30th row: As 22nd row.
31st to 50th rows: Repeat 21st to 30th rows twice.
These 50 rows form the pattern. Now work the first 30 rows again; work 1 extra row here when working right front.
To slope the front edge: Maintaining the continuity of the pattern as set, dec. 1 st. at the end of the next row and the 2 following 6th rows.
Work 1 row back to armhole edge.
To shape the armhole and continue to slope the front edge: Cast off 5 sts. at the beginning of the next row, work 1 row straight, then dec. 1 st. at the armhole edge on each of the next 8 (9) (10) rows *and at the same time* dec. 1 st. at the front edge on the 3rd (3rd and 9th) (3rd and 9th) of these rows—23 (23) (24) sts.
Pattern 19 (18) (17) rows, decreasing 1 st. at the front edge on the 1st (6th) (5th) of these rows and on the 3 (2) (2) following 6th rows.
On 19 (20) (21) sts. pattern 15 (17) (19) rows.
To slope the shoulder: Cast off 9 sts. at the beginning of the next row. On 10 (11) (12) sts. work 1 row, then cast off.

The right front:
Work as given for left front noting the variation in the number of rows before sloping the front edge.

The pocket tops *(both alike)*:
With right side of work facing rejoin wool to the 26 sts. left on stitch-holder at front of work and using No. 5 needles work 6 rows in single rib, then cast off loosely.

The sleeves *(both alike)*:
With No. 5 needles cast on 52 (54) (56) sts. and work 30 rows in single rib.
Continuing in rib and working extra sts. in rib as they occur inc. 1 st. at each end of the next row and the 6 following 10th rows.
On 66 (68) (70) sts. rib 19 rows.
To shape the sleevetop: Cast off 5 sts. at the beginning of the next 2 rows then dec. 1 st. at each end of the next row and the 5 (6) (7) following alternate rows.
Work 1 row straight, then dec. 1 st. at each end of the next 10 rows.
Cast off 3 sts. at the beginning of the next 6 rows, then cast off the 6 remaining sts.

The left front band and collar:
With No. 5 needles cast on 16 (18) (18) sts. and work 86 rows in single rib.
***To shape the collar:* Continuing in rib, inc. 1 st. at the beginning of the next row and the 15 following alternate rows—32 (34) (34) sts.
Work 43 (47) (49) rows in rib, cast off.

The right front band and collar:
With No. 5 needles cast on 16 (18) (18) sts. and work 6 rows in single rib.
1st Buttonhole row: Rib 6 (7) (7), cast off 4, rib to end.
2nd Buttonhole row: Rib 6 (7) (7), turn, cast on 4, turn, rib to end.
Rib 24 rows.
Repeat the last 26 rows twice more then work the 2 buttonhole rows again.
Now work as given for left front band and collar from ** to end.

To make up the jacket:
Press all parts lightly on the wrong side with a warm iron over a damp cloth. Join shoulder seams. Set in sleeves. Join sleeve and side seams. Sew pocket backs and row ends of pocket tops in place. Join cast off edges of collar. Neatly sew front bands and shaped row end edges of collar in place. Press seams. Turn back 3 in. cuffs.

LACEY

By day or by night, be ultra feminine in one or both parts of this twinset. Beige, white, *bois de rose* or raw amber (a lovely brown) are among the many colours available in this pure soft mohair.

Materials:
For the sweater: 13 25 gram balls of 'Woollybear' 100% Mohair; a pair each of size 6 mm (No. 4) and size 5½ mm (No. 5) Aero knitting needles.
For the waistcoat: 10 25 gram balls of 'Woollybear' 100% Mohair; a pair each of size 6 mm (No. 4) and size 5½ mm (No. 5) Aero knitting needles; 4 large buttons. The 'Woollybear' mohair for these garments is available by mail order from the Patricia Roberts Knitting Shop, 60 Kinnerton Street, London SW1; price inclusive of postage and V.A.T. for the sweater £10 for the waistcoat £7.70
Tension:
10 stitches—1 repeat of the pattern—to 7.5 cm (3 in.) in width and 16 rows—2 repeats of the pattern to 9 cm (3½ in.) in depth over the Rosebud lace pattern using size 6 mm (No. 4) knitting needles.
Abbreviations:
K., knit; p., purl; st., stitch; tog., together; dec., decrease (by working 2 sts. tog.); inc., increase (by working twice into the same stich); single rib is k. 1 and p. 1 alternately; up 1., pick up the loop, which lies between the needles, slip it onto left hand needle, then k. into back of it; s.s., stocking stitch is k. on the right side and p. on the wrong side; y.r.n., yarn round needle; sl., slip; p.s.s.o., pass sl. st. over; k. 1b., k. 1 through back of st.; s.s.k. sl. 1, k. 1, p.s.s.o.
Note:
The instructions are given for the small size. Where they vary work the figures in the first brackets for the medium size or the figures in the second brackets for the large size.
Measurements:
The measurements are given in centimetres followed by inches in square brackets.
THE SWEATER

small	medium	large
All rounds at underarms		
95 [38]	100 [40]	
Side seam		
41 [16½]	41 [16½]	
Length		
66 [26½]	67.5 [27]	
Sleeve seam		
42.5 [17]	42.5 [17]	

THE WAISTCOAT
All round at underarms
95 [38]   102.5 [40]
Side seam with hem sewn in place
31 [12½]   31 [12½]
Length with hem sewn in place
56 [22½]   57.5 [23]
Special Note:
The rosebud lace pattern does not maintain the same number of stitches after each pattern row, therefore do not count stitches after rows 2 and 3.
THE SWEATER
The back:
With size 5½ mm (No. 5) needles cast on 63 (67) sts. and work 23 rows in single rib. Change to size 6 mm (No. 4) needles and work in rosebud lace as follows:
1st row: (wrong side): All p.
2nd row: (right side): K. 1 (3), k. 2 tog., * y.r.n., k. 3, y.r.n., k. into front and back of next st., y.r.n., k. 3, y.r.n., sl. 1, k. 2 tog., p.s.s.o.; repeat * ending last repeat s.s.k., k. 1 (3) instead of sl. 1., k. 2 tog., p.s.s.o.
3rd row: And every wrong side row: All p.
4th row: K. 1 (3), s.s.k., * y.r.n., sl. 2, k. 1, p. 2 s.s.o., y.r.n., k. 2 tog., y.r.n., s.s.k., y.r.n., sl. 2., k. 1, p. 2 s.s.o., y.r.n., sl. 2, k. 1, p. 2 s.s.o.; repeat from * ending last repeat k. 2 tog., k. 1 (3) instead of sl. 2, k. 1, p. 2 s.s.o.
6th row: K. 3 (5), * k. 2 tog., y.r.n., k. 3, y.r.n., s.s.k., k. 3; repeat from * ending last repeat k. 3 (5).
8th row: K. 2 (4), * k. 2 tog., y.r.n., k. 1b., y.r.n., sl. 1, k. 2 tog., p.s.s.o., y.r.n., k. 1b, y.r.n., s.s.k., k. 1; repeat from * ending last repeat k. 2 (4).
The last 8 rows form the pattern; repeat them 5 times more, then work the first 7 rows again. Mark each end of the last row with coloured threads to mark armholes.**
Pattern 45 (47) rows more.
To slope the shoulders: Cast off 21 (23) sts. at the beginning of the next 2 rows—21 sts.
Change to size 5½ mm (No. 5) needles and work 6 rows in single rib, then cast off in rib.
The front:
Work as given for back until ** is reached. Pattern 29 (31) rows more.
Now divide the sts. for the neck: Next row: P. 28 (30) and leave these sts. on a spare needle until required for right front shoulder, cast off 7, p. to end and continue on these 28 (30) sts. for the left front shoulder.
The left front shoulder: Dec. 1 st. at the neck edge on each of the next 7 rows.
Pattern 8 rows more.
To slope the shoulder: Cast off the remaining 21 (23) sts.
The right front shoulder: With right side of working facing rejoin yarn to inner edge of sts. left on spare needle and work as given for left front shoulder to end.
The sleeves *(both alike):*
With size 5½ mm (No. 5) needles cast on 32 (34) sts. and work 16 rows in single rib.
Increase row: Rib 1, * up 1, rib 1; repeat from * to end—63 (67) sts.
Now work 63 rows in pattern as given for back then cast off.
The front neck band:
With right side of work facing rejoin yarn and using size 5½ mm (No. 5) needles pick up and k. 39 sts. from all round front neck edge.
Work 5 rows in single rib, then cast off in rib.
The pocket backs *(two alike):*
With size 6 mm (No. 4) needles cast on 21 sts. and work 50 rows in stocking stitch, then cast off.
To make up the sweater:
Pin out to size and press all parts except the ribbing on the wrong side with a warm iron over a damp cloth. Join shoulder seams, continuing seams across neckband. Set in sleeves between the marking threads on back and front. Fold pocket backs in half and join row edges, then join sleeve and side seams, inserting pockets at side seams above the ribbing.

THE WAISTCOAT

The main part:
With size 6 mm (No. 4) needles cast on 146 (150) sts. and beginning with a k. row s.s. 16 rows, marking each end of the 11th of these rows with coloured threads.
Decrease row: K. 6 (8), * k. 2 tog., k. 4; repeat from * ending last repeat k. 6 (8)—123 (127) sts.
Now work 52 rows in rosebud lace pattern given for back of sweater.
Now divide the sts for the armholes: Next row: P. 30 (31), and leave these sts. on a spare needle until required for left half front, p. next 63 (65) sts. and leave these sts. on a spare needle until required for back, p. to end and continue on these 30 (31) sts. for the right half front.
The right half front:
To shape the neck: Dec. 1 st. at the beginning—front edge of the next row—and the 8 following 4th rows.
Pattern 12 (14) rows more.
Cast off the 21 (22) remaining sts.
The back:
With right side of work facing rejoin yarn to the 63 (65) sts. left on spare needle and pattern 45 rows.
To slope the shoulders: Cast off 21 (22) sts. at the beginning of the next 2 rows—21 sts.
Increase row: P. 3, * up 1, p. 5; repeat from * ending last repeat p. 3—25 sts.
Beginning with a k. row s.s., 16 rows, then cast off.
The left half front:
With right side of work facing rejoin yarn to inner edge of sts. left on spare needle and work to end of row. Now work as given for right half front to end.
The left front edging:
With right side of work facing rejoin yarn at left front shoulder, using size 6 (No. 4) needles pick up and k. 40 sts. down to first front edge dec. then pick up and k. 52 (54) sts. between first front dec. and marking thread on hem—92 (94) sts.
Beginning with a p. row s.s. 16 rows, then cast off loosely.
The right front edging:
With right side of work facing rejoin yarn at marking thread on hem and using size 6 (No. 4) needles pick up and k. 52 (54) sts. up to first front dec., then 40 sts. up to shoulder.
1st Buttonhole row: P. 40, * y.r.n., p. 2 tog., p. 13; repeat from * ending last repeat from * ending last repeat p. 5.
Beginning with a k. row s.s. 15 rows, then cast off loosely.

The left and right back and front armhole edgings *(both alike):*
With right side of work facing rejoin yarn and using size 6 (No. 4) needles pick up and k. 80 sts. from row end edges of armhole.
Beginning with a p. row s.s. 16 rows, then cast off.

To make up the waistcoat:
Pin out to size and press all parts on the wrong side with a warm iron over a damp cloth. Join shoulder seams, continuing seam along armhole edgings and neck edgings. Roll all edgings in 3 to right side so that the reversed side of the stocking stitch shows. Neatly sew in place—so that the edging at right front is sewn in place at outer edge of buttonhole. Press seams, but do not press the rolled edgings. Sew on buttons.

PLAIN DEALING

The little teddy bear scarf, which is knitted in two shades of mohair, is an ideal garment for a beginner to attempt. The jacket is quite simple, too, as you only need to know what K. (knit plain) means to be able to knit it. It's thick and warm and striped with so many colours and different yarns that it will match up with almost any of your clothes—whatever the season.

Materials:
For the jacket and the scarf: 3(4)(4) 100 gram hanks of Jaeger Naturgarn in each of 3 contrasting colours, 3(4)(4) 50 gram balls of Jaeger Catkin and 6(7)(8) 25 gram balls of Jaeger Mohair in each of 2 contrasting colours; a pair of No.5 knitting needles; 5 buttons.
For the scarf only: Two 25 gram balls of Jaeger mohair in each of 2 contrasting colours; a pair of No.5 knitting needles.

Tension:
7 stitches to 5 cm (2 in.) in width and 32 rows—1 repeat of the pattern to 11 cm ($4\frac{1}{2}$ in.) in depth over the garter stitch using No.5 needles. If you cannot obtain the correct tension using needles of the size suggested, use larger or smaller ones accordingly.

Abbreviations:
K., knit; st., stitch; tog., together; dec., decrease (by working 2sts. tog.); inc., increase (by working twice into same st.); sl., slip; p.s.s.o., pass sl. st. over; garter stitch is k. plain on every row; m., main colour—Naturgarn; a., first contrast colour—mohair; b., second contrast—Naturgarn; c., third contrast—mohair; d., fourth contrast—Naturgarn; e., fifth contrast—Catkin.

Note:
The instructions are given for the small size. Where they vary, work the figures in the first brackets for the medium size or the figures in the second brackets for the large size.

Measurements:
The following measurements are given in centimetres first, followed by inches in brackets.

small (10)	medium (12)	large (14)
All round at underarms		
85(34)	90(36)	95(38)
Side seam		
58($23\frac{1}{2}$)	58($23\frac{1}{2}$)	58($23\frac{1}{2}$)
Length		
79(32)	79(32)	79(32)
Sleeve seam		
36($14\frac{1}{2}$)	36($14\frac{1}{2}$)	36($14\frac{1}{2}$)

The back:
With No.5 needles and m. cast on 76(80)(84)sts. and work in garter stitch in stripes sequence as follows: 6 rows m., 4 rows a., 6 rows b., 4 rows c., 6 rows d., 6 rows e.
These 32 rows form the stripes sequence.
Continuing in garter stitch in stripes as set, work 8 more rows straight.
1st Decrease row: K.18(20)(22), sl.1, k.2 tog., p.s.s.o., k.34, sl.1, k.2 tog., p.s.s.o., k. to end—72(76)(80)sts.
Work 31 rows in garter st. in stripes as set.
2nd Decrease row: K.17(19)(21), sl.1, k.2 tog., p.s.s.o., k.32, sl.1, k.2 tog., p.s.s.o., k. to end—68(72)(76)sts.
Work 31 rows in stripes as set.
3rd Decrease row: K.16(18)(20), sl.1, k.2 tog., p.s.s.o., k.30, sl.1, k.2 tog., p.s.s.o., k. to end—64(68)(72)sts.
Work 31 rows in stripes as set.
4th Decrease row: K.15(17)(19), sl.1, k.2 tog., p.s.s.o., k.28, sl.1, k.2 tog., p.s.s.o., k. to end—60(64)(68)sts.
Work 31 rows in stripes as set.
To shape the armholes: Cast off 5(6)(7) sts. at the beginning of the next 2 rows.
On 50(52)(54)sts. work 58 rows in garter stitch in stripes as set.
To slope the shoulders: Cast off 14(15)(16)sts. at the beginning of the next 2 rows.
Join in m. and on 22sts. with m. k.2 rows, then cast off.

The pocket backs *(both alike):*
With No.5 needles and m. cast on 20sts. and work 38 rows in stripes as given for back, then leave these sts. on a stitch holder until required.

The left front:
With No.5 needles and m. cast on 38(40)(42)sts. and work 40 rows in garter stitch in stripes sequence given for back.
Continuing in garter stitch stripes as set work as follows:
1st Decrease row: K.18(20)(22), sl.1, k.2 tog., p.s.s.o., k. to end—36(38)(40) sts.
Work 29 rows in stripes as set—ending with 6 rows m.
***Pocket row:* With a. k.8(9)(10) then k. across the 20 sts. of one pocket back, rejoin m. and cast off 20sts. at centre front, then with a. work to end.
Work 1 row straight as set—work 2 rows here on right front.
2nd Decrease row: K.17(19)(21), sl.1, k.2 tog., p.s.s.o., k. to end—34(36)(38) sts.
Work 31 rows in stripes as set.
3rd Decrease row: K.16(18)(20), sl.1, k.2 tog., p.s.s.o., k. to end—32(34)(36) sts.
Work 31 rows as set.
4th Decrease row: K.15(17)(19), sl.1, k.2 tog., p.s.s.o., k. to end—30(32)(34)sts.
Work 31 rows as set.
To shape the armhole: Cast off 5(6)(7) sts. at the beginning of the next row.
On 25(26)(27)sts. work 34 rows.
To shape the neck: Cast off 11sts. at the beginning of the next row.
On 14(15)(16)sts. work 24 rows, then cast off.

The right front:
With No.5 needles and m. cast on 38(40)(42)sts. and work 41 rows in garter stitch in stripes as given for back.
Continuing in stripes as set work as follows:
1st Decrease row: K.18(20)(22), sl.1, k.2 tog., p.s.s.o., k. to end—36(38)(40)sts.
Work 28 rows in stripes.
Now work as given for left front from ** to end, noting the variation in the number of rows before working 2nd Decrease row.

The sleeves *(both alike):*
With No.5 needles and m. cast on 56 sts. and work 32 rows in stripes sequence as given for back.
Continuing in stripes as set, inc.1st. at each end of the next row and the 2 following 32nd rows.
On 62sts. work 7 rows marking each end of the last row with coloured threads.
Work 10 more rows, then cast off.

The left front edging:
With right side of work facing rejoin m. and using No.5 needles pick up and k.100 sts. from left front edge.
K.1 row, then cast off loosely.

The right front edging:
With right side of work facing rejoin m. and using No.5 needles pick up and k.100sts. from right front edge, ending at neck edge.
Buttonhole row: K.2, turn, cast on 5sts., turn, * k.20, turn, cast on 5sts., turn; repeat from * 3 more times, then k. to end.
Cast off the 125sts.

The left front neckband:
With right side of work facing rejoin m. and using No.5 needles pick up and k.14 sts. from row ends of neck edge, then 15sts. from front neck edge.
1st row: K.14, k.2 tog., k.13.
Cast off.

The right front neckband:
With right side of work facing rejoin m. and using No.5 needles pick up and k.15 sts. from front neck edge and 14sts. from left front neck edge.
1st row: K.13, k.2 tog., k. to end.
Cast off.

To make up the jacket:
Press all parts lightly on the wrong side with a warm iron over a damp cloth. Join shoulder seams. Set in sleeves so that the sts. cast off underarms are sewn to the row end edges above the marking threads. Join sleeve and side seams. Sew pocket backs in place. Sew on buttons. Press seams.

The scarf:
With No.5 needles and a. cast on 32sts. and k.24 rows. Break off a., join in c. and k.16 rows, repeat the last 40 rows 7 more times, then with a. k.24 rows. Cast off.

COWBOY KID

Here is a real cowboy waistcoat, for a little boy keeping up with the best of the men.

Materials:
4 (5) (6) 25 gram balls of Paton's Purple Heather 4 ply in main colour and 1 ball in each of the four contrast colours; a pair each of size 2¾ mm (No. 12) and size 2¼ mm (No. 13) Aero knitting needles; 5 buttons.

Tension:
16 stitches and 20 rows to 5 cm (2 in.) over the stocking stitch using size 2¾ mm (No. 12) needles; 16 stitches and 28 rows to 5 cm (2 in.) over the moss stitch using size 2¼ mm. (No. 13) needles.

Abbreviations:
K., knit; p., purl; st., stitch; tog., together; dec., decrease (by working 2 sts. tog.); inc., increase (by working twice into same st.); s.s., stocking stitch is k. on the right side and p. on the wrong side; m., main colour; a., first contrast; b., second contrast; c., third contrast; d., fourth contrast.

Note:
The instructions are given for the first size. Where they vary work the figures in the first brackets for the second size or the figures in the second brackets for the third size.

Measurements:

The measurements are given in centimetres followed by inches in square brackets.

small	medium	large
To fit chest sizes		
55 [22]	60 [24]	65 [26]
All round at underarms		
55 [22]	60 [24]	65 [26]
Side seam		
12.5 [5]	15 [6]	17.5 [7]
Length		
26 [10½]	30 [12]	34 [13½]

The back:
With size 2¼ mm (No. 13) needles and m. cast on 89 (97) (105) sts. and work in moss stitch as follows:
1st row: K. 1, * p. 1, k. 1; repeat from * to end.
2nd row: K. 1, * p. 1, k. 1; repeat from * to end.
The last 2 rows form the pattern continuing in moss stitch as set, work in colour sequence as follows: 2 rows a., 2 rows b., 2 rows c., 2 rows m., 2 rows d., 2 rows m.
The last 12 rows form the colour sequence repeat them 4 (6) (7) times more then work the first 8 (nil) (2) rows again.
To shape the armhole: Continuing in moss st. in stripe sequence as set, dec. 1 st. at each end of the next row and the 5 (7) (9) following alternate rows.
On 77 (81) (85) sts. pattern 55 (65) (75) rows more.
To slope the shoulders: Cast off 12 sts. at the beginning of the next 2 rows and 11 (12) (13) sts. on the 2 following rows.
Cast off the remaining 31 (33) (35) sts.

The pocket backs *(both alike):*
With size 2¼ mm (No. 13) needles and m. cast on 23 (25) (27) sts. and work as given for back until 22 (24) (26) rows have been worked in moss stitch stripe pattern, then leave these sts. on a spare needle until required.

The left front:
With size 2¼ mm (No. 13) needles and m. cast on 3 sts. and work 2 rows in moss st. as given for back.
Continuing in moss st. as set and working the extra sts. into the pattern as they occur inc. 1 st. at each end of the next 24 (26) (28) rows.
On 51 (55) (59) sts. work 11 rows in moss st. as set.
Now divide the sts. for the front bands as follows:
Next row: Pattern 12 and leave these sts. on a safety pin until required for front band, pattern 8 (9) (10), cast off next 23 (25) (27) sts. for pocket, pattern to end.**.
Change to size 2¾ mm (No. 12) needles and continue in s.s. as follows:
2nd Pocket row: K. 8 (9) (10), k. across the 23 (25) (27) sts. of one pocket back in place of those cast off, k. to end—39 (43) (47) sts.
Beginning with a p. row s.s. 1 (5) (9) rows.
Now work the cowboy motif as follows: This is worked entirely in s.s. so only the colour details are given. Take great care not to pull colours not in use tightly across the back of the work or it will become puckered.
1st row: 30 (32) (34) m., 6 a., 3 (5) (7) m.
The last row sets the position of the pattern given in the chart. Now work the 2nd to 40th rows from the chart as set.
Continuing with m. only in s.s. work nil (6) (12) rows, ending at side seam edge.
***To shape the armhole and to slope the front edge: S.s. 6 (8) (10) rows decreasing 1 st. at the armhole edge on each row *and at the same time* decreasing 1 st. at the front edge on the 1st of these rows and the 1 (1) (2) following 4th rows.
S.s. 31 (33) (35) rows decreasing 1 st. at the front edge on the 3rd (1st) (3rd) of these rows and the 7 (8) (8) following 4th rows.

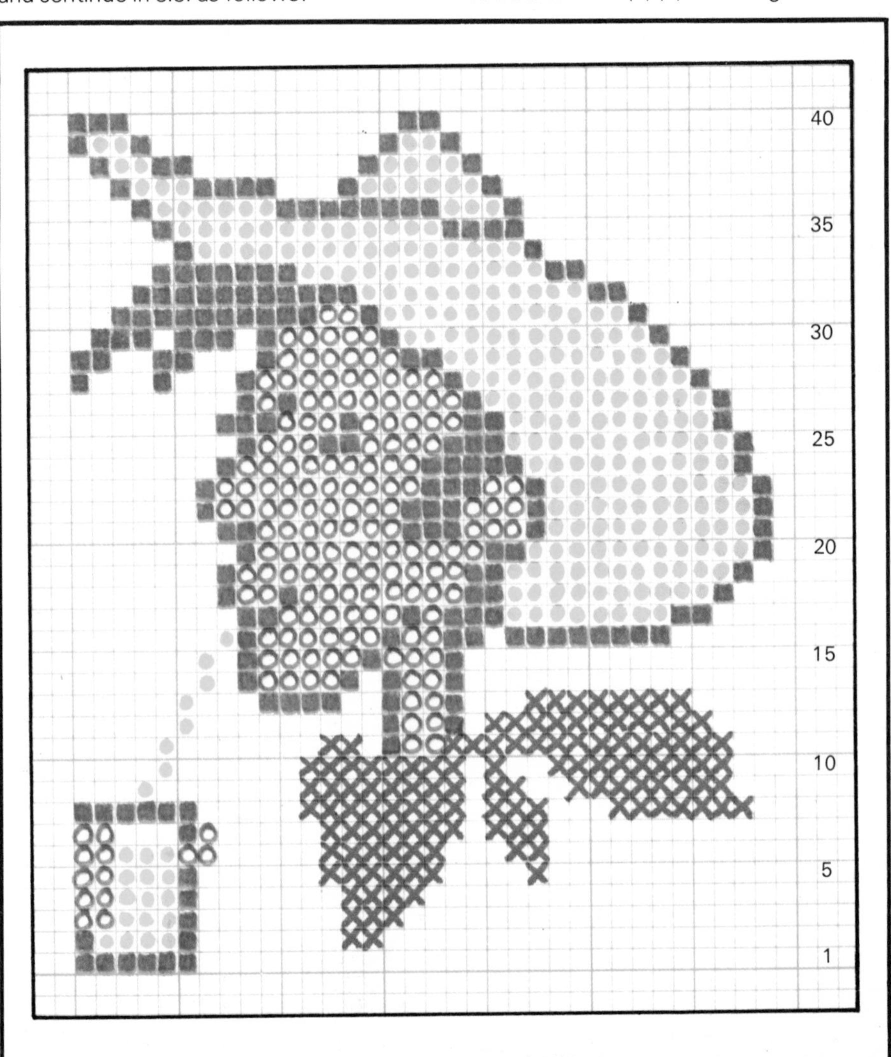

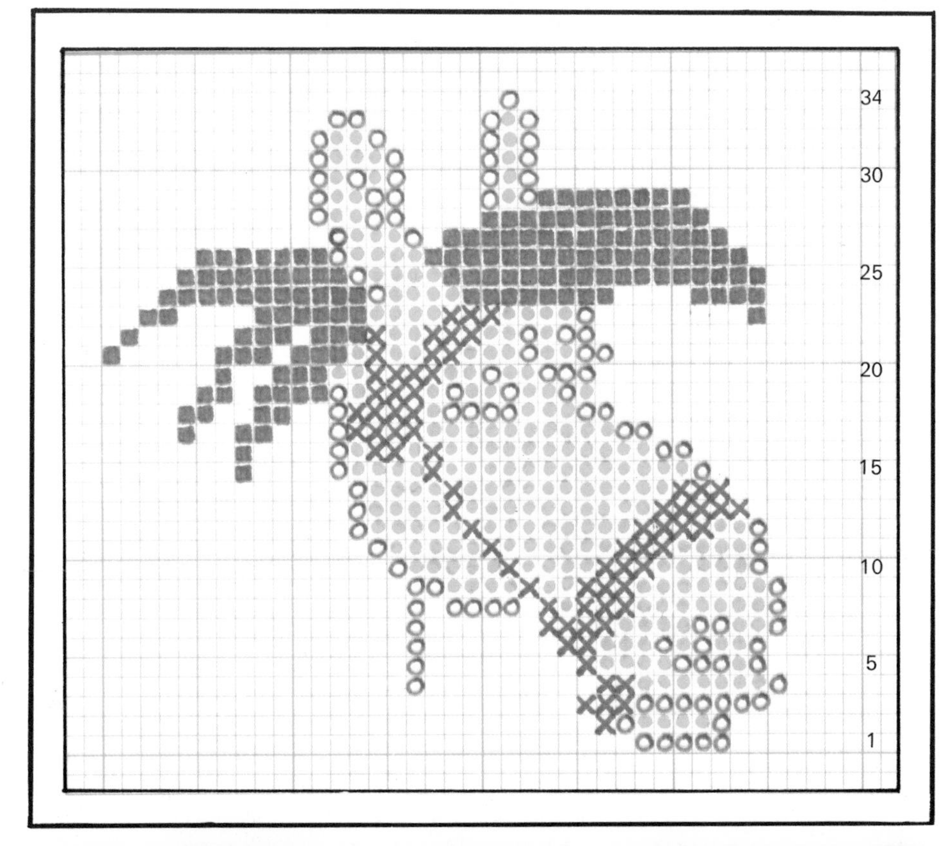

On 23 (24) (25) sts., s.s. 9 (15) (21) rows.
To slope the shoulder: Cast off 12 sts. at the beginning of the next row.
On 11 (12) (13) sts., work 1 row, then cast off.

The right front:
Work as given for left front until ** is reached.
Change to size 2¾ mm (No. 12) needles and continue in s.s. as follows:
2nd Pocket row: P. 8 (9) (10), p. across other pocket back, p. to end.
On 39 (43) (47) sts. beginning with a k. row s.s. 6 (10) (14) rows.
Now work the horse motif as follows:
1st row: 6 (8) (10) m., 5 d., 28 (30) (32) m.
The last row sets the position of the horse motif given in the chart, now work the 2nd to 34th rows from the chart as set.
Continuing with m. only in s.s. work 1 (7) (13) rows ending at side seam edge.
Now work as given for left front from *** to end.

The pocket flaps *(both alike):*
With size 2¼ mm (No. 13) needles and m. cast on 3 sts. and work 2 rows in moss st., continuing in moss st. as set inc. 1 st. at each end of the next 4 rows.
1st Buttonhole row: Inc. in first st., moss st. 3, cast off 3 sts., moss st. next 2 sts., inc.
2nd Buttonhole row: Inc., moss st. 4, turn, cast on 3, turn, work until 1 remains, inc.
Inc. 1 st. at each end of the next 4 (5) (6) rows.
Cast off these 23 (25) (27) sts.

The right front band and half collar:
Rejoin m. to inner edge of the 12 sts. left on safety pin and using size 2¼ mm (No. 13) needles work 50 (62) (74) rows in moss st., as set—ending at inner edge.
***To shape the collar:* Continuing in moss st. as set, inc. 1 st. at the beginning of the next row and the 11 (12) (13) following 4th rows—24 (25) (26) sts.
Work 1 row as set, then cast off.

The left front band and half collar:
Rejoin m. to inner edge of the 12 sts. left on safety pin and using Size 2¼ mm (No. 13) needles work in moss st. as follows:
1st Buttonhole row: Moss st. 4, cast off 4, work to end.
2nd Buttonhole row: Moss st. 4, turn, cast on 4, turn, work to end.
Moss st. 22 (28) (34) rows.
Repeat the last 24 (30) (36) rows once more then work the 2 buttonhole rows again.
Now work as given for right front band and half collar from ** to end.

The back collar:
With size 2¼ mm (No. 13) needles and m. cast on 63 (73) (83) sts. and work 22 (26) (30) rows in moss st. as given for back.
Dec. 1 st. at each end of the next row and the 7 following alternate rows.
Cast off the remaining 47 (57) (67) sts.

The armhole edgings *(both alike):*
First join shoulder seams. With right side of work facing rejoin m, and using size 2¼ mm (No. 13) needles pick up and k. 88 (96) (104) sts. from all round armhole edge.
Work 12 rows in moss st., then cast off.

To make up the waistcoat:
Pin out to size and press all parts on the wrong side with a warm iron over a damp cloth. Join side seams. Sew front bands and half collars in place. Neatly sew shaped row end edges and cast off edge of back collar in place. Sew pocket backs in place. Sew cast off edge of pocket flaps in position. Sew on buttons. Press seams.

POWWOW

SEE GIRL MODEL, PREVIOUS PAGE

A jacket specially designed for eight to thirteen year-olds. A young teenager might even knit it for herself–or for her brother for a birthday present!

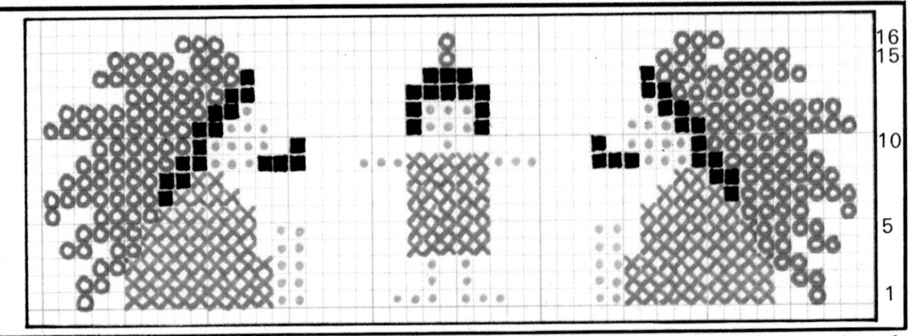

Materials:
4 (5) (6) 100 gram hanks of Jaegar Naturgarn in main colour and 1 hank in each of the 4 contrast colours; a pair each of size 6 mm (No. 4) and size 5¼ mm (No. 5) Aero knitting needles; 4 buttons.

Tension:
15 stitches and 18 rows to 10 cm (4 in.) over the stocking stitch using size 6 mm (No. 4) knitting needles.

Abbreviations:
K., knit; p., purl; st., stitch; tog., together; dec., decrease (by working 2 sts. tog.); inc., increase (by working twice into same st.); s.s., stocking st. is k. on the right side and p. on the wrong side; m., main colour; a., first contrast colour; b., second contrast colour; c., third contrast colour; d., fourth contrast colour.

Note:
The instructions are given for the small size. Where they vary work the figures in the first brackets for the medium size or the figures in the second brackets for the large size.

Measurements:

The measurements are given in centimetres followed by inches in square brackets.

small	medium	large
To fit chest sizes		
65 [26]	70 [28]	75 [30]
All round at underarms		
72.5 [29]	77.5 [31]	82.5 [33]
Side seam		
32.5 [13]	35 [14]	37.5 [15]
Length		
49 [19½]	54 [21½]	59 [23½]
Sleeve seam		
35 [14]	37.5 [15]	40 [16]

The back:
With size 5½ mm (No. 5) needles and m. cast on 55 (59) (63) sts. and work in moss stitch as follows: Moss st. row: K. 1, * p. 1, k. 1, repeat from * to end.
Repeat the last row 9 times more.
Change to size 6 mm (No. 4) needles and beginning with a k. row s.s. 2 rows.
Now work in pattern as follows: This is worked entirely in s.s. so only the colour details are given. Take great care not to pull colours not in use tightly across the back of the pattern or it will become puckered.
1st row: 1 a., 2 b., * 2 a., 2 b., repeat from * to end.
2nd row: * 2 b., 2 a.; repeat from * ending last repeat 1 a.
3rd row: 1 b., 2 a., * 2 b., 2 a.; repeat from * to end.
4th row: * 2 a., 2 b.; repeat from * ending last repeat 1 b.
5th and 6th rows: As 1st and 2nd rows.
7th to 10th rows: All m.
11th row: All c.
12th row: 1 c., * 1 d., 1 c.; repeat from * to end.
13th row: 1 d., * 1 c., 1 d.; repeat from * to end.
14th row: All d.
15th row: As 13th row.
16th row: As 12th row.
17th row: All c.
18th to 20th rows: All m.
Now work the Indian motif as follows:
1st row: 5 (7) (9) m., 1 c., 2 m., 9 a., 2 b., 5 m., 3 b., 1 m., 3 b., 5 m., 2 b., 9 a., 2 m., 1 c., 5 (7) (9) m.
The last row sets the position of the Indians motif given in the chart. Now work the 2nd to 16th rows from the chart as set. This completes the motif.
With m. only s.s. 2 rows.
Now continuing to work in the 20 row repeat pattern given at beginning, pattern 10 (14) (18) rows. Mark each end of the last row with coloured threads to mark armhole.
Continuing in pattern as set work 28 (32) (36) rows.
To slope the shoulders: Cast off 19 (20) (21) sts. at the beginning of the next 2 rows.
Cast off the remaining 17 (19) (21) sts.

The left front:
With size 5½ mm (No. 5) needles m. cast on 25 (27) (29) sts. and work 10 rows in moss st. as given for back.
Change to size 6 mm (No. 4) needles and beginning with a k. row s.s. 2 rows.
Now work in pattern as follows:
1st row: 1 a., * 2 b., 2 a.; repeat from * ending last repeat 2 a. (2 b.) (2 a.).
2nd row: 2 a. (2 b., 2 a.) (2 a.); * 2 b., 2 a.; repeat from *ending last repeat 1 a.
The last rows sets the position of the 20 row pattern given for back now work the 3rd to 20th rows as set.**
Now work one Indian motif as follows:
Next row: 5(7) (9) m., 1 c., 2 m., 9 a., 2 b., 6 m.
The last row sets the position of the Indian on right hand side of chart. Now work the 2nd to 16th rows from the chart as set.
With m. s.s. 2 rows.
Work the first 10 (14) (18) colour pattern rows again. Mark the end of the last row with a coloured thread to mark armhole.
To slope the front edge: Continuing to work in the 20 row repeat pattern as set, dec. 1 st. at the end of the next row and the 5 (6) (7) following 4th rows.
On 19 (20) (21) sts. pattern 7 rows.
To slope the shoulder: Cast off.

The right front:
Work as given for left front until ** is reached.
Now work the Indian motif as follows: *Next row:* 6 m., 2 b., 9 a., 2 m., 1 c., 5 (7) (9) m.
The last row sets the position of the Indian motif given at left hand side of chart. Now work the 2nd to 16th rows from the chart as set.
With m. s.s. 2 rows.
Now work the first 11 (15) (19) colour pattern rows, mark the end of the last row with a coloured thread to mark armhole.
To slope the front edge: Work as given for left front to end.

The sleeves *(both alike):*
With size 5½ mm (No. 5) needles and m. cast on 47 (55) (63) sts. and work as given for back until the 20 row pattern had been worked. Work these 20 rows again, then work the first 10 (14) (18) of these rows again.
Cast off.

The pocket backs *(two alike):*
With size 6 mm (No. 4) needles and m. cast on 15 (17) (19) sts. and s.s. 36 (40) (44) rows, then cast off.

The left front band and half collar:
With size 5½ mm (No. 5) needles and m. cast on 7 sts. and work 60 (64) (68) rows in moss st. as given for back.
** Continuing in moss st. inc. 1 st. at the beginning of the next row and at the same edge on each of the next 13 (15)(17) rows.
On 21 (23) (25) sts. pattern 26 (30) (34) rows, then cast off.

The right front band and half collar:
With size 5½ mm (No. 5) needles and m. cast on 7 sts. and work 4 (8) (6) rows in moss st. as given for back.
1st Buttonhole row: Moss st. 2, cast off 3, moss st. to end.
2nd Buttonhole row: Moss st. 2, turn, cast on 3, turn, moss st. to end.
Moss st. 16 (16) (18) rows.
Repeat the last 18 (18) (20) rows twice more, then work the 2 buttonhole rows again.
Now work as given for left front band from ** to end.

To make up the jacket:
Pin out to size and press all parts on the wrong side with a warm iron over a damp cloth. Join shoulder seams. Set in sleeves between the marking threads on back and front. Fold pocket backs in half and join row end edges. Join sleeves and side seams, inserting pockets 4 inches above lower edge at side seams. Join cast off edges of left and right half collars. Neatly sew frontbands and collar in position, so that the shaped row end edge of collar is sewn to neck edge, with the first front dec. on front edge in line with first increase on collar. Press seams. Sew on buttons.

IBBLE-OBBLE

SEE MODEL ON RIGHT, FOLLOWING PAGE

A really warm, woolly coat that will keep you snug in winter: and certainly a garment that a beginner could knit. Cream is the only colour available in the two beautifully-textured 100 per cent wools used.

Materials:
6½ lbs of main wool—twisted wool slub; 1½ lbs of contrast wool thick/thin soft spun wool; a pair of No.1 knitting needles; 5 buttons. The wool for the coat is available from The Patricia Roberts Knitting Shop, 60 Kinnerton Street, London, S.W.1. Mail order service available.

Tension:
Work at a tension of 5 stitches and 8 rows to 5 cm (2 in.) over both the garter stitch and the bobble pattern using No.1 needles. If you cannot obtain the correct tension using the size needles suggested, use larger or smaller needles accordingly.

Abbreviations:
K., knit; p., purl; st., stitch; tog., together; dec., decrease (by working 2sts. tog.); inc., increase (by working twice into same st); garter st. is k. plain on every row; s.s., stocking stitch (k. on the right side and p. on the wrong side); y.r.n., yarn round needle; m.b., make bobble thus, k. 1, y.r.n., k. 1, y.r.n., k. 1, turn, k. 5, turn, p. 5, turn, k. 5, turn, p. 5, pass the 2nd, 3rd, 4th and 5th sts. on left hand needle over first st., k. 1 through back of st.; m., main wool; a., contrast wool; sl., slip; p.s.s.o., pass sl. st. over.

Note:
The instructions are given for the small size. Where they vary work the figures in the first brackets for the medium size or the figures in the second brackets for the large size.

Measurements:
The measurements are given in centimetres followed by inches in square brackets.

small (10)	medium (12)	large (14)
All round at underarms		
95 [38]	100 [40]	105 [42]
Side seam		
90 [36]	90 [36]	90 [36]
Length		
112.5 [45]	112.5 [45]	112.5 [45]
Sleeve seam (with cuffs folded back)		
40 [16]	40 [16]	40 [16]

The back:
With No.1 needles and m. cast on 65 (67) (69) sts. and work in pattern as follows:
1st to 24th rows: With m. in garter st. Break off m., join in a.
25th to 28th rows: With a beginning with a k. row s.s. 4 rows.
29th row: With a. k. 4 (5) (6), * m.b., k. 7 repeat from * ending last repeat k. 4 (5) (6).
30th to 34th rows: With a. all s.s.
35th row: With a. k. 8 (1) (2), * m.b., k. 7; repeat from * ending last repeat k. 8 (1) (2).
36th row: With a. all p., break off a., join in m.
The last 36 rows form the pattern. Repeat the last 36 rows once more, then work the first 24 pattern rows as set. Break off m., join in a.
1st dec. row: With a. k. 6 (7) (8), * sl. 1, k. 1, p.s.s.o., k. 1, k. 2 tog., k. 11; repeat from * ending last repeat k. 6 (7) (8)—57 (59) (61) sts.
With a. beginning with a p. row s.s. 3 rows.
Next row: With a. k. 3 (4) (5), * m.b., k. 7, m.b., k. 5; repeat from * ending last repeat k. 3 (4) (5).
With a. s.s. 5 rows.
Next row: With a. k. 7 (8) (1), * m.b., k. 6; repeat from * ending last repeat k. 7 (8) (1).
With a. p. 1 row, break off a., join in m.
With m. work 24 rows in garter st. Break off m., join in a.
2nd dec. row: With a. k. 5 (6) (7), * sl. 1, k. 1, p.s.s.o., k. 1, k. 2 tog., k. 9; repeat from * ending last repeat k. 5 (6) (7)—49 (51) (53) sts.
With a. beginning with a p. row s.s. 3 rows.
Next row: With a. k. 3 (4) (5), * m.b., k. 5; repeat from * ending last repeat k. 3 (4) (5).
With a. s.s. 5 rows.
Next row: With a. k. 6 (1) (2), * m.b., k. 5; repeat from * ending last repeat k. 6 (1) (2).
With a. p. 1 row, break off a., join in m.
The last 2 bobble rows set the position of the pattern for the rest of the back.
To shape the armholes: Continuing in pattern as set cast off 6 (7) (8) sts. at the beginning of the next 2 rows.
On 37 sts. pattern 34 rows as set.
To slope the shoulders: Cast off 10 sts. at the beginning of the next 2 rows.
Cast off the remaining 17 sts.

The pocket backs *(both alike)*:
With No.1 needles and a. cast on 13 sts. and beginning with a k. row s.s. 24 rows, then leave these sts. on a spare needle until required.

The left front:
With No.1 needles and m. cast on 29 (30) (31) sts. and work as given for back until 28 rows have been worked in pattern.
29th Pattern row: With a. k. 4 (5) (6), * m.b., k. 7; repeat from * ending last repeat k. 8.
30th to 34th rows: With a. in s.s.
35th row: With a. k. 8 (1) (2), * m.b., k. 7; repeat from * ending last repeat k. 4.
36th row: With a. all p. break off a., join in m.
The last 36 rows form the pattern.
Repeat the last 36 rows once more, then work the first 24 pattern rows again. Break off m., join in a.
1st dec. row: With a. k. 6 (7) (8), sl. 1, k. 1, p.s.s.o., k. 1, k. 2 tog., k. 11, sl. 1, k. 1, p.s.s.o., k. 1, k. 2 tog., k. 2—25 (26) (27) sts.
With a. p. 1 row.
Pocket row: K. 6 (7) (8), cast off 13 sts. and in their place k. across the 13 sts. of one pocket back, k. 6.
With a. p. 1 row.
Next row: With a. k. 3 (4) (5), m.b., k. 7, m.b., k. 5, m.b., k. 7.
With a. s.s. 5 rows.
Next row: With a. k. 7 (8) (1); * m.b., k. 6; repeat from * ending last repeat k. 3.
With a. p. 1 row. Break off a., join in m.
With m. k. 24 rows. Break off m., join in a.
2nd dec. row: With a. k. 5 (6) (7), sl. 1, k. 1, p.s.s.o., k. 1, k. 2 tog., k. 9, sl. 1, k. 1, p.s.s.o., k. 1, k. 2 tog., k. 1—21 (22) (23) sts.
With a. s.s. 3 rows.
Next row: With a. k. 3 (4) (5), * m.b., k. 5; repeat from * to end.
With a. s.s. 5 rows.
Next row: With a. k. 6 (1) (2), * m.b., k. 5; repeat from * ending last repeat k. 2.
With a. p. 1 row.
The last 8 rows set the pattern for the rest of the left front.
***To shape the armhole:* Continuing in pattern as set cast off 6 (7) (8) sts. at the beginning of the next row—15 sts.
Work 1 row straight.
To slope the front edge: Dec. 1 st. at the end—front edge of the next row and the 4 following 6th rows.
On 10 sts. pattern 9 rows.
To slope the shoulder: Cast off the remaining 10 sts.

The right front:
With No.1 needles and m. cast on 29 (30) (31) sts. and work as given for back until 28 rows have been worked in pattern.
29th pattern row: With a. k. 8, * m.b., k. 7; repeat from * ending last repeat k. 4 (5) (6).
30th to 34th rows: With a. in s.s.
35th row: With a. k. 4, * m.b., k. 7; repeat from * ending last repeat k. 8 (1) (2).
36th row: With a. all p. Break off a., join in m.
Repeat the last 36 rows once more. With m. k. 24 rows. Break off m. Join in a.
1st dec. row: With a. k. 2, sl. 1, k. 1, p.s.s.o., k. 1, k. 2 tog., k. 11, sl. 1, k. 1, p.s.s.o., k. 1, k. 2 tog., k. 6 (7) (8)—25 (26) (27) sts.
With a. p. 1 row.
Pocket row: K. 6, cast off 13 and in their place k. across the 13 sts. of one pocket back, k. 6 (7) (8).
With a p. 1 row.
Next row: With a. k. 7, m.b., k. 5, m.b., k. 7, m.b., k. 3 (4) (5).
With a. s.s. 5 rows.

Next row: With a. k.3, * m.b., k.6; repeat from * ending last repeat k.7 (8) (1).
With a. p.1 row. Break off a., join in m.
With m. k. 24 rows. Break off m., join in a.
2nd dec. row: With a. k.1, sl.1, k.1, p.s.s.o., k.1, k.2 tog., k.9, sl.1, k.1, p.s.s.o., k.1, k.2 tog., k.5 (6) (7).
With a. s.s. 3 rows.
Next row: With a. k.5 * m.b., k.5, repeat from * ending last repeat k.3 (4) (5).
With a. s.s. 5 rows.
Next row: With a. k.2, * m.b., k.5; repeat from * ending last repeat k.6 (1) (2).
With a. p.1 row.
The last 8 rows set the position of the pattern for the rest of the right front.
Break off a., join in m. and k.1 row.
Now work as given for left front from ** to end.

The sleeves *(both alike)*:
With No. 1 needles and m. cast on 44 sts. and k.76 rows, mark each end of the last row with coloured threads. K.10 (11) (13) rows, then cast off.

The buttonband:
With No.1 needles and m. cast on 6 sts. and k.146 rows. Cast off.

The buttonhole band:
With No.1 needles and m. cast on 6 sts. and k.70 rows.
1st Buttonhole row: K.2, cast off 2, k. to end.
2nd Buttonhole row: K.2, turn, cast on 2, turn, k. to end.
K.16 rows.
Repeat the last 18 rows 3 times more then work the 2 buttonhole rows again.
K.2 rows, then cast off.

The collar:
With No.1 needles and m. cast on 44 sts. and k.10 rows.
Dec. 1 st. at each end of the next row and the 12 following alternate rows.
On 18 sts. k.1 row, then cast off.

To make up the coat:
Pin out to size and press all parts on the wrong side with a warm iron over a damp cloth. Join shoulder seams. Set in sleeves so that the row ends above the marking threads are sewn to the sts. cast off at underarms. Join sleeve and side seams. Sew pocket backs in position. Sew front bands in place up to first front edge dec. on each front. Sew collar in place, so that the 17 sts. cast off at end are sewn to back neck edge, the shaped row end edges are sewn to the sloped neck edges and the first 10 straight row end edges are sewn to the cast off edges of front bands. Press seams. Sew on buttons.

TEA COSY

SEE MODEL ON LEFT, PREVIOUS PAGE

Textures and subtle colouring make this jacket look like a work of art. The main parts are knitted in bobbly wool which is very thick, but the patchwork squares are in Shetland. Cream is the only colour available in the thick wool, with toning shades in Shetland.

Materials:
36 ounces of 'Woolly bear' chunky wool; 4 ounces of cream Shetland, one ounce of Shetland in each of 4 contrast colours—pale oatmeal, grey, green, pale grey; a pair each of No. 12 and No. 2 knitting needles; 4 buttons; a cable needle. The wools for this garment are available from The Patricia Roberts Knitting Shop, 60 Kinnerton Street, London, S.W.1. Mail order service available.

Tension:
5 stitches and 8 rows to 5 cm (2 in.) over the chunky wool knitted in garter stitch using No. 2 needles. The Fair Isle square should measure 11 cm ($4\frac{1}{2}$ in.) in width and 22.5 cm (9 in.) in length. The Nosegay square should measure 12.5 cm (5 in.) in width and 22.5 cm (9 in.) in length.

Abbreviations:
K., knit; p., purl; st., stitch; tog., together; dec., decrease (by working 2 sts. tog.); inc., increase (by working twice into same st.); s.s., stocking stitch (k. on the right side and p. on the wrong side); garter st. is k. plain on every row; m., cream Shetland; a., pale grey Shetland; b., grey Shetland; c., oatmeal Shetland; k. or p. b., k. or p. through back of st. or sts.; c.2 f., cable 2 front thus, slip next st. on to cable needle at front of work, k.1, then k.1 from cable needle; c.2 b., cable 2 back, as c.2 f., but leave sts. at back of work; cr.2 f., cross 2 front, slip next st. on to a cable needle at front, p.1, then k.1 from cable needle; cr.2 b., cross 2 back thus, slip next st. on to cable needle at back, k.1, then p.1 from cable needle; cr.4 f., cross 4 front thus, slip next 2 sts. on to cable needle at front, p.2, then k.2 from cable needle; cr.4 b., cross 4 back, slip next 2 sts. on to cable needle at back, k.2, then p.2 from cable needle; cr.3 f., cross 3 front thus, slip next 2 sts. on to cable needle at front, p.1, then k.2 from cable needle; cr.3 b., cross 3 back, thus, slip next st. on to cable needle at back, k.2 then p.1 from cable needle; c.4 b., cable 4 back thus, slip next 2 sts. on to cable needle at back, k.2, then k.2 from cable needle; c.4 f., cable 4 front thus, slip next 2 sts. on to cable needle at front, k.2 then k.2 from cable needle; m.b., make bobble thus, k.1, y.r.n., k.1, y.r.n., k.1 all from next st., turn, p.5, turn, slip 2nd, 3rd, 4th and 5th sts. over first st. on left hand needle, then k.1 b; y.r.n., yarn round needle.

Measurements:

To fit sizes small to medium.	
All round at underarms:	100 cm [40 in.]
Side seam:	45 cm [18 in.]
Sleeve seam (before folding back cuff):	45 cm [18 in.]
Length:	67.5 cm [27 in.]

The Fair Isle squares *(4 alike)*:
With No. 12 needles and m. cast on 41 sts. and beginning with a k. row s.s. 4 rows.
Now work in pattern as follows. This is worked entirely in s.s. so only the colour details are given. Take great care to avoid pulling colours not in use tightly across the back of the work or it will become puckered.
1st row: 2 m., * 1 a., 2 m., 1 b., 2 m.; repeat from * ending last repeat 1 a., 2 m.
2nd row: 1 m., 3 a., 1 m., * 1 b., 1 m., 3 a., 1 m.; repeat from * to end.
These 2 rows set the position of the pattern given in the chart. Now work the 3rd to 14th rows from the chart.
15th row: 9 c., * 7 a., 11 c.; repeat from * ending last repeat 7 c.
The last row sets the position of the rest of the pattern. Now work the 16th to 42nd rows from chart as set.
Repeat the 1st to 42nd rows once more, then cast off.

The Nosegay squares *(4 alike)*:
With No. 12 needles and m. cast on 51 sts. and work in pattern as follows:
1st row (wrong side): P.2 b., k.2, p.2, k.4, p.2, k.2, p.2 b., k.7, p.2, k.7, p.2 b., k.5, p.5, k.5, p.2 b.
2nd row (right side): K.2 b., p.5, k.2, m.b., k.2, p.5, k.2 b., p.6, c.2 f., c.2 b., p.6, k.2 b., p.2, k.2, p.4, k.2, p.2, k.2 b.
3rd row: P.2 b., k.2, p.2, k.4, p.2, k.2, p.2 b., k.5, cr.2 f., p.2, cr.2 b., k.5, p.2 b., k.5, p.5, k.5, p.2 b.
4th row: K.2 b., p.5, m.b., k.3, m.b., p.5, k.2 b., p.4, cr.2 b., c.2 b., c.2 f., cr.2 f., p.4, k.2 b., p.2, cr.4 f., cr.4 b., p.2, k.2 b.
5th row: P.2 b., k.4, p.4, k.4, p.2 b., k.3, cr.2 f., k.1, p.4, k.1, cr.2 b., k.3, p.2 b., k.5, p.5, k.5, p.2 b.
6th row: K.2 b., p.5, k.2, m.b., k.2, p.5, k.2 b., p.2, cr.2 b., p.1, cr.2 b., k.2, cr.2 f., p.1, cr.2 f., p.2, k.2 b., p.4, (cr.4 f.), p.4, k.2 b.
7th row: P.2 b., (k.4, p.2, k.6), p.2 b., k.2, p.1, k.2, p.1, k.1, p.2, k.1, p.1, k.2, p.1, k.2, p.2 b., k.5, p.5, k.5, p.2 b.
8th row: K.2 b., p.4, cr.3 b., p.1, cr.3 f., p.4, k.2 b., p.2, m.b., p.1, cr.2 b., p.1, k.2, p.1, cr.2 f., p.1, m.b., p.2, k.2 b., (p.6, cr.3 f., p.3), k.2 b.
9th row: P.2 b., (k.3, p.2, k.7), p.2 b., k.4, p.1, k.2, p.2, k.2, p.1, k.4, p.2 b., k.4, p.2, k.1, p.1, k.1, p.2, k.4, p.2 b.
10th row: K.2 b., p.3, cr.3 b., k.1, p.1, k.1, cr.3 f., p.3, k.2 b., p.4, m.b., p.2, k.2, p.2, m.b., p.4, k.2 b., (p.7, cr.3 f., p.2), k.2 b.
11th row: P.2 b., (k.2, p.2, k.8), p.2 b., k.7, p.2, k.7, p.2 b., k.3, p.3, k.1, p.1, k.1, p.3, k.3, p.2 b.

12th row: K.2 b., p.2, cr.3 b., p.1, k.1, p.1, k.1, p.1, cr.3 f., p.2, k.2 b., p.6, c.2 f., c.2 b., p.6, k.2 b., (p.3, m.b., p.4, k.2, p.2), k.2 b.
13th row: P.2 b., (k.2, p.2, k.8), p.2 b., k.7, p.2, k.7, p.2 b., k.2, p.2, k.1, p.1, k.1, p.1, k.1, p.1, k.1, p.2, k.2, p.2 b.
14th row: K.2 b., p.2, k.3, p.1, k.1, p.1, k.1, p.1, k.3, p.2, k.2 b., p.4, cr.2 b., c.2 b., c.2 f., cr.2 f., p.4, k.2 b., (p.7, cr.3 b., p.2), k.2 b.
15th row: P.2 b., (k.3, p.2, k.7), p.2 b., k.3, cr.2 f., k.1, p.4, k.1, cr.2 b., k.3, p.2 b., k.2, p.2, k.1, p.1, k.1, p.1, k.1, p.1, k.1, p.2, k.2, p.2 b.
16th row: K.2 b., p.2, cr.3 f., p.1, k.1, p.1, k.1, p.1, cr.3 b., p.2, k.2 b., p.2, cr.2 b., p.1, cr.2 b., k.2, cr.2 f., p.1, cr.2 f., p.2, k.2 b., (p.6, cr.3 b., p.3), k.2 b.
17th row: P.2 b., (k.4, p.2, k.6), p.2 b., k.2, p.1, k.2, p.1, k.1, p.2, k.1, p.1, k.2, p.1, k.2, p.2 b., k.3, p.3, k.1, p.1, k.1, p.3, k.3, p.2 b.
18th row: K.2 b., p.3, cr.3 f., k.1, p.1, k.1, cr.3 b., p.3, k.2 b., p.2, m.b., p.1, cr.2 b., p.1, k.2, p.1, cr.2 f., p.1, m.b., p.2, k.2 b., (p.4, c.4 b., p.4), k.2 b.
19th row: P.2 b., k.4, p.4, k.4, p.2 b., k.4, p.1, k.2, p.2, k.2, p.1, k.4, p.2 b., k.4, p.2, k.1, p.1, k.1, p.2, k.4, p.2 b.
20th row: K.2 b., p.4, cr.3 f., p.1, cr.3 b., p.4, k.2 b., p.4, m.b., p.2, k.2, p.2, m.b., p.4, k.2 b., p.2, cr.4 b., cr.4 f., p.2, k.2 b.
21st to 40th rows: Work as given for 1st to 20th rows but substituting the instructions in brackets below for those given in brackets above where appropriate as follows:
21st to 25th rows: As 1st to 5th rows.
26th row: (Cr.4 b.)
27th row: (K.6, p.2, k.4).
28th row: (P.3, cr.3 b., p.6).
29th row: (K.7, p.2, k.3).
30th row: (P.2, cr.3 b., p.7).
31st row: (K.8, p.2, k.2).
32nd row: (P.2, k.2, p.4, m.b., p.3).
33rd row: (K.8, p.2, k.2).
34th row: (P.2, cr.3 f., p.7).
35th row: (K.7, p.2, k.3).
36th row: (P.3, cr.3 f., p.6).
37th row: (K.6, p.2, k.4).
38th row: (P.4, cr.4 f., p.4).
39th and 40th rows: Exactly as 19th and 20th rows.
The last 40 rows form the pattern. Repeat them once more then work the first 10 rows again. Cast off.

The garter stitch lower piece:
With No.2 needles and chunky wool cast on 95sts. and k.36 rows, then cast off.

The back yoke:
With No.2 needles and chunky wool cast on 38sts. and k.34 rows.
To slope the shoulders: Cast off 10sts. at the beginning of the next 2 rows. Cast off the remaining 18sts.

The left and right front yokes *(both alike as the fabric is reversible)***:**
With No.2 needles and chunky wool cast on 19sts. and k.12 rows.
To slope the neck: Continuing in garter st. dec. 1st. at the beginning of the next row and the 8 following alternate rows.
On 10sts. k.5 rows more.
To slope the shoulder: Cast off these 10sts.

The button band and half collar:
With No.2 needles and chunky wool cast on 5sts. and k.84 rows.
***To shape the collar:* Inc. 1st. at the beginning of the next row and at the same edge on each of the next 10 rows—16sts.
K.40 rows more, then cast off.

The buttonhole band and half collar:
With No.2 needles and chunky wool cast on 5sts. and k.10 rows.
Buttonhole row: K.2, y.r.n., k.2 tog., k.1.
K.23 rows.
Repeat the last 24 rows twice more, then work the buttonhole row again.
K.1 row, then work as given for button band and half collar from ** to end.

The sleeves *(both alike)***:**
With No.2 needles and chunky wool cast on 45sts. and k.72 rows, marking each end of the last row with coloured threads.
K.8 rows more, then cast off.

The pocket backs *(2 alike)***:**
With No.12 needles and m. Shetland cast on 40sts. and beginning with a k. row s.s. 50 rows, then cast off.

To make up the jacket:
Pin out all the pieces to size and press lightly with a warm iron over a damp cloth. Join the Fair Isle and Nosegay squares together. Sew these to the chunky wool lower stripe, leaving openings for pockets. Sew pocket backs in place. Join shoulder seams. Set in sleeves. Join sleeve seams up to marking threads. Join top to top of Nosegay and Fair Isle squares. Join cast off edges of the 2 collar pieces. Neatly sew front bands and the straight row end edges of collar in place. Sew on buttons. Press seams. Fold bottom of sleeves to right side for cuffs.

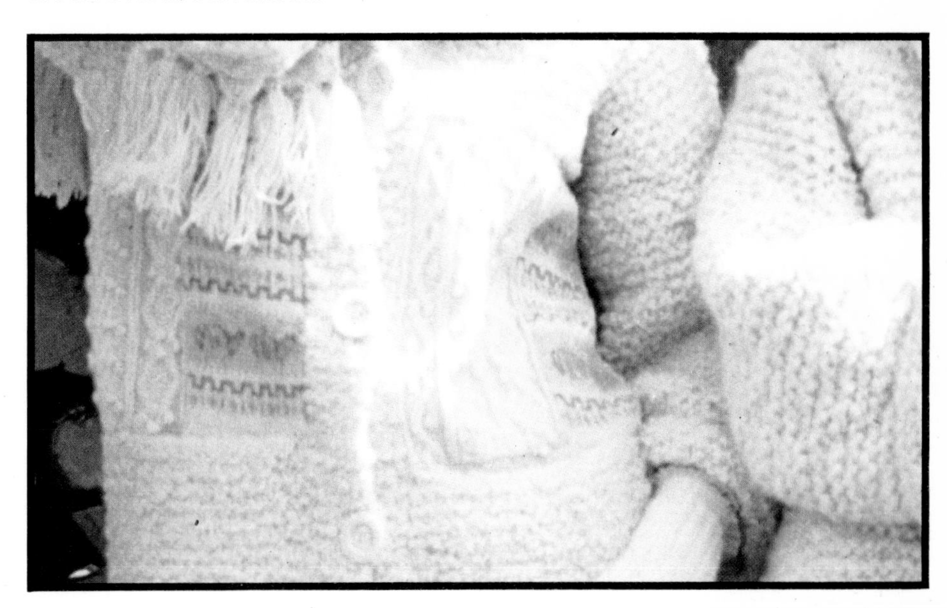

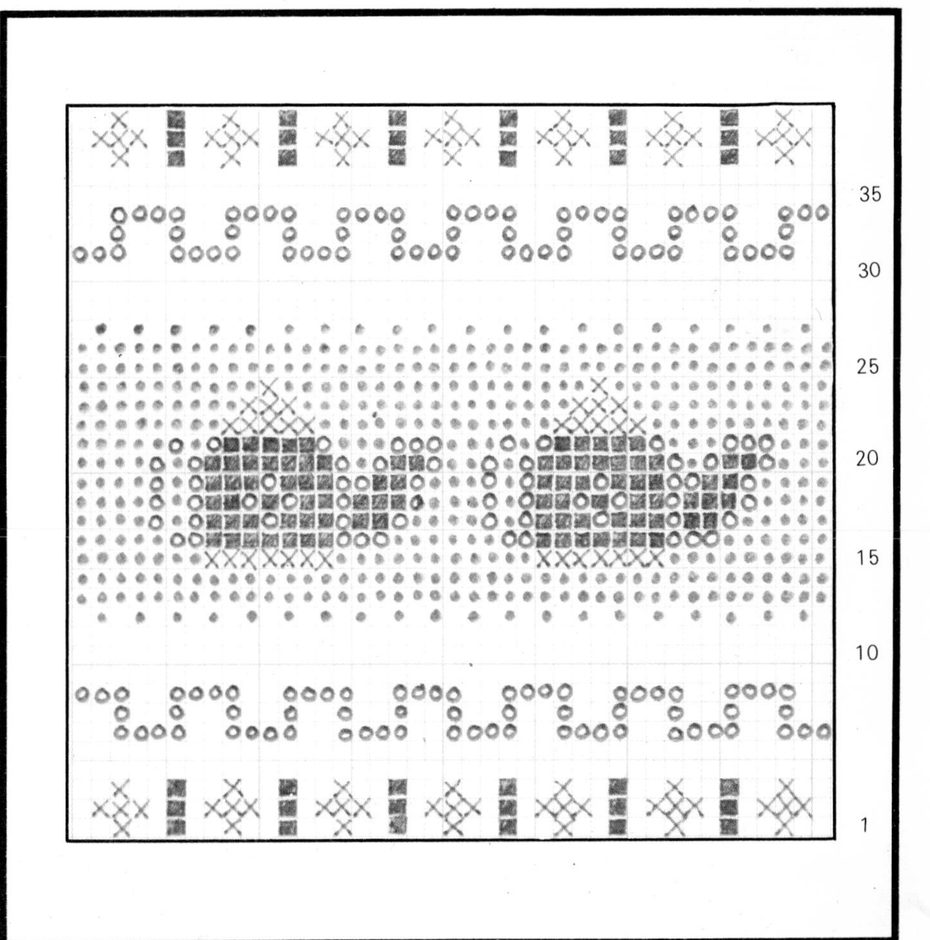

FROM HIGHLANDS TO HIGH STREET

Use Shetland shades for this classic Fair Isle sweater for men—grey, oatmeal, black, charcoal, mulberry or blue, which also make attractive base colours. The Shetland wools you will need are available from The Patricia Roberts Knitting Shop, 60 Kinnerton Street, London S.W.1. Mail order service available.

Materials:
7 ounces of Shetland in main colour; 4 ounces in first contrast; 2 ounces in each of second, third and fourth contrast colours; a pair each of No.12 and No.13 needles.

Tension:
16 stitches and 20 rows to 5 cm (2 in.) over stocking stitch using No.12 needles.

Abbreviations:
K.,knit; p.,purl; st.,stitch; tog.,together; dec.,decrease (by working 2sts. tog.); inc.,increase (by working twice into same st.); s.s.,stocking stitch; double rib is k.2 and p.2 alternately; up1,pick up the loop that lies between the needles, slip it onto left-hand needle, then k. into back of it; m.,main colour; a.,second contrast colour; b.,first contrast colour; k.2 tog.b., knit 2 tog. through back of sts.

Note:
The instructions are given for the extra-small size. Where they vary, work the instructions in the first brackets for the small size; the figures in the second brackets for the medium size; or the figures in the third brackets for the large size.

Measurements:
The following measurements are given in centimetres first, followed by inches in brackets.

ex-small	small	medium	large
All round at underarms			
86($34\frac{1}{2}$)	90(36)	94($37\frac{1}{2}$)	98(39)
Side seam			
40(16)	40(16)	40(16)	40(16)
Length			
62.5(25)	63($25\frac{1}{4}$)	64($25\frac{1}{2}$)	64.5($25\frac{3}{4}$)
Sleeve seam			
47.5(19)	47.5(19)	47.5(19)	47.5(19)

The back:
With No.13 needles and m. cast on 122 (128) (134) (140) sts. and work 47 rows in double rib.
Increase row: Rib 5(8) (11) (14), * up 1, rib 7; repeat from * ending last repeat rib 5 (8) (11) (14)—139(145) (151) (157) sts.
Change to No.12 needles and beginning with a k. row s.s. 2 rows.
Now work in Fair Isle pattern in the following way. This is worked entirely in s.s. so only the colour details follow. Take great care not to pull colours not in use tightly across the back of the work.
1st row: 1 a., * 5 m., 1 a.; repeat from * to end.
2nd row: 2 a., * 3 m., 3 a.; repeat from * ending last repeat 2 a.
3rd row: 1 m., * 2 a., 1 m.; repeat from * to end.
4th row: 2 m., * 3 a., 3 m.; repeat from * ending last repeat 2 m.
These 4 rows set the position of the Fair Isle pattern given in the chart. Work the 4th to 15th rows from the chart.
16th row: 5 b. (1 a., 7 b.) (3 b., 1 a., 7 b.) (6 b., 1 a., 7 b.), 9 a., * 7 b., 1 a., 7 b., 9 a.; repeat from * until 5(8) (11) (14) remain, 5 b.(7 b., 1 a.)(7 b., 1 a., 3 b.) (7 b., 1 a., 6 b.).
17th row: 4 b., (2 a., 5 b.) (2 b., 3 a., 5 b.) (5 b., 3 a., 5 b), 11 a., * 5 b., 3 a., 5 b., 11 a.; repeat from * until 4(7) (10) (13) remain, 4 b., (5 b., 2 a.) (5 b., 3 a., 2 b.) (5 b., 3 a., 5 b.).
18th row: As 17th row.
The last 3 rows set the position of the pattern; now work the 19th to 68th rows from the chart, then work the first 50 rows again.

To shape the armholes: Maintaining the continuity of the pattern as set, cast off 6 sts. at the beginning of the next 2 rows, then dec.1 st. at each end of the next 10 (12) (14) (16) rows — 107(109) (111) (113) sts.
Pattern 72 rows.
To slope the shoulders: Cast off 8sts. at the beginning of the next 4 rows and 9 sts. on the 2 following rows—57(59) (61) (63) sts.
Change to No.13 needles and work 16 rows in double rib, then cast off in rib.

The front:
Work as given for back until the 68 pattern rows have been worked once, then work the first 41 rows again.
Now divide the sts. for the neck: *Next row:* Continuing in pattern as set work across 69(72) (75) (78) sts., and leave these sts. on a spare needle until required for right front shoulder, p.2.tog., pattern to end and continue on these 69(72) (75) (78) sts. for the left front shoulder.
The left front shoulder: To shape the neck: Continuing in pattern as set dec.1 st. at the

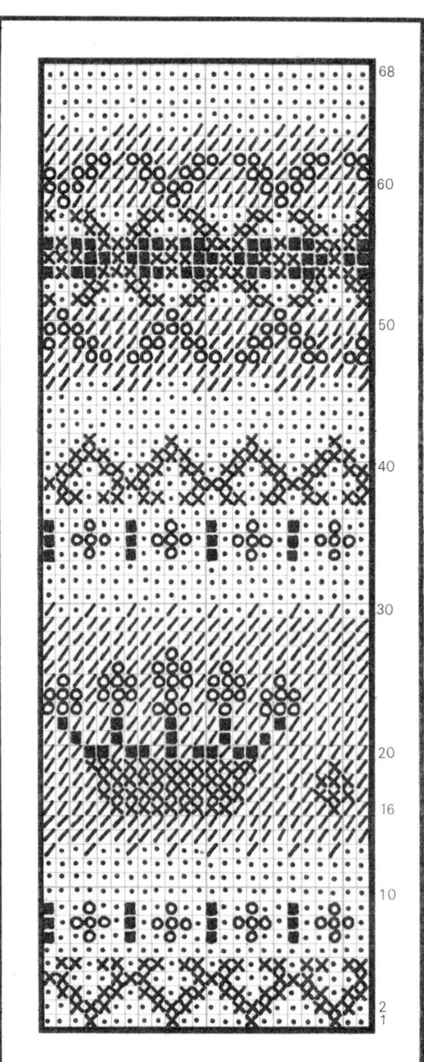

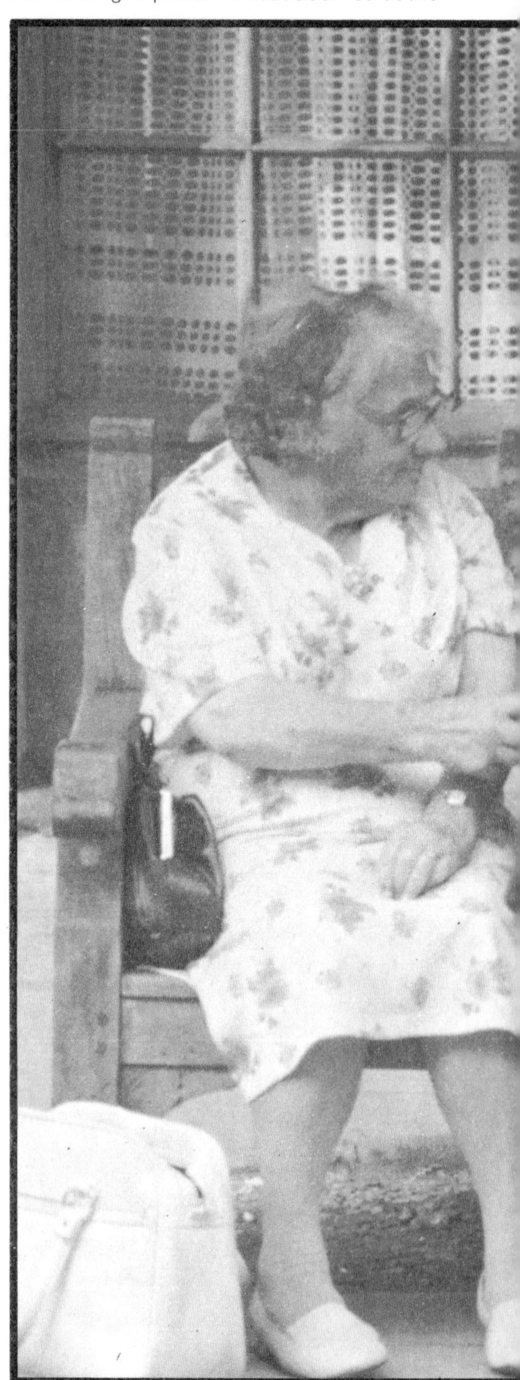

end—neck edge on the next row and at the same edge on the 2 following 3rd rows. Work 1 row back to armhole edge.
To shape the armhole and continue to slope the neck edge: Continuing in Fair Isle pattern as set and decreasing at neck edge on every 3rd row as before, cast off 6 sts. at the beginning of the next row, work 1 straight, then dec. 1 st. at armhole edge on each of the next 10 (12) (14) (16) rows.
Work 62 (63) (64) (65) more rows decreasing 1 st. at neck edge on every 3rd row as before.
On 25 sts. work 10 (9) (8) (7) rows as set.
To slope the shoulder: Cast off 8 sts. at the beginning of the next row and following alternate row.
On 9 sts. work 1 row, then cast off.
The right front shoulder: With right side of work facing rejoin yarn and work 1 row as set to armhole edge, then work as given for left front shoulder to end.

The front neckband:
With right side of work facing rejoin m. and using No. 13 needles pick up and k. 81 (83) (85) (87) sts. from left front neck edge, and 81 (83) (85) (87) sts. from right front neck edge—162 (166) (170) (174) sts.
Work in rib as follows: *1st row:* P. 2, * k. 2, p. 2; repeat from * to end.
Next row: Rib to within 2 sts. of centre front, k. 2 tog.b., k. 2 tog., rib to end as set.
Next row: Rib to within 2 sts. of centre front, p. 2 tog.b., p. 2 tog., rib to end as set.
Repeat the last 2 rows 6 more times, then cast off in rib.

The sleeves (*both alike*):
With No. 13 needles and m. cast on 76 sts. and work 72 rows in double rib, increasing 1 st. at the end of the last row—77 sts.
Change to No. 12 needles and beginning with a k. row s.s. 2 rows.
Now work in Fair Isle pattern as follows, taking great care not to pull colours not in use tightly across the back of the work, beginning with the 29th pattern row as follows:
29th row: All b.
30th row: 2 m., * 1 b., 2 m.; repeat from * to end.
Now work the 31st to 48th rows from the chart.
Now maintaining the continuity of the pattern and working the extra sts. into the pattern as they occur, inc. 1 st. at each end of the next row and the 13 (15) (17) (19) following 10th (8th) (8th) (6th) rows.
On 105 (109) (113) (117) sts., pattern 9 (19) (3) (25) rows.
To shape the sleevetop: Cast off 6 sts. at the beginning of the next 2 rows, then dec. 1 st. at each end of next row and the 18 following alternate rows—55 (59) (63) (67) sts.
Work 1 row, then dec. 1 st. at each end of the next 6 (8) (10) (12) rows—43 sts.
Cast off 3 sts. at the beginning of the next 10 rows, then cast off the remaining 13 sts.

To make up the sweater:
Pin out carefully all pieces of knitting to correct measurements and press all parts except ribbing on the wrong side with a warm iron over a damp cloth. Press ribbing lightly. Join shoulder seams. Set in sleeves. Join sleeve and side seams. Press seams.

EASY RIB

The real beginner's knitting. It's as easy as easy.

Materials:
For the jacket: 9 (9) (10) 100 gram balls of Jaegar Naturgarn; 6 buttons; a pair each of size 6 mm (No. 4) and size 5½ mm (No. 5) Aero knitting needles.
For the scarf: 4 100 gram balls of Jaegar Naturgarn; a pair of size 6 mm (No. 4) Aero knitting needles.
Tension:
15 stitches—3 repeats of the pattern—to 9 cm (3½ in.) in width and 10 rows to 5 cm (2 m) in length over the rib pattern using size 6 mm (No. 4) needles.
Abbreviations:
K., knit; p., purl; st., stitch; tog., together; dec., decrease (by working 2 sts. tog.); inc., increase (by working twice into same st.); single rib is k. 1 and p. 1 alternately; s.s., stocking stitch is k. on the right side and p. on the wrong side; up 1., pick up the loop which lies between the needles, slip it onto left hand needle than k. into back of it.
Note:
The instructions are given for the small size. Where they vary work the figures in the first brackets for the medium size or the figures in the second brackets for the large size.

Measurements:
The measurements are given in centimetres followed by inches in square brackets.

The jacket:

small	medium	large
All round at underarms		
100 [40]	105 [42]	110 [44]
Side seam		
41 [18]	45 [18]	45 [18]
Length		
70 [28]	71 [28½]	72 [29]

The scarf: 21 cm (8½ in.) in width by 160 cm (64 in.) in length.

THE JACKET
The back:
With size 5½ mm (no. 5) needles cast on 73 (78) (83) sts and beginning with a k row s.s. 9 rows.
Increase row: P. 3 (6) (8), * up 1., p. 5; repeat from * ending last repeat p. 5 (7) (10)—87 (92) (97) sts.
Change to size 6 mm. (No. 4) needles and work in rib pattern as follows:
1st row: P. 2, * k. 3, p. 2; repeat from * to end.
2nd row: k. 2, * p. 3, k. 2; repeat from * to end.
The last 2 rows form the rib pattern; repeat them 41 times more.
To shape the armholes: Cast off 4 sts at the beginning of the next 2 rows—79 (84) (89) sts.
Rib 46 (48) (50) rows more as set.
To slope the shoulders: Cast off 25 (27) (29) sts. at the beginning of the next 2 rows.
Change to size 5½ mm (No. 5) needles and work 4 rows in single rib, then cast off the remaining 29 (30) (31) sts.
The left front:
With size 5½ mm (No. 5) needles cast on 35 (38) (40) sts. and beginning with a k. row s.s. 9 rows.
Increase row: P. 2 (4) (5) * up 1, p. 5; repeat from * ending last repeat p. 3 (4) (5)—42 (45) (47) sts.
Change to size 6 mm (No. 4) needles and work in rib as follows:
1st row: P. 2, * k. 3, p. 2; repeat from * ending last repeat p. 2 (k. 3) (p. 2).
2nd row: K. 2 (p. 3, k. 2) (k. 2), * p. 3, k. 2, repeat from * to end.

The last two rows form the rib pattern; repeat them 41 times more.
***To shape the armhole:* Cast off 4 sts at the beginning of the next row.
On 38 (41) (43) sts. rib 26 (28) (30) rows.
To shape the neck: Cast off 3 (4) (4) sts. at the beginning of the next row, then dec. 1 st. at the neck edge on each of the next 10 rows.
On 25 (27) (29) sts. work 10 rows.
To slope the shoulder: Cast off.
The right front:
Work as given for left front until the increase row has been worked.
Change to size 6 mm (No. 4) needles and work in rib as follows:
1st row: P. 2 (k. 3, p. 2) (p. 2), * k. 3, p. 2; repeat from * to end.
2nd row: K. 2, * p. 3, k. 2; repeat from * ending last repeat k. 2 (p. 3) (k. 2).
Repeat the last 2 rows 41 times, then work the first row again.
Now work as given for the left front from ** to end.
The armbands *(both alike):* With size

5½ mm (No. 5) needles cast on 5 sts. and work 100 rows in single rib, then cast off.
The buttonhole band:
With size 5½ mm (No. 5) needles cast on 7 sts. and work 4 (6) (6) rows in single rib.
1st Buttonhole row: Rib 2, cast off 3, rib to end.
2nd Buttonhole row: Rib 2, turn, cast on 3, turn, rib to end.
Rib 20 rows.
Repeat the last 22 rows 4 times more then work the 2 buttonhole rows again.
Rib 4 (4) (6) rows.
Cast off.
The button band:
With size 5½ mm (No. 5) needles cast on 7 sts. and work 120 (122) (124) rows in single rib, then cast off.
The left and right front neckbands *(both alike):*
With right side of work facing rejoin yarn and using size 5½ mm (No. 5) needles pick up and k. 23 (24) (24) sts. from front neck edge.
Work 3 rows in single rib, then cast off in rib.
The pocket backs *(two alike):*
With size 6 mm (No. 4) needles cast on 22 sts. and beginning with a k. row s.s. 50 rows, then cast off.
The chord:
Cut 3 lengths of yarn each 500 cm (200 in.) long. Knot one end. Twist together firmly in one direction; fold in half allowing the 2 halves to twist together in the opposite direction. Knot ends.
To make up the jacket:
Pin out to size and press on the wrong side with a warm iron over a damp cloth. Join shoulder seams continuing seams across neckband. Neatly sew armbands in place; so that the cast on and off edges are sewn to the sts. cast off at underarms. Fold pocket backs in half and join row end edges. Join side seams, inserting pockets at side seams 4 inches above cast on edge. Fold s.s. rows at lower edges in half to wrong side and neatly sew cast on edge in position. Neatly sew button and buttonhole bands in position, sewing them to the back part only of the s.s. at lower edge, thus leaving openings at front in the hem. Slot chord through hem. Press seams. Sew on buttons.

THE SCARF
To work:
With size 6 mm (No. 4) needles cast on 37 sts. and work 320 rows in rib pattern given for back. Cast off.
To complete:
Pin out to size and press as for jacket. Fold in half lengthways and knot each end.

WALKING THE DOG

Look closer at this doggie bowl and you will see that it is in fact a pocket on this easy-to-wear smock. Wear it with casual clothes such as jeans, and you'll look good walking in the park—with or without a dog.

Materials:
10(11)(12) 100 gram hanks of Jaeger Naturgarn in main colour; one hank of the same yarn in first contrast colour; one 25 gram ball of Jaeger Mohair in each of three colours; a pair each of No. 5 and No. 6 knitting needles.

Tension:
8 stitches and 10 rows to 5 cm (2 in.) over stocking stitch using No. 5 needles. If you cannot obtain the correct tension using needles of the size suggested, use larger or smaller ones accordingly.

Abbreviations:
K., knit; p., purl; st., stitch; tog., together; dec., decrease (by working 2 sts. tog.); inc., increase (by working twice into same st.); single rib is k.1 and p.1 alternately; s.s., stocking stitch (k. on the right side and p. on the wrong side); m., main colour; a., first contrast colour Naturgarn; b., second contrast—mohair; c., third contrast—mohair.

Note:
The instructions are given for the small size. Where they vary, work the figures in the first brackets for the medium size or the figures in the second brackets for the large size.

Measurements:
The following measurements are given in centimetres first, followed by inches in brackets.

small (10)	medium (12)	large (14)
All round at underarms		
85 (34)	90 (36)	95 (38)
Side seam		
50 (20)	50 (20)	50 (20)
Length		
70 (28)	71 (28¼)	73 (28¾)
Sleeve seam		
32.5 (13)	32.5 (13)	32.5 (13)

The back:
With No. 6 needles and m. cast on 88 (92) (96) sts. and k.4 rows. Join in a. and with a. k.2 rows; break off a.; with m. k.4 rows.
Change to No. 5 needles and beginning with a k. row s.s. 10 rows **
Dec. 1 st. at each end of the next row and the 9 following 8th rows.
On 68 (72) (76) sts. s.s. 7 rows.
To shape the armholes: Cast off 7 (8) (9) sts. at the beginning of the next 2 rows.
On 54 (56) (58) sts., s.s. 16 (18) (20) more rows.
The yoke: Next row: Cast on 7 (8) (9) sts., work in single rib to end, turn, cast on 7 (8) (9) sts.—68 (72) (76) sts.
Work 23 rows in single rib.
To slope the shoulders: Cast off 20 (22) (24) sts. at the beginning of the next 2 rows.
For the collar back: On 28 sts. work 30 rows in single rib, then cast off loosely.

The front:
Work as given for back until ** is reached.
Dec. 1 st. at each end of the next row, then work 1 row straight—86 (90) (94) sts.
Now work the dog motif in the following way. This is worked entirely in s.s. so only the colour details follow. *Use mohair double throughout.* For easier working use separate balls of m. at each side of the dog motif.
1st row: 43 (45) (47) m., 7b., 4m., 4b., 28 (30) (32) m.
2nd row: 27 (29) (31) m., 16b., 2m., 3b., 38 (40) (42) m.
These 2 rows set the position of the dog motif given in chart. Now work the 3rd to 43rd rows given in chart, *and at the same time* decrease 1 st. at each end of the 7th pattern row and the 4 following 8th rows.
With m. only on 76 (80) (84) sts. s.s. 3 rows.
Dec. 1 st. at each end of the next row and the 3 following 8th rows.
On 68 (72) (76) sts. s.s. 6 rows.
Now divide the sts. for the neck: *Next row* (wrong side): P.24 (25) (26) and leave these sts. on a spare needle until required for right front shoulder, cast off 20 (22) (24) sts., then p. to end and continue on these 24 (25) (26) sts. for the left front shoulder.
The left front shoulder: To shape the armhole and slope the neck: Cast off 7 (8) (9) sts. at the beginning and dec. 1 st. at the end of the next row.
S.s. 2 (4) (6) rows.
Dec. 1 st. at the neck edge on each of the next 15 rows then fasten off.
The right front shoulder: With right side of work facing rejoin m. to inner edge of sts. left on spare needle and work to end of worked entirely in s.s. so only the colour details follow:

The pocket:
With No. 5 needles and a cast on 20 sts. and beginning with a k. row s.s. 12 rows.
Now work the word 'dog' in the following way. Use the mohair double. This is worked entirely in s.s. so only the colour details are given:
1st row: 4a., 1c., 15a.
2nd row: 4a., 4c., 1a., 3c., 1a., 3c., 4a.
3rd row: 6a., 1c., 1a., 1c., 1a., 1c., 1a., 1c., 1a., 1c., 5a.
4th row: As 2nd row.
Continuing with a. only s.s. 2 rows.
K.4 rows, then cast off.

The left and right front yokes
(both alike—the fabric being reversible):
With No. 5 needles and m. cast on 20 (22) (24) sts. and work 3 (5) (7) rows in single rib. Continuing in rib as set inc. 1 st. at the beginning of the next row and at the same edge on each of the next 15 rows—36 (38) (40) sts.
Cast on 7 (8) (9) sts at the beginning of the next row, then on 43 (46) (49) sts. work 23 rows in single rib.
To slope the shoulder: Cast off 20 (22) (24) sts. at the beginning of the next row. On 23 (24) (25) sts. rib 31 rows, then cast off.

The sleeves *(both alike):*
With No. 6 needles and m. cast on 64 (66) (68) sts. and k.4 rows. Join in a. and with a. k.2 rows, break off a. With m. k.4 rows.
Change to No. 5 needles and beginning with a k. row s.s. 55 rows, marking each end of the last row with coloured threads.
Now divide the sts. for the sleevetop: *Next row:* P.13 (14) (15) and leave these sts. on a spare needle until required, cast off the next 38 sts., p. to end and continue on these 13 (14) (15) sts.
On 13 (14) (15) sts. s.s. 8 (9) (10) rows, then cast off.
Rejoin m. to the 13 (14) (15) sts. left on spare needle and s.s. 8 (9) (10) rows, then cast off.

To make up the smock:
Press all parts on the wrong side with a warm iron over a damp cloth. Join shoulder and collar seams. Neatly sew back and front yokes in place so that the 7 (8) (9) sts. cast on groups at each side of yokes are sewn to the row ends at inner edges of sleevetops and the row ends above the marking threads on sleeves are sewn to the cast off groups at underarms. The cast on edge of right front yoke should be sewn to the cast off group of sts. at centre front and the left front cast on edge behind it. Join sleeve and side seams. Neatly sew pocket in place so that the dog appears to be drinking out of it. Press seams.

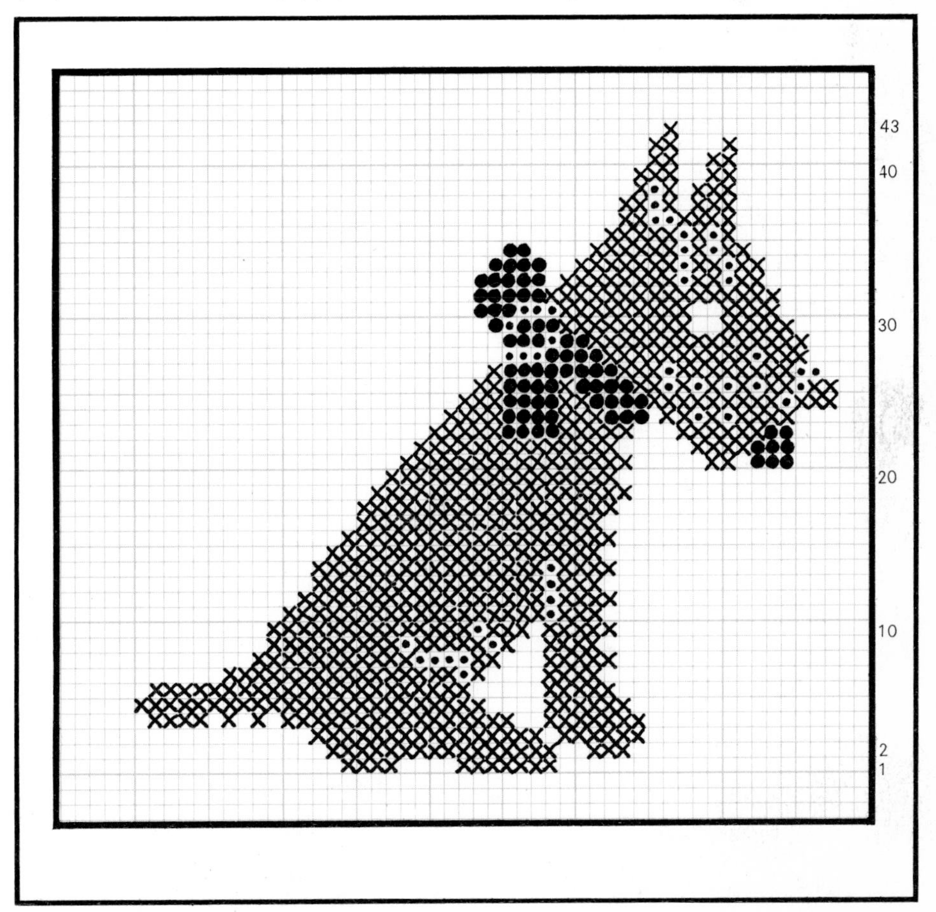